Innovative Teaching and Learning in Higher Education

Innovative Teaching and Learning in Higher Education

John Branch, Sarah Hayes,
Anne Hørsted and Claus Nygaard

THE LEARNING IN HIGHER EDUCATION SERIES

LIBRI
PUBLISHING

First published in 2017 by Libri Publishing

Copyright © Libri Publishing

Authors retain copyright of individual chapters.

The right of John Branch, Sarah Hayes, Anne Hørsted and Claus Nygaard to be identified as the editors of this work has been asserted in accordance with the Copyright, Designs and Patents Act, 1988.

ISBN 978-1-911450-08-5
A CIP catalogue record for this book is available from The British Library

Cover design by Helen Taylor

Design by Carnegie Publishing

Libri Publishing
Brunel House
Volunteer Way
Faringdon
Oxfordshire
SN7 7YR

Tel: +44 (0)845 873 3837

www.libripublishing.co.uk

Contents

Foreword

Having been invited to write this foreword, I started by thinking about the title of this book, which contains three vitally important words/ ideas – teaching, learning, and innovation – in the context of Higher Education.

I am sorry to say I can't name the speaker but I remember a conference keynote, some decades ago, in which she argued that if you had been an ancient Greek abducted by time travelling aliens and transported to the present day there would not be much that you would recognise, one exception being higher education. In virtually every room you would see someone at the front, probably standing, talking to a silent group of people, almost certainly seated. The lecture, as the prime method of teaching, has certainly stood the test of time. When I started as an educational developer in Higher Education, over 30 years ago, it was not uncommon for an academic in a workshop to take issue with being described as a teacher. "I am described and employed as a lecturer; teaching is what happens in schools," was the gist of what was said to me on more than one occasion.

It is good to reflect that I have not heard that argument for a while, and to think that at least that battle as to the role of the academic as an educator in Higher Education has maybe been largely won: although clearly, there are still a very large number of lectures being given. Of course, it is also arguable that over that time students have also changed. Whether or not there is a danger of a rose-tinted spectacle view of the past, it is certainly true that, in the UK, far more school-leavers are now going to university (around 50%) and they are paying fees. Subsequently, a common complaint of colleagues is that students do not appear particularly interested in learning, will only do work if marks are attached, and having been encouraged to see themselves as customers and consumers, seem to feel that they have 'bought' a degree. I particularly like the following response to this that I have heard suggested by Sally Brown. As part of induction, it should be made to clear to students that they are customers in the same way as people who join a gym or fitness club are customers. They have every right to expect good facilities, expert coaching and appropriate fitness programmes. But they have not bought fitness! That can only be achieved by them putting in sufficient time and effort; similarly, with learning at university. This is a comparison I think students can recognise and understand.

It has been noted before that it is interesting, and probably not helpful, that in English we have the two distinct words – teaching and learning – that makes it all too easy to think of them as two distinct and different activities. At best, the linkage is implicit. I have memories of a "Peanuts" cartoon by Schultz, in which Charlie Brown is asked what he has been doing all day. "Teaching my dog [Snoopy] to play dead," is his reply. "Play dead," says the inquisitor to the dog, but Snoopy shows no reaction and just sits there. "I said I'd been teaching him," says Charlie Brown. "I didn't say he'd learnt it!" In similar vein, I remember a keynote presentation by Tom Angelo, in which he observed, "Teaching without learning is just talking." So in order that we don't lose sight of this linkage, there being no single word (pedagogy just not quite doing it, for a number of reasons), as the focus on pedagogy and the quality of the student learning experience has grown, we have been forced to repeatedly use the somewhat cumbersome pairing, teaching and learning.

And arguably this is still not really sufficient. Of particular interest to me over many years has been the importance of assessment in the teaching and learning process, and I and others would argue that there is an 'out-of-sight out-of-mind' problem if we just refer to learning and teaching and that assessment can then easily get forgotten. But to insist that inclusive reference should always be made to learning, teaching *and* assessment is, not unreasonably, considered too cumbersome by many. I have to say, I was a little disappointed that this book does not include more on innovations in assessment, but I guess that's fair considering that last year's compendium was totally focussed on the assessment of learning. And as a proponent of authentic assessment, wherever possible, I found the examples in section 5 of authentic learning – an essential concomitant – both interesting and useful.

This brings me to the third idea in the title – innovation. I have always found this quite a difficult concept for several reasons. To be innovative something has to be 'new, advanced, original' and someone has to be 'original and creative'. My first problem is with originality. What might be very original in one context may be decidedly traditional and mainstream in another – so by whose yardstick, and in what contexts are we making the judgement that something is innovative? My second problem is that once innovation is seen to be a 'good thing' and starts to be seen as a performance indicator – either formal or informal – there is the danger of a slippery slope leading to 'change-for-change-sake'. I am reminded of a conference, to promote pedagogic research, if memory serves, where controversially Graham Gibbs argued in a keynote that we don't really need any more research into teaching and learning. What we actually need is for the sector to act on, and implement, what we already know from the existing research literature that we have already.

However, certainly in the UK, even after thirty years or more of initiatives, projects, and targeted funding, the Government this year expressed concern that universities are not offering "the quality and intensity of teaching" expected to justify the fees that students are paying and the universities minister has stated the aim to wipe out "mediocre teaching", describing some teaching as "lamentable", and warning that bad teaching is damaging the reputation of British Higher Education. Based on my travels and experience, I suspect the quality of university teaching is similarly patchy in other countries too. Now while in the UK there may well be another agenda, associated with fees, and the proposed Teaching Excellence Framework will inevitably fail to assess the quality of teaching, given the metrics chosen and the focus on whole institutions, nevertheless there would still appear to be a very real need for books like this, offering academics clear, practical examples of innovative ways to improve their teaching and the students' learning.

This book is impressive in the range of types of innovation covered: role play and games; student partnerships; technology and e-learning (two separate sections); case-based teaching; authentic learning; and field work – surely, something for everyone? I am also confident that many university teachers who are already innovative and providing students with an excellent learning experience will still find much of interest in this book. It would be invidious to pick out individual chapters, but for me (in addition to Section 5, already mentioned), given my experience and interest in promoting research-based learning, I found Section 2, and the range of other ways of including students in partnerships that that covers particularly inspiring (along with chapter 17, in Section 4). And for those interested in the increasingly popular idea of the flipped classroom, Section 3 will be of especial interest.

Of course, ideally, picking up Graham Gibb's earlier point about research, we need the sector as a whole to be sufficiently motivated to engage with, and implement as appropriate, the kind of approaches detailed in this book to the point that they cease to be innovatory.

Professor Chris Rust.

Chapter 1

An Introduction to Innovative Teaching and Learning

John Branch, Sarah Hayes, Anne Hørsted & Claus Nygaard

Cassettes, Compact Discs, and Creative Destruction

Three of us are children of the eighties (Anne is the baby among us). It is not to say that we were born in the eighties. Oh, how we wish! No, it means that our coming of age—especially in terms of music—occurred during that wonderful decade of *Billie Jean* by Michael Jackson, Madonna's *Like a Virgin*, and really anything which was sung by a band with 'big hair'.

The eighties also offered us the rare opportunity to witness—with the launch of the compact disc player in 1982 by Philips and Sony—the beginnings of the digital music revolution which continues to this day. Indeed, prior to the advent of the compact disc, our lives were filled with cassettes, which themselves had supplanted vinyl, the dominant format of the music industry from the first days of commercial music sales. And then, if by magic, came the almost ethereal beauty of the compact disc!

John recalls buying his first player (a JVC model, by the way) one day in early September 1986 when he began his university studies in London, Canada. He even remembers the first five compact discs which he bought that same Autumn afternoon:

Brothers in Arms by Dire Straits

Pink Floyd's *The Wall*

Upstairs at Eric's by Yaz

Air Supply's *Greatest Hits* (in hopes of romantic evenings in his dormitory room)

Some Great Reward by Depeche Mode

But the compact disc not only provided music listeners unprecedented convenience and sonic bliss, it also served as the harbinger of a flurry of development in music technology. In 1987, for example, Sony launched DAT—Digital Audio Tape which promised similar aural quality and the ability to record. Then came Mini-Disc, HDCD, Super Audio CD, DVD-Audio, MP3, MP4, and doubtless several other formats which we have forgotten.

What was it about the compact disc, however, which caused it to catch on, and effectively kill cassettes? Likewise, why have compact discs all but disappeared today, with music listeners now favouring MP3 files? And equally importantly, why did all those other music formats not take off in a similar way?

The answer is simple: innovation. We define innovation with the following equation:

$$INNOVATION = INVENTION + VALUE$$

As such, an invention is never guaranteed, simply because it is new. On the contrary, an invention must be better. And better is judged by the customer. That is to say, the market is the arbiter of innovation. In other words, a company does not innovate, it invents. It puts a new product to the market, and hopes that it 'catches on' among customers. And if it does, the new product diffuses in the market, displacing previous instantiations (like the case of the compact disc)... a process which Joseph Schumpeter (1975) called creative destruction.

To illustrate, John was in the health and beauty section of a local department store a few years back, when he discovered a new product being launched by Colgate-Palmolive. It was a pump-style tube of toothpaste. Nothing new there, except that in the cap of the toothpaste was a roll of dental floss. Hmm, interesting! When John returned to the department store two weeks later, however, the tube had disappeared from the shelves. You see, customers did not derive any additional value from the invention, and consequently, it had not diffused. In other words, it was an invention, not an innovation.

Contrast the toothpaste with a gardening invention which John also witnessed. Traditionally, insect-killing chemicals are purchased in large plastic bags (sometimes up to 20 kg) which are difficult to transport, open, and store. To add insult to injury, an additional piece of equipment (a spreader) is also required in order to apply the chemicals in the garden. All in all, not such a convenient product for the customer.

In the early 2000s, however, Senoret Company in the U.S.A. began distributing its chemicals in a new type of container. It held about 3 pounds (almost 1.5 kg), and had a self-opening and re-sealable mouth. But best of all, it had a special plastic filter-like mesh in the mouth which, when combined with the built in handle in the bag, allowed the user to shake the chemicals on the garden without the need for the additional spreader (See Figure 1.). Invention or innovation? Well, the proof is in the pudding as they say, because the new shaker-bag became the best-selling product among customers in Walmart's gardening centre that year, and quickly diffused throughout the industry as other companies adopted it. Innovation indeed!

Figure 1: Shaker Bag.

In the context of higher education, therefore, this definition of innovation suggests that any new teaching or learning practice is not an innovation but instead an invention. And like the compact disc, it becomes an innovation not because it is novel, but because it adds value... because it improves the practice of teaching or, more importantly, enhances student learning in higher education.

LiHE

This anthology is the product of *Institute for Learning in Higher Education* (LiHE), an academic association which, as intimated by its name, focuses entirely on learning at the post-secondary level. The focus of the association reflects the shift from a transmission-based philosophy to a student-centred, learning-based approach. And its scope is limited to colleges, universities, and others institutions of higher education.

The main activity of the association is the symposium. About 10 years ago, Claus noted that professors attend conferences at which they present their scientific research in a 10--20 minute session, receive a few comments, then very often 'head to the bar for a drink'. He proposed an alternative, therefore, which *au contraire* returns to that ancient Greek format— the symposium— at which co-creation is key.

So, about 6 months prior to a symposium, a call for chapter proposals which has a relatively tightly focused theme is announced on the association's website and on various electronic mailing lists. The June 2015 symposium which was held in Aegina, Greece, for example, had the theme *Assessing Learning in Higher Education*; previous themes have revolved around games and simulations, classroom innovations, and learning spaces (in higher education).

So, authors submit chapter proposals, which are then double-blind reviewed. If a proposal is accepted, its author is given 4 months to complete it. The whole chapter is then double-blind reviewed, and if it is accepted, the author is invited to attend the symposium. There, all authors revise their own chapters, work together to revise each other's chapters, and collaborate to assemble an anthology which, about a month later, goes off to the publisher.

The 2016 Copenhagen Symposium

For this symposium we (the editors) sought teaching and learning innovations, within the domain of higher education and with an emphasis on learning, as per the focus of LiHE. We aspired to publish an anthology which was diverse in nature and which showcased concrete examples of innovative teaching and learning practices in higher education from around the world. We welcomed practices from all scientific disciplines and in all teaching and learning contexts. The call for chapter proposals resulted in submissions from around the world which described a variety of different innovative teaching and learning practices. The subsequent review and re-submission process, whittled the submission down to the 28 chapters which follow in this anthology. The LiHE symposium at which the chapters were revised and the anthology was assembled was held in May 2016 in Copenhagen. In addition to the academic symposium activities, authors explored the city's many bridges and canals, toured the famous Carlsberg brewery, and acted like kids again at Tivoli Gardens.

The Editors and Innovative Teaching and Learning Practices

As editors, of course, we bring our own perspectives to the role, which are based on our own experiences with innovative teaching and learning practices. We have our own disciplinary backgrounds, which come with their own specific boundaries and biases. And we have our own philosophical assumptions about pedagogy which, in turn, influence our views about innovative practices.

John

After completing my MBA in 1993, I moved to France to take up a position as a marketing lecturer at a new business school. Deriving inspiration from Robin Williams in *Dead Poets Society*, I aspired to be the greatest lecturer in the history of business schools. And consequently, I spent hours scripting every course session (See Figure 1.), with colour-coded prompts to remind me to 'give example', 'change transparency slide', and even 'tell joke'.

But as I grew more comfortable with the idea of relinquishing control to students, and more importantly, as I began to realise that students could learn more effectively from action-based experiential methods, I started to experiment with alternatives to my traditional lectures. One of the first innovations which I adopted was a computer-based marketing simulation. Entitled *Markstrat*, the simulation pits students against each other in a simulated marketplace in which the various activities of marketing—segmentation, targeting, positioning, product mix, promotional campaigns—are managed over a several year period. I knew that I was onto something when I met a group of students at Blueberry Hill (the bar and restaurant in Saint Louis which is owned by the famous guitarist/singer Chuck Berry) late one Saturday. Rather than enjoying a drink or dancing, the students were huddled in a booth talking *Markstrat* tactics.

Over the past decade, I have also been experimenting with international study tour courses. In these courses, I usually require students to keep and reflect on a journal, in service of the development of their cross-cultural competence. The course always revolves around a group project which calls for on-the-ground field research. But this year I 'pulled out all the stops', also integrating a challenge from the local government economic development agency, and an in-country home-stay as part of the cultural experience.

Figure 2: Example Scripts.

The most recent invention (not yet deemed innovative by my students) with which I have been experimenting is a syllabus template which draws on the European Credit Transfer System notion of learning hours. In North America, courses have traditionally been measured in terms of contact hours. As such, syllabi are often a mish-mash of schedule, required books, and office hours. My new syllabus template focuses on learning activities and their corresponding learning hours. The course is organised by week, and details exactly which activities are to be completed, in which order, and the time which they ought to take. Although admittedly it is quite simple in practice, it seems to be paying dividends, both to me and my students. I find that it forces me to identify the learning objectives very clearly, and subsequently consider thoughtfully the different instructional tools for achieving these learning objectives. Anecdotally, the new template is much appreciated, especially with my part-time MBA students, who find it a great scheduling device given their busy schedules.

Week	Learning Activities (Learning Hours)
27 June to 3 July	1. Participate in Marketing Forum (1 hour) 2. Read these articles on the meaning of marketing, and then develop your own definition of marketing (1 hour): • AMA Marketing Definitions (Canvas) • 72 Marketing Definitions (Canvas) • History of the Word 'Marketing' (Canvas) • The Word on the Street (Canvas) 3. Read these articles on the importance of marketing, and then articulate the role of marketing in today's organisations (1 hour): • Marketing Concepts (Canvas) • Marketing in the Driver's Seat (Canvas) • The Decline and Dispersion of Marketing Competence (Study.net) • Can Marketing Regain Its Seat at the Table? (Canvas) 4. Complete John Smith Exercise (2 hours) 5. Read Chapter 1. An Introduction to Marketing Research, and then contemplate the research challenge of identifying the most popular exhibit at an aquarium (1 hour): • Introduction to Marketing Research 6. Read this article on the marketing context, and then identify some contextual factors which impact marketing at your organisation (1 hour): • PEST and PESTEL Analysis (Canvas) 7. Read this guide on business ecosystems, and consider the history of companies such as Eastman Kodak or Blackberry, for example (1 hour): • Mapping Business Ecosystems

Figure 3: Syllabus Template.

What next? Well, I have just reviewed the literature on blended-learning/flipped-classrooms, and I am gearing up to push myself to relinquish even more control of the classroom to my students. I have been revising the layout for a new introduction to marketing textbook which takes a novel 'going to market' decision-making approach, rather than the typical dictionary-like *modus operandi*. And I have been toying with the idea of programming a computer-based simulation for teaching and learning international business.

Sarah

I like to think that creativity and innovation in my teaching has its roots back in the 1980s, when I completed my BA (Hons) Degree at Edinburgh College of Art (listening to cassette tapes of Bruce Springsteen, Chaka Khan, Frankie Goes to Hollywood, Talking Heads, Sade and U2). I didn't teach students until many years later, but I did innovate after my graduation, running my own business: *Bare Threads* and selling my tie-dyed 'creations' at craft fairs during the Edinburgh Festival.

Figure 4: Sarah's carved Bare Threads sign from her 1980s stall.

I have to say that when visiting Freetown Christiania in Christianshavn, Copenhagen during the symposium, with my new friends and colleagues from around the world, I felt very much at home! Alas, my hippie spirit soon had a mortgage to pay... and I found myself working in finance for several years, before entering higher education in 1998 and re-training. Since then, over the years, I have taught in Business, Computing, Sociology and Education, but always with the sense that the varied groups I am teaching are 'partners' with me in the process of learning. Between 2005 – 2009 I found ways to bring innovation to my teaching of web design, project management and e-learning to undergraduates, by running online discussion forums alongside class sessions, and by taking students into virtual worlds, such as *Second Life*. I completed my Masters degree in Educational Research, based on case studies in E-learning, but this also reminded me of how much I enjoy social theory.

Whilst at school, after Art & Design, Sociology was my favourite subject and, when developing my PhD, this was the field I chose to research in. In particular, I liked applying social theory to everyday events and artifacts, that are otherwise treated as simply 'there'. When I wrote my course on *Technology & Social Theory*, I challenged my students to notice the politics inherent in the design and deployment of technologies of all kinds in society, including the construction of, and access to, public spaces. I introduced peer assessment techniques where students gave each other feedback on their ideas about technology, society and power. My chapter in the LiHE book: *Learning to Research – Researching to Learn* (2015) is about students learning to 'live' their research, as advised by C Wright Mills (1959) in *The Sociological Imagination*. When I wrote the popular culture course this chapter is based on, I found myself in the privileged position of being able to facilitate students to critically notice things about everyday popular culture (soap operas, popular music, film, reality TV, tattoos, 'chick-lit' and celebrities), through classic sociological theory. Thus every student submission I marked was an original and personally creative article, as it was 'crafted' through the student's combined choice and comprehension of media, topic and theorist. A few years later now, as Director of a Post Graduate Diploma and Masters in Higher Education, I find I can once more encourage my students (actually higher education educators also) to consider themselves as 'reflexive projects' (Giddens, 1991:75–77), as they develop innovative research projects to transform their academic practice.

By using techniques like 'free writing' these teaching staff are encouraged to critically re-visit their teaching identity and share their ideas on a social media platform, in this case: Yammer. The added value here comes from gaining new perspectives on the ways that personal and professional life is intertwined for both ourselves and our students. In recent years I have sometimes found myself teaching about quality in higher education internationally, in places like Italy, Vietnam and India. In such cultural exchanges, mutual ideas about what constitutes innovative teaching are shared between international partners, adding rich dimensions to my understanding of what constitutes innovative teaching. Reflecting on how I continue to innovate in teaching, I would say that many of my ideas develop through interaction with other educators, in the same manner that has enabled this book to come together.

Anne

While the other editors were wearing pastel colours, headbands and short tight Lycra I had my first meeting with the Danish education system in late 1980's. For many years I struggled with wanting to please my teachers. I took directions and followed the rules. And at the same time I was feeling creatively unfulfilled as I always searched for an alternative explanation. I had an urge to try something in a different way. I loved learning and spend a lot of time studying on my own. I read books, watched movies, I observed and I used my imagination. So school turned into an uninspiring place. I saw school as a necessary commitment, but not much else. Gradually, I transformed into a student who challenged authority and caused disruption. This went on until I met a teacher who made a difference. He was able to inspire, motivate and involve students in their own learning process. He focused on collaboration both in relation to the academic content and in relation to our own learning process. To him, we were all explorers who had to find our own way, and he was a supportive guide who was able to make a connection between the subject and students' interests.

So in my mind —collaborating and benefiting from diversity are the keystones of innovative teaching and learning. Throughout history, most of the great scientific breakthroughs and important innovations came through collaboration and through the stimulation of other people's ideas. Nobody lives in a vacuum and we all draw from the cultures we are a part of and from the influence of other people's minds and achievements. In my own practice, I try my best to switch my focus from teaching creativity and innovation to teaching for creativity and innovation by a pedagogy that is designed to encourage other people to think creatively and to engage in innovative processes. I try not to give many answers but instead giving students the tools they need to find out what the answers might be or to explore new avenues. Within particular domains, I find it is perfectly appropriate to say, "I'm interested in new and original ways you can approach these issues". However, teaching for creativity and innovation is not always an easy process either for students or for university staff. When most students set foot on a campus, they are often being taught to produce rather than create, to follow rather than lead, and to fear instead of learning from failure.

Nevertheless, as I have had the opportunity to learn from this anthology – and from the symposium that supported its creation – my understanding of ways to teach for innovation in Higher Education has matured. This anthology is a result of collaboration of ideas and experiences that can be useful to stimulate our ideas of innovative teaching and learning in Higher Education.

Claus

In my first years as ph.d.-student, I was given the task to coordinate a bachelors' course with 450 students at Copenhagen Business School. My task was to lecture in a 150-people capacity theatre, which meant that each 2-hour lecture should be repeated back-to-back three times a day. It was a nightmare to teach in this way. During the third round, it was often impossible for me to remember, if I had said something or it was just my memory of the first and second lecture. But the idea was that all students had to hear the same lecture, so there was nothing else to do than to repeat myself three times on lecture days. One could say that this was not very innovative.

A year later I got involved in the development of a CD-ROM, which contained case-material from a Danish company in the hearing aid industry. It had been decided that students should be more actively engaged during class, so we produced a CD-ROM with video interviews, annual reports, photos, podcasts (at that time podcasts were called tape-recordings), budgets, organisation charts, etc. All the material documented the life of the company. Students now had the task of analysing the company as part of their studies. It was a great success, because students became "field researchers" and overall learned much more about the use of theory for analysing empirical situations. It was a great way to use technology to promote case-based learning. Technologically it was an innovation in teaching and learning too (this was before the Internet Browser). With the Internet came the possibility to develop even further case-based learning, and the day before Christmas Eve 2004, I wrote a prospect for a piece of software called CaseMaker. In 2005 we started to develop a beta-version of the software, and it was used at Copenhagen Business School at a trial basis. Following the positive feedback of students, I gathered a group of international colleagues from the LiHE-network, and we wrote an application for EU-funding of proper development of the CaseMaker-software. Due to other obligations I withdrew from the work to bring "my" baby to life, but I followed the project from the side-line, and was happy to see the completion of CaseMaker in 2015 (www.casemaker.dk). One interesting thing is that this book actually contains a chapter about the CaseMaker software and its use at Birmingham City University. Much to my surprise, when we received the submissions for this handbook.

Innovations in teaching and learning are many. Of course it is obvious to point to the use of technology as is most probably the most recent game-changer of higher education. However, I have also been involved in live role-plays, teaching with live-cases, outdoor learning, inquiry based learning, and problem-based project-work (Meier & Nygaard, 2008). All somewhat innovations in teaching and learning, where the focus has shifted from teacher-governance to student-governance, and from syllabus-driven to problem-driven. It is my experience, and belief, that if you work systematically to empower students to take governance in their learning process, and develop problem-driven education, students will learn differently, more and better.

The Anthology – overview

This anthology holds 28 chapters which all discuss and showcase innovative teaching and learning practices in higher education. The chapters are grouped into 6 sections:

+ Section 1: Innovation through Play, Role-Play and Games in Higher Education;

+ Section 2: Innovative Teaching and Learning Practices Using Student Partnerships;

+ Section 3: Teaching and Learning Innovations Using Modern Technologies;

+ Section 4: Innovation through Case-based Teaching and Learning;

+ Section 5: Innovation through Authentic Learning - Environments, Experiences and Field Work;

+ Section 6: Innovative Teaching and Learning practices using E-learning.

Section 1, *Innovation through Play, Role-Play and Games in Higher Education*, holds 4 chapters.

In chapter 2, *Managing conflict through Role-Play*, Salh provides a practical exercise that reflects a multi-layered workplace dispute explored via a role play scenario. Drawing upon academic and practical knowledge, students work together to unpack a range of issues. This collective approach ensures students emerge through this process with an enhanced understanding of their subject area by using fun.

In chapter 3, *Role playing in the Traditional Classroom, Blended Learning, and eLearning*, Mackey explores the strengths and challenges of three modalities for role playing. The chapter includes practical advice and examples of role playing in the traditional instructor-led classroom; in blended learning, which combines technology-enhanced learning with the traditional classroom; and in eLearning, in which students learn entirely online, whether synchronously or asynchronously.

Chapter 4, *Language Learning through Engaging in Online Role Play*, highlights the advantages offered by interactive online role-play in language learning. This practical example presented by Ludewig-Rohwer demonstrates how flexibility and anonymity can be used to create a fun and safe learning environment that encourages autonomous learning through creative discussion.

Chapter 5, *Assisting Pre-service Educators to Understand Lesson Planning. Planning not to Fail*, by Jansen van Vuuren, provides lecturers with three ideas for teaching lesson planning. These ideas incorporate a variety of learning styles, intelligences and human drives to ensure that as many students as possible are reached in an effective, yet fun way. A computer-based lesson planning exercise is complemented by a floor puzzle and board game to enrich the learning experience.

Section 2, *Innovative Teaching and Learning Practices Using Student Partnerships*, holds 6 chapters.

In chapter 6, *Exploring feelings through reflective poetry writing*, Jack presents the use of reflective poetry writing as a way to explore thoughts and feelings about nursing practice.

In chapter 7, *STA(r)s in the Classroom: Supporting Collaborative Learning with Student Teaching Assistants*, Bale describes the use of Student Teaching Assistants (STAs) in Modern Language lessons. He shows how the use of STAs goes a step further than peer-assisted learning, as students have a visible presence in the classroom and help plan lesson content based on their knowledge of their fellow students' needs.

In chapter 8, *Beyond engagement and enhancement – piloting a 'digital student partnership' to co-teach academic staff on our Post Graduate Diploma in Higher Education*, Hayes explains how she had success by engaging undergraduate students to co-teach a group of educators with her, in a student-staff partnership.

In chapter 9, *TAPs – Text Analysis Presentations*, Bhoola presents how students can improve major language skills, reading comprehension, critical thinking, discussion skills and group work by giving Text Analysis Presentations (TAPs).

In chapter 10, *Connecting Theory Through Practice: Transformational Learning in Pre-Service Teacher Education*, Kalyn shares how teacher candidates connect practical learning experiences and knowledge acquisition in a Physical Education methods course.

In chapter 11, *Extended Flipped Classroom – using peer dynamics for integrative learning*, Johnsson *et al.* introduce a novel method that uses peer dynamics for integrative learning referred to as Extended Flipped Classroom (EFC). Its aim is to enhance learning and mimic work-life learning situations.

Section 3, *Teaching and Learning Innovations Using Modern Technologies*, holds 3 chapters.

In chapter 12, *Utilizing recorded lectures and simple mobile phone Audience Response Systems in a Modified Flipped Classroom-Peer Instruction format*, Fadel is using a combination of recorded lectures and a simple mobile phone application as an ARS in a Modified Flipped Classroom-Peer Instruction format to provoke peer discussion and learning.

In chapter 13, *Enhancing the Physical World with Augmented Reality (AR)*, Watson on the other hand is using AR to create digitally interactive 360° physical learning environments in a hybrid style of Flipped Classroom.

In chapter 14, *The Application of Tangible User Interfaces for Teaching and Learning in Higher Education*, De Raffaele *et al.* are making use of TUIs for non-front loaded Flipped Classrooms to aid in the Teaching and Learning of Abstract Concepts within Higher Education.

Section 4, *Innovation through Case-based Teaching and Learning*, holds 3 chapters.

In chapter 15, *Collaborative engagement in case-studies through Learning Technology*, Eley & Faniglione look at an approach to address, at least in part, the issue of limited collaborative case-study engagement by students outside the classroom environment. They describe a trial study of an innovative platform for collaborative and progressive work on, and use of, case-studies.

In chapter 16, *Teaching Responsible Management Practices via Cases*, Svendsen gives an insight into the reflections of the teacher in connection with organizing a course on corporate communication and including reflections on responsible management practices to fulfill the strategic aims of the university. Her chapter also contains reflections on how best to facilitate student learning through the use of cases that play into the corporate communication and responsible management philosophy and what the teacher's role should be in this process.

In chapter 17, *Psychology students as co-creators in designing an innovative case-study based learning resource*, Faniglione *et al.* present innovative approaches related to students as partners at Birmingham City University. Academic staff and students have been working in partnership to identify areas of the Psychology curriculum which could benefit from greater links between theory and practice. Consequently, the proposed solution was the co-creation of an interactive multimedia resource that allows learners to explore all the stages involved in taking a clinical, assessment or developmental history interview.

Section 5, *Innovation through Authentic Learning Environments, Experiences and Field Work*, holds 4 chapters.

In chapter 18, *Integration method to create innovative business ideas and to learn multicultural team working skills*, Ahonen & Heikkinen focus on developing and testing business ideas. This is a method used to demonstrate to business students what kind of aspects they have to consider when creating new business ideas. The method aims to create an authentic learning experience for students. The authentic experience creates strong memories which can be used later in their studies as a framework for knowledge to be attached into. Simultaneously it is offering the students opportunities to identify their own strengths and become familiar with their fellow students.

In chapter 19, *Teaching academic writing against the grain: A project-based approach,* Ip introduces the innovative teaching and learning practice designed for an academic writing course. Students experience a complete, systematic and authentic research process organized according to the project-based learning approach. The process is achieved through an inter-university collaboration. Students in small teams collect data relevant to any social issues of their own interest. The data are used to generate two outcomes – an academic research paper for students of one university and a business plan for students of the other university. With this practice, students develop hands-on research skills and learn academic literacy more effectively. The collaborative experience also enhances their social and communication skills through working in multidisciplinary and multicultural teams.

In chapter 20, *Multiple tools for innovative interdependent learning techniques in higher education to foster employability skills,* Younis describes an actual experience of the multiple tools that are used to ensure the transfer of knowledge from theory to practical field work application. The tools are used in the British University in Egypt where a variety of modules are taught in the Business department to ensure meeting the intended learning outcomes and developing transferable skills in order to ensure a high degree of employability in the market. The intention is to prepare graduates for both local and international employment through the application of several methods in the course of their higher education at university.

In chapter 21, *Building motivated student engagement through demonstrated curriculum relevance,* Benvenuti describes an approach to curriculum design and implementation that encompasses not only consideration of what students need to know and be able to do, but a broader view that looks at the context in which they will one day need to do it. Learning outcomes for the courses include a focus on the personal attributes and values related to students' future careers, and an aspect of self-directed learning in which students define their own specific learning outcomes and ways in which to develop these. By strongly emphasizing the relevance of the curriculum to their future desired careers, it is hoped that high student engagement over a sustained period of time will be encouraged.

Section 6, *Innovative Teaching and Learning practices using E-learning*, holds 7 chapters.

In chapter 22, *Promoting Self-Regulated Language Learning through a Technology Enhanced Content-based Classroom*, Koç shows how the use of technoogy can encourage students to be independent learners. The concordance analysis program extended students' vocabulary by allowing them to see and search for lexical combinations used in different contexts on their own. The Moovly tool gave students an opportunity to work together to create presentations independently while they decided what kind of information was to be extracted from the different websites they accessed. By using these tools students improved their cognitive and social strategies. Students not only scan and search for information but they also evaluated information and made independent decisions. They worked collaboratively and with peers in groups.

In chapter 23, *Promoting Language Skills through Teacher-structured out-of-class ICT Activities in Higher Education Context*, Inozu & Gorgun show how the use of blogging and podcasting provide students with ample amount of listening experience in foreign language learning process. The main motive for using these digital tools was to extend in-class work to outside of the classroom, so that the students could have access to teacher-structured materials and activities delivered in a self-study mode. Integration of digital technologies enables the teacher to extend the class-room beyond its physical borders and allows the students to study in their private or preferred environment without time and place constraints. Lower levels of anxiety, improved self-efficacy perceptions and increased motivation are the further benefits of this instructional design.

In chapter 24, *Impact of eLearning: Looking past the hype. The impact of two Life Science courses on global learners*, Perumalla *et al.* present the online courses in Faculty of Medicine at the University of Toronto (UofT) using the Blackboard (Bb) Learning Management. The flexibility and robustness of Bb provides instructors in creating a "virtual learning environment" by ability to manage the course content including posting videos and other learning modules, administer online assessments (quizzes), submit assignments and also to manage Grade Book where students can access their respective grades. For the students, it provides a "one stop shop", where they access course material, create a community of learners through chat and discussion boards, and can easily and conveniently access bulk announcements.

In chapter 25, *Stimulating Self-Regulated and Self-Directed Learning Through Technology Enhanced Learning Environment*, Koç shows examples that allow freedom for learners to create their own learning path using Webspirationpro with feedback from teachers in the form of a concept map. As the learners choose their own path, they can use the necessary resources from the videos uploaded by the teacher. Also the freedom of learners was extended to create evaluation schemes by negotiating with the teacher and peers in line with self-directed learning principles. Moodle and YouTube were used for assignment and resource sharing.

In chapter 26, *Modelling the use of Google Applications for Education and social media as building blocks for student teachers' TPACK*, Du Plessis at University of Mpumalanga in South Africa proposes the use of freely available solutions such as Google Applications. The absence of a Learning Management System necessitated the use of time-saving scripts such as Doctopus in conjunction with Google Drive and Flubaroo in conjunction with Google Sheet. This proved particularly useful for efforts to teach technology as part of the students' teacher training and the implementation of certain social media applications created opportunities to model these applications' to help facilitate teaching about technology.

In chapter 27, *A reduced attendance model of delivery that engages remote learners in the workplace*, Lewis shows the utilisation of a range of digital technologies in Dental studies. Adobe Connect Pro (videoconferencing software) is used for polls, presentations, collaboration, and breakout groups. This increased access to the programme for geographically remote and academically disparate learners. Moodle (VLE) is used for Lessons, Books, Quizzes, and Mahara for eportfolio. Work Based Learning and Professional Practice outcomes provides a single point of access for learning resources (to increase access and consistency of material presentation and format). YouTube allows access to practical demonstrations. The benefits to students are that we provide contextualisation and application of learning to the workplace – and workplace activity to the learning. Access to practical demonstrations of processes through video clips and rewards work related activity with academic credit.

In chapter 28, *How Do We Hybridise x and c MOOC Architectures to Create a Course on Online CVs?*, McGuire describes his work with an online course at the University of Glasgow. It is a global, free, completely open, online course, with no entry requirements, not targeted at a specific group. It is a trans-discipline initiative that is cross-cutting in that it is targeted at all careers and is also supportive of academic-professional/ work transitions. Its aim was to improve employability through the development of 'digital' or online *curriculum vitae* (CV) writing skills and it involved liaison with a wide range of internal and external partners.

Together these inspiring examples show a large diversity in their approach to being innovative in teaching and learning practices. And at the same time they somewhat show a homogeneous effect on both student engagement and student learning outcomes. They all argue that their innovative approach has helped student learn different, better, and more. If we take their words for granted, there is a lot to gain from reading the narrative accounts of innovative teaching and learning in this book. Happy reading!

About the Authors

John Branch is Academic Director of the part-time MBA programmes and Assistant Clinical Professor of Business Administration at the Stephen M. Ross School of Business, and Faculty Associate at the Center for Russian, East European, & European Studies, both of the University of Michigan in Ann Arbor, U.S.A. He can be contacted at this e-mail: jdbranch@umich.edu

Sarah Hayes is Senior Lecturer in Technology-Enhanced and Flexible Learning in the Centre for Learning Innovation and Profession Practice at Aston University in Birmingham, England. She can be contacted at this e-mail: s.hayes@aston.ac.uk

Anne Hørsted is Adjunct Professor at Syddansk Universitet, Senior consultant at cph:learning in Denmark, and Adjunct Professor at the Institute for Learning in Higher Education. She can be contacted at this e-mail: anne@lihe.info

Claus Nygaard, professor, ph.d., is executive director at Institute for Learning in Higher Education (LiHE) and executive director at cph:learning in Denmark. He can be contacted at this e-mail: info@lihe.info

Bibliography

Giddens, A. (1991). *Modernity and Self-Identity. Self and Society in the Late Modern Age*. Stanford University Press.

Hayes, S. (2015). Encouraging the intellectual craft of living research: tattoos, theory and time. In C. Guerin; P. Bartholomew & C. Nygaard (Eds.) *Learning to Research – Researching to Learn*. Oxfordshire: Libri Publishing Ltd.

Meier, F. & C. Nygaard (2008). Problem Oriented Project Work in Higher Education. In C. Nygaard & C. Holtham (Eds.) *Understanding Learning-Centred Higher Education*. Copenhagen: Copenhagen Business School Press.

Schumpeter, J. (1975). *Capitalism, Socialism and Democracy*. New York, U.S.A.: Harper.

Wright Mills, C. (1959). *The Sociological Imagination*, Oxford University Press.

Section I: Play, Role-Play and Games

An Introduction to Play, Role-Play and Games in Higher Education

Eurika Jansen van Vuuren, Iris Ludewig-Rohwer,
Terry Mackey & Sukhwinder Salh

Introduction

The benefits of playing in higher education have long been underappreciated, despite ample theoretical evidence of its advocacy. As Geurts & Duke (2012:X) succinctly observed, *"Those in higher education do not play enough."* This chapter overviews the theory and concepts of role play and learning games, providing concrete applications in higher education. A brief definition of key practices will provide a foundation for these concepts.

Play

Play makes a valuable contribution to the learning process throughout life and is a natural way of exploring the world. Play in higher education, however, is structured to achieve instructional goals and evolves through a process of rules and regulations, thus enhancing learning. Complex concepts of theory and knowledge explored in an enjoyable way are less intimidating and enable learners to work in a safe environment. An inclusive environment creates a real opportunity for all students to be involved in ways that match their learning styles. This interactive and engaging practice not only encourages collaboration but also permits creativity and interpersonal skills to develop.

Role play

Wills *et al.* (2011:2) describes role plays as *"situations in which learners take on the profiles of specific characters or representatives of organizations in a contrived setting"*. Designing situations in which learners are required to understand and express the viewpoints and experiences of others not only deepens their learning of a given character type or experience; it encourages empathy and builds communication and collaboration skills.

Games

Percival & Ellington as quoted by Leigh (2003:85) defined games as activities that are "time-limited", "role-oriented", "outcome – driven" and "scored". They give two main requisites for a game: competition (which may include a learner competing against him- or herself) and rules. Games often involve cooperation and conflict. A learning game includes overcoming challenges and solving problems through thoughtful decision-making (Kapp, 2014). Although many games are now computer-based, it is still relevant to use board and paper based or other non-digital games to encourage the development of interpersonal skills and collaboration in a more relaxed way, where the fun element of a game contributes to a less intimidating learning experience.

Overall, role playing and game-based learning are excellent applications of problem-based learning, which emphasizes active learning that centres on the resolution of real-world problems. First used in medical education, problem-based learning engaged students by presenting them with medical issues to be resolved in small group situations; this approach increased motivation and enhanced students' ability to move from concept to practice, offering learners the opportunity to collaborate on solutions and learn from each other (Walker *et al.*, 2015). Much like other learner-centred techniques, role playing empowers students to take responsibility for their own education, increasing motivation as well as learning (Mackey, 2016).

Bringing reality into the classroom

The use of role plays within higher education offers a practical insight into real life scenarios and enables students to develop the necessary skills and knowledge within their discipline. Role play represents a form of learning through experience and is endorsed by Kolb (1984:41), who claims *"knowledge is created through transformation of experience"*. Baker *et al.* (2002) views learning as an integrated process with each stage being mutually supportive of and feeding into the next. It is possible to enter the cycle at any stage and follow it through its logical sequence. The four stages include:

(1) a concrete experience;

(2) observation of and reflection on that experience;

(3) the formation of abstract concepts (analysis) and generalizations (conclusions);

(4) generalisations used to test hypothesis in future situations.

Each of these stages is explored and embedded within many of the exercises included in this chapter. This collection of innovative teaching practices offers a unique way in which the learning in the classroom is brought to life.

Building emotional intelligence

When students are actively involved in role play and games they advance an important component of emotional intelligence – intrapersonal skills (Mayer & Salovey, 1993). They are provided with the opportunity to evaluate their own thinking and enhance their higher level reasoning skills. Gaming activities aid in the understanding of the self in relation to others by giving students the opportunity to be aware of their own feelings and to express them in their interaction with fellow students and others.

Learning through these practical exercises is seen as a social process that enables development of a wider range of skills that students don't necessarily gain through the traditional modes of teaching. Creating an environment for reflective learning through practical exercises not only builds an engaging dialogue but shifts the focus from the teacher to the student. (Brockbank & McGill, 2007). This opportunity brings with it a high degree of empowerment, autonomy and engagement for the students' learning and allows them to manage their own journey of learning in a more effective and collaborative manner. The exercises shared within this chapter aim to support a range of learning styles and offer each individual student the opportunity to engage with the process using their preferred learning style. In a climate of increased competition and focus on employability it is vital that higher education professionals embrace the opportunity to learn from doing. Developing interpersonal skills through interactive exercises allows students to emerge through this process with a broader degree of professional competence. Professional competence goes beyond the simple acquisition of knowledge; skills acquired through these exercises allow students to market themselves more effectively and provide a foundation from which they can progress further both in their careers and life.

Challenges for instructors

Role play and game-based learning offer both challenges and advantages for instructors. One of those challenges involves time. Initial preparation can be more time-intensive than traditional lecture, particularly in the case of media-rich online learning and many types of game-based learning. For technology-enhanced lessons, time may need to be spent teaching the technology rather than the lesson. The payoff, however, is that once the plans and resources for lessons using these modalities have been created, they can be reused for future classes, albeit with any tweaks necessitated by differing class makeup, content changes, or lessons learned in previous iterations. Game pieces will have already been created; online modules will have been developed and tested; role descriptions and scenarios will have already been designed. Thus, preparation time for future classes will be greatly reduced.

Another challenge for instructors is the variability that comes from the creative license inherent in these learning strategies: students may wander down paths previously unanticipated, rules may not be precisely followed, interpersonal communication challenges may emerge, or emotions may be inappropriately engaged. Each of these challenges, however, presents rich opportunities to enhance the lesson. Each offers an essential teaching moment: perhaps an insight into the interpersonal challenges that emerge in handling HR or political issues, the miscommunications that can result from a misstep in a foreign language, a content question that deserves exploration. Just as an awkward question in a lecture class can lead to a productive discussion, a misstep in a role play or learning game can be a pedagogical gift. In some cases, these challenges also provide insight into how a lesson might be enhanced or expanded.

Practical examples

Included within chapter 2, Salh provides a practical exercise that reflects a multi-layered workplace dispute explored via a role play scenario. Drawing upon academic and practical knowledge, students work together to unpack a range of issues. This collective approach ensures students emerge through this process with an enhanced understanding of their subject area by using fun.

In "Role playing in the Traditional Classroom, Blended Learning, and eLearning" (chapter 3), Mackey explores the strengths and challenges of three modalities for role playing. The chapter includes practical advice and examples of role playing in the traditional instructor-led classroom; in blended learning, which combines technology-enhanced learning with the traditional classroom; and in eLearning, in which students learn entirely online, whether synchronously or asynchronously.

Chapter 4 "Language Learning through Engaging in Online Role Play" highlights the advantages offered by interactive online role-play in language learning. This practical example presented by Ludewig-Rohwer demonstrates how flexibility and anonymity can be used to create a fun and safe learning environment that encourages autonomous learning through creative discussion.

Chapter 5 entitled "Assisting Pre-service Educators to Understand Lesson Planning. Planning not to Fail", by Jansen van Vuuren, provides lecturers with three ideas for teaching lesson planning. These ideas incorporate a variety of learning styles, intelligences and human drives to ensure that as many students as possible are reached in an effective, yet fun way. A computer-based lesson planning exercise is complemented by a floor puzzle and board game to enrich the learning experience.

We believe that these four chapters on Role Play and Games will encourage you to try similar learning-centred activities in your own teaching and learning. We end with a quote for inspiration: *"Man only plays when he is in the fullest sense of the word a human being, and he is only fully a human being when he plays."* (Schiller, 1795).

About the Authors

Dr Eurika Jansen van Vuuren is a senior lecturer at the newly established University of Mpumalanga in South Africa, specializing in Life Skills for the Foundation Phase (Arts, Physical Education, Social Sciences, Natural Sciences and Personal and Social Well-being). She can be contacted at one of these e-mails: eurikajansenvanvuuren@gmail or eurika.jvvuuren@ ump.ac.za

Iris Ludewig-Rohwer is a postgraduate student at the University of Western Australia with a special interest in the use of online role play in language learning. She works as tutor for German as a second language in higher education and adult education, and can be contacted at this e-mail at: iris.ludewig-rohwer@research.uwa.edu.au

Dr. Terry Mackey is Vice President of Learning and Member Engagement at AcademyHealth in Washington, D.C., USA. She can be reached at this e-mail: terry.mackey@gmail.com

Sukhwinder Salh is a Senior Lecturer at the Business School; Birmingham City University, England. She is contactable at this e-mail: Sukhwinder. salh@bcu.ac.uk

Bibliography

Baker, A. C.; P. J. Jensen & D. A. Kolb (2002). *Conversational learning: An experiential approach to knowledge creation.* Westport: Greenwood Publishing Group.

Brockbank, A. & I. McGill (2007). *Facilitating reflective learning in higher education.* Maidenhead, UK: McGraw-Hill Education (UK).

Geurts, J. & R. D. Duke (2012). Foreword. In C. Nygaard, N. Courtney and E. Leigh (Eds.) *Simulations, Games and Role Play in University Education.* Faringdon, UK: Libri Publishing, pp. IX-XVIII.

Kapp, K. (2014). *Gamification. Separating fact from fiction, Chief learning office,* Vol. 13, No. 3, pp. 45–52.

Kolb, D. A. (1984). *Experiential Learning: Experience as the Source of Learning and Development.* Englewood Cliffs, NJ: Prentice-Hall.

Lean, J.; J. Moizer; M. Towler & C. Abbey (2006). Simulations and games. Use and Barriers in higher education. *Active Learning in Higher Education,* Vol. 7, No. 3, pp. 227–242.

Leigh, E. E. (2003). *A practitioner researcher perspective on facilitating an open, infinite, chaordic simulation: learning to engage in theory while putting myself into practice.* Diss.

Mackey, T. (2016). Learner-Centered Techniques. In S. L. Danvers (Ed.) *Encyclopedia of Online Education.* Sage Publishing.

Mayer, J. D. & P. Salovey (1993). The intelligence of emotional intelligence. *Intelligence* Vol. 17, No. 4, pp. 433–442.

Schiller, F. (1795). *Ueber die aesthetische Erziehung des Menschen. Brief 15.*

Walker A.; H. Leary; C. Hmelo-Silver & P. A. Ertmer (Eds.) (2015). *Essential Readings in Problem-Based Learning: Exploring and Extending the Legacy of Howard S. Barrows.* West Lafayette, USA: Purdue University Press.

Wills, S.; E. Leigh & A. Ip (2011). *The power of role-based e-learning: designing and moderating online role play.* New York: Routledge.

Chapter 2: Play, Role-Play and Games

Managing Conflict through Role-Play

Sukhwinder Salh

Background

As students prepare to leave higher education and embark on their chosen career paths they are faced with a number of challenges from employers. Employers do not merely want evidence of a qualification but require a student to be equipped with professional competence together with a high degree of academic knowledge. It is with this in mind that I was keen to explore how to bring the workplace into the classroom and offer the opportunity to develop skills and academic knowledge in a simultaneous fashion. Having worked both in industry and academia my aim was to use the stories that I had acquired from the workplace to bring a sense of reality to the learning process.

In order to improve the student experience looking at alternative ways to engage students became a priority. Feedback traditionally is led by the lecturer but the power of peer feedback breaks away from the notion that *"assessment is something done to learners"* (Brown & Glasner, 1999:157). Encouraging peers to contribute to formative feedback on activities related to role-play exercises; expose students to developing a range of skills and taking on the *"roles of assessors (rating and commenting upon peer's work) and assesses (viewing and acting upon feedback)"* (Li, 2011:3). Using exercises such as role-plays was seen as an ideal vehicle by which students could engage and question their own decision making process.

The power of learning through a reflective lens facilitates students self

-development. Self -reflection is a learning approach whereby individuals redefine their current perspective in order to develop new patterns of understanding, thinking and behaving. It requires learning as well as new learning (Mezirow 1985). Hence it should be seen as a continuous process which has the potential to impact students approach and attitude to a range of situations beyond the classroom. Other outcomes from adopting such innovative learning practices is the opportunity to encourage dialogue and form communities of practice. Interaction within groups allow individuals to not only expand their own knowledge, but benefit from doing this in a connected way (Schuck 1996). Wenger *et al.* (2002:4) define communities of practice as *"groups of people who share a concern, a set of problems or a passion about a topic, and who deepen their knowledge and expertise in this area by interaction on an ongoing basis"*. Reflective practice is gaining momentum within higher education and already professions such as nursing and teaching implement such approaches within their educational training. However Hunt (2005) suggests critical reflection is not necessarily a natural skill. However being taught or assisted to reflect in an informal or formal classroom setting through processes of coaching, mentoring and action learning can be highly effective (Gray 2007). The practice described within this chapter draws upon the comments above and incorporates these views within the role-play exercise. Keen to ensure students not only acquire knowledge and theory but also understand the "how" we do things was a key priority when developing the role-play exercise.

The Practice

The innovative teaching practice described is designed for students undertaking a business related degree and in particular it is relevant to the topic area of "Managing people" & "Employee relations". Any business degree which hopes to provide students with exposure on how to deal with difficult situations will find the learning from this exercise valuable. The exercise is linked to developing skills in a management role and enhances understanding of "good practice". Key Learning outcomes are outlined below:

+   developing key skills through reflection on how to deal with conflict
     & disputes;

- identifying and applying the rules of "good practice" when dealing with conflict within the workplace;

- exploring solutions to conflict issues and developing negotiation skills with confidence and professionalism.

The role play exercise focuses on a conflict / dispute between an employee and line manager. The chosen dispute is centered on a request for "time off" by the employee, who is scheduled to work the weekend but wants to take annual leave. The line manager, however, refuses to give time off, and the employee as a result of this has raised a grievance (Role-play 1 hears the grievance). This issue escalates and students are advised after role-play 1, that the employee calls in "sick", which also happens to be the weekend that the employee initially wanted to take as leave. The employee, by not working his scheduled shift, puts the operational needs of the business at risk. The line manager doesn't believe the employee was sick and wants the matter investigated.

Hence role-play 1 deals with a complaint from the employee with respect to refusing time off, and role-play 2 deals with the line manager's request to investigate his absence, as he believes it was a lie to get time off and hence a potential conduct issue. It is possible to use any conflict scenario that is typical within the workplace in order to develop learning through role play. For example a dispute can arise where an employee has not been selected to attend a training event and the line manager uses budget / operational needs as the reason, or even a disagreement between a line manager and employee over a performance rating. Using relevant everyday real life disputes from the workplace can enhance the reality of the exercise.

Role-Play 1

There are two stages to the role-plays: the first one relates to hearing a grievance appeal, and the second involves a disciplinary investigation. The aim of the exercise is to focus students attention on the "how" to deal with difficult employees and develop a range of skills in relation to managing people. The students receive a brief, which includes background to the organization and explains the organization's internal rules and policies. In preparation for this role- play the students are expected to examine the brief and use the information provided to evaluate the rights and obligations that may or may not have been breached. Examining the brief will also enable students to develop relevant questions for when they meet with the employee and line manager (Both acted out by role –players). Students initially attend a lecture, which aims to share what is considered to be "good practice" when managing people and difficult situations. This lecture provides a good grounding on "grievance & disciplinary" issues within the workplace. The lecture provides the basis for understanding relevant rules and identifies approaches / skills needed when dealing with difficult situations.

Essentially the Student brief provides students with a staffing structure, rules on shifts, union agreements, grievance & disciplinary policy and a background on the employee and line manager. The key issue for this role-play exercise is the refusal of the line manager of an employee to take annual leave when he has been scheduled to work for the weekend. The line manager refuses based on operational needs of the business and the employee is challenging this view as he is asking for time off to support the work of the army reserve, which is an initiative supported via the union agreement. The overall brief should reflect the rules that apply to weekend working (e.g. A minimum number of staff are required at the weekend for health & safety reasons).

Role-play 1 will require students to hear the grievance appeal. Based on the information provided by the role player actors, students must make a decision whether to grant the employee time off or side with management (Management claims that the business needs must prevail.) The outcome should be that that the employee is advised he cannot be given leave for that weekend due to the number of staff already having time off; however when the weekend in question arrives the employee calls in sick. Management are suspicious and want to investigate this matter further; this forms the issue for role-play two, and this role play takes place the following week. Your role – player actors should be briefed adequately and a script outlining to them the role to portray is detailed below as Figures 1 and 2. The role-players who play the role of employee and line manager are actors and should have management experience, as this enables them to give effective feedback to the students in order to enhance their learning.

Steven Dale (Employee)	Barry Morris (Manager)
Role player instructions	Role Player instructions
• Steven will emphasise that Barry has not supported the agreement between union and management.	• Barry will share the rota and this demonstrates he is already overstretched as he has 7 people currently off & the rules are only 6 are allowed time off at any given time. Hence he is already in breach of internal rules.
• Steven will claim that Barry doesn't like him and this is largely due to personal issues (Role players can be as imaginative as they wish here).	• Barry will justify having seven off as two employees are on long term sick and one of them was due to return, however he had another heart attack.
• Steven will allege not all options have been explored (Overtime, extra shift worked and or agency staff).	• Other employees had pre-booked their holiday over a year ago and as they are going abroad this cannot be altered.
• Steven will allege management is not supportive.	• Bringing in agency staff means training and induction – no time for this, hence this option can be dismissed.
• Steven will comment on his commitment and that he is a long serving employee.	• Doing overtime puts existing staff at risk of overworking. Must think of everyone's health and safety.
• Steven will be quite dismissive of HR and may even raise his voice to assess how students deal with a difficult employee.	• Barry emphasises budget constraints and the need to maintain operational needs is the priority and not personal issues.

Figure 1: Grievance Appeal: Role play 1 instructions for actors.

Steven Dale Employee	Barry Morris Line manager	Karen Bailey (Witness)
<ul><li>Steven is adamant he was ill and did not attend the camp.</li><li>Steven emphasises he is being victimized.</li><li>Steven claims he was too ill to phone in and therefore asked his wife to call in.</li><li>Steven stresses he is angry at the mis-trust.</li></ul>	<ul><li>Barry is furious that Steven let the team down and put the service being delivered at risk.</li><li>Barry is convinced that Steven is lying and therefore this is a matter of misconduct as he failed to follow a reasonable order, which was simply "he had to come into work on the weekend".</li><li>Barry believes further action should be taken against Steven.</li><li>If students ask probing questions and fully explore the incident, Barry will share with them that Karen also attends the camp and could verify the situation, but this will only be revealed if the students ask the relevant questions.</li></ul>	<ul><li>Karen works in admin support and keeps herself to herself.</li><li>When asked about the camp and whether she went she will say yes.</li><li>If students ask the right questions, Karen will disclose that Steven was at the camp.</li><li>Karen is nervous about sharing information as she doesn't want to get anyone at work in trouble (Students should re-assure her).</li></ul>

Figure 2: Grievance Appeal: Role play 1 instructions for actors.

Preparation for role-play exercise

The lecturer is required to deliver the lecture on "managing people & disputes" and this covers adherence to legal rules, management practices and skills needed to deal with difficult situations. Following on from this the students are advised to form groups of up to 4 people in order to take part in the exercise. The students are then presented with a background to the dispute and advised to explore & identify the following points:

(1) what are the key issues;

(2) what questions need to be asked in order to gather information;

(3) what solutions could be explored;

(4) finally to ensure that all members of their group participate and rotate the roles.

The students should incorporate role of observer, note-taker and up to two student interviewers; who manage the questions during the grievance and disciplinary investigatory interviews. The Lecturer will then schedule the groups for the following week with meetings booked with both the employee and line manager (role-played by actors) in order for students to gather information. The final meeting with the employee will require students to confirm the way forward, and at the end of this exercise the students will receive feedback from the role-player actors on their approach. All the feedback guidelines and schedules are produced by the lecturer. (Feedback guide is made available below in Figure 3). Once the first role play exercise is complete, the lecturer is informed by each group of the outcome, and then the lecturer shares with students whether this is the correct outcome. The lecturer (After role-play 1) will also inform students that matters have progressed and the new information has come to light; the employee raising the grievance has claimed he is too ill to come into work, and this also happens to be the weekend the employee so desperately wanted time off for, but was refused.

+ did students develop rapport or cold 'off-hand';

+ questioning – to gather information: used open questions; probes; clarifying or leading questions; prejudicial questions, good use of closed questions?

+ listening: active listening displayed? eye-contact; body posture; note taking evident;

+ to understand your points and feelings; or 'tell and sell'

+ assertiveness;

+ knowledge of internal procedures;

+ summarising at end;

+ explored solutions and advised of way forward or left employee wondering what happens next.

Figure 3: Feedback forms collate evidence on the following areas.

Role players provide evidence of behavior under these headings to support the feedback process to students.

Role-play 2

Going forward the students are advised in role-play 2 they will need to address the issue of un-authorized absence. The lecturer is then required to devise another timetable scheduling meetings between both the employee and line manager to enable them to resolve this new matter and identify if the employee has been dishonest in order to get time off work. Once the exercise is complete the role –player actors will give further feedback to the students about their approach. In week 3 students are asked to present their learning to the whole class. The Lecturer will facilitate the learning shared in week 3, and students are asked to focus on 3 main questions when presenting back:

"Student groups will be asked to present back (5–10 minutes overview) on the following:

+ one skill that role players said you did well;

+ one skill that Role players said you need to develop;

+ one skill that you as a team think you did well or need to develop

Students are expected to use their reflection and feedback received to complete this last exercise." Hence the lecturer is responsible for managing this whole process and supporting students and facilitating their learning by getting students to reflect on their actions.

Student's preparation for exercise

Students are expected to use the initial lecture on good management practices as a guide to developing an approach to tackle the dispute. The students will need to make time as a group to fully examine the role play brief and formulate an understanding of legal rules, policies and organizational practices. As students familiarize themselves with the dispute they will be expected to begin formulating questions that are necessary in order to gather information. Investing time outside of the classroom to conduct wider reading, use of library resources and reviewing rules on good practice; is a key ingredient for preparation. Employing a range of open / closed questions and ensuring students adequately allocate roles to all group members; ensures full participation from all members of the group. When students conduct the role plays they should be acting in a professional manner ensuring introductions, purpose of meeting, identify key issues and explain next steps; all of this should be covered by the students as part of their preparation. Students are required to speak to both employee and line manager (Role-played by actors) as they would in any real life scenario. Meetings should include a note-taker and the decision should be based on the information gathered. The feedback should then be used by students to reflect on their approach and incorporate learning for week 2's role –play. In the final week students will present back as a group what their learning was and will also have an opportunity to review what their peers have learnt through this exercise. This part of the exercise will enable students to identify their strengths and development needs.

Outcomes

The role-play exercise is different to traditional methods of teaching as it is focused on student needs and self-expression. There is less direct intervention by the lecturer and the students are managing their own learning. Some initial input from the lecturer is used as a basis to build their own development, however students take ownership of their own learning. Gaining feedback on their participation enables students to reflect and grow the necessary skills that focus more on "how" things should be done when managing people. The opportunity to work in a group encourages students to build teamwork skills and enhance their communication. This is an opportunity to be exposed to deep learning as opposed to surface learning and learning by doing adds another approach to their student experience. Students also get to see and hear from their peers in the final presentations, and hence the learning encourages peer feedback as well as lecturer's feedback.

Students walk away having learnt "how" to deal with difficult situations. They gain further knowledge on how different types of questions, such as probing, open and closed should be used. They also receive a range of feedback, which includes points such as; were any potentially discriminatory questions asked? Were assumptions made that could reflect poor management practice? Were internal polices adhered to? Was there an understanding and appreciation of body language / emotional intelligence? Having participated with the exercise and observed /reflected during the process; enables participants to arrive at conclusions which they can take forward with them as part of their learning. Hence through the role-play exercise it is possible to employ what Kolb (2002) suggests is a form of experiential learning. It is also important to acknowledge how this exercise impacts on the confidence levels and building of a range of interpersonal skills for students.

Moving Forward

It is possible to take this exercise further by developing a summative assessment based on reflective learning gained from the whole process. Such practices create options to play even further with the exercise and engage as many characters or situations of conflict as possible. Use of role-plays is a fun way of implementing learning and enabling students to acquire transferable skills for life. Viewing the learning as an interactive process adds a further dimension of fun and enhances not only the student experience but their ability to evolve as a critical thinker. As student's progress through their studies it is possible to use this story and build on it further, to reflect learning that can be gained from other management theory and practices. Characters and similar professional settings can be re-visited in other modules; thereby integrating the whole teaching and learning process. As we tell stories we create opportunities, to express views and reveal emotions. As suggested by Alterio & McDrury (2003) linking the art of storytelling with the art of reflective practice allows students to use the tool to inform, develop and advance their learning.

About the Author

Sukhwinder Salh is a Senior Lecturer at the Business School; Birmingham City University, England. She is contactable at this e-mail: Sukhwinder.salh@bcu.ac.uk

Bibliography

Alterio, M. & J. McDrury (2003). *Learning through storytelling in higher education: Using reflection and experience to improve learning.* Routledge.

Baker, A. C.; P. J. Jensen & D. A. Kolb (2002). *Conversational learning: An experiential approach to knowledge creation.* Greenwood Publishing Group.

Brown, S. & A. Glasner (1999). Part 4 Towards Autonomous Assessment. In S. Brown & A. Glasner (Eds.) *Assessment matters in higher education: choosing and using diverse approaches.* Buckingham Society for research into Higher Education & Open University Press, pp. 157–158.

Gray, D. E (2007). Facilitating management learning developing critical reflection through reflective tools. *Management Learning*, Vol. 38 No. 5, pp. 495–517.

Hunt, C. (2005). Reflective practice. In J. P. Wilson (Ed.) *Human Resource Development: Learning and training for individuals and organizations.* London: Kogan Page, pp. 234–51.

Li, L. (2011). How Do Students of Diverse Achievement Levels Benefit from Peer Assessment? *International Journal for the Scholarship of Teaching and Learning*, Vol. 5, No. 2, pp. 11–16.

Mezirow, J. A. (1985). A critical theory of self-directed learning'. In S. Brookfield (Ed.) *Self-Directed Learning: From theory to practice*. San Francisco, CA: Jossey-Bass.

Schuck, G. (1996). Intelligent technology, intelligent workers: a new pedagogy for the high tech workplace'. In K. Starkey (Ed.) *How organizations learn*. London: International Thomson Business press, pp. 199–213.

Wenger, E.; R. McDermott & W. M. Snyder (2002). *Cultivating communities of practice*. Boston, MA: Harvard Business School Press.

Chapter 3: Play, Role-Play and Games

Role-Playing in the Traditional Classroom, Blended Learning, and eLearning

Terry Mackey

Background

Story-based learning has become an increasingly popular topic in instructional design and eLearning discussions, with new perspectives and methods now reflecting the age-old concept that stories engage learners and enhance retention (Andrews, 2009). A form of story-based learning, role-playing allows learners to draw from their own experiences and interests. It makes learning personal and timely for students at all levels and in all fields, providing or clarifying contexts and empowering students to shape their own educational experiences (Bender, 2005). Because students help to create the narrative, role-playing requires higher-order thinking, which facilitates students' ability to apply the new knowledge in real-world situations. Technology-based and technology-enhanced role-playing instructional possibilities have become increasingly available, popular and robust, leading to the question of which modality—traditional classroom, blended learning or eLearning—will best suit the needs of content to be taught, the audience of learners, and the desired learning outcomes. This chapter explores the possibilities and strengths of each modality, including concrete examples, instructional recommendations and technical guidance.

The Practice

Role-Playing in the Traditional Classroom

Virtually any subject area has the potential for instructionally sound role-playing exercises. In a literature or history class, students might assume the roles of literary or historical characters; in business, political science or economics, they might explore the challenges of key stakeholders. In the hard sciences, too, role-playing increases students' ability to integrate new knowledge into existing knowledge (Francis & Byrne, 1999). In medicine, it is an excellent way for emerging practitioners to develop empathy and appreciate the whole patient (MacKinnon & Young, 2014).

The simplest role-playing exercise would be an interview: one or more students research and portray a key character or player, and other students interview him/her. More interesting and effective versions, however, involve situations that explore alternate outcomes or situations. What if a different event had occurred? What if a piece of information emerged that was not available then, or had been suppressed? These situations can be staged in a classroom and acted out. While students can be asked to script their responses, the experience will be substantially richer if they must think on their feet: students are likelier to find themselves identifying with and understanding characters and situations if they must solve challenges while acting out that character. Shy students and other students who may be disinclined to participate actively can be engaged in ways more conducive to their preferences and learning styles; they might participate as researchers, (written) commentators, or audience members who vote on an outcome.

"What if?" discussions are key in helping students understand that small influences and factors can have large consequences. What might have caused Rasputin to be discredited, and what would have been the result in Russia? What might have caused Othello to suspect that the information about Desdemona was incorrect, and how would the plot evolve? What might have led to a different outcome in World War II? What if scientific research had been planned or influenced differently? Such questions set the stage for role-playing.

Outlining, staging, and acting these scenarios offer a deeper understanding of concepts, genres and events. In a psychology or sociology class, role-playing might explore individual or personal dynamics in role-playing that require a personal space requirement that differs from that of their own culture. As students find themselves unconsciously moving closer or further away from their interlocutors, they recognize the importance and challenge of personal space in interacting cross-culturally. In a political science, government or history class, assigning roles and specifying motivations can be invaluable in helping students understand political realities and influences. Students might be given specific roles in a mock United Nations Security Council meeting or international political summit. In researching their character's motivations and the assigned country's interests, students gain a deeper understanding of the influences of history and the give-and-take of politics. What compromises might one make – political, ethical, or social – if a country's economic or political survival is at stake? What is most important to gain, and least important to lose? Which arguments are compelling, and which irrelevant?

Goals and objectives for role-playing exercises will vary with the subject matter but should be clarified before the exercises begin. For a history class, historical accuracy/appropriateness might be paramount; for psychology, appropriate portrayals and analyses of motivations and character might be more important; for political science, realistic presentations of the socio-political and historical moment and characters' political values and motivations may be essential, etc.

The amount of information and number of resources provided to students will vary with the level of the class and assumptions of student preparedness. For introductory classes, some source material should be supplied, including supplementary resources or guidance on finding appropriate resources. Students often do not realize that sources found on the internet may be wildly inaccurate; where such naiveté is anticipated, it can be helpful to have them submit a list of their sources together with an explanation of why each should be considered valid (e.g., a historical source written by a historian with a doctorate in the field). For more advanced classes, or classes where motivation and preparedness are higher, more minimal guidance would generally suffice.

Focused Example of Role-Playing in the Traditional Classroom

Involving students in a mock-trial encourages research, collaboration, and creativity across subjects. It can also enhance quantitative skills (Bair, 2000). The foundation might be a famous case from history, such as the trial of Socrates or Sir Thomas More; a situation in a literary work, such as "A Jury of Her Peers"; or a hypothetical situation relevant to the core course, such as a situation that might come before the International Court of Justice. Ideally, the choice should involve genuine questions of guilt/culpability or innocence; a simple re-enactment has fewer possibilities for creativity or in-depth exploration of themes and motivations, though it can still be useful. Roles should include the accused, key witnesses, a prosecutor, a defense attorney/barrister, and research associates; the latter role allows students who may be uncomfortable with acting to play a meaningful part in the exercise. The role of judge might be given to a student, or the instructor might play that role. If the class is large, members not assigned roles become the jury. If a class is very large, non-participants might be assigned an analysis paper from which participants are exempted; this has the dual purpose of motivating participation.

After assigning readings, a short discussion or overview of the issues should occur: enough to engage interest and provide focus but not enough that research is no longer necessary. What questions or uncertainties exist in the readings? What are alternative viewpoints or interpretations? What insights might emerge in a new trial? What new information might affect the outcome? If students are unfamiliar with the mechanics of a trial, the instructor should overview basic procedures, including how the classroom exercise will differ from an actual trial (e.g., it might be a class requirement that witnesses cannot refuse to testify).

The next step is to assign roles, which may be done either by asking for volunteers or by writing roles in folded slips of paper and having students choose blindly, with or without the option to trade with other students. In addition to "Prosecutor", etc., some roles might be marked "New Witness", to allow each side to add witnesses who might have been asked to testify; these might be people who might have observed or been involved in the situation or those with particular expertise (e.g., psychologist, forensic scientist).

Next, students separate into two teams: defense and prosecution. The instructor visits each group to ensure discussion is productive and all are involved. Guided by the instructor as needed, students map out their initial strategy: which facts need to be brought out, what information might emerge to damage their case, what strategies the other side might involve, which additional witnesses are needed, what new witnesses might emerge, etc. This motivates a close reading of the texts to determine what additional information would be helpful. The outcome of the discussion is a list of individual assignments, their homework assignments.

The homework assignment for day 1 will vary by assigned role. Attorneys/barristers are responsible for creating lists of questions for witnesses, including notes on what information must be brought out in court. They also need to prepare their opening statements. Witnesses list questions they expect might be asked by defense or prosecuting attorneys; prepare responses; and research their characters' motivations, actions and backgrounds as well as any cultural influences (e.g., how gender, class or time period affect their portrayal). Judges research era-appropriate points of law so they can rule appropriately, listing out reasons that affect whether testimony is acceptable and whether attorney's objections should be sustained or overruled, including any variations for the time period. Research associates research cultural, historical and psychological influences and potentially relevant facts so that they can advise the attorney and witnesses as needed during the course of the trial.

Depending upon case's complexity and the degree of student preparedness, an additional class period and/or independent study meeting(s) may be needed for each team to review findings and strategies, practice responses, and anticipate issues. It is helpful for students to practice testimony, critique each other's believability and predict jury reactions. Where possible and practical, students might dress in a way that reflects their characters.

On Mock Trial Day(s), desks are arranged to mimic a courtroom. This may vary in different countries but will be limited by the size and layout of the classroom. One possible arrangement might be the following:

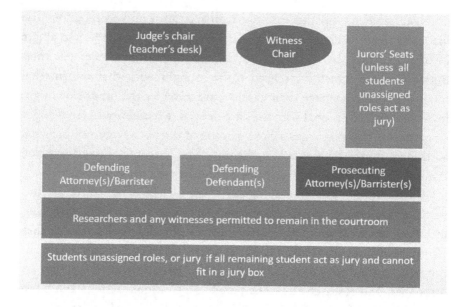

Figure 1: Possible Classroom Arrangement for a Mock Trial.

The judge might begin by providing instructions to the jury. Each attorney then gives an opening statement, then calls witnesses to testify. Opposing attorneys cross-examine witnesses and may object to any evidence presented. Research associates may be asked to research additional information and suggest questions or strategies, as needed, using any resources they have gathered. If the trial is complex, more than one class period may be needed.

At the trial's conclusion, the judgment is made. If a jury is involved, jury members must discuss evidence and make a decision; if the trial is by judge, the judge must explain his/her ruling.

As a homework assignment, or during an additional class day, a follow-up discussion allows students to analyze their experience, using criteria specific to the class's focus. Was it historically accurate? Were all relevant facts introduced? Were any inaccuracies introduced? Were proper legal procedures followed? Did characters appropriately communicate motivations, formative experiences, etc., both verbally and nonverbally? In hindsight, were any good strategies or important testimony missed? What was learned beyond what could be found in the original readings?

Any students who did not participate might also be asked to complete a paper analyzing such factors.

Advantages of Role-Playing in the Traditional Classroom

Role-playing motivates a very close reading of assigned texts and additional resources, since students know their portrayal of a character must be informed by these. They explore motivations and influences, the uses (and abuses) of rhetoric, historical influences, socioeconomic factors, the limits and possibilities of political structures for political science, etc., more deeply than in the passive learning of readings and lectures. They better appreciate other perspectives and motivations, and they confront the role of chance—what might another player say or do?

The element of competition inherent in a trial or other role-play tends to increase motivation to read and research, and the element of creativity inherent in role-playing allows students to showcase their talents in creating and acting roles. It encourages collaboration, as students work together to unravel issues and motivations. In addition, the immediacy of personal contact—real people acting believable roles, watching and observing others' role-playing—makes the experience memorable and greatly increases retention. As with all problem-based learning, it gives students an important stake in their own learning, increasing motivation and depth of learning (Mackey, forthcoming).

Role-playing using Blended Learning

A combination of technology-enhanced learning and traditional instructor-led learning, blended learning offers a broader range of possibilities for role-playing. Since most students now have smartphones or other mobile devices, even in developing countries, and since computer-equipped classrooms are now common, blended learning models have become both easier and more frequently employed. Most students are reasonably adept at internet searches, and many are adept at media production (e.g., creating graphics, YouTube style videos), which increases the possibilities for presentations.

All of the role-playing models suggested in the previous section could be used in blended learning scenarios. In the mock trial example, internet access would allow on-the-spot research as unexpected questions emerge or as witnesses introduce unanticipated information. Computers also provide the opportunity for multimedia presentations for the jury (historical accuracy allowing) and the presentation of documents that would otherwise need to be printed. Photographs or video clips can be presented as evidence. Documents and other evidence can be created or produced (e.g., a letter that might have been sent).

In a role-playing exercise involving international politics, students can access a wide variety of virtual props and means of communications. Where students are asked to play the roles of governmental figures, initial negotiations might take the form of emails, introducing students to formal communications—and to the dangers of putting certain things in writing. They can explore the differences between face-to-face negotiations and virtual negotiations, comparing advantages and disadvantages of each. They might create supporting documents to support their negotiations, such as spreadsheets sheets to support economic arguments, or gather or create media, such as video or audio clips as evidence.

Focused Example of Role-Playing using Blended Learning

Involving students in simulated journalism is a role-playing exercise that works well across many subject areas. Journalists are involved in a wide range of content and are sometimes subject experts themselves; in addition, good journalists interview experts and witnesses to create their copy. The requirements of specific publications, or publication types, add an additional layer of learning: students must consider requirements of reading level, focus, and perspective/objectivity. This particular example assumes a computer-equipped classroom in which computers have some type of word-processing program, or where students can be asked to bring laptops or mobile devices that include word-processing.

The instructor invents a situation in which writers are on a deadline to produce content: students have a precise amount of time to research, write, and format a breaking story, which may be based entirely in fact or partially or fully in fiction. They are given a specific word count or column inch requirement. As in the mock trial, roles may be drawn from a hat or taken by volunteers.

On day 1, the instructor introduces the situation, overviews the roles in a general way and ensures that each student has a computer has internet access and a word processing program. Next, roles are distributed. In this example, the story involves an environmental protest involving the use of pesticides, since this topic spans multiple subject areas: environmental science, journalism, language/writing, sociology, political science, history, psychology, etc. The instructor provides the basics of the story: for example, a protest involving the use of DDT.

Students open and read their roles, which they are asked to keep private. Some will be witnesses; their paper provides short details (e.g., "You were a participant in the environmental protest; you only heard about the police response but you hate the police and exaggerate what you saw"; "You were one of the responding police. You did not use force but saw others who did; unfortunately, they are your friends."). Other roles involve experts (e.g., a chemist who is an expert on the tear gas used in the protest, an environmentalist who knows the dangers of a pesticide, an agricultural expert or a corporate economist who knows the economic consequences of not using the pesticide). Journalists also receive descriptions (e.g., "You write for a conservative, pro-corporate newspaper with an educated audience", "You write for a liberal publication that focuses on green endeavors", "You write for a mass-market newspaper that seeks to be objective and has an audience in which most readers are not college graduates", "You are submitting an opinion piece or letter for a scientific journal in which most readers have doctorates in a scientific field.").

At least the first 30 minutes of the class are devoted to interview and internet-based research. Witnesses to the protest must research other environmental protests to determine what might have happened; witnesses may collaborate. Subject matter experts, such as environmental scientists, research the specifics of what they might be asked. Journalists research similar situations and compile questions for witnesses.

The next time block involves interviewing and writing. Students assigned to be journalists conduct interviews, assess the accuracy of what they hear, and write the final story. Those assigned non-journalist roles become bloggers. This might take 45 minutes. In a writing class, the last 15 minutes involve collaboration with an editor. At the end of the class, the final stories are emailed or otherwise distributed to all students.

For homework for Day 1, or for a follow-up discussion on the next class day, students compare and contrast the journalistic accounts. How does the actual information—the inclusion or exclusion of facts—differ across the articles? What did each journalist's goal seem to be? How did word count limits affect presentation and choice of facts?

On the following class day, the instructor leads a deeper discussion of the articles. Students discuss challenges they encountered: how to assess honesty, get good quotes, get the right column length, address the paper's audience and mission without compromising journalistic integrity. They also discuss differences across papers. Did any of the accounts cross the line from perspective into intentional inaccuracy? Is there such a thing as objectivity? Is omitting information dishonest? At what point did the writer's perspective become obvious, if at all? This role-playing exercise introduces students not only to the pressures of journalism but to the challenge of accuracy and objectivity, and the diversity of perspectives, in any writing. It also introduces them to the challenges of writing copy that is both compelling and accurate.

Feedback for this type of exercise is always positive. Students report that it is stressful in a good way—they must fight the clock to write a compelling and accurate story in the allotted time, since print deadlines are typically non-negotiable. Students not only learn about the subject matter they have researched; they become more aware of the problem of "slant" in written accounts, the challenges of conflicting information and the importance of consulting multiple sources to get a complete understanding of an issue.

Advantages of Role-Playing in Blended Learning

Adding computer-based and/or internet based resources to classroom instruction expands the possibilities of the classroom. Students can do on-the-spot research when they are challenged on points of fact or choice of language. Printed resources can be supplemented with online visual media to help students visualize content. They discover when a visual is more effective than words, or how visuals might affect how words will be read.

Role-playing in eLearning

eLearning has become a major force in higher education: as stand-alone classroom assignments; as regularly planned modules in a "flipped classroom" structure (where students access primary instruction independently online, with classroom time focused on application, practice, and discussion); or as entire courses, whether MOOCs (massive online open courses) or as standard university courses. In a well-designed eLearning module or course in which students learn independently, role-playing can be powerful. As in classroom-based role-playing, role-playing via eLearning enables students to step into a role, make choices for a character and explore the outcomes of those choices. The added possibility of role-playing in the virtual world, as opposed to the classroom, is that the consequences of unwise, even dangerous choices can be experienced more fully in the safe virtual environment. Since students often learn best from mistakes, this an effective instructional tool. Incorporating game elements (gamification) into role-playing scenarios online also increases learner engagement and effectiveness.

Another advantage of role-playing via eLearning is that multiple students can play the same role, whereas in the classroom, there might be only one protagonist or antagonist. It is also easier to go back and explore the results of different choices online; it would be awkward to replay a choice with physical characters. Additionally, students feel more free to explore choices they know are wrong when no one else is watching and potentially judging.

Creating eLearning modules has become increasingly easy and affordable. Many types of software are available, and even the more robust professional software choices (e.g., Adobe Captivate) generally offer special pricing for academics. It is no longer difficult to build online modules in which students choose a role from a finite number of choices, make choices for their character, and explore the results of those choices. Creating an online role-playing scenario can take anywhere from a day to a few weeks, depending on the length of the module, the amount and quality of media used, the instructor's comfort level with software and the complexity of the scenarios. For instructors who lack the time or inclination to create online role-playing scenarios, many examples can be found on the internet for free or very low cost (e.g., Will Interactive, online).

Nearly every subject area is represented. In addition, some universities offer instructional design and/or programming support to instructors interested in customized online modules.

Virtual role-playing is particularly useful in situations in which it is difficult, dangerous, or unrealistic to explore negative consequences or results in the real world, or in which positive and/or negative consequences are difficult to envision. In medical training, the results of a bad choice might involve permanent harm or even death to a patient; in a simulation, medical students can view consequences (e.g., they see the "blue baby" that results if the airway is not cleared, a smiling baby once the correct measures are applied)—the need for a fast response is visible onscreen. In psychology, political science, sociolog, and ethics, there are major benefits to viewing the results of inappropriate decision-making or cultural insensitivity, and these are obviously best explored without jeopardizing or alienating humans. In computer science or information technology, it is important to know how to handle system failures and outages, but it is at best a major inconvenience to take a system down so that a prospective system administrator knows how to handle this crisis. In laboratory sciences, mistakes are also best made in the safe virtual environment than with chemicals. In economics, the results of various investment strategies can be explored without actual financial risk.

Focused Examples of Role-Playing via eLearning

As with classroom-based lessons, the first step in building an eLearning module is to determine learning objective(s). In a chemistry class, for example, objectives might include laboratory safety practices and following research protocols. The next step is choosing roles; these should be realistic as well as interesting enough that a student will choose that character and care about the consequences to him/her. Ideally there should be at least two options, preferably with a choice of gender/gender identity (n.b.: the number of characters will impact production time). A full online course might include multiple role-playing scenarios, with the same or different characters. Choices for the chemistry course might include a male undergraduate student who works as a lab assistant and a female Research Associate.

Media for the characters can be still images (photographs) or videos (smart phone quality is generally fine). Multiple images of characters will be needed, so a copyright-free media library for still images is needed for multiple images of each character (e.g., a faculty member on the phone, standing, talking, happy, angry....). There is a wealth of free images online, but finding multiple shots of the same person in the same clothing can take time. If video is used, it will be important to get release forms from the people who donate their time; it is wise to consult your university for rules on using students and/or employees. Video is more compelling, but it is also harder to edit—the same actors may not be easy to find, scenes may change, etc.—so still images are the simpler choice.

The next step is to map out decision points and consequences on paper. What situations might be encountered that would illustrate the teaching points? What decisions would the character need to make? What are realistic options and potential consequences? Instructionally, difficult choices are best; a compelling story will present the learner with real dilemmas. In a 20-minute module, there might be 5 decision points. The most effective scenarios involve real dilemmas, not obvious answers, and students learn a lot by exploring multiple ways to address an issue. A module on ethics or psychology, for example, might pose a situation in which a character suspects that a friend is the victim of abuse. Should the character confront the friend, call the police, attempt to intervene, notify campus security, offer support but not interfere? Any of these might be reasonable—what are potential consequences?

Once the basic story and decision points are determined, the course can be built. For each descriptive screen, upload an appropriate image, enter a description or dialogue. For each screen that involves a decision point, insert a button for each choice; typically a drop-down menu will provide options for the button (e.g., if this choice is clicked, go to screen X). If the course is to be accessible to the differently abled (e.g., blind students, students who cannot use a mouse), it is important to use software that supports this: software that enables course navigation via arrow keys, that allows text equivalents for images can be uploaded so assistive technologies such as screen readers can provide a description of what sighted learners can see. Another technical consideration is whether the module should be accessible on mobile devices; since most students use these, it is a good practice to choose software that supports responsive projects (i.e., projects that automatically adjust to different screen sizes and ensure that media, such as video clips, play properly on all devices). Below are samples of two simple, easy-to-build text screens: the first sets up the story, and the second shows a simple decision point screen:

Figure 2: Narrative screen showing dialogue.

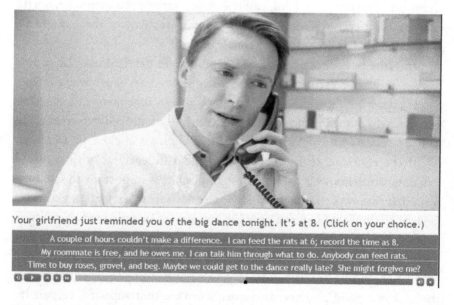

Figure 3: Choice screen in which learners choose an outcome.

Which screen the student encounters after each choice screen depends upon the choice made. Choosing to feed the rats two hours before schedule might or might not have consequences—perhaps he is not caught but hears about someone else who lost an assistantship for the same thing; perhaps the professor notices minor anomalies in animal weights, discovers the deception, and puts him on notice that he will be fired if he departs from protocol again. Having the roommate feed the rats might lead to the rats escaping, with no clear indication which rats belong in A cages or B cages. The experiment is compromised; the student loses his assistantship; he now washes dishes in the cafeteria; end of scenario, with an option to Replay. Going late to the dance may cause him to lose a relationship that is extremely important—or result in an act of revenge, which the girlfriend has threatened earlier in the sequence.

Additional screens would extend out the results of each choice, or the narrative could move to the next choice. As it is time-consuming and expensive to have every decision point branch continue indefinitely, it is easiest to build a narrative in which the step after each consequence is the same for everyone. Assuming that the character was not fired, the action might move to an email or phone call unrelated to the previous decision, such as an email requiring a decision about ordering lab supplies (can he substitute generic?) or a phone call from a fellow student needing guidance on labeling chemicals (label all, label only those that post no danger?), or text message about a student who claims to have been hurt in the lab class. Any or all of these might occur in the sequence.

Audio can be easily added to these screens; this is generally as simple as clicking a *Record Audio* button and speaking into the computer microphone. Still graphics can be replaced by video clips in which students or other volunteers act out each segment. Viewing examples of online role-playing scenarios can be helpful (e.g., Will Interative). Video can enhance learner engagement and the ability of students to identify with a character, but video-based modules can be more time-intensive to create. For instructors who lack the time or technical facility for video and/or audio, still graphics and on-screen text will still yield a memorable and effective learning experience. Alternatively, an instructor might investigate whether the university provides instructional design or programming assistance. Yet another alternative is to access modules already available online, since many are free or low-cost.

eLearning role-playing can also be created to include game elements, such as playing against a clock to resolve issues, points earned/lost for good/bad decisions, "help" lines that can only be used a finite number of times, badges for exploring more than one role, leaderboards to compare scores, etc. Game-based learning provides powerful motivation for learning reinforcements; while few students would retake an online quiz to get a higher score or view non-required alternate screens (unless doing so impacts their grade), the lure of a game motivates them to try to beat their original scores, earn badges that not everyone will earn, etc. The very sense of playing a game, as opposed to being a passive or semi-passive recipient of knowledge, increases the attractiveness of online role-playing, and with it the probability that students will replay the experience, thus deepening their learning (Kapp, 2012). Many effective learning games are available online (e.g., Jensen); these can also provide inspiration for game creation.

Advantages of Role-Playing via eLearning

Because Gen X, Gen Y, and Gen Z students tend to be media-focused, role-playing via eLearning is an effective engagement strategy. This model motivates students to explore the "what if?" of many situations, developing a deeper understanding of issues and consequences (Nygaard et al., 2013). The inclusion of humor and the gamification of learning encourage students to replay modules, particularly when humor or game elements, such as the possibility of being virtually fired, are involved. Whereas few student replay traditional instructional modules that are purely pedagogical in turn, students are very likely to replay role-playing scenarios to explore the results of different decisions or perspectives, increasing learning. Adding the lure of game-based elements increases this probability.

Outcomes

Role-playing is an invaluable pedagogical strategy that encourages higher-order thinking, increases retention, and maximizes learner engagement. It is effective across subject areas (Bender, 2005) (Rao & Stupans, 2012). Whether in the traditional classroom, a blended learning model, or eLearning (synchronous or asynchronous), the opportunity to step into another's shoes, actively participate in key situations, and explore the range of historical, cultural, and other variables and influences is invaluable. With creative thinking, it can be used in virtually any subject area to enrich the teaching and learning experience. In role-playing exercises, students become much more deeply engaged in the subject matter because it becomes personal and emotional, particularly as they become immersed in roles. They spend more time with readings, retain more information, and are better able to apply what they learn because, in a sense, they have already applied it. Students often comment on these assignments years after the class. Such memorable assignments are key in ensuring that students remember key facts, insights, and procedures.

Moving Forward

The use of the internet and internet-based technologies is now commonplace in education. As learning technologies become more affordable and easier to use, and as students increasingly expect wider use of multimedia in the classroom, the use of blended learning will continue to grow. Fully online courses are already a global phenomenon: MOOCs and for-cost eLearning courses have become widely available, expanding access to higher education for many students who lack the time or resources to attend traditional classes and attracting the growing percentage of students who prefer to access education online. The software for creating eLearning modules has become increasingly robust, affordable and user-friendly. Smartphones make it easy to record and incorporate video and still visuals in eLearning modules. In addition, increasing numbers of online modules and learning games are available for free or low-cost for educational use. Role-playing via eLearning or blended learning has never been easier, and the possibilities continue to expand.

While blended learning and asynchronous eLearning modalities are highly likely to become more widely used for role-playing, they are not always the best choice. Traditional face-to-face role-playing remains the best choice for certain content, such as practicing cross-cultural communication skills and conflict management, and for certain audiences, such as those who lack access or comfort level with technologies. By contrast, asynchronous eLearning works best for other types of content and other audiences. In the virtual world, students can safely explore potentially dangerous consequences, and they can better appreciate situations that may be difficult to visualize without media. Online modules also allow a single role to be played by multiple students, and for students to reverse course to explore the results of different choices. The middle ground is blended learning, which can incorporate many of the advantages of each. Whichever the choice, role-playing is an invaluable teaching and learning practice.

About the Author

Dr. Terry Mackey is Vice President of Learning and Member Engagement at AcademyHealth in Washington, D.C., USA. She can be reached at this e-mail: terry.mackey@gmail.com

Bibliography

Andrews, D. H.; T. D. Hull & J. A. Donahue (2009). Storytelling as an Instructional Method: Definitions and Research Questions. *Interdisciplinary Journal of Problem-Based Learning*, Vol. 3, No. 2, pp. 6–23.

Bender, T. (2005). Role playing in online education: A teaching tool to enhance student engagement and sustained learning. *Innovate*, Vol. 1, No. 4, pp. 1–7.

Bair, E. S. (2000). Developing Analytical and Communication Skills in a Mock-Trial Course Based on the Famous Woburn, Massachusetts Case. *Journal of Geoscience Education*, Vol. 48, pp. 454.

Francis, P. J. & A. P. Byrne. (1999). The Use of Role-Playing Exercises in Teaching Undergraduate Astronomy and Physics. *Publications of the Astronomical Society of Australia*, Vol. 16, pp. 206–211.

Jensen, R. *50 Great Sites for Serious, Educational Games.* http://www.onlinecolleges.net/50-great-sites-for-serious-educational-games/. [Accessed online May 11, 2016].

Kapp, K. (2012). *The Gamification of Learning and Instruction.* San Francisco: Pfeiffer, 2012.

Mackey, T. (2016). Problem-Based Learning. *The Sage Encyclopedia of Online Education.* S. L. Danvers (Ed.). London: Sage Publishing.

MacKinnon, K. & L. E. Young. (2014). Story Based Learning: A Student Centred Practice-Oriented Learning Strategy. *Quality Advancement in*

Nursing Education – Avancées en formation infirmière. Vol. 1, Issue 1, Article 3, pp. 1–12.

Nygaard, C.; N. Courtney & E. Leigh (Eds.) (2013). *Simulations, Games and Role Play in University Education.* Learning in Higher Education series. Libri Publishing Ltd., Oxfordshire.

Pierce, D. & J. Middendorf. (2008). Evaluating the effectiveness of role playing in the sport management curriculum. *International Journal of Sport Management and Marketing,* Vol. 4, Nos. 2–3, pp. 277–294.

Rao, D. & I. Stupans. (2012). Exploring the potential of role play in higher education: development of a typology and teacher guidelines. *Innovations in Education and Teaching International,* Vol. 49, No. 4, pp. 427–436.

Will Interactive. (Various examples of robust video-based role-playing for academic audiences; some are free or low-cost for academic use.) http://willinteractive.com/products/category/youth-education [Accessed online May 11, 2016].

Chapter 4: Play, Role-Play and Games

Language Learning in Higher Education through Engaging in Online Role Play

Iris Ludewig-Rohwer

Background

Employers require graduates leaving university to possess both advanced communication skills and the ability to adapt to new situations and challenges. Role play and simulation have found their way into higher education, allowing students to practise and develop these employment skills, as well as empathy and dealing with the unknown in a safe learning environment (examples provided by Salh & Mackey in this volume). The idea behind the role play approach is to get students involved in online discussions by taking on a role. Trying to understand someone else's point of view teaches the students empathy. Applying knowledge and building on social and linguistic proficiency by fostering skills in a context where unfolding events cannot always be predicted mirrors real life. Students (and teachers) can only anticipate to a certain degree how communication and events will unfold, how other people will respond, and what impact the players' intervention will have on the course of events (Van Ments, 1989; Wills *et al.*, 2011).

In online role play the interaction and communication between players are shifted from the classroom to a virtual space, offering additional flexibility with regard to participation. Online role play facilitates cross-disciplinary and cross-institutional collaboration and can foster both oral and written communication skills. A learning design that allows for asynchronous and anonymous discussion can assist in reducing the level of intimidation in traditional role play settings (Horwitz *et al.*, 1986) by allowing for more time to respond, thus benefitting language learners as well as those who require more time to respond (Bell, 2001; Freeman & Capper, 1999; Ludewig & Ludewig-Rohwer, 2012).

There are a variety of technical approaches that can be used to structure an online role play based on written communication, including email, chat, discussion boards and blog postings (Hardy & Totman, 2012; Freeman & Capper, 1999).

The online role play presented in this chapter is designed for intermediate level (B1) students of German at the University of Western Australia. It is particularly aimed at those students who want to increase their written communication and fluency, and those who feel that there is not enough time to practise their communication skills in class. It focuses on written communication only to allow the students to participate in character and keep a secret identity.

The role play was part of a unit consisting of four contact hours (a one hour lecture on contemporary Germany and language, a two hour language class and a one hour conversation class). In lectures and language classes of 20 or more students there is only limited time to actively engage in discussion and to practise productive (speaking/writing) language skills.

In this unit students could choose between three assessment pathways, each including an essay, an oral presentation and a final exam. One of the choices was participation in an online role play, thus allowing the students at least one extra hour per week for communication. Participating in the online role play meant that their other assessments were reduced in length and value. Six students decided to take up this opportunity, either because they preferred open-ended activities, more creative learning and assessment opportunities, wanted to challenge themselves or try something new, had heard about it from the previous year's students, or simply because they anticipated receiving a better grade compared to the other assessment options.

Practice

This online role play is set up as a learning and assessment activity in which students take on the roles of historically significant persons in order to understand and relive German history. Within set challenges, predetermined by the course of history, students discuss issues online in character without revealing their true identity. The assessment is based on the quality of contributions to event pages, discussion boards and their online profile.

The learning outcomes were met as follows: To varying degrees, students demonstrably

- 'experienced' the 1970s in West Germany through the eyes of a key figure in German history (e.g. a political leader, journalist or terrorist);

- built up vocabulary and practised vocabulary in context;

- expressed their opinions in a text-based forum;

- reacted to other messages instantly (online meeting);

- maintained a discussion over the period of a week (asynchronous contribution);

- understood the format of a German CV; and

- practised their oral skills through individual in-character presentations to the rest of the class at the end of the role-play.

As a first assessment and to stimulate initial engagement with their character, students were required to create a CV and a diary entry (100 words) in character, which they then published on their character's webpage, allowing others to get to know their fellow players. Both documents were guided by templates and examples provided by the tutor.

Students travelled through time, following a series of events, with each event represented by a page, a collaborative learning space, where editing can be undertaken by any group member. The teacher might start to set the scene by creating character pages and event pages, embedding historically relevant sources such as newspaper articles and videos. At the same time students are invited to research events and to add their own resources, an opportunity that is usually taken up once they have familiarised themselves with the new learning format. Every page has a bulletin board that allows for discussion of the events. Inspired by the material provided, players posted their character's opinions on bulletin boards (employing a linear structure), using references and threads to organise their posts. Students could contribute to the discussions at any time (at least two contributions per meeting), but there was also a fixed weekly discussion time to encourage the flow of communication, as taking full advantage of an asynchronous setting could mean waiting for days to get a reply. Although a response might take five minutes or longer to formulate, the students felt that they had to respond 'on the spot'. In general they liked the idea of being 'forced' to participate in discussion and felt surprised that they had the capacity to do so.

What software to use?

The software needs to be easy to use and up-to-date in features and design. This role play is facilitated by 'wikispaces classroom', an open classroom management platform that provides a safe environment for students. Wikispaces is free educational software which allows for collaboration in design and participation, as well as easy tracking of participants' contributions. Authentic material, such as newspaper clips, images and videos, can easily be embedded. Characters and events can be set up as individual pages. Language students might find it helpful if vocabulary lists are provided. Students communicate in bulletin boards, but can also send individual messages.

How long does it take?

This particular role play was set to run over five weeks, including an introduction week to get used to the software and the character, as well as overcoming some barriers in participating in an unfamiliar learning and assessment activity. A role play can easily expand to a whole semester, as is common practice in the simulation of complex global business and political situations, or be reduced to one intensive week. However, we found that after four weeks, interest and participation decrease. A role play, despite its playful nature, is work-intensive for students and teachers alike.

How is it different from traditional teaching and learning practices?

The teacher may set a course, but the students 'sail the boat' and could head in any direction. As in in-class role plays, the teacher gets to see and review how students interact; however, unlike communicative learning activities in class, the teacher can spend more time considering how students communicate with each other and their relative language proficiency, rather than relying on individual assessments such as tests and essays. While students need to be spontaneous and quick with their responses, teachers can also immerse themselves in the discussion, knowing that there will be time later for reflection and assessment when browsing through discussion boards. Assessment tracking also allows for filtering participants' discussions, facilitating evaluation and focusing on individual feedback.

Student evaluation has shown that students find this setting very challenging and work/study intensive, but appreciate being forced to communicate intensively over the period of an hour in a less intimidating environment.

The level of engagement was high. As written communication other than essay writing is more important in daily life, (SMS, messages, posting, blogging, etc.) students learn to communicate more effectively and are more prepared to participate in online communication in the target language.

Online teaching comes with certain expectations. Social media, email etc. have created a demand for access and availability 24/7. By agreeing to a discussion time once a week for an hour, we removed some of the flexibility of the role play, but at the same time accommodated students' expectations in receiving quicker responses and aiding the flow of communication. Although one hour per week might not seem long, the fact that language learners are required to be immersed in the foreign language for this hour is perceived as a challenge.

Tips for teachers

Provide a starting point, establish a story line with conflicting interests between characters and outline the learning outcomes and assessment criteria. Plan for more scaffolding and easy-to-comprehend material in the first weeks, and then slowly withdraw your online presence and only interfere when absolutely necessary, allowing the students to take over the role play.

Be prepared to be available 24/7 to provide guidance and feedback. As it is an unfamiliar learning format, students will ask for more feedback. With visual tracking available, be prepared to spend more time providing more detailed feedback. However, setting a fixed time for discussion also reduces the workload for the language tutor, as there is less need to monitor communication and participation. One way of supplying feedback is by interacting with the students in character, clarifying content by asking questions, as well recasting and rephrasing posts. Plan for at least one interim feedback process to take place after one or two weeks. Inform students about the frequency of feedback and negotiate with them as to what type of feedback they will find helpful. A role play 'party' at the end revealing the characters' true identity will allow for a playful and enjoyable reflection process.

There are many parameters to play with, including software, introduction of cross-institutional student cohorts, inclusion of native speakers, variation of length and intensity, synchronity versus flexibility, anonymity versus inclusion of students' audio or video posts, assessed versus non-assessed interaction.

In an assessed learning activity the assessment value needs to reflect the students' workload, but should not over-emphasise the role play, especially if there is no assessment alternative. Assessed participation requires a clear guide with regard to the quantity and quality of posts and other resources uploaded by students to represent their characters.

Outcomes

Students of varying language abilities and learning styles were more active (in written communication) and their responses were more considered (with regards to research and empathy) than would generally be expected when they are put on the spot in a live classroom situation. Moving the role play to an online environment provided students with a safe and anonymous learning space that they took to with great enthusiasm.

Students also developed their presentation skills, in addition to the language-specific learning outcomes (vocabulary, fluency, reading comprehension, writing skills), and improved their intercultural knowledge, empathy and confidence in dealing with challenging situations.

The participating students voiced their enthusiasm about their involvement in the role play. They were keen to try out something new and had no previous experience in educational online role play. Considering they had been given the choice of participating either in this innovative, open-ended, blended role play or focussing on traditional assessment (essay-writing) only, none of the participating students regretted their involvement. This is a success in itself, as assessment is rarely appreciated. Moreover, students felt their learning was aided by the discussion in character and enjoyed the playful nature and their 'immersion' in the material, as well as the challenge of actively communicating for an extended period. Students felt that they gained a better understanding of German history; they connected their in-character experiences with the content of lectures; improved their vocabulary; and felt they had found a space where they could practise newly-acquired grammatical structures. Although the collaborative work on a vocabulary page failed, all students applied individual strategies to enhance their reading comprehension and productive language skills, from using (online) dictionaries to Google Translate, from free creative writing to pre-writing their responses in English and then translating them. Students noted that they had become more spontaneous and confident in using the target language and felt that they were learning autonomously.

Moving Forward

Although common practice in many social sciences (e.g. business, politics), as well as in nursing and other subjects which have adopted a problem-based learning approach, some disciplines still struggle to acknowledge the advantage of online role play and simulation in the classroom. On reflection, however, language learning benefits greatly from role play situations, as immersing students extends their communicative potential, and encourages and enriches the learning experience.

The success of any learning activity is defined by how it is perceived by learners and instructors. Planning an interactive online role play does not mean that it will be perceived as such, and the feedback process between students and tutors therefore needs to be well-established.

The EnRole repository (Australian Teaching and Learning Council) contains more than 60 examples across all disciplines and provides further guidance on the design of online role play.

About the Author

Iris Ludewig-Rohwer is a postgraduate student at the University of Western Australia with a special interest in the use of online role play in language learning. She works as tutor for German as a second language in higher education and adult education, and can be contacted by e-mail at: iris.ludewig-rohwer@research.uwa.edu.au

Bibliography

Australian Teaching and Learning Council. EnRole. Encouraging role based online learning environments. Online Resource: http://enrole.uow.edu.au [Accessed May 20, 2016].

Bell, M. (2001). Online Role-Play: Anonymity, Engagement and Risk. *Educational Media International*, Vol. 38, No. 4, pp. 251–260.

Freeman, M. A. & J. M. Capper (1999). Exploiting the web for education: an anonymous asynchronous role simulation. *Australian Journal of Educational Technology*, Vol. 15, No. 1, pp. 95–116.

Hardy M. & S. Totman (2012). From Dictatorship to Democracy: Simulating the Politics of the Middle East. In C. Nygaard; N. Courtney & E. Leigh (Eds.). *Simulations, Games and Role Play in University Education*, Oxfordshire, UK: Libri Publishing, pp. 257–276.

Horwitz, E. K.; M. B. Horwitz & J. Cope (1986). Foreign Language Classroom Anxiety. *Modern Language Journal*, Vol. 70, No. 2, pp. 125–132.

Ludewig, A. & I. Ludewig-Rohwer (2012). "We are the people!" Empowering Students in German Studies. In C. Nygaard; N. Courtney & E. Leigh (Eds.) *Simulations, Games and Role Play in University Education*, Oxfordshire, UK: Libri Publishing, pp. 257–276.

Van Ments, M. (1989). *The effective use of role-play: A handbook for teachers and trainers.* London: Kogan Page, New York: Nichols Pub.

Wills, S.; E. Leigh & A. Ip (2011). *The Power of Role-based e-Learning.* New York: Routledge.

Chapter 5: Play, Role-Play and Games

Assisting Pre-service Educators with Lesson Planning: Planning not to fail

Eurika Jansen van Vuuren

Background

As lecturer in a new university in rural South Africa I came across several challenges when teaching Foundation Phase educators in the Early Childhood Education program. Due to a mostly deprived background, many students find the language of teaching, English, a challenge. Coupled with a language backlog there is also a lack of general Western knowledge systems which need to be addressed due to the curriculum being westernized.

Students, who are in their 1st, 2nd and 3rd year of study attend lesson planning support sessions a week prior to doing their practicum teaching which is done on a rotational basis in several cycles. The university teaching school is utilized as a centre for observation and practical work. Lesson planning, being the heart of any lesson is an important section of the module of Teaching Methodology but also features in each individual content subject. In the South African context the content modules offered in the degree are Mathematics, Life Skills, Home Language and English First Additional Language.

During the support sessions, students are assisted with teaching ideas and with aligning the lesson topics given to them by the university teaching school teachers with the national curriculum. After the meeting, lessons and resource materials are prepared in groups and submitted online to be reviewed. I then make remarks and suggestions and return it to the group for finalisation and adjustment. On the day of the lesson presentation a name from the group is drawn to determine who is going to teach the particular lesson in an effort to ensure that all students are fully involved in the planning. During the presentation of the lesson, the students are assessed by the class teacher and appointed lecturer. A process of reflection and mentoring takes place shortly after the presentation where the teacher, lecturer and students collaborate.

Lesson plan reviewing and practicum teaching assessment highlighted a myriad of challenges experienced by students – language hurdles, terminology confusion and inability to weave a topic through an entire lesson to ensure effective teaching, learning and assessment. I saw evidence that the conventional teaching they were getting (teacher-centred direct approach) on how to do a lesson plan on the prescribed template was not successful.

After receiving poorly executed lesson plans weekly and getting more and more despondent due to the repeated remedial efforts (repeating and repeating) not showing any positive results, I realized that I had to find a new teaching strategy. In an effort to enhance my teaching skills I looked to the following concepts for inspiration:

- VARK teaching styles (Visual, Aural, Read/write, and Kinaesthetic sensory modalities) of Fleming (2011).

- Gardner's (2003) eight learning intelligences, namely Linguistic intelligence, Logical-Mathematical intelligence, Visual-Spatial intelligence, Musical intelligence, Bodily-Kinaesthetic intelligence, Interpersonal (Social) intelligence, Intrapersonal intelligence and Naturalistic intelligence.

- Silver & Perrini's (2010) four basic human drives (mastery, interpersonal, self-expression, and understanding) coupled with the 8 C's of engagement (Competition, challenge, cooperation, connection, choice, creativity, curiosity, and controversy).

Keeping the above teaching styles, learning styles and learning intelligences in mind I came up with three interventions to accommodate as many teaching and learning styles and human drives as possible – a computer-based exercise, a floor puzzle and a board game. The computer-based exercise can be done by the students in their own time. The other two interventions – floor puzzle and board game – take place simultaneously during the planning sessions and work on a rotational basis. Whilst some groups are working on the floor puzzles, other groups play the board game.

The Practice

The three interventions that I used are discussed in the following section. Please refer to figure 1 for a visual impression of intervention 1.

Intervention 1

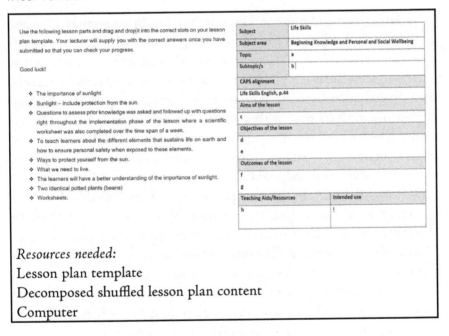

Figure 1: Computer-based lesson planning exercise.

I compiled a computer-based lesson plan exercise. In this exercise the students are given the correct lesson template and have to drag and drop the decomposed lesson plan content into the correct spaces. Students mostly compete against themselves and can request a memorandum with answers. Extra decomposed lesson plans are available and students can work towards improving their own scores. The length of the game will depend on the competence of the player. See figure 1 for an extract from the exercise. This method uses the visual teaching style, accommodates the linguistic and intrapersonal intelligences and the human drives of mastery and understanding.

South African students from rural areas mostly have a very low computer literacy rate due to a mostly underprivileged background and limited exposure to computers. Due to this they find it novel to do something on the computer. The simple drag and drop activity on the computer assists in honing computer skills whilst learning to plan a lesson properly.

Intervention 2

In an attempt to add more variation into my teaching methods, I made large lesson plan template headings using cardboard and also decomposed several lesson plans' content onto cardboard strips. In this exercise the lesson template is not given in the correct order so it is more advanced than the computer-based version where the template is given. Each group of students receive a pack with a lesson plan outline and content. Originally the lesson plan was used against a wall but moving it to a horizontal level on the floor with students gathered in a circle format around it proved to be more successful and ensured that all students were drawn into the activity (See figure 2). In the floor puzzle exercise, each student is given a few lesson components and the group then collaborates to firstly place the lesson plan outline and then the content of the given lesson plan correctly. Finally the links between the objectives and outcomes and the different lesson sections (introduction, input and implementation, and conclusion) must be indicated to ensure that all aspects are pulled through the entire lesson. This is done by using a specific peg colour for each objective. The peg colour must be seen in each section of the lesson plan to ensure that each objective was met. The winning group is the group that finishes the puzzle correctly in the shortest time. It takes students approximately 15 minutes to complete a lesson floor puzzle.

Resources needed:
Lesson plan template on cardboard
Lesson plan contents on separate cards (variety of lesson plans)
Pegs of different colours – 10 per colour

Figure 2: Lesson plan floor puzzle.

By using a floor puzzle, the visual and kinaesthetic teaching styles as well as the linguistic, visual-spatial, bodily-kinaesthetic and intra- and interpersonal intelligences are accommodated. The basic human drives that are covered are those of mastery, interpersonal and understanding, whilst the forms of engagement covered include challenge, cooperation, connection and choice.

Intervention 3

Whilst some groups are building floor puzzles, others play the board game called PLAN (See figure 3.) I devised a board game consisting of multiple choice question cards and a board that contains instructions that must be followed. Up to five players can be involved. A dice determines the distance each player's game token is moved. If a player lands on a 'pick a card' block, a multiple choice card is read to the player by an administrator. A correct answer results in a player moving forward. This game tests lesson plan format and lesson part recognition. The board game can continue from 15 minutes up to an hour depending on the knowledge of the players, the number of players and the instruction blocks on which the students land.

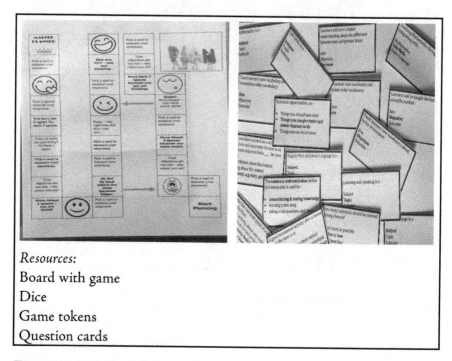

Resources:
Board with game
Dice
Game tokens
Question cards

Figure 3: PLAN board game.

This board game covers the visual teaching style, and considers and develops the strengths of inter- and intrapersonal intelligence. The human drives of mastery and understanding is accommodated and competition and challenge are the ways of engagement.

Outcomes

Intervention 1

Students in rural South Africa are not optimally exposed to computers at university and thus find it more exciting doing a computer exercise than just sitting in a formal lecture. They can do it in their own time and retry until they are successful in a non-threatening environment. With the current student generation being used to cellular phones, they find a computer exercise more aligned to the digital era.

Intervention 2

When doing the floor puzzle activity, a higher participation rate is obtained from the students. It has also encouraged academic conversation between the students and me, which shows students are thinking about how they plan and understand how to do it. I leave the students to make mistakes and argue about the way the lesson should be organized and only intervene when necessary. After all the previous attempts of teaching the lesson plan, I have heard students saying, 'Oh – is that how it works? But then it is easy!' It is evident that the light has gone up for many students. Students also commented that they had the opportunity to interact with me as lecturer in a less formal way and in smaller groups where they did not feel embarrassed to make mistakes and ask for assistance. When specifically asked about the method, students concurred that it was 'way easier than just talking about it.' In addition, some students have started copying the idea of unpacking certain learning material on the floor, which is evidence of pre-service educators breaking the traditional teaching mould and embracing alternative methods.

This teaching method is different from my usual teaching style and is much less stressful than trying to lecture using a Power Point presentation and giving each student a lesson plan template to complete. It cannot be done in a theatre style lecture hall but works well outside or on any other flat surface. It needs substantial preparation when you start off but then the material can be used for a couple of years which eventually cuts down on preparation. You have more time to mingle with students and guide them where necessary.

Intervention 3

Students playing the board game generally tend to focus on the game rather than on the lecturer and find it less intimidating and threatening than a normal activity where their knowledge is exposed and assessed. The board game to enhance the understanding of the lesson plan has guided students into thinking about the different aspects and terminology of the lesson plan and it assists in solidifying the content in a fun interactive way. The general improvement of lesson plans prepared by the students has convinced me that these practical playful activities are the key to the planning door.

Moving Forward

For these games to remain relevant some changes will need to be made. The computer-based lesson needs to be fully computerized by developing it into a format like HTML 5 where the score is automatically generated and the competition element enhanced, whether it is self-competing or playing in competition with others.

The floor puzzle can be enhanced by adding more lesson plans covering a variety of subjects and topics.

A different version of the board game can be developed to make the game more accessible for first years who are just starting to learn lesson planning. Extra question cards will assist to keep the game relevant.

About the Author

Dr Eurika Jansen van Vuuren is a senior lecturer at the newly established University of Mpumalanga in South Africa, specializing in Life Skills for the Foundation Phase (Arts, Physical Education, Social Sciences, Natural Sciences and Personal and Social Well-being). She can be contacted at one of these e-mails: eurikajansenvanvuuren@gmail or eurika.jvvuuren@ump.ac.za

Bibliography

Fleming, N. (2011). The VARK modalities.

Gardner, H. & T. Hatch (1989). Educational implications of the theory of multiple intelligences. *Educational Researcher*, Vol. 18, No. 8, pp. 4–10.

Gardner, H. (2003). Multiple intelligences after twenty years. *American Educational Research Association, Chicago, Illinois*, No. 21.

Silver, H. F. & M. J. Perini (2010). The Eight C's of Engagement: How Learning Styles and Instructional Design Increase Students' Commitment to Learning. *On Excellence in Teaching*, pp. 319–344.

Tulbure, C. (2011). Do different learning styles require differentiated teaching strategies? *Procedia-Social and Behavioral Sciences*, Vol. 11, pp. 155–159.

Section 2: Student Partnerships

An Introduction to Innovative Teaching and Learning Practices Using Student Partnerships

Sarah Hayes, Richard Bale, Tracy Bhoola,
Kirsten Jack, Charlotta Johnsson & Brenda Kalyn

Introduction

Collaborative partnerships for learning in higher education constitute a coming together of stakeholders who each contribute important aspects to the learning process. In this case, we refer to partnerships between students and teaching staff primarily. Learning without one of these connective partners lessens the potential for exploration. Through learning and teaching partnerships, ideas are shared, listening and observing become crucial, thinking and wondering are a part of generating new knowledge and ideas around important themes. Partners are supportive and share the power in learning. There has been a shift from the idea of authoritative, knowledgeable educators lecturing as though students have no experiences or ideas to bring to their learning contexts. Partnerships are respectful, exciting and recognise that we all become learners within the contexts of the goals and outcomes of our courses. Such a two-way transmission challenges the lack of agency students typically have within university educational structures and processes, endorsing change that is more meaningful and fruitful (Hassan & Hayes, 2016). As partnership participants, it is important to be 'present' in the sharing of knowledge, contributing to the process, and being accountable (Ryan,

1988). Learning becomes personal, active and combines integration of doing and knowing (Hutchings & Wutzdorff, 1988).

There are many definitions of partnerships. According to Healey *et al.*, (2014:12) the development of partnerships in learning and teaching is considered to be one of the most important issues in higher education today. The authors discuss that: *"partnership is understood as fundamentally about a relationship in which all involved … are actively engaged in and stand to gain from the process of learning and working together. Partnership is essentially a process of engagement, not a product. It is a way of doing things, rather than an outcome in itself."*

In our writings, we have moved beyond the traditional practice of defining partnerships. We have chosen instead to demonstrate our ideas of partnerships through explanations and applications as they emerged within our work and academic practices. Partnership innovations have added value as students and teachers experience personal and professional growth. Student and teacher partnerships must also be authentic for genuine learning to occur. The breadth and depth of knowledge develops through collaboration that begins in the classroom and continues to the home and the workplace. Partners collaborate to create new ideas and knowledge, adopt roles, solve problems, and present their findings in reciprocal, meaningful contexts. Subsequently, students and teachers learn from each other in supportive and safe environments. An effective way of generating a deeper understanding and making real connections to any type of information is to teach the content. Acknowledging how to target capabilities, weaknesses, ambitions and learning styles can help learners and educators plan effective and engaging curricular assignments, assessments and activities. Partnerships can inform and inspire new and effective practices in higher education and curriculum innovation.

Partnerships are also a way of working that is interpreted and actively shaped by the individuals involved. Through mutual trust and a strong focus around institutional and individual change, it requires shifts in power dynamics. When successful, it empowers students to become active contributors rather than passive recipients (Kellner, 2000; Kolb & Kolb, 2005). This is personally meaningful because it can go well beyond the policy rhetoric of 'student engagement', which frequently results in students sitting on the side-lines of their experiences. Given the 'marketisation' of education (Molesworth *et al.*, 2009), learning experiences can become viewed as isolated commodities, with no clear link between previous knowledge and new knowledge. In a *surface* approach, Marton & Säljö (1976) suggest we may discuss 'student engagement', but in a *deep* approach towards partnership, a more holistic view is possible and one where all participants develop critical analysis and interpretation of their shared context. Partnerships provide us with the opportunity to demonstrate care within our teaching and learning practices. There is much to be gained, both academically and humanly, by including themes of care in our curricular teachings (Noddings, 1995). When we care about the contexts of learning for our students and ourselves as teachers, we demonstrate attentiveness to the processes of learning.

Student partnerships encourage writing and collaborations that allow us to explore our experiences in a deep and meaningful way and to focus on our past, our current, and future work. There is the potential to share information about who we are and what we feel and think. These are our personal stories, which as narratives, reveal meanings that were previously unrecognised. As such they have potential to *"transform life and elevate it to another level"* (Crosseley, 2000:537). When we read and write we share our thoughts and feelings, and what is written on paper comes to life. We invite others into our world and we share experiences, working towards common goals in our work and our learning. Through the process we learn to empathise and understand more deeply about another's context. Partnerships operate on multiple levels and the educator becomes a partner in the learning, developing their own self-knowledge and awareness. Trust is central to this process, and learning expands and comes to life in new ways. Reflection is also an important part of learning through partnerships. The ability to step back and ponder personal learning experiences is to abstract and piece together meaning and knowledge relevant to specific contexts of learning. Many of these experiences are transferable pieces that transform experience into learning (Hutchings & Wutzdorff, 1988).

Benefits

Higher education is valued for its contributions to the global economy, which can lead to prioritisation to meet the needs of industry and competition. This emphasises to students the role of a degree to secure future material affluence, but less so, the opportunities to study as an on-going investment in the self (Molesworth *et al.*, 2009). Students are consumers in this model, and come to view their development in isolation from the transformative potential that university education offers for the whole of life. Assignments can be perceived as discrete items to 'pass' and move on from, rather than learning elements, within a whole curriculum, linked to life skills and future employment. In addition, students may not reflect upon, nor gather their own feedback. Teachers encouraging students to ask critically reflective questions, such as: 'what did I get from doing this assignment?' and: 'how might I do it differently in the future?' is not a priority in a fragmented modular system. Educators can perceive students to be dis-engaged and may question their own teaching methods, as attendance in lectures declines. Teachers may not ask the deeper, probing, reflective questions that genuinely effect change. Therefore, developing a partnership approach enables shared understandings that are advantageous for all parties. The benefits of establishing partnerships include:

+ sharing interpretations of the higher education environment;

+ understanding and challenging each other's points of view;

+ empowering learners;

+ developing autonomy;

+ preparing students for work life;

+ preparing students to participate in teaching-related activities;

+ considering a different approach towards teacher presence;

+ fostering a shift in educators to recognise that they are also learners;

+ valuing students as co-creators of knowledge;

+ honouring students' experiences and building on their ideas;

+ creating possibilities to write, publish, or present collaboratively.

As students work more closely with educators, both parties can begin to appreciate each other's positions and interpretations of the wider political context around them. This new understanding and challenging of each other's practice provides an exchange that can begin to change the higher education landscape. For example, students are empowered to take control of and be responsible for their own learning as well as to build a learning community with their peers. They can also begin to interact within wider forms of academic and professional practice, such as running a mentoring programme, being active participants on panels or committees, and perhaps writing into institutional or departmental policy. With sufficient support from educators, students can chair meetings autonomously, design lesson plans, or write in ways that they connect with their emotions, and thereby gain confidence and achieve success relevant to them. Students can carry these skills and experiences into the future and recognise their value when applied in the workplace, or life in general.

From an educator's point of view, a student partnership can cause the teacher to reconsider the form of presence he or she has within a class. The partnerships become instruments for personal and institutional change and may lead to a shift in the balance of power often found in classrooms. A reflexive approach can enable staff to confront their own assumptions and learn from what this reveals; as such students become valued as co-creators of knowledge. In honouring students' experiences and building on their ideas, teachers and students can come together to create lesson ideas that will inspire students to reach academic, personal and professional goals. For example, providing fresh routes into writing or publishing research papers collaboratively, or taking responsibility for delivery of some content within a lesson and being prepared to share thoughts and opinions with peers.

Considerations

Quality in education is often measured on the basis of quantifiable information using module evaluation questionnaires and student surveys, for example. However, partnership working is also assessed in terms of creative processes, with results that cannot necessarily be quantified and measured using traditional metrics. With less quantifiable evidence of success, compared with traditional metrics, educators might initially be dissuaded from adopting these approaches. In addition, other considerations might include:

+ the perception of giving away 'power and control';

+ an increased risk taking in the classroom;

+ a concern that these approaches are (initially) more time-consuming;

+ the necessity of 'moving into the unknown';

+ anxiety about lack of student engagement;

+ a requirement to justify and explain the underlying pedagogy.

By inviting students to take an active role in shaping the learning context, the educator may feel as if s/he is relinquishing control, leading to a more unpredictable situation. This entails the willingness to take risks concerning the design and delivery of learning and assessment activities. Moving from a familiar approach to something new may be perceived as time-consuming, both at the planning and the delivery stages. For example, educators may be willing to adopt a new approach but may not feel empowered to explore their options due to the multiple demands on their time. In addition, there may be several new activities to prepare when rethinking the planning and implementation of the new approach.

Within an already busy curriculum, it may be daunting to experiment with unfamiliar approaches which offer uncertain outcomes and rewards for student learning. It is this 'moving into the unknown' which can cause anxiety for both educator and student. This leads on to the possibility that students themselves may not initially be willing to engage with a new approach. They may also feel that they are being asked to work harder than those whose learning is facilitated using a more traditional method. With unfamiliar pedagogies, students may question why they are learning in unconventional ways, and it is therefore important to explain the reasoning behind the approach.

Innovations in learning and teaching need to be valued highly at an institutional level, in order to promote the adoption of new methods of working. However, considering the benefits outlined above, it seems worthwhile for all parties involved in the partnership to pursue new, innovative and exciting approaches.

Introduction to the Chapters

The chapters which follow will share insights into six different and inspiring innovations in teaching in higher education that involve the extensive use of partnerships, reciprocal sharing, and deep contextual learning. In chapter 6 Kirsten will present the use of reflective poetry writing as a way to explore thoughts and feelings about nursing practice. In chapter 7 Richard will describe the use of Student Teaching Assistants (STAs) in Modern Language lessons. In chapter 8 Sarah will explain how she engaged undergraduate students to co-teach a group of educators with her, in a student-staff partnership. In chapter 9 Tracy will present how students can improve major language skills, reading comprehension, critical thinking, discussion skills and group work by giving Text Analysis Presentations (TAPs). In chapter 10 Brenda will share how teacher candidates connect practical learning experiences and knowledge acquisition in a Physical Education methods course. In chapter 11 Charlotta, Carl-Henric and Givi will introduce a novel method that uses peer dynamics for integrative learning referred to as Extended Flipped Classroom (EFC). Its aim is to enhance learning and mimic work-life learning situations.

We hope that these six chapters on student partnerships will encourage you to further develop learning-centred higher education including students as collaborative partners.

About the Authors

Sarah Hayes is a Senior Lecturer in Technology-Enhanced and Flexible Learning in the Centre for Learning Innovation and Profession Practice at Aston University in Birmingham, UK. She can be contacted at this e-mail: s.hayes@aston.ac.uk

Richard Bale is Head of Modern Languages in the Brunel Language Centre at Brunel University London, United Kingdom. He can be contacted at this e-mail: richard.bale@brunel.ac.uk

Tracy L. Bhoola is an English as a Second Language (ESL) professor at the York University English Language Institute at the School of Continuing Studies, York University in Toronto, Ontario, Canada. She can be contacted at this e-mail: tgoode@yorku.ca.

Kirsten Jack is Reader in Learning and Teaching Development at Manchester Metropolitan University, England, United Kingdom. She can be reached at this e-mail: k.jack@mmu.ac.uk

Charlotta Johnsson is Associate Professor at Department of Automatic Control, Faculty of Engineering at Lund University, Sweden. CJ was co-program director for the Technology Management program 2008–2015.She can be reached at this e-mail: charlotta.johnsson@control.lth. se

Dr. Brenda Kalyn is a faculty member in the Department of Curriculum Studies, College of Education, University of Saskatchewan. Brenda can be reached at this e-mail: brenda.kalyn@usask.ca

Bibliography

Crossley M. l. (2000) Narrative psychology, trauma and the study of self/identity. *Theory & Psychology*, Vol. 10, No. 4, pp. 527–546.

Hassan, I., & S. Hayes (2016). Transforming the relationship between staff and students to effect change. *The Journal of Educational Innovation, Partnership and Change*, Vol. 2, No. 1.

Healey, M.; A. Jenkins & J. Lea (2014). *Developing research-based curricula in college-based higher education*. York: Higher Education Academy.

Hutchings, P. & A. Wutzdorff (1988). Experiential learning across the curriculum: Assumptions and Principles. In P. Hutchings & A. Wutzdorff (Eds.), *Knowing and Doing: Learning through experience*. San Francisco: Jossey-Bass, pp. 5–19.

Kellner, D. (2000). *Multiple Literacies and Critical Pedagogies, in Revolutionary Pedagogies – Cultural Politics, Instituting Education, and the Discourse of Theory*, Peter Pericles Trifonas, Routledge.

Marton, F. & R. Säljö (1976). On qualitative differences in learning: Outcome and process. *British Journal of Educational Psychology*, Vol. 46, pp. 4–11.

Molesworth, M; E. Nixon & R. Scullion (2009). Having, Being and Higher Education: the Marketisation of the University and the Transformation of the Student into Consumer, *Teaching in Higher Education*, Vol. 14, No. 3, pp. 277–287.

Noddings, N. (1995). Teaching Themes of Care. *Phi Delta Kappan International*, Vol. 76, No. 9, pp. 675–679.

Ryan, M. (1988). The teachable moment. In P. Hutchings & A. Wutzdorff (Eds.), *Knowing and Doing: Learning through experience* San Francisco: Jossey-Bass, pp. 30–47.

Chapter 6: Student Partnerships

Exploring Feelings through Reflective Poetry Writing

Kirsten Jack

Background

My innovative teaching practice involves student nurses writing reflective poems about their nursing experiences. The writing and subsequent group analysis of the poems supports deeper levels of learning about, and engagement with, students own feelings and those of service users and carers, when compared to traditional methods. This innovation is not restricted to health care students and could be used more broadly, for example, to engage students from any discipline in self-development or encourage them to think more creatively about their own speciality.

In undergraduate nurse education it has been suggested that there is too much emphasis on the scientific model and less time devoted to the interpersonal aspects of nursing practice (Rolfe, 2014). This is particularly evident during care delivery where there is more of a focus on the completion of tasks than the relational aspects of care. This is problematic, not only from the service user perspective but it can leave student nurses feeling negative about the care they provide and can even contribute to students discontinuing their studies (Jack & Wibberley, 2013). The seminal work of Carper (1978) reminds us that there are four fundamental patterns of knowing in nursing; empiric, aesthetic, ethic and personal, and each are of equal importance. As a nurse educator based in a higher education setting, I wanted students to engage more coherently with the aesthetic and personal nature of nursing rather than a continued focus on the science, and I developed an innovative method to support a change in educational practice

The Practice

The overarching aim of this innovation was for student nurses to consider their thoughts and feelings about nursing practice with a view to supporting their self-awareness development and emotional sensitivity to others. Using poetry supports a deeper understanding of professional issues by engaging the student in creative thinking, for example, through the use of metaphor and imagery and offers opportunities for a more liberating writing experience than the use of traditional methods. The process of poetry writing is a personal one and learning gain will differ from one student to the next. However, the specific objectives are that by taking part in the process the student will be able to:

+ Analyse their thoughts and feelings about important professional nursing issues;

+ Discuss their experiences with others using poems as a form of creative expression;

+ Discuss the experiences of other students in a supportive way;

+ Analyse the issues raised in the poems and subsequent discussion, from a service user perspective.

I introduced the concept of reflective poetry writing to the students, as a way to explore their nursing experiences in a deep and meaningful way. Reflective practice is a familiar concept to most nurses and is an educational and professional requirement. It has been described by Jasper (2013:3) as a way of learning which involves "...*thinking about things that have happened to us and looking at them in a different way, which enables us to take some kind of action*". It supports the development of interpersonal competence and helps students to cope with the emotional nature of their work. However, in recent years reflective practice, as a way of learning from experiences, has been criticised for its overuse and misuse. Reflective pieces are sometimes assessed as part of undergraduate nursing outcomes, making it difficult for student nurses to reflect honestly and they might be tempted to write what they think is 'correct' and not discuss how they truly feel.

In the early stages of a first year module I deliver a one-hour workshop to introduce the concept of poetry writing to the students. Students are introduced to different styles of poem in the introductory session and are shown examples of poems written by their peers from previous groups. However, they are advised that their poems do not need to follow a particular format and can be written in any style. Students often worry about the need for their work to rhyme or that the poem needs to be a particular length. For many students, their only experience of poetry was during their school days and often this leaves them with a dislike of this style of writing. It is important to repeatedly reassure the students at this stage and support the process of self-expression rather than focusing on the end product of the poem itself. Students are then given private study time to write their poem. Two weeks later the students return to share their poem with their peers in a group session comprising of approximately 15 – 20 students. This session is facilitated by an educator who writes and shares their own poem, becoming a co-learner in the group, in a transformatory style of learning like that described by Mezirow (1997). Discussion of the poems in the small group supports different ways of thinking about the issues raised and encourages an openness to the views and perspectives of others in the group.

Reflective poetry writing is different to traditional reflective writing, for example, when students use a reflective model, as it leads to deeper levels of discussion and learning. This is because it affords the students more freedom, acting as a welcome change to traditional reflective models which might be viewed as restrictive and impersonal. This is beneficial as it helps students to understand their own feelings in a more meaningful way and supports the view that nursing practice is more than merely a set of tasks to be completed.

Writing poems enables students to articulate their feelings more easily (Chan, 2013). It supports their understanding of difficult concepts such as empathy and compassion and encourages thinking about areas they might not normally consider (Speare & Henshall, 2014; Jack, 2015). In the discussion session, educators share their own poems as part of the group, leading to more of a joint learning experience than afforded by traditional methods. This gives an opportunity for the educator to discuss their feelings as part of the norm, thereby acting as a role model for effective practice. It encourages students to engage with their creative side and to express themselves more effectively and pleasurably than traditional methods. Being able to think more creatively is an important skill for students, who often need to find creative answers to the multiple challenges faced when they are working in the clinical environment (Chan, 2013).

Students engage well with this style of teaching and learning practice as it gives them an opportunity to think and write in an unrestricted way. All too often, the only time students are invited to write is for an assignment or examination, and being overly prescriptive can be unhelpful to their academic writing development (Whitehead, 2002). Students prefer a more creative style of writing as it is more 'personal' thereby reflecting the unique nature of their feelings. It encourages them to talk about how they feel and increases understanding of, and empathy for, their peers in the group. Students report that the drafting and redrafting process required when writing poems helps them to take more time and contemplate their experiences than they would normally do when completing the traditional reflective templates. By doing this they reach different and more meaningful conclusions about their practice. Even the students who do not enjoy the process of poetry writing, still engage with it and like the fact that is it a different way to learn and think about their experiences.

Often students write poems from the service user perspective which helps them consider how others might be feeling. This gives them an opportunity to practice empathy which can then be applied in the practice setting. Poetry writing supports thinking about concepts such as compassion and communication, and it helps students articulate their role as caring professionals, in terms of where they are now, and where they would like to be upon qualification as a nurse. They write about both current and future concerns relating to their nursing practice. Reading a poem aloud to a group can feel daunting although the experience has a beneficial effect on students' confidence. The ability to speak aloud in a confident way is an important skill in nursing practice, for example, when acting as an advocate or during nursing handovers in the clinical setting.

Students are enabled in their writing through the use of metaphor. Metaphor helps them to discuss their feelings in ways they might not normally feel comfortable, enabling them to 'express the inexpressible' (Barker, 2000:98). This is helpful to students as it can lead to catharsis which then enables them to move on from situations they have encountered. When using this method, students learn more about themselves and how they feel about situations, which supports self-awareness development. This is important as it is only when we begin to understand ourselves that we can start to understand another person. The process helps them to explore their emotions and how they identify and manage their feelings in practice; this supports the development of emotional sensitivity to themselves and others.

There are some particular issues which require consideration when implementing this style of approach, which might be helpful to support its success:

+ Website: The Caring Words website www.caringwords.mmu.ac.uk was designed to create an online poetry community to support students in thinking about their feelings and experiences. Students can read poems written by other students, which lessens feelings of isolation and loneliness. The poems can be used by educators as examples when inspiring others to write creatively;

+ Timing: Some students might not perceive poetry writing to be relevant to their chosen course. Therefore, introducing the innovation around, for example, assessment time, might not encourage students to engage with the activity. Introducing the idea early on in the module encourages students to engage with it as part of the norm, and to start thinking creatively well in advance of them having to write and share their poems with others;

+ Emphasis on the process: When preparing for this innovation, it is important for educators to place emphasis on the *process* of poetry writing, rather than the end product; the poem itself. Students worry that their poems might not be 'good enough' therefore it is important that educators respect all contributions and not judge them as 'good' or 'bad';

+ Educator Involvement: It is helpful if educators prepare for the session by writing their own poem to be shared with the group. This is important, as it models a style of critical reflection expected from the group. It also helps develop a more equal relationship between student/educator. Educators need to feel comfortable in letting go of their traditional role, as the leadership of the group is shared and the educator is more of a co-learner than teacher;

+ Safety: Due to the increased levels of engagement, students might feel vulnerable as they expose more personal issues and emotions through poems, leading to a more unpredictable learning environment. However, it is important as educators, that we are aware of any current or potential problems that students might be facing, so that we can offer appropriate support. Learning about students' emotional needs in this way enables us to be proactive in our approach rather than wait until a problem occurs, by which time students might have already become very distressed or disillusioned about nursing practice. It is to be expected that this method of learning will mean that students might require more emotional support than they would do normally and educators need to be more prepared for challenging situations, and the potential need to bring their pastoral role into the classroom. There needs to be opportunities for private discussion between student and educator after the session and time for de-brief to ensure student safety.

Outcomes

Using this innovation, I am able to engage with students in a more meaningful way in comparison to traditional methods, such as reflective pieces using models as a template. This leads to a greater understanding of their emotional needs, meaning I can tailor my support for them more adequately. Using this method, students develop academically in terms of their writing, and personally, as they begin to understand themselves and others better. Through their poems they engage more meaningfully with other students and this has a beneficial effect on their confidence and ability to communicate.

The poems give the students an opportunity to consider the unique and individual interactions they have with service users, helping them to explore their role as nurses and the important concept of 'patient centred care'. Poetry writing helps them to make sense of the feelings they have around experiences, rather than merely describe and focus on the events themselves and this has importance for their ongoing self-awareness development. Often poems do not make sense when we first hear them and we need time to contemplate the meaning of what is being said. Therefore by listening to poems, students can rehearse for the often complex nature of nursing practice and the need to listen carefully to service users, so that they can care for them effectively. The nature of poems help students see beyond the medical model, exposing the important relational aspects of nursing practice.

Writing my own poems sustains my understanding of the realities of nursing practice faced by students on a daily basis. This supports feelings of empathy for them as I remember the emotional challenges faced by myself as a novice nurse. Working in higher education can lead nurse educators away from the practice setting, as they become consumed with administrative and other duties as part of their role. Remembering the realities of nursing practice through poems enables a return to the complexity of the lived experience of being a student nurse. The culture of nursing practice is one which does not always value the process of reflection or the contributions students make through engaging with it (Coleman & Willis, 2015). Therefore it is essential that students are provided with opportunities to reflect meaningfully on their work in the university setting, and with someone who values the contributions they make.

Students report through module evaluations that poetry writing enables them to think about important topics in more depth and detail than using traditional methods. The innovation helps them to explore situations in creative ways, igniting their imagination and the ability to express their feelings in a more honest way than before. It helps them to slow their thinking down as they consider the best word or phrase to include in their poem. Hearing the poems of other students helps them to develop empathy and explore the different ways their peers experience similar situations to themselves. This method reduces feelings of isolation and supports students in thinking about who they are both as people and novice professionals. Students report that being able to work creatively boosts their confidence in both themselves and their writing ability.

All of the students' poems are posted on the Caring Words website, so they can see their work published. Some students continue to write poems, after the class based sessions, and these have been successfully used in different ways. For example, one poem written by a student was used to educate primary school children about the basic rules of first aid if faced with an unconscious patient. Another poem was used at a conference launching the 6 'C's (an initiative designed to raise compassion in nursing) and then tweeted about positively by the Experience of Care Lead at NHS England.

Moving Forward

This chapter has outlined how student authored poetry can support the exploration of thoughts and feelings about practice. Looking forward, an alternative approach, whilst still using poetry, might be to use published work. This can be helpful when educators want to focus on a certain aspect of practice, as they can choose a piece of work which might direct a discussion in a particular way (Foster & Freeman, 2008). Some suggestions of published work include; *Sudden Collapses in Public Places* (Darling, 2003); a collection of moving and often humorous poems about the authors experience of cancer and, *Final Chapters* (Kirkpatrick, 2012); a collection of poems and short stories about end of life experiences. Students might be invited to choose their own examples of published work for discussion in the classroom. This can be helpful when attempting to develop a diverse range of issues for discussion, and can support the involvement of the service user by bringing their voice into the classroom, using the medium of poems.

There is great potential for the use of the arts to support health care education. When we engage the imagination, we open up endless opportunities for learning, both theoretically and in terms of self-development. Growth occurs on both sides of the student/educator relationship and engaging with the arts helps us as educators to remember ourselves as students, how it felt and the challenges we faced. It is up to us to continue to explore how the arts can be used to support educational development. We then uncover new meanings, and opportunities for discovery, not only for our students but for ourselves.

About the Author

Kirsten Jack is Reader in Learning and Teaching Development at Manchester Metropolitan University, England, United Kingdom. She can be reached at this e-mail: k.jack@mmu.ac.uk

Bibliography

Barker, P. (2000). Working with the metaphor of life and death *Medical Humanities* Vol. 26, pp. 97 – 102

Carper, B. (1978). Fundamental patterns of knowing in nursing. *Advances in Nursing Science* Vol. 1, No. 1, pp. 13–23.

Chan, Z. C. Y. (2013). A systematic review of creative thinking/creativity in nursing education *Nurse Education Today* Vol. 33, No. 11, pp. 1382–1387.

Coleman, D. & D. S. Willis (2015). Reflective writing: The student nurse's perspective on reflective writing and poetry writing *Nurse Education Today* Vol. 35, pp. 906–911.

Darling, J. (2003). *Sudden Collapses in Public Places.* Todmorden: Arc Publications.

Foster, W. & E. Freeman (2008). Poetry in general practice education: perceptions of learners *Family Practice* Vol. 25, pp. 294–303.

Jack, K. (2015). The use of poetry writing in nurse education: An evaluation *Nurse Education Today* Vol. 35, No. 9, pp. e7–e10.

Jack, K. & C. Wibberley (2013). The meaning of emotion work to student nurses: A Heideggerian Analysis *International Journal of Nursing Studies* Vol. 51, No. 6, pp. 900–907.

Jasper, M. (2013). *Beginning Reflective Practice* Hampshire: Cengage

Kirkpatrick, R. (2014). *Final Chapters: Writings about the End of Life* London: Jessica Kingsley Publications.

Mezirow, J. (1997). Transformative Learning: Theory to Practice *New Directions for Adult and Continuing Education* Vol. 74, pp. 5–12.

Rolfe, G. (2014). Editorial: Educating the good for nothing student. *Journal of Clinical Nursing* Vol. 23, pp. 1459–1460.

Speare, J. & Henshall, A. (2014). 'Did anyone think the trees were students?' Using poetry as a tool for critical reflection *Reflective Practice: International and Multidisciplinary Perspectives* Vol. 15, No. 6, pp. 1–14.

Whitehead, D. (2002). The academic writing experiences of a group of student nurses: a phenomenological study *Journal of Advanced Nursing* Vol. 38, No. 5, pp. 498–506.

Chapter 7: Student Partnerships

STA(r)s in the Classroom: Supporting Collaborative Learning with Student Teaching Assistants

Richard Bale

Background

This approach to learning and teaching capitalises on the multilingual and multicultural student populations often found on university campuses by recruiting students with native-level competence in a foreign language to act as Student Teaching Assistants (STAs) in Modern Language classes, which students attend as additional modules alongside their degree subjects.

The decline in the number of UK universities offering Modern Languages as a degree subject presents opportunities to reconsider models of language provision as a co-curricular option. Language classes at our institution are popular, and courses are often full. The STA model offers a way of continuing to meet high student demand for foreign language tuition, whilst also increasing the personalised support students receive, and providing STAs with valuable work and volunteering experience, thus enhancing their employability. In this way, there are benefits for all parties involved in the learning partnership. This approach complements peer-assisted learning (PAL), which is now commonplace in many higher education institutions. PAL has its origins in the USA, where it is commonly referred to as supplemental instruction (Bidgood *et al.*, 1994;

Topping *et al.*, 1996; Capstick *et al.*, 2004). There is also much interest in the use of *online* peer learning and peer feedback, with pedagogic research in this area starting in the 1990s (Warschauer, 1996; Liang, 2010; Shih, 2010).

The use of STAs goes a step further than PAL, however, as students have a visible presence in the classroom and help plan lesson content based on their knowledge of their fellow students' needs. Boud *et al.* (1999:413–14) define peer learning broadly as *"the use of teaching and learning strategies in which students learn with and from each other without immediate intervention of a teacher."* According to this definition, the STA approach is not strictly peer learning, as the Student Teaching Assistant assumes a leading role in the learning interaction. Nevertheless, it can be seen from the feedback from Student Teaching Assistants (see Outcomes below) that the learning is indeed reciprocal, with STAs also gaining many benefits from the experience.

Thus far, there is little evidence of students assuming a visible teaching role in the classroom (whether as a fellow learner or in the role of teaching assistant), as opposed to the activities usually associated with peer-assisted learning. By contrast, STAs are not part of the learners' class (as they are already native speakers of the language of study), but instead join the group in the role of learning facilitator. A small study in the USA reported on the use of Peer Teaching Assistants (PTA) in Spanish classes, with undergraduate students taking responsibility for agreed sequences of learning content. Rodríguez-Sabater (2005) reports that over 90% of the students involved claimed to have improved their Spanish speaking skills more than in previous semesters. The STA model builds on Rodríguez-Sabater's study, and we have gathered evidence of positive outcomes for language learners as well as Student Teaching Assistants in classes across six different languages.

The Practice

STAs are recruited through the University's on-campus Volunteering Service and attend a one-day Student Teaching Assistant training session with an external provider (see next section for an overview of training content). Applicants attend a brief interview to explore their motivation for applying, and to ensure that they have native-level competence in the language they wish to teach. Candidates for the role of STA are studying a range of subjects, from engineering, to business administration, to life sciences. During the interview, it is explained that, whilst teaching assistantship is conducted on a voluntary basis, applicants must be sure that they are able to commit to helping a group of language learners for at least one hour per week, without impacting negatively on their own degree studies.

Once selected and trained, STAs work alongside language tutors to assist with language learning. The STAs perform various activities in collaboration with the tutor, but the role mostly involves working with small groups of students for conversation and pronunciation practice. STAs also take the students' learning beyond the classroom by organising language cafes where language learners can practise the foreign language in an informal environment while drinking coffee with their friends and fellow learners. Another activity frequently facilitated by the STAs is the delivery of short presentations about cultural and social aspects of the countries where the language is spoken. This allows learners to hear about the country(ies) from a perspective other than that of the usual class tutor.

Ideally, STAs commit to working with a particular class either for one semester or for a whole course, which lasts two semesters. This enables the language learners and the STAs to establish fruitful working relationships. It also enables the class tutor to develop a high degree of continuity in the ways in which the STA is employed in the classroom. Language classes are generally timetabled in the evenings (after 4pm), when most of the degree teaching has finished. This enables students to attend a language class and/or volunteer as a STA without clashing with the main academic timetable.

This approach is different from traditional practices as it places the student at the centre of the learning – both as learner and learning facilitator. It also emphasises the UK Higher Education Academy's philosophy of *students as partners* (HEA, 2014), which focuses on student engagement and co-designing of the learning environment. Language learners also have the opportunity to learn collaboratively with their peers, placing responsibility for learning, and thus autonomy, firmly in the hands of the students.

There are rich learnings for all parties involved in this approach. From a practical point of view, STAs gain valuable professional and teaching experience. Through their work as Student Teaching Assistants, they increase their self-confidence and ability to communicate clearly and effectively. They also gain experience of presenting, both in their native language and in English. Finally, they learn more about their native language from the perspective of second language acquisition. The language learners themselves also benefit from this approach, most notably by having access to another person who speaks the target language, other than the usual class tutor. Students also receive more individual attention, as the STA is able to work with learners one-to-one and in small groups. As mentioned above, learners often have the opportunity to meet with the STA after lesson time, so the learning experience is no longer confined to the timetabled sessions in the classroom.

This approach does not only bring advantages for language learners and STAs, however. Language tutors also benefit from having Student Teaching Assistants in their classrooms, as STAs provide a wealth of up-to-date knowledge about the countries where the target language is spoken. This enables tutors to enrich their lesson content by drawing on the STA's cultural knowledge and experiences.

Training of Student Teaching Assistants

Before the semester begins, STAs are recruited to volunteer in language classes. Each applicant is interviewed face-to-face in order to explain the role in more detail and to verify that the student has the required level of skill in the language in question. In our institution, volunteering activities are linked to a scheme which allows students to collect points so that they can gain volunteering awards. Students can record the hours they spend on volunteering projects, both on and off campus, and are awarded a bronze award if they complete 25 hours of volunteering over an academic year, a silver award for 50 volunteering hours, or a gold award for 100 hours. Students are then invited to a ceremony and a gala dinner, where the awards are presented.

Before teaching begins, STAs attend a compulsory one-day training workshop. In the workshop, STAs learn about the following:

• the role of a STA, drawing on the teaching assistantship literaure (Burnham, 2011; Kamen, 2011; Morgan, 2007):

- o checking students' work;

- o encouraging students to correct their own mistakes;

- o keeping an individual student or group on task;

- o repeating instructions given by the teacher;

- o clarifying meaning and/or ideas;

- o explaining difficult words to learners;

- o reading and clarifying textbook/worksheet activities for a learner;

- o listening to students while they read;

- o playing a game with an individual learner or small group;

- o observing/recording learner progress during an activity;

- o reporting problems and successes to the teacher;

- o contributing to class discussions under the direction of the teacher.

- how the role of a STA differs from that of a teacher; what a STA should *not* be expected to do (Burnham, 2011; Kamen, 2011; Morgan, 2007):

- o planning the lesson;

- o teaching a lesson unsupervised;

- o differentiating tasks according to the individuals' needs;

- o giving learners regular written feedback and grades;

- o marking homework;

- o maintaining achievement records.

- STA interactions with students; how to correct students' linguistic errors; correcting pronunciation;

- typical difficulties associated with learning particular languages (French, German, Russian, etc.);

- ◆ how to support weaker students;

- ◆ dealing with problematic scenarios in class;

- ◆ facilitating small-group activities.

STAs explore these topics in small discussion groups, mainly on the basis of video stimuli, which were filmed specifically for the training session. The videos explore various scenarios, showing problematic situations that can arise in the classroom, initially with a 'what went wrong' scenario (see Figure 1). This is then discussed in the group, before playing a video sequence showing a more appropriate way of handling the situation in question.

Figure 1: Photographic still from STA training videos.

Reflection and Evaluation

This approach requires the use of a video camera to record training videos and for ongoing recording of lesson sequences, subject to agreement of STAs and language learners. Recordings of lesson sequences serve as a useful training and development tool, as STAs can review and reflect upon their practice in the classroom. The language learners and STAs signed consent forms, giving permission for their learning interactions to be filmed and reported on in publications.

At the end of the language courses, there is an evaluation question-naire which forms part of the quality assurance of all modules taught at the institution. Questions related to the STA model were added, in order to obtain feedback from language learners about their experiences of working with a STA. STAs and tutors also completed questionnaires, in order to gauge the views of all parties involved in the partnership. These views will be presented in the following section.

Outcomes

A particular strength of this approach to learning and teaching is the emphasis on students as partners and collaborators in the learning process. Those volunteering as STAs take an active role in the delivery of learning content. Similarly, those in the role of language learners realise, through learning with and from their peers, that they are valued stake-holders in the learning process. This inevitably leads to a student-centred and student-led approach, which empowers learners and STAs to engage in learning and teaching alongside their tutors. From lesson observa-tions and questionnaire responses, it is evident that the STAs enhanced classes by carrying out a broad range of roles in the six language classes – summarised as follows:

+ helping students to revise vocabulary;

+ helping students to prepare/conduct role plays;

+ working with students who missed the previous class while other students completed exercises with a partner or individually;

+ task modelling: the STA conducted short role plays / Q&A with the tutor;

+ checking pronunciation and helping students during pair work;

+ helping during presentations or revision of vocabulary by miming words and concepts;

+ delivering presentations about business and cultural etiquette;

+ helping students prepare for oral assessments;

+ organising *whatsapp, wechat* or *Facebook* groups, so that students can continue learning with other learners and the STA online and via text message (see Figure 2);

+ arranging to meet with students informally outside of lesson time, for example in a 'language café' setting, where students sit and drink tea/coffee whilst practising the target language.

Figure 2: STA adding a learner to a Mandarin wechat group to enable discussions and learning to continue via text message after class.

As mentioned above, STAs enable learners to receive greater individual attention, as the STA can work with students one-to-one and in small groups. The class tutor is then able to monitor the progress of students more closely. In the end-of-course evaluation, the tutors across the six languages provided feedback on their experiences of working with STAs, with comments summarised as follows:

+ students benefit from hearing different accents;

+ more students receive individual feedback;

- students are able to work in smaller groups with a native speaker for support / feedback (see Figure 3);

- students can see and hear the target language being used authentically by watching the tutor and STA model the language / task;

- students can hear about the target language, country and culture from a young(er) person's perspective, adding a sense of authenticity to the learning experience.

Figure 3: STA working with a group of four students in a German class.

Following on from the final point above, it is important to note that the STA is an invaluable contemporary cultural resource which can help to bring the language to life. I, as well as many other tutors in the department, have not lived in the target language country for some time, so it can be difficult to maintain up-to-date knowledge of sociocultural developments in the countries where the target language is spoken. In this case, the STA becomes a vital source of information, helping to provide a context for the language learning and, ultimately, inspiring students to continue with their language learning and even work abroad upon graduation.

In order to gauge language learners' views about this approach, responses on the end-of-course questionnaire were analysed. The language learners were largely positive in their responses, with 95% of respondents stating that they found the approach *useful* for their learning progress and 95% stating that they found the approach *enjoyable*. The minority of students who did not find this learning practice useful or enjoyable stated quite honestly that they were not engaged during the course and that they did not attend many of the lessons. Their negative judgements therefore referred to the learning experience as a whole, and not about the use of Student Teaching Assistants specifically.

Students found it particularly useful to be able to see and hear authentic conversations take place between the tutor and the STA, rather than relying on recorded voices on audio(visual) media. As mentioned above, it was also useful for students to have access to an additional person who could help on an individual basis. Interestingly, some students also stated that they felt more comfortable making linguistic errors when working with the STA, as opposed to when they were speaking with the tutor. Therefore, students were more willing to experiment with more complex structures, rather than 'playing it safe'. This led to students feeling less inhibited, thus allowing learning to take place more rapidly and in a more relaxed way. A similar outcome arises from Kirsten Jack's contribution in this volume, which explores the use of poetry and creativity to empower students to express themselves and reflect on their learning in less conventional ways, and without the fear of being judged and assessed.

Learners also noted that they enjoyed having contact with a fellow student (in the form of a STA) outside of lesson time. As mentioned above, this was often in the form of online and text-message communication via *whatsapp* or *wechat* groups, or at informal language cafés, which involved meeting up with language learners for conversation practice while drinking coffee or playing games.

In addition to the feedback from language learners, the STAs also provided very useful insights about their experiences with this initiative, with several themes emerging, allowing for a qualitative analysis of the perceived success of this approach. All STAs made reference to improved communication skills and increased confidence through participating in this initiative, for example:

"Being a STA helped me explain things to other people in various way [sic] patiently, which obviously improved my overall communication skills, an overall plus to all of my careers to come."

"As well as teaching students, it also helped me on how to explain what I know to students."

There were also some comments which alluded to the fact that teaching their own language made STAs more aware of the structures in their native language, as follows:

"It's just a very nice experience to help people from all over the world to learn about your own language and culture. That also gets me thinking about the way I speak and the way languages are structured."

Some students also made explicit reference to the usefulness of the experience for a potential teaching career after university:

"Very nice is also the way the teacher is explaining the value and purpose of particular tasks to me while the students are working on it, so that I understand the structure of teaching."

Finally, all STAs mentioned various skills and attributes which they feel they gained or developed through their work as STAs. These were mainly communication skills, organisational skills, teamwork and increasing self-confidence, as evidenced by the following:

"I think I got more experience of teamwork and I felt more confidence [sic]."

"As skills that I have gained I can include mainly communication, also organisation skills and working with students which also has provided me with intercultural skills."

So it is clear that the STAs found the experience useful for their own personal and professional development, as it provided them with an opportunity to place themselves in the role of learning facilitator in a partnership with fellow students and language tutors. They also gained an insight into the difficulties associated with learning their own language, and they were able to appreciate the complexities of designing and delivering effective teaching and learning opportunities. This new understanding encouraged the STAs to become more engaged in the process of learning as a whole, thus increasing their engagement with their lecturers and tutors in their degree subject areas.

Moving Forward

The STA model described above outlines one possible way of forming student-student and student-educator learning partnerships, placing students, both as language learners and as Student Teaching Assistants, at the centre of the learning experience. Initial feedback about this approach is positive from all parties involved. However, the use of STAs with further cohorts will enable more detailed feedback to be gathered, thus providing additional information about how STAs can be employed in the classroom and beyond. It will also be necessary to produce training materials specifically for language tutors, in order to ensure that both educators and STAs are able to collaborate with maximum benefits for all parties.

Finally, it is important to note that this approach can be useful in other subject areas. It is already very common for postgraduate students to work as 'demonstrators' in science laboratories, for example. With the promising results from this project, it is possible to see how such a model could be relevant in other subject areas, with students at higher levels of study (final-year undergraduate, Masters, Doctoral) acting as STAs in first-year undergraduate classes, for example. This therefore points towards the potential of establishing a STA model institution-wide across multiple subject areas.

Acknowledgements

I wish to thank the STAs, language learners and language tutors in this year's cohort of language classes. I would also like to thank Angela Agbanubu and Daniel Webber for creating the content for the STA training videos. This initiative was developed with support from the Teach Brunel Fund.

About the Author

Richard Bale is Head of Modern Languages in the Brunel Language Centre at Brunel University London, United Kingdom. He can be contacted at this e-mail: richard.bale@brunel.ac.uk

Bibliography

Bidgood, P. (1994). The Success of SI – The Statistical Evidence. In C. Rust & J. Wallace (Eds.) *Helping Students to Learn From Each Other: Supplemental Instruction*, Birmingham: Staff and Educational Development Association, pp. 71–79.

Boud, D.; R. Cohen & J. Sampson (1999). Peer Learning and Assessment. *Assessment and Evaluation in Higher Education*, Vol. 24, No. 4, pp. 413–426.

Burnham, L. (2011). *Brilliant Teaching Assistant: What You Need to Know to be a Truly Outstanding Teaching Assistant*. Harlow: Pearson Education Ltd.

Capstick S.; H. Fleming & J. Hurne (2004). Implementing Peer Assisted Learning in Higher Education: The Experience of a New University and a Model for the Achievement of a Mainstream Programme. In *Peer Assisted Learning Conference Proceedings*, 2004, Bournemouth University, UK.

Kamen, T. (2011). *Teaching Assistant Handbook Level 3*. Oxford: Hodder Education.

Liang, M. Y. (2010). Using Synchronous Online Peer Response Groups in EFL Writing: Revision-related Discourse. *Language Learning & Technology*, Vol. 14, No.1, pp. 45–65. Online Resource: http://llt.msu.edu/vol14num1/liang.pdf [Accessed on 16 May 2016].

Morgan, J. (2007). *How to be a Successful Teaching Assistant*. London: Continuum International Publishing Group.

Rodríguez-Sabater, S. (2005). Utilizing Undergraduate Peer Teaching Assistants in a Speaking Program in Spanish as a Foreign Language. *Foreign Language Annals*, Vol. 38, No. 4, pp. 533–543.

Shih, Ru-Chu. (2010). Blended Learning Using Video-based Blogs: Public Speaking for English as a Second Language Students. *Australasian Journal of Educational Technology*, Vol. 26, No. 6, pp. 883–897.

Topping, K. J. (1996). The Effectiveness of Peer Tutoring in Further and Higher Education: A Typology and Review of the Literature. *Higher Education*, Vol. 32, pp. 321–345.

Warschauer, M. (1996). Comparing Face-to-face and Electronic Discussion in the Second Language Classroom. *CALICO Journal*, Vol. 13, No. 2, pp. 7–26.

Beyond Engagement and Enhancement – Piloting a 'digital student partnership' to Co-teach Academic Staff on our Post Graduate Diploma in Higher Education

Sarah Hayes

Background

My innovative teaching and learning practice entailed hiring two final year undergraduate students to co-teach with me in a collaborative digital student-staff partnership on my PG Diploma module: *Embedding Technology into Campus-Based and Distance Learning Modules*. For more details on the concept of a 'digital student partnership' see the reference section under Joint Information Systems Committee (JISC) Digital Student. To place myself into this context for readers, I will briefly mention my motivation for developing student-staff partnerships. Prior to my current role as a Senior Lecturer and Programme Director of the PG Dip and Masters in Education in the Centre for Learning, Innovation and Professional Practice (CLIPP), at Aston University, I taught Sociology undergraduates. Critical theory and critical pedagogy (Freire, 1972; Giroux, 1989) are personal, theoretical drivers for me to teach in partnership with my students. Race (2014:34) observes: *"influencing is not achieved by talking at anyone!'*. However, my teaching identity, in itself, does not effect wider change across an institution. In UK Higher Education (HE) (globally, too) market-based agendas reinforce treatment of students as *customers*, as for example in UK Government White Paper: *Higher Education: Students at the heart of the system* (BIS, 2011). Students treated as 'consumers' may view their development in isolation from the transformative potential that university education offers for the whole of life. They may not collect their own feedback, seeing assignments as discrete items to 'pass' and move on, rather than learning elements in a whole curriculum, linked to life skills and future employment.

Encouraging students to ask questions, such as: 'what did I get from this assignment?' and: 'how might I do it differently in the future?', or 'how do I use what I have learned in other modules?' is not a priority in a fragmented modular system. Staff can in turn perceive students to be dis-engaged and begin to question their own methods, as the numbers of students in lectures drop. However, universities can choose to respond differently to this agenda, and begin to work with students as *partners* in HE instead (Hayes & Bartholomew, 2015). This is important, given the global competition that universities now face from private providers and from Massive Open Online Courses (MOOCs). Lecturers can benefit from learning what engages MOOC participants. They can also experiment with 'flipped' forms of delivery, where typically the lecture element is placed online to be viewed before a class and the in-class time is used for active participation from students in seminar discussions, projects and tasks. There are possibilities to improve the digital capabilities of both staff and students via digital student-staff partnerships. Though some authors have claimed that young people immersed in a digital world think, act and learn differently, doing many things at once and with a low tolerance for lectures (Prensky, 2001; Tapscott, 2009), others have urged caution, reminding us that: 'young students do not form a generational cohort and they do not express consistent or generationally organised demands' (Jones & Shao, 2011). Given too some recent concerns that both academics and students may have very variable digital skills, it is necessary to adopt a partnership approach towards developing both the curriculum and the technologies we use to support it. There is a lot of educational literature that stresses collaborative and inclusive approaches towards teaching, so extending this into design of learning, as a partnership, enables fruitful discussions where both staff and students might gain shared interpretations of what it means to learn and teach in a digital world.

Whilst Universities commonly involve students in course evaluations and staff-student committees, thereby eliciting a 'student voice' with the aim of raising awareness of student experiences of teaching and learning at university. More recently, emphasis has been placed not merely on consulting students, but rather on treating them as legitimate equals in a student-staff partnership (Hassan & Hayes, 2016) whose parties jointly make decisions relating to the design of teaching approaches, courses and curricula (Healey *et al.*, 2014). Following our Higher Education Review (HER) in April 2015, we needed to illustrate our engagement and enhancement strategies with actual practices. I therefore wanted to:

- Go beyond a rhetoric often found in policy about 'student engagement', which frequently results in students sitting on the sidelines in committees, to seek a more honest *partnership*, to discover benefits and pitfalls, scope student needs to be able to co-teach with staff and explore powerful values. This links with the UK Professional Standards Framework (UKPSF) and with Part B of the QAA Quality Code, we are currently required to work to.

- Demonstrate to the academic staff on the PG Dip that this is one way they might consider strengthening student engagement. This sort of change supports effective student consultation, as part of our new university-wide curriculum design guidelines. It was recommended in our HE Review in 2015 and is valued in new UK quality frameworks and a proposed Teaching Excellence Framework (TEF). For further information see the Green Paper: *Teaching Excellence, Social Mobility and Student Choice* (BIS, 2015).

Centrally, my role is also linked with improving quality and changing culture. I Chair the University Learning Technology Management Committee, which is responding to the challenge of developing the digital capabilities of both staff and students. So from these standpoints I will describe the stages of my innovative practice, which was a pilot digital student partnership, where students were supported to take the lead in co-teaching staff about what engages them online.

The Practice

Overall approach

- Students research and deliver co-taught sessions to staff, at a University-wide Continuing Professional Development (CPD) Day on designing effective blended learning, from a student perspective;

- As a student-staff partnership, the students are supported to lead the day;

- They produce re-usable video and textual materials to demonstrate and make available on the Virtual Learning Environment (VLE);

- This introduces new skills for the students, such as researching their approach, screencasting, designing a survey for staff to provide feedback;

- It provides staff with resources they can consult about new techniques;

- Students evaluate the day with staff – see below for the survey questions;

- Evaluation feedback supports change thinking in our broader work about student-staff partnerships in curriculum design and online learning;

- This feeds into dissemination events and strategic planning;

- Students write about the partnership in a co-published research article (Hassan & Hayes, 2016).

Recruiting students as educational developers and digital partners

+ I created an advertisement that explained the partnership role as an Educational Mentor undertaking 40 hours of work. See Figure 1 for details;

+ I shortlisted the 11 student applications I received;

+ I interviewed the student applicants jointly with our Quality Officer;

+ I appointed 2 final year students from diverse subject areas and backgrounds.

Timescale and distribution of hours

+ Following their appointment, in April 2015 the students met with me once, before mutually agreeing time to complete their final year examinations;

+ On the very same day of their last exam though, they came to see me to enthusiastically ask about the next stage of this work;

+ We had just under 2 months before the day when they would co-teach;

The distribution of hours is shown in Figure 1 below:

Vacancy: 2 final year undergraduate educational mentors

2 final year undergraduates are sought to undertake up to 40 hours each of educational development and mentoring work on a small pilot student/staff partnership project.

Led by Dr Sarah Hayes, this work involves working closely with Sarah. In partnership, you will research and deliver co-taught sessions to staff, at a Continuing Professional Development (CPD) Day on 'Student Engagement for Learning in the Digital Environment' on 15 July in MB512.

The CPD event will be attended by current academic staff participants on the CLIPP PG Dip module: *Embedding Technology into Campus-based and Distance Learning Programmes* (20 credits) and by staff who want to know more about ways to engage students in online learning environments.

Skills required and benefits for your CV

+ An interest in using technology to engage student learning
+ Ability to research how technology has been used to do this
+ Sharing your findings, opinions and experience with staff
+ Gaining experience of co-teaching at a university-wide event
+ Possibility to jointly publish an article based on this work

Start date: 5 May

Rate of pay: £8.70 per hour

Distribution of the 40 hours of work

+ 2 hours: either 5 or 8 May: first meeting with Sarah Hayes
+ 27 hours: 3 hours per week spent on research/preparation with Sarah, leading up to the event on 15 July. Hours can be arranged with some flexibility, in discussion with Sarah.
+ 3 hours: 13 July: final planning meeting with Sarah Hayes
+ 8 hours: active participation in the event on 15 July

If you are interested and would like to know more about this opportunity email Sarah Hayes s.hayes@aston.ac.uk

Figure 1: the advertisement for the student partnership role

Developing our partnership

In our early meetings the students were polite and sought a lot of guidance from me as to what they should do. I wanted them to plan a draft agenda for the taught day in July. However, the first draft turned out to be the sort of day that a staff member might have designed. We discussed this and the students then developed an agenda that was based on their experience to challenge staff:

> "You have been very attentive to our ideas Sarah, and the guidance you provided so far has been really constructive. For instance, bringing us back to recognise the focus of the day should be what students would like to engage with online."

Maintaining an on-going dialogue

We evaluated our experiences constantly in a critically reflective way, as illustrated by this comment from one of the students:

> *"I have found our meetings productive in terms of discussing general ideas and trying to move forward with these ideas with the event on the 15th of July in mind. I also think we have developed a positive partnership, and I feel comfortable bringing my own ideas to the table."*

Different from traditional teaching and learning practices?

Yes, very! The students needed to create materials themselves and practice the sessions they would run on the day. Below you can see a recording of the students teaching, together with example questions they asked the teaching staff.

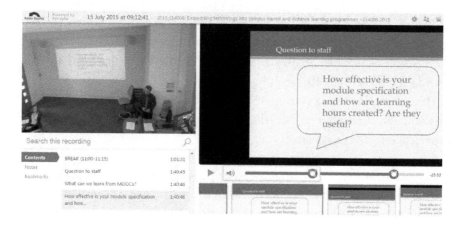

Figure 2: A recording of the students teaching created in Panopto.

However, in the fortnight before the taught day we had been planning, I was out of the country presenting at a conference and teaching at another institution. This meant I could not meet with the students until the day on which they were due to teach. This was a real test of our earlier planning. The students pulled the day together themselves, practiced it all without me and then assigned presentation slots to the Quality Officer and myself. I was delighted to see the confidence with which they then delivered the teaching on the actual day.

What did the day look like?

9:30: Welcome and overview (Sarah Hayes, Course Leader)

9.45: Interactive exercise (Student-led)

Students asked staff: What tools do you currently use? What would you use with support?

10:00: Feedback

10.15: Student perceptions of current use of technology in the University (Student-led)

After reviewing their impressions of their limited courses in Blackboard, the students discussed creative presentation tools, clickers, and social media for class collaboration, such as Google hangouts and Babele. They asked staff questions about assessment and feedback practice and demonstrated what engages them through examples and case studies

11.00: Break

11.15: What can we learn from MOOCs? (Student-led)

MOOCs the students had accessed were demonstrated, including video welcomes to the course and simulation technology recreating real-world challenges and situations

12.00: Do we have a problem? *A critical student-led evaluation* (Student-led)

An exchange between students and staff on what is valued and what is less useful and with reference to case studies at other universities

12:30: Read Opinion Pieces & Complete a Survey and Feedback Form (Student-led)

Staff read and commented on the draft articles written by the students for publication

1.00: Lunch

2.00: Student-staff partnership (Quality Officer and Course Leader)

This gave some of the national quality context and reasons for student-partnership

2:30: Group task (Student-led)

An action learning discussion to find out from each other how some ideas might be developed in people's own contexts to effect and evaluate a change.

Question: What factors make for effective instructional design in Web-based learning in higher education? This involves examining students' and lecturers' perceptions of what elements make for effective online learning environments. This also involves an investigation into how existing principles of instructional design can be applied to online learning.

2.45: Break

3.00: Group task (Student-led)

An action learning discussion to find out from each other how some ideas might be developed in people's own contexts to effect and evaluate a change.

Question: What are the learning strategies that influence students' successful learning in Web-based learning environments? This involves examining how students are being instructed on how to use online learning and what learning strategies do lecturers encourage their students to use. This also involves an investigation into students' satisfaction towards the use of online learning.

3:25: Group presentations on ideas discussed

3:45: Survey and feedback (Student-led)

4:00: Round up, questions and post-event communication (All)

Figure 3: The agenda for the day that the students created.

Reflections

By empowering the students to run the sessions and also to write a publication about this (Hassan & Hayes, 2016), we each experienced rich engagements. For me it was transformational due to the students' enthusiasm and approach, which provoked me re-think how I might teach future sessions. Essentially I felt such refreshment from the exchange of ideas with the students leading up to the taught day. Also all core stakeholders had been involved, including colleagues from Learning Technology Support and our Quality Team. There was positive student feedback and I personally learned a great deal from this partnership. The students (now graduates) stay in touch and I have written references for each of them. The most important preparation is an honest and legitimate ongoing dialogue with your student partners. They need to feel empowered to plan and design materials that are meaningful to them, and not simply to create sessions designed to please staff, which only reinforces existing power relations. A student-staff partnership involves re-negotiating the distribution of power between the students and you as a teacher. It is really important to go much further than consultation. In empowering students to take a *leading* role, the member of academic staff acknowledges a shared authority and values the knowledge and experience that students bring.

The students produced screencasts with free software such as Screen Cast O Matic. In the example in Figure 4, one of the students gave staff an overview on why creating an introductory video of themselves explaining to students what a course will entail, is a really engaging approach. She explains that seeing and hearing the academic explaining what the course will involve helps both prospective and current students to feel more connected with the teacher.

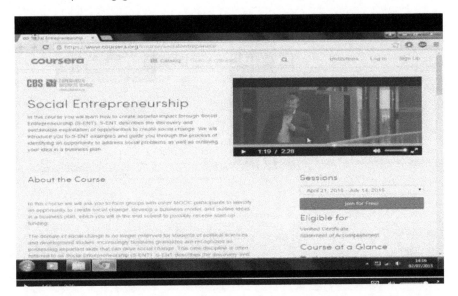

Figure 4: A student-created screencast explaining the value of introductory videos.

She shows a clip from a MOOC where the tutor is walking through his campus describing what is to come on the course. She recounts how in her own experience younger students have approached her with questions about courses to come. She suggests that teachers create engaging introductory videos to visually explain what their course is about, the technology and resources they will use and perhaps also to get former students to comment on their experiences of the course. This may sound a simple concept, but it is felt by students to be personal and inviting.

MOOCs certainly provide many free resources that my student partners were able to demonstrate to staff to explain how such techniques might work in the Virtual Learning Environment (VLE). Below I list some further useful resources on MOOCs, student-staff partnerships and a really helpful benchmarking toolkit.

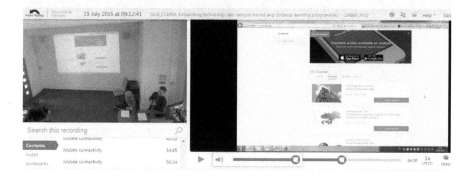

Figure 5: The students explain to academic staff what engages them in a MOOC.

Other useful resources

+ Hayes, S. (2015). MOOCs and quality: a review of the recent literature. https://research.aston.ac.uk/portal/files/18622357/ MOOCs_and_quality_a_review_of_the_recent_literature.pdf

+ Developing Successful Student-Staff Partnerships: https://www. jisc.ac.uk/guides/developing-successful-student-staff-partnerships

+ JISC NUS Benchmarking Toolkit: http://tsep.org.uk/resource/ jiscnus-benchmarking-tool-the-student-digital-experience/

Designing effective blended learning from a student perspective

Survey and feedback

Please indicate how much you agree or disagree with each sentence below:

1. Overall I found the event day useful

Strongly agree	Agree	Neutral	Disagree	Strongly disagree
❏	❏	❏	❏	❏

2. I was provided with new information

Strongly agree	Agree	Neutral	Disagree	Strongly disagree
❏	❏	❏	❏	❏

3. I gained a better understanding of what students find engaging in the learning environment

Strongly agree	Agree	Neutral	Disagree	Strongly disagree
❏	❏	❏	❏	❏

4. The exercises and tasks structured within the day were engaging

Strongly agree	Agree	Neutral	Disagree	Strongly disagree
❏	❏	❏	❏	❏

5. The video and paper resources created were beneficial

Strongly agree	Agree	Neutral	Disagree	Strongly disagree
❏	❏	❏	❏	❏

6. I was inspired to improve the way I use technology in my teaching (if applicable)

Strongly agree	Agree	Neutral	Disagree	Strongly disagree
❏	❏	❏	❏	❏

7. What specifically did you enjoy, or take away from this day?

8. Was there anything that you feel should have been included or focused on more?

9. What resources discussed today are you most interested in using or becoming more familiar with?

10. What are your opinions and/or experiences of student-staff partnerships? Do you think they can bring about significant change?

Figure 6: The students designed this survey to get staff feedback.

Outcomes

The feedback from my student partners has been really positive about the partnership process as a whole – and not just the taught day. Feedback from staff who attended was also supportive in the survey responses: "*I love the interaction between students and teaching staff on this module*".

One of the students particularly enjoyed researching about different approaches to teaching with technology and she published an article with me (Hassan & Hayes, 2016), despite having been apprehensive in the early stages of the partnership:

> "*Although I have worked in other mentoring and teaching roles, teaching on the PG Dip module was a new, exciting but also daunting prospect for me as this was the first time I would be interacting in this kind of way with academic professionals.*" (Final Year Psychology Student).

The other student was confident in a range of technologies and studying on MOOCs. He particularly enjoyed the networking opportunities:

> "*Teaching on the PG Dip Programme was a very enriching experience. It allowed for a unique cross-reference of experiences between students, staff, and teachers to reach an unprecedented viewpoint on learning and technology. I personally benefited from networking opportunities, professional development, and additional research and presentation skill refinement. I can't wait to do it again.*" (Final Year Optometrist).

An honest approach from all parties is advisable from the beginning. It is important that the students feel they can voice their ideas and know they are valued:

> "*Looking back, what really made the sessions worthwhile and of value was that academics/staff who partook were honest and open about their opinions and thoughts regarding the ideas presented – and this led to fruitful discussions. I also felt well-equipped and positive when taking part in this module due to the excellent support that was in place.*" (Final Year Psychology Graduate).

Moving forward

More undergraduates have been recruited since this partnership to work in liaison with the Director of our unit, to input into policy for their engagement and representation across the University.

This partnership work gained me a "SEDA-JISC Institutional Change Leader Award" in September 2015, and since then, I have been asked if I would consider becoming a tutor for colleagues on this course. I believe this to be valuable work for a number of reasons. Firstly, learners expect their courses of study to include digital practices that will equip them for work as well as support their academic progress at university. Secondly, they expect activities to be mediated by teachers who are digitally confident and proficient (Beetham, 2016). Thirdly, it is simply incorrect if we write policy that discusses 'the student experience' are though it were a singular entity, given significant cultural differences in how diverse learners engage in online spaces.

About the Author

Sarah Hayes is a Senior Lecturer in Technology-Enhanced and Flexible Learning in the Centre for Learning Innovation and Profession Practice at Aston University in Birmingham, UK. She can be contacted at this e-mail: s.hayes@aston.ac.uk

Bibliography

Beetham, H. (2016). Digital Student – What Have We Learned? https://digitalstudent.jiscinvolve.org/wp/2016/05/20/digital-student-what-have-we-learned/ [Accessed May 22, 2016].

BIS (2011). *Higher education: Students at the heart of the system.* London: TSO

BIS (2015). *Teaching Excellence, Social Mobility and Student Choice.* London: TSO

Freire, P. (1972). *Pedagogy of the Oppressed,* Harmondsworth, Middlesex: Penguin Education.

Giroux, H. A. and P. McLaren (1989). *Critical Pedagogy, the State and Cultural Struggle.* Suny Press.

Hassan, I. & S. Hayes (2016). Transforming the relationship between staff and students to effect change. *The Journal of Educational Innovation, Partnership and Change*, Vol 2, No. 1.

Hayes, S & P. Bartholomew (2015). Where's the Humanity? Challenging the Policy Discourse of Technology Enhanced Learning. In J. Branch; P. Bartholomew & C. Nygaard (Eds.) *Technology Enhanced Learning in Higher Education*. Oxfordshire, UK: Libri Publishing Ltd.

Healey, M.; A. Flint & K. Harrington (2014). Engagement through partnership: students as partners in learning and teaching in higher education. York: Higher Education Academy.

JISC Digital Student https://digitalstudent.jiscinvolve.org/wp/exemplars/ [Accessed May 22, 2016].

Jones, C. & B. Shao (2011). The net generation and digital natives: implications for higher education. Higher Education Academy.

Prensky, M. (2001). Digital Natives, Digital Immigrants, part 2: Do they really think differently? On the Horizon.

Prensky, M. (2010). Teaching Digital Natives: Partnering for Real Learning. London: Sage Publishers.

Quality Assurance Agency. UK QAA. http://www.qaa.ac.uk/AboutUs/Pages/default.aspx [Accessed April 25, 2016].

Race, P. (2014). *The lecturer's toolkit: a practical guide to assessment, learning and teaching*. Routledge.

Tapscott, D. (2009). Grown up digital: How the Net generation is changing your world. New York: McGraw-Hill.

Chapter 9: Student Partnerships

TAPs – Text Analysis Presentations

Tracy L. Bhoola

Background

I designed Text Analysis Presentations (TAPs) for an English as a Second Language class, but it is highly adaptable to non-ESL subjects and courses in higher education such as science, languages, history, law, psychology, business or technology. That is, any course in which students need to think, read and discuss topics critically. I have taught TAPs at a community college, adult continuing education programs and at a university over approximately 12 years. My students, currently, are university students who hold undergraduate degrees and are pursuing graduate degrees. However, in the English Language Institute there are students at various levels from beginner English learners to advanced to undergraduate students.

I developed TAPs as a creative, engaging and inspiring assignment that encompasses major and minor English language learning skills. Initially, my primary goal was to create an assignment that would lessen the fear and apprehension my students had when tasked with reading and comprehending Canadian texts of various levels of difficulty and diverse topics. I also wanted to take their learning with their classmates a step further with enriching critical thinking and discussion abilities. Through TAPs activities, students learn and practice their speaking, reading, writing, listening and vocabulary skills, along with developing their comprehension, group work, critical thinking and presentation competencies in an all-inclusive setting rather than practicing skills or topics in isolation. I often refer to TAPs as a 360° project in which the student presenters, classmates and teacher are all engaged simultaneously during the presentation and afterward during evaluations.

TAPs is different from a traditional teaching/learning method such as a 'pen and paper test' in which one subject or one skill is tested with limited forms of questions i.e.: multiple choice. It is an all-encompassing assignment that enables students to use technology or paper, practice and strengthen their major (reading, writing, listening, speaking) and minor English skills (vocabulary, grammar, pronunciation) and learning strategies all under the guidance of the teacher and their classmates in a highly communicative and supportive setting. It is a remarkably adaptable assignment in regard to course, English proficiency level, vocabulary, article length and topic, discussion length and presentation style.

As I continued to develop TAPs, I realized it aligns with some theoretical concepts. I have integrated Felder and Solomon's Learning Styles (n.d.), Gardner's Multiple Intelligences (Gardner, n.d.; Gardner, 2006), Bloom's Taxonomy Revised (Anderson & Krathwohl, 2001), to a small degree the Theory of Student Development (Chickering & Reisser, 1993) and Team-based learning (TBL) (Team Based Learning Collaborative, 2016; Brame, 2016). Worth mentioning for teachers interested in the instruction design process is Gagne's Nine Events of Instruction (Northern Illinois University, 2012). Gagne developed a framework of nine steps that can help teachers plan and deliver academic content. Sections of TAPs lend themselves to student learning styles for visual learners who can create outlines, diagrams and presentation notes, or other visual representations of the text. Verbal learners can rehearse orally, brainstorm and discuss work with partners, write summaries and explain ideas and information. Active learners can thrive in the group setting, they can use real life examples with difficult concepts, circulate during class discussions and move while presenting. Sensing learners appreciate choosing texts with some facts, solving problems, and connecting to the real world. Intuitive learners can grasp new concepts more easily and can be innovative. In relation to Gardner's Multiple Intelligences (Gardner, n.d., 2006), TAPs encourages intrapersonal intelligence by researching and reflecting; interpersonal intelligence by cooperatively solving problems, answering questions, collaboratively discussing and taking on group roles; spatial intelligence by representing ideas with pictures, diagrams, and handouts; verbal/linguistic intelligence by reading and analyzing written information; musical intelligence by including music or a video; and kinesthetic intelligence by demonstrating movements and gestures during the preparation and presentation stages. At least one of Chickering's (1993) vectors, developing competence, is applicable. Throughout the TAPs process, students are intellectually and interpersonally working to understand and analyze the TAPs article and establish a working relationship with their classmates in a small group. Next, Bloom's Taxonomy Revised (Anderson *et al.*, 2001) provides the teacher and students with a framework of knowledge and cognitive processes from remembering, to applying, to creating. Using Bloom also provides students with question stems to create their critical thinking questions to be used during the discussion section and these are illustrated in Table 1. Depending on the class level, teachers can determine which level(s) of question stems from Bloom's Taxonomy to use with the students. Finally, TBL (Brame, 2016; TBLC, 2016) provides the students opportunities to: form groups; work and prepare as a team both in and out of the classroom; reflect and then evaluate themselves and their group mates upon completion; have consistent group interaction; and to have the teacher as a guide in the learning process by establishing TAPs objectives and guiding them as they solve problems and complete the tasks.

QUESTION STEMS FOR BLOOM'S TAXONOMY REVISED

LEVEL 1

REMEMBERING

Exhibit memory of previously learned material by recalling facts, terms, basic concepts, and answers.

Key Words	Questions
Choose	What is .....?
Define	Where is .....?
Find	How did ....happen?
How	Why did ....?
Label	When did ....?
List	How would you show .....?
Match	Who were the main ...?
Name	Which one ....?
Omit	How is ....?
Recall	When did ...happen?
Relate	How would you explain .....?
Select	How would you describe ....?
Show	Can you recall ....?
Spell	Can you select ....?
Tell	Can you list the three .....?
What	Who was ....?
When	
Where	
Which	
Who	
Why	

LEVEL 2

UNDERSTANDING

Demonstrate understanding of facts and ideas by organizing, comparing, translating, interpreting, giving descriptions, and stating main ideas.

Keywords	Questions
Classify	How would you classify ....?
Compare	How would you compare ....?
Contrast	How would you contrast ....?
Demonstrate	State in your own words ....?
Explain	Rephrase the meaning .....?
Extend	What facts or ideas show ....?
Illustrate	What is the main idea of ....?
Infer	Which statements support .....?
Interpret	Explain what is happening ...?
Outline	What is meant by ....?
Relate	What can you say about ....?
Rephrase	Which is the best answer ....?
Show	How would you summarize?
Summarize	
Translate	

LEVEL 3

APPLYING

Solve problems to new situations by applying acquired knowledge, facts, techniques and rules in a different way.

Key Words	Questions
Apply	How would you use ...?
Build	What examples can you find to .....?
Choose	How would you solve....using what you've learned?
Construct	How would you organize...to show .....?
Develop	How would you show your understanding of?
Experiment	What approach would you use to .....?
Identify	How would you apply what you learned to develop.....?
Interview	What other way would you plan to .....?
Make use of	What would result if .....?
Model	Can you make use of the facts to .....?
Organize	What elements would you choose to change.....?
Plan	What facts would you select to show....?
Select	What questions would you ask in an interview with....?
Solve	
Utilize	

LEVEL 4
ANALYZING

Examine and break information into parts by identifying motives or causes. Make inferences and find evidence to support generalizations.

Key Words	Questions
Analyze	What are the parts of ....?
Assume	How is related to ....?
Categorize	Why do you think ....?
Classify	What is the theme of .....?
Compare	What motive is there ...?
Conclusion	Can you list the parts ...?
Contrast	What inference can you make .....?
Discover	What conclusions can you draw?
Dissect	How would you classify....?
Distinguish	How would you categorize....?
Divide	Can you identify ....?
Examine	What evidence can you find .....?
Function	What is the relationship .....?
Inference	Can you distinguish
Inspect	between .....?
List	What is the function of .....?
Motive	What ideas justify .....?
Relationships	
Simplify	
Survey	
Take part in	
Test for	
Theme	

LEVEL 5

EVALUATING

Present and defend opinions by making judgments about information, validity of ideas, or quality of work based on a set of criteria.

Key Words	Questions
Agree	Do you agree with the actions/outcome....?
Appraise	What is your opinion of .....?
Assess	How would you prove/disprove.....? Assess the value /
Award	importance of....?
Choose	Would it be better if .....?
Compare	Why did they choose.....?
Conclude	What would you recommend....?
Criteria	How would you rate the.....?
Criticize	What would you cite to defend the actions .....?
Decide	How could you determine....?
Deduct	What choices ....?
Defend	How would you prioritize ....?
Determine	What judgment can you make .. ..?
Disprove	Based on what you know, how would you explain ....?
Dispute	What information would you use to support the view....?
Estimate	How would you justify ....?
Evaluate	What data was used to make the conclusion....?
Explain	What was it better that ....?
Importance	How would you compare the ...ideas?
Influence	the....people?
Interpret	
Judge	
Justify	
Measure	
Opinion	
Perceive	
Prioritize	
Prove	
Rate	
Recommend	
Select	
Support	
Value	

LEVEL 6

CREATING

Compile information together in a different way by combining elements in a new pattern or proposing alternative solutions.

Key Words	Questions
Adapt	What changes would you make to solve ....?
Build	How would you improve ...?
Change	What would happen if ....?
Choose	Can you elaborate on the reason .....?
Combine	Can you propose an alternative....?
Compile	Can you invent .....?
Compose	How would you adapt....to create a different .....?
Construct	How could you change (modify) the plot (plan) ...?
Create	What could be done to minimize/max ....?
Design	What way would you design....?
Develop	What could be combined to improve (change) ....?
Discuss	Suppose you could what would you do ....?
Elaborate	How would you test .....?
Estimate	Can you formulate a theory for .....?
Formulate	Can you predict the outcome if .....?
Happen	How would you estimate the results for .....?
Imagine	What facts can you compile .....?
Improve	Construct a model that would change....?
Invent	Think of an original way for the .....?
Make up	
Maximize	
Minimize	
Modify	
Original	
Originate	
Plan	
Predict	
Propose	
Solution	
Solve	
Suppose	
Test	
Theory	

Table 1: Question Stems for Bloom's Taxonomy Revised*
*Reprinted from Quick Flip Questions for the Revised Bloom's Taxonomy by Linda Barton with permission of Edupress, a Trademark of Highsmith, LLC.

The Practice

Before I introduce the TAPs assignment to the students, I model a version of it for them. I take a Canadian newspaper to class and have the students work in pairs to read an assigned paragraph. Then, I have the students take turns reading it orally to each other, and then I orally summarize the paragraph and show them my printed version of the summary. Next, I present 3–4 new words from the paragraph and produce the definitions, words families, collocations, parts of speech and example sentences. I give them a short quiz on the vocabulary to ensure comprehension is accurate, but also to model a way to 'test' their understanding, which they can replicate during their TAPs. Finally, I ask 3–4 critical thinking questions based on the article. For those critical thinking questions, I refer to Bloom's Taxonomy Revised (Anderson *et al.*, 2001) for the question stems and then complete the stems with my ideas. The students (individually, in pairs, or in triads) then skim and scan the article for the answers and we share the answers as a whole class. Once TAPs has been modeled, I then introduce the assignment that the students will complete by giving each student a detailed handout shown in Table 2 below. Each section of TAPs can easily be assigned a time frame (appropriate to each teacher's schedule and level of students) so that the work is completed over more than one class. I generally have students working over a one to one-and-one-half-week period in and out of class with presentations beginning the following week. This is based on my current course which runs five days per week at four hours per day. Depending on student or class level and TAPs requirements (article length, number of words, discussion length etc.), each group may take anywhere from 25 to 60+ minutes to present. Table 3 illustrates an example timeframe I have implemented, but it is flexible for the needs of every teacher.

SAMPLE TAPs – Text Analysis Presentation

This type of presentation encourages you to read and understand an English academic article related to your graduate major; to learn new English, graduate-level or +6.0 IELTS level vocabulary; to ask/answer critical thinking questions; to practice summarizing, conducting pair/group discussion, and pronunciation skills. *You do not need Prezi or PPT for this presentation.*

Requirements

1. Choose 1 (one) English academic journal article or critical reading article with your partner(s).

- Length of the article should be approximately 2–3 pages.
- Make sure the article is of interest to you and your partner(s).
- If you understand less than 80% of the article, then stop and choose another article. (See Tracy for help)

2. Choose 5 new words from the journal article and provide the following information for each word on a handout for your classmates:

   a) The word
   b) An English Dictionary definition
   c) Part of Speech and its word family (noun, verb, adjective...)
   d) Collocations – if any
   e) An Example Sentence – you must use the word in your own sentence

3. Write a summary of your article and BRIEFLY explain it to the class (do not read it).

4. Write 3 Critical Thinking Questions (Bloom's levels 4,5,6) based on the article and ensure you know the answers.**Be prepared to ask the questions and lead a discussion with the class.**

5. Prepare a handout for your classmates with the following information:

   1) The title and source of your article
   2) The article photocopied (see Tracy if necessary)
   3) 5 new words with a-e above included
   4) The 3 Critical Thinking Questions (no answers)

6. Present the following information:

   1) The title and source of your article
   2) The summary of your article
   3) The 5 new words and all the information from a-e above
   4) Ask the 3 questions and *lead a discussion* with the whole class.

Evaluation: 44 marks – See attached rubric

Due Date: Preparation begins April 11, 2016 and Presentations begin week of April 18, 2016

Table 2: Sample TAPs Assignment Handout for Students.

Day	Time	TAPs
Monday	1–2 hours + any work after class the group does	Assignment Introduction with handout, choose a partner(s), search, find and choose an article, receive approval, read article
Tuesday	1.5–2.5 hours + any work after class the group does	Continue reading article, comprehension, choose 10 new words, complete vocabulary work, check with teacher
Wednesday	2–3 hours + any work after class the group does	Continue with vocabulary work if necessary, write a summary of the article, edit and revise summary as necessary, check with teacher
Thursday	1–1.5 hours + any work after class the group does	Write 3 critical thinking questions, write answers, edit and revise questions as necessary, if applicable – create a PPT/ Prezi, check with teacher
Friday	2–3 hours + any work after class the group does	Prepare a handout, rehearse the TAPs (timing etc), continue editing and revising any section as necessary, check with teacher, submit any materials to teacher for copying if necessary
Saturday/ Sunday		Rehearse
Monday		TAPs Group #1 presents and so on

Table 3: Example of a TAPs timeframe.

After I have modelled TAPs and in order to achieve the assignment requirements, I have students choose an article, read and understand it, complete vocabulary work, summarize it, edit and revise, create critical thinking questions and answers for discussion, prepare a handout, organize a group presentation, and practice. Then, the students are ready to do their TAPs and present to the class their article, summary, vocabulary, questions and conduct a class discussion. I use a rubric while the students present and it is a rubric that I share with all students previous to the presentations. The categories I include on my rubric are:

+ timing;

+ content;

+ summary;

+ vocabulary;

+ critical thinking;

+ organization;

+ critical thinking discussion questions;

+ eye contact;

+ body language;

+ vocabulary;

+ grammar.

After TAPs, I meet with each group and review the completed rubric with them and then I give the students the peer and self-evaluations to complete and submit within one to three days afterward. Now, there are times when I do not provide the peer and self-evaluations, so it is up to each teacher's discretion. For example, beginner ESL learners may not know how to effectively complete such evaluations due to language and cultural barriers and inexperience. So for a first TAPs, I may not require the evaluations and instead wait until I can teach students about the assessment process and when they have a better grasp of assignments, expectations and collaboration.

Materials Required

The main materials required are newspapers or magazines or journal articles (print or digital), and excerpts from textbooks or course reading packs are useful too. Depending on the teacher's requirements being digital or paper-based TAPs, students may need access to computers to prepare a PowerPoint or Prezi or a traditional approach would have students using chart paper and markers. Access to a whiteboard or blackboard along with a photocopier or a projector would be useful to help students, if necessary, to make copies of the articles and handouts.

Outcomes

As comfort and confidence grow during TAPs preparation and practice stages, students cultivate their critical thinking skills, enhance their oral communication abilities, and practice conversation strategies while engaging in small talk about the articles with their classmates and with Canadian English speakers. This serves to help them become more aware of and learn about Canadian culture, their communities and current events and continue to read authentic Canadian material after TAPs is completed. Of course, this is applicable to any culture and language beyond Canada and English. In addition, learners are able to practice pronunciation of new vocabulary, identify concordances, and use an English dictionary (paper or digital) and vocabulary strategies to delve into the word families, collocations and idioms associated with the new words. This would satisfy at least one objective of integrating the new words into their daily personal, academic, or vocational lives.

From a teacher's perspective, I consider TAPs an innovative teaching practice because it is highly flexible, functional and engaging. For example, teachers can adapt the level of difficulty to any caliber of ESL student, or non-ESL student from elementary to university. Moreover, the skills and strategies inherent to TAPs are transferrable to higher education and the workplace. TAPs can also be adapted to include long or short texts or video lectures; academic journals, magazines or newspapers; individual or small groups; multi-media, technology or paper-based work; and just about any course or subject – all of which encourage students to read and think critically and construct and convey knowledge.

From my students' perspective, I consider TAPs an innovative learning practice because I have discovered that my students are more engaged when the text is Canadian, current and of interest to them which is why I tend to let them choose their own articles. From the beginning to end of one TAPs and also with repetition of TAPs, the learners' ability to communicate in written and verbal formats improves along with their aptitude for collaboration and cooperation with classmates. It is wonderful to see their confidence grow in their overall achievement in all of the major English language skills and learning strategies being applied and practiced. Moreover, the inherent flexibility of TAPs makes it an activity that the students can do, more informally, at home with their families and friends, as well as adapting it to meet those needs. So, given the appropriate time, support and inspiration, students are able to complete a well-rounded project.

My students have provided feedback, both written and oral, that touches on the necessity of practicing major/minor English skills and that working on TAPs covers all of the skills in one place. They feel that TAPs gives them the time and flexibility they need to be successful in their own ways and are able to take on group roles that challenge their weaknesses and complement their strengths. The students have commented that their improvement is "more obvious" and "faster" than with standard tests or activities. The learners feel that TAPs is fun and allows them to be creative and independent but still dependent on group-mates and classmates. They also appreciate the opportunity to work closely in small groups and to get to know each other personally and as a result, they gain cross-cultural awareness and understand and respect diversity. Students have also stated that they have a chance to be leaders and followers at different times during the TAPs process and therefore they do not feel as "stressed out" as when they have to complete a project or essay alone. Lastly, students have commented that doing TAPs helps them to learn organizational and time-management skills in part due to the layout of the requirements.

Moving Forward

This chapter has endeavoured to describe an innovative teaching practice for the educational, personal and professional benefits of students. If you find yourself asking, "what else can be done with TAPs?" then I believe teachers and students are only limited by their imaginations. Following are possible extension activities for TAPs, if a teacher so chooses. Apps or educational technology tools could be used during the preparation and presentation stages with particular sections of TAPs such as Animoto, Edmodo, emaze, Google Docs, Kaizena, Podio, Recordium, Simple Mind, Vocaroo and Voxer. These tools enable students to practice individually or prepare together, and they are not bound by geography or time. Furthermore, to extend learning, the teacher could add another section to the TAPs assignment in which students produce their TAPs in a style reminiscent of a TED talk, or a YouTube video, or a flipped classroom version of TAPs. Another possibility is to allow students to integrate an artistic piece of work that represents their topic or a related theme in photographs, a sketch, a painting, or a poem. Lastly, with organization by the teacher, students could present to other classes within their programs or schools. Moreover, I briefly mentioned meeting with students after their TAPs in order to discuss a marked rubric, give feedback and ask reflective questions. Another avenue is for teachers to provide their own critical reflection questions for students to answer over a designated period of time and to later meet with the teacher for a more in-depth review. The benefits of reflection in teaching and learning are numerous and would augment the learners' experiences. Also, conducting peer and self-evaluations are valuable. I have sometimes implemented these techniques with my students only after I conduct lessons on types of evaluations, the essential vocabulary, and how to complete evaluations.

Finally, one other concept to explore for its application to TAPs is Vygotsky's theory of social development and the aspect of the zone of proximal development (Vygotsky, 2012). Educators can look at how interaction with peers and teachers influences learning; how students learn through a cultural lens and its impact upon knowledge; and how language and literacy can be promoted across the curriculum.

Overall, with TAPs, rubrics, evaluations and reflections, it is important to know where your students are at and start from there. It is a sentiment that has served me well and I hope it does for you too.

About the Author

Tracy L. Bhoola is an English as a Second Language (ESL) professor at the York University English Language Institute at the School of Continuing Studies, York University in Toronto, Ontario, Canada. She can be contacted at this e-mail: tgoode@yorku.ca.

Bibliography

Anderson, L. W. & D. R. Krathwohl (2001). *A taxonomy for learning, teaching, and assessing: A revision of Bloom's taxonomy of educational objectives.* New York: Longman.

Barton, L. (2010). *Quick flip questions for the revised Bloom's taxonomy.* Janesville, WI: Edupress.

Brame, C. J. (2016). *Team-Based Learning.* Online Resource: https://cft.vanderbilt.edu/guides-sub-pages/team-based-learning/[Accessed April 12, 2016].

Chickering, A. W. & L. Reisser (1993). *Education and Identity.* San Francisco: Jossey-Bass.

Felder, R. M. & B. A. Soloman (n.d.). *Learning styles and strategies.* Online Resource: http://www.ncsu.edu/felder-public/ILSdir/styles.htm [Accessed May 22, 2016].

Gardner, H. (n.d.). The components of multiple intelligences. Online Resource: http://multipleintelligencesoasis.org/about/the-components-of-mi/ [Accessed May 22, 2016].

Gardner, H. (2006). *Multiple intelligences: New horizons.* Basic Books: New York.

Northern Illinois University Faculty Development and Instructional Design Center. (2012). Gagne's Nine Events of Instruction. In *Instructional Guide for University Faculty and Teaching Assistants.*

Team Based Learning Collaborative. (2016). Definition – Team-Based Learning Collaborative. Online Resource: http://www.teambasedlearning.org/definition/ [Accessed June 6, 2016].

Vygotsky, L. (2012). *Thought and Language Revised and Expanded.* Cambridge, Mass: MIT Press.

Connecting Theory Through Practice: Transformational Learning in Pre-Service Teacher Education

Brenda Kalyn

Background

As a professor in teacher education, I wondered how teacher candidates (TCs) were connecting personal learning experiences and knowledge acquisition when involved in a practical learning environment within a physical education methods course. These environments often produce less note taking than traditional lecture courses as TCs engage in a great deal of practical experience. TCs are immersed in the "doing" and consider the classes "fun." I found students asking the question, "Do we have to write this down?" which caused me to wonder how they were learning through practical experiences and how they valued the course content.

Practical classes are different because the theory is embedded within the practical and it was of interest to learn how TCs experience this knowledge in relation to the "fun" and the curriculum that was planned for their learning. TCs vary in their entry-level class knowledge with some students having a major or minor in PE, to those who have no experience teaching PE at all. Some TCs, in-fact are afraid of the class because they had negative PE experiences as students themselves and they just do not want to experience those issues again. At the end of the class the TCs would say the class was "great" and I wondered what that really meant. I also noted many conversions. TCs who were initially nervous about the class emerged believing they could be good teachers of physical education. This was a desired outcome of course; however, as educators we need to understand what occurs for our students during this process of learning. This innovation in teaching sheds light on their experiences and furthers understanding of TC's experiences relating to physical education methods, specifically. The goal of this work is to understand how students connect theory through the practical and build knowledge towards sound pedagogy. The innovation and the outcomes are an intersection of teaching, learning, observations, and the value that TCs place on this learning experience. Hopper and Bell (2016) agree that teaching strategies are learned best through field experiences or in other practical environments related to PE pedagogy. Providing practical, learner-centered opportunities assists TCs in understanding practice more authentically.

The Practice

In light of the questions that I wondered about in the background section, I decided to attract TCs attention by designing learner- centered assignments that would all link together, profit their knowledge, and lead up to a final 30 minutes show case teaching assignment that would be video-taped and presented back to them for self-analysis. This strategy focused on TCs being immersed in teaching real students – real lessons. I wanted to insert an element of "tension" as they realized their final assignment would put them in the spot light! This strategy proved very successful. The following descriptions outline the processes of the course. Although the focus here is physical education, I welcome the reader to envision possibilities within your own course work.

This innovation in pre-service teacher education assists (TCs) in connecting theory through the practice of teaching physical education with children from Pre K-Grade 8 (ages 3–13) in a natural setting. The class runs once a week for a three- hour block. This time frame is very important to accommodate large numbers of students and TCs learning together as well as to consider the school day and time the students can spend at the university or we can spend within the partner school.

Initially, this approach is time consuming in planning; however, once up and running it flows very smoothly.

Over the 39 hours of in-class experiences the TCs spend approximately 62% of their time actively involved in teaching and learning with over 450 students throughout the term. Most of the students visit the university during our class time. TCs also attend class at our partner school and engage in learning along side the PE specialist, my-self, school students, and their peers. Strong school partnerships are the key to accessing school students. The partnership is a connection between our class and a school; or a school based PE teacher/specialist and his classes. Partnerships can be acquired through direct 'shoulder-tapping' of colleagues in the field, through field based experience placements within your college, or a combination of both. I simply call colleagues and invite them to my classes, former students remember their experiences in the class and they call me to see if they can bring their students in, and my specialist colleagues in the field are eager to participate. Students walk to the university if they are close enough; otherwise, buses are provided from the university or school budgets.

One school based partnership in an elementary school is established where my colleague is a PE elementary specialist. We visit the school twice during the term and work directly with the teacher whereby the TCs observe students during their formal PE instruction and participate in the activities with them. Debriefing sessions are held afterwards in the school library and we discuss observations and answer questions the TCs might have. This is a highlight of their experience to be in the school, with a real teacher and real students, as they describe it. As a result of these interactions at the school the TCs are comfortable in the environment and have met most of the students they might teach for their final 30-minute teaching assignment described further down.

The instructional process is a reversal of a typical lecture-practice-discussion method. This innovation immerses TCs in practice-observation-discussion, theory, connecting the theoretical links in relation to practical methods. TCs develop greater understanding of a variety of curricular contexts in relation to children, learning, and physical education. The underlying goal is to engage TCs within their learning and transform their knowledge and practice. Hutchings & Wutzdorff (1988:7) agree that in order to engage students in their learning, the learning must be active, involve the students, and be engaging. The authors affirm that knowing and doing must be learned together through interactive activities and integrative learning. Their research points out that *"knowing and doing are not simply a matter of application but rather an ongoing interactive process in which both knowledge and experience are repeatedly transformed"*.

During all teaching opportunities, the TCs are not required to take notes during the class time; however, I observe several of them taking a minute or two to write something on their computers that they want to recall for their questions and reflections. Planning and teaching in the elementary PE methods course includes these primary areas:

Figure 1: Curriculum Components for Elementary PE Methods.

Also included are curriculum; adaptive learning; Laban's Movement Concepts (Boorman, 1969; Graham, 2007; Pangrazi, 2009) (Body, Effort, Space, Relationships) which is the fundamental framework for movement; manipulatives (over 12 different apparatus from balloons, balls, yo-yo, skipping, hoops, bean bags, scooters, scoops, racquets, etc.); gymnastics, dance, developmental games; Indigenous games; and large scale activity days with 75 grade one students visiting our class. These conceptual pieces of learning are centered around and inter-related through a body of knowledge, pedagogy, and instructional strategies that have been researched and can be learned by TCs (Pangrazi & Gibbons, 2009).

TCs engage in planning a series of lessons (described below) that are progressive in length and complexity moving from general exploratory movement activities with pre-k students to more sophisticated skill acquisition and learning up to grade 8. Every teaching opportunity includes directly teaching children, observing children moving and responding to lessons, participating directly in the lessons, discussing outcomes, and generating questions and answers in regards to effective pedagogical strategies they will be assessed on in their final 30 minute teaching assignment. While TCs are teaching their lessons I move throughout the teaching spaces and record observations and general themes that I see emerging from their lessons. Noted are both the strengths and the weaknesses I observe and after each teaching opportunity we debrief and share what learning has occurred, the suggestions and accolades I have for their considerations, and address the questions they might have as a result of their lessons.

The role of the instructor changes with this type of innovation in teaching. In essence, the instructor gives up the notion of power and control over the class but is still very present. The instructor becomes a guide, a learning friend, and a knowledgeable resource. The orchestration of the learning environment rises out of the expertise of the instructor and the perceived need of the TCs. Weimer (2002) applauds the redistribution of power so that the learner is motivated and empowered by their experiences. It is important to realize that teaching is not about lecturing, disregarding the students' experiences and knowledge, and being a sole source of knowledge. Learner-centered teaching is not only about the student experience. The instructor is also immersed within the teaching and learning and the rewards of watching students emerge and shine through these experiences is indeed magical.

The key goals for the class:

+ Understand and implement a quality PE program for elementary students; moving beyond the sports orientated framework;

- Introduce students to a wide variety of activities to develop physical skills, healthy social/emotional responses to movement and peers, cognitive understanding of movement, and where applicable apply spiritual/Indigenous connections to movement;

- Become critical observers of children moving;

- Become effective practitioners who provide quality instruction, feedback, and maximum participation in class for all students regardless of ability;

- Develop an appreciation for PE in the daily lives of children.

Organization

As an organization example, I will use 30 TCs in the class. The TCs place themselves into working groups of 6 called SALT (Student Active Learning Groups) for a total of 5 class groupings. They remain in these working groups for the duration of the course. Each group receives a numbered and color-coded file folder with all of the assignments, locations, and dates on the front of the folder. TCs sign up for their lessons on the folders and place any written assignment components within these folders that are stored in a file box that I always bring to class. This is an organizational piece that works extremely well. The TCs always know where they can find their assessed work, assignments, and class information. I also keep attendance records on this folder for teaching assignments.

All lessons are individually taught by the TCs within their groups with some exceptions such as teaching in pairs. School students who participate in the lessons are divided into 5 groups and those students join the TCs groups (culminating in 5–15 students per group plus the TCs). TCs are expected to participate fully in all lesson activities along with the school students who join their groups. Sometimes groups remain in their teaching space and other times the groups rotate through stations. The spaces used are the 4 quadrants of the gymnasium, the hallway, the smaller gym, the squash court, or outside. Space is can be a premium in some facilities so think creatively without being disruptive to others. The following example of assignments is stapled to the front of the file folder.

These are sample assignments and you may use more or less assignments depending on your needs and what you wish to accomplish. Percentages may vary as well. All assignment details are within their course outline.

1. Teaching: Day Care (Please sign up for one concept) (Some will have to go in pairs)	Sept 18 (10%) (U of S Ed. Gym)
BODY	Day Care Kids
EFFORT	7 minute lesson
SPACE	
RELATIONSHIP	
2. Teaching Indigenous Games (Games will be taught in pairs. A separate sign-up sheet will be provided.)	Sept 25 (15%) (U of S Ed. Gym) Grade 7/8 15 minute lesson
3. Issue Presentation (SALT Group presentation. Issue of choice or from a selected list provided in class)	Oct 8 (20%) Classroom 1009
4. Teaching: Manipulatives (Please sign up for one concept)	Oct 29 (15%) (U of S Ed. Gym) Grade 4/5 15 minute lesson

Hoops	Bean Bags
Hacky Sack	Jump Rope
Rhythmic Ribbons	Ankle Hop
Dance	Buddy Walkers
Lummi Sticks	Chinese Skipping
Yo-Yo	Elastic Bands
Balloon Activities	
Frisbee	

5. Teaching Physical Education Activity Day – 75 Grade 1/2 students will participate in station work. You will each teach 2 stations.	Nov 19 (Credit) (U of S Ed. Gym) Grade ½ 7 minute stations
6. In Class Writing – this is a formal in class writing assignment based on pedagogies learned and discussed to date.	Nov 26 (15%) Classroom 1009

7. 30 minute teaching opportunity – Sign up to teach according to your availability during this week	Nov 24–28 Partner School
8. Reflection in action + 30 minute analysis (teaching) Your critical reflection of your DVD and your ongoing class reflections will culminate in this assignment. (Max. 10 pages)	Dec 3–7 (25%)
*We also have 2 classes held in our partnership school during our semester.	Oct 15 Nov 12

Table 2: Student Active Learning Groups (SALT): Assignments.

Assignment Descriptions

All lessons are progressive in duration and technique. At the end of the teaching time I play music over the general loud-system and that signals a change in teachers and/or a change in location for teaching if it is station work where they rotate through the spaces. All information for the content of the assignments is from our text, our lectures, and the internet/library sources.

1. Day Care (7 minute lesson)

Teach one concept of Body, Effort, Space, Relationship to a group of Day Care children and your participating peers for 7 minutes. A short lesson plan is required to be handed in describing: 1) equipment needs, 2) learning outcomes (what do you want the children to experience as a result of your lesson through the Physical Emotional/Social, Cognitive, Spiritual learning domains; 3) observations; 4) and how will you know if your lesson was successful?

2. Indigenous games (15 minute lesson)

In pairs, research and prepare one Indigenous game. The written context of your game should include:

+ Name of the game;

+ Origin/history of the game and who played it originally;

+ State the learning outcomes of the game from the PE curriculum;

+ A complete description of how to play the game;

+ Number of player;

+ Playing space needed with diagrams;

+ Equipment required and instructions on how to make the equipment (you should have the equipment or a modified version ready to play the game; this is your responsibility as the teacher/s);

+ Outline the skills needed to play the game;

+ Include the learning cues you would use to teach the skills;

+ Adaptations for younger/older players;

+ Include references and any other materials you wish to include.

3. Issue presentation *(30 minutes in class)*

Each group (of 6) gives one oral presentation on an issue of choice following these criteria:

+ Outline the issue;

+ Summarize the literature and what you have learned about the issue to date. (Each group member should contribute one solid article on the issue);

+ Discuss why the issue important to consider as a teacher;

+ Discuss the impact this issue has on students;

+ Demonstrate how this issue can be addressed through PE/integrated subjects;

+ Share any personal stories or experience inside this issue;

+ Include your audience within the presentation;

+ Recommendations to address the issue from the teacher and students' perspective.

Potential topics/issues:

Energy Drinks and Youth

Weight Training and Youth

Eating Disorders and Body Image

Cultural considerations and PE

Coaching vs teaching

Technology in PE

Innovative Programs in PE

Nutrition and PE

Obesity and Youth

Physical Activity and Diabetes

Student Inactivity

Adaptive PE

Outdoor Education

Long distance running and kids

Co-ed PE vs gendered

Fitness Testing

Competition vs Cooperation

4. Manipulatives *(15 minutes lesson)*

The students will:

+ experience outcomes related to the curriculum;

+ explore concepts through the equipment;

+ learn vocabulary related to the concept learned;

+ acquire new skills;

+ experience progressions and creative play.

Sample lesson plan to be submitted includes these components:

+ Concept focus;

+ Equipment/supplies needed;

+ Instructional strategies used;

+ Objectives/Outcomes describe the learning that should occur as a result of units, lessons, etc. (The outcomes are holistic and include the four aspects of human nature from the Indigenous culture/s: cognitive, physical, affective, spiritual);

+ Motivational Set;

+ Warm Up;

+ Learning tasks within the lesson (procedures);

+ Closure;

+ Assessment/Indicators.

5. Physical Education activity day *(7 minutes per station)*

(Brenda plans all stations attached below). TCs engage with large groups of children (75 grade 1's) to explore educational learning stations and rotate through these stations as examples. TCs take turns teaching the concepts.

BALANCING/LANDINGS	ROTATIONS
Purpose: to have students understand what a good landing and a strong balance should look like	Purpose: To rotate the body in different ways around the horizontal and vertical body axis.
+ Landing: safely on toe/ ball/heal of the foot + Be in control/soft landings/ use arms for balance Balancing: Balance should be strong, straight lines, held, good focus ahead + On the floor + Using the floor lines + Different body bases (feet, hands, elbows, shoulders, side, front (parachute fall: arms and legs up in the air to stretch) + Low balance beam + Benches + Jump boxes	+ Using the body on the floor/mats + Log roll + Side roll + Forward roll + Down the incline matt/up the incline matt

GYMNASTICS POSITIONS/ANIMAL MOVEMENTS

Purpose: to enjoy moving the body in different ways to imitate shapes, designs, animals

+ Tuck
+ Pike
+ Straddle
+ Back support
+ Front support
+ Lunge
+ Arabesque
+ Kangaroo jump
+ Bear walk
+ Gorilla walk

PARTNER STUNTS

Purpose: to explore movements with a partner in a safe way. Stunts must be safe and bear no weight on each other.

+ Bouncing Ball
+ Wring the dishrag
+ Partner toe touches
+ Seat circle
+ Frog jump

RHYTHMIC RIBBONS

Purpose: to explore rhythmic movements using a manipulative using both arms, different levels, pathways and effort changes

+ Make small/large circles, zigzag, straight lines, change levels (high/medium/low) (change hands)
+ Skipping, galloping while twirling the ribbon
+ Follow the leader in small groups where the leader designs an activity and then someone else takes a turn (keep the pace up with this)
+ Respond to a piece of music with the ribbon by moving in a variety of ways

STUFFY DANCE

Purpose: to sequence simple movements together with the music and explore manipulating a stuffed animal (supplied for you)

+ Stretch up high, down low, turn in a circle, push the stuffy out-front of you, wrap it around your body, through your legs, swing it back and forth
+ Toss and catch your stuffy lightly

Sequence

+ Sway back and forth
+ Lift stuffy up high and turn slowly in a circle/reverse direction
+ Melt to the floor and slowly spin on your bum in a circle while hugging your stuffy
+ Stretch out on your back and raise your stuffy to the ceiling/lift your legs and hold stuffy on the bottom of your feet for a moment.... Carry on!

BALLOONS	HOOPS
Purpose: To manipulate the object and explore body and special awareness	Purpose: To manipulate the object and explore body and special awareness
• Have extra incase of breakage • Make sure the students don't bite them • Tap with different finger tips to keep in the air • Lob back and forth in an arc to keep it in the air • Volley off of different body parts from head to toe • Two students face each other/hold hands/one balloon in-between their chest/can they walk from A to B without dropping it • Keep the balloon in motion as you move from A to B forward/backward/sideways • Walk through a hoop someone is holding while keeping the balloon moving Other activities	• Jump in and out of the hoop • Jump in and freeze into a shape • Jump out and freeze • Balance by walking around the hoop • Step inside and outside (alternating) around the hoop • Change directions • Hoola hoop • Teachers roll the hoop past the students and see if students can jump through the hoop (watch spacing so they don't jump to close to the wall) • Spin the hoop and run around it until it stops • Join hands/place the hoop on one shoulder/pass the hoop around the circle by maneuvering the body

Table 1: Sample Station Work.

6. In class writing.

TCs watch a video of a master teacher teaching a PE lesson, record and discuss the pedagogical practices the teacher uses to teach the class. This is a formal essay piece.

7. 30-minute teaching opportunity: *Your time to shine!*

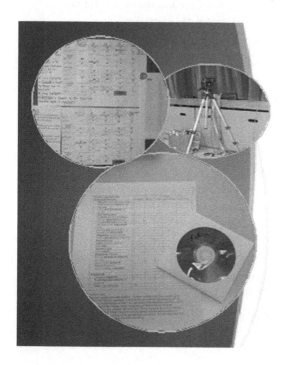

Figure 2: 30 minute teaching sign up, camera, DVD, rubric.

TCs choose a grade to teach one 30-minute lesson at our partner school at the end of the semester. A sign up sheet is provided. The students are from Kindergarten to Grade 8 in our partner school. A Functional Life Skills Class (FLS) is also included in this opportunity. These students have a variety of exceptionalities ranging from physical, verbal, and behavioral issues and this provides TCs an opportunity to observe and engage in teaching students with exceptionalities. (The University, the parents, and the school administration prior to taping approve all permission and ethical concerns. If students are not permitted to be filmed they participate in the lesson in a side space and are not in the camera view).

Their lesson must be curriculum related and any concept they choose is fine. During the lesson they are live recorded. I am present in the gym, observe their lessons, and assess their lessons with the following rubric of researched PE strategies listed below. The major rubric themes are:

- Knowledge & Curriculum;

- Planning;

- Management & Discipline;

- Instruction.

TCs are provided written comments at the end of their rubric sheet and at the end of the lesson we debrief for a short period. A technician at the university transfers the lessons to a DVD and TCs are provided with a copy; as well as a copy of the assessment I have done. They usually have these back within 5 days after they teach their lesson. TCs analyze their lesson based on the criteria we discussed in our course, this rubric, and sound pedagogy. They are required to de-construct their lesson and determine the percentage of time spent: 1) instructing; 2) managing students and equipment; 3) engaging students in on task movement in relation to learning outcomes; and 4) the amount and type of feedback generated to students. This reflective analysis becomes a part of their reflective writing paper. This brings everything we have learned, observed, discussed, and practiced through our course to a grand finale!

Sound pedagogy and instructional strategies have been researched within the field of physical education. There are many resources that outline these important pieces of practice that are paramount within any methods course in PE for TCs (Graham, 2007; NASPE, 2007; Seidentop, 1991; Pangrazi & Gibbons, 2009). For this innovation, important thematic criteria were selected from these resources to create a rubric that represented researched pedagogies that would align with our course work.

Lesson Components and Pedagogical Strategies	5 Exemplary	4 Strong	3 Good	2 Needed Improvement	1 Unsatisfactory
Objectives outlined to the students					
Students actively **engaged** in the outcomes					
Lesson **flow /transitions** are smooth					
Time Management is evident					
Quality Feedback provided to students					
Actively **supervised** learning					
Clear **progressions** are evident					
Developmentally **appropriate** tasks					
Learning **cues** are provided					
Active learning time (strive for maximum)					
Learning **cues** are provided					
Assisted with **motor skills**					
Teacher **placement** for instruction					
Demonstrations					
Angles of demonstrations					
Gym **voice**					
Attention signal					
Class **control**					
Enthusiastic teaching					
Pleasant **learning environment**					
Appeared well **prepared**					
Dressed for success					
Active Learning					
Management					
Equipment **organized**					
Distribution and **collection** of equipment efficient					
Safety issues addressed					
Written Comments: ½ –3/4 page					

Table 3: Assessment Rubric. Graham, (2007); (NASPE (2007); Pangrazi & Gibbons, (2009); Seidentop, (1991).

8. Reflection in Action

This reflective writing assignment is a culmination of your observations and experiences during this PE course. I invite you to observe critically, think, reflect, wonder, question and formulate a deeper understanding of what it means to teach physical education. When you go out to schools, watch your own kids play and move, observe other kids in activities on playgrounds, and in other active venues, try to be a critical observer/ educator and consider these questions. This is a guide to help you critically think about your practice as a teacher; it is not a checklist. These are reflective questions that will help to shape your experiential learning and guide your reflective writing:

+ What are children "doing" inside of their physical activities/physical education classes?

+ What does it mean to be "doing"?

+ What motor skills, levels of motor learning did you observe?

+ Did the learning tasks reflect the intent of the lesson?

+ How engaged are the children in the activities? Do you wonder about their levels of engagement? What might predicate this?

+ Do the activities complement their levels of motor learning?

+ Do you see adaptive strategies?

+ What is the teacher doing in terms of: managing students and equipment; instruction; safety; inclusive, adaptive activities; being enthusiastic; pacing the lesson?

+ What vocabulary did you hear?

+ Did you hear any teacher feedback? How deep was it?

+ Can you identify the whole child in the lesson? Cognitive, Affective, Emotional, Psychomotor, Spiritual?

+ What did the students learn as a result of the lesson?

+ Can you pick out the "competent bystander"?

+ Are you becoming a critical thinker in terms of physical education?

- What do you wonder about in relation to teaching PE?
- How do you see yourself teaching in this environment?
- Who are you in terms of your teacher identity at this point?
- What have you learned?

Equipment and cost considerations

This program is cost effective and can be run with the existing equipment in my (well stocked) education equipment room and with the partner school equipment resources. Use what you have and design your ideas and assignments around these. You can see from the assignments a wide variety of common and unique pieces of equipment are used. If you receive funding in any way for equipment then add to your resources. As mentioned, invite students who are within walking distance of your institution, tandem with another instructor in science, math, language arts, fine arts, for example and bring the children in for a full day to be more cost effective when busing.

Outcomes

Research Grant

After three years of piloting this class innovation, I received a University of Saskatchewan Research Praxis Grant ($1250 for two years) to conduct research around the class to learn about the TC's experiences connecting theory through practice and to understand how the innovation impacted their learning. The grant provided:

- Equipment rental (audio headset/receiver, batteries);
- Video camera and equipment;
- Research assistant for data analysis;
- Teacher time release (conferencing);
- Unique equipment used in the lessons was purchased and left for the partner school (rhythmic ribbons, lummi sticks);

+ Busing to the university for elementary students;

+ The school had plenty of equipment and our university PE equipment supply is very strong;

+ After the grant expired there was no problem continuing with the program.

Students' responses (N 87) strongly applauded their experiences teaching and learning within the practical environment. The opportunities to be immersed in planning and teaching increased knowledge gains in a variety of pedagogical areas that supported learning within the practical environment.

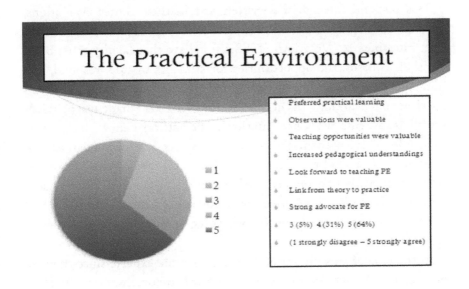

Figure 3: TC's response to the practical learning environment.

This innovation is an intensive but very rewarding approach to teaching physical education methods to TCs. The exchange in learning between the TCs and myself is exciting. I am able to observe my students teaching and learning alongside the children they work with. I hear their conversations with children and the evolving vocabulary they use to teach. I observe them moving with the children, instructing, managing, organizing, and engaging students. I observe areas that need to be addressed and through my observations raise questions to elicit linking their theory with practice. I hear them think. I learn from my students. They teach me what they are learning and how that impacts their vision for their future teaching. I readily observe if the outcomes of this course are reflected in their practice. As they reflect through verbal and written contexts, key elements of their learning are defined. TCs are extremely committed to the process and they enjoy the immersion within the activities. Some TCs have rediscovered the joy of movement for movement's sake. These experiences transform their learning, their attitudes towards physical education as an important curricular experience, their personal motivation for movement, and their practice.

TCs respond through the written text in their course evaluations, reflective writing assignments, and reactions to questions that I might pose. Huthings & Wutzdorff (1988:15) believe that faculty must build into their courses, the opportunities for students to stop, respond, and think about their experiences. Reflection, they affirm, is what *"transforms experience into learning"*. In their work, they have also made use of video-recording students' work presentations. The authors believe that anyone being able to review themselves on a play back is indeed quite an experience where students have the opportunities to recognize their strengths and identify areas that require further work. Reflection is a way to self-assess and it is also imperative for students to recognize learning and how far they have come from the beginning of their learning journey in a particular situation.

In the case of this innovation the TCs are the experts since they are the ones who have been immersed within this innovative practice. Their words and thoughts are of value and are shared within. Sarah commented that her experiences were both transferable and authentic:

> *"In this class I was participating in a lived curriculum, which brought theory to life. One particular example was the power of observation. We were shown a short video clip during class of a "competent bystander" (a student who appears involved in play but is really positioning himself/ herself to avoid the play). We were taught what this term actually looked like and when I began to observe this in reality with students I was amazed that this is so overlooked in practice by teachers. It's easy to spot*

these kids who are really quite disengaged; yet so often we think their actively playing. It's one thing to learn a theory, but another to actually put that theory into action. In this class the theory complimented my practical learning."

Other comments that students shared:

"This is such a valuable class because it provides a great balance of theory and practice where teacher candidates are given the opportunity to teach lessons they have created and use the techniques taught in the course immediately. We learn by doing. We don't have to "imagine" how the lesson might go; we get to experience it."

"We plan, teach, and then discuss our learning and observations. It all fits into the theory we learn in class about children and teaching Physical Education. The feedback we receive is immediate and so helpful to help us grow as teachers. I really enjoyed the wide range of diverse learning opportunities. The assignments were very applicable to future lessons/ unit planning. The class has provided me with many tools to help me progress in my career."

TCs were asked to respond to Hutchings & Wutzdorff's (1988:11–15) quote in relation to their experiences linking theory through practice: *"The best results were obtained by leaving theory until later and beginning with [university] students' experiences, and instead of building theories out of air, building theories on that experience. Rather than assuming all students had experiences relevant to the topic, the instructors made the class itself the needed experience. Reflection is the ability to step back and ponder one's own experience, to abstract from it something meaningful. The capacity for reflection is what transforms experience into learning".*

Colton's response:

"I completely agree. Whether pre-or post intern, we appreciated the ability to have experiences first and connect it to theory afterwards. We were truly able to reflect after every teaching experience. If I were taught by the traditional theory-first approach, I believe we would have simply been less interested and less engaged. This was my first experience with this type of learning and I have become a strong advocate of it, especially

at the university level. I appreciate the structure and content provided in this course and am excited and encouraged to utilize it moving forward in my career."

Brilene commented:

"When you have an experience, discuss what you experienced and then introduce the theory (like we did in this course), the theory resonates with you at a deeper level. That theory is directly tagged to a memory that you can relate to. You are able to remember what that theory is instead of wondering if your experience later on could possibly fit or be an example of that theory you discussed. Instead of making assumptions about a theory and just memorizing it for the test, the theory has been applied to our learning and we will remember the theory long after the class is over."

Moving Forward

This innovation has been in operation for five years and small adjustments have been made along the way. The process moves very smoothly and TCs, partner teachers, administrators, and the teacher education program have all responded positively to their participation and particular outcomes.

There are situation where slight changes might have to occur. For example, if my partner PE specialist has an intern for a semester we do not enjoy the 30-minute teaching opportunity; however, the outcomes are still very positive for the TCs. Thinking creatively inside your educational practice and adjusting for program and student needs is a consideration. The important piece here is to continue to provide TCs with much appreciated practical experiences. Even TCs who have already interned are excited to keep teaching and learning and generally they are enlightened within their PE methods practice due to their internship experiences. Many comment at how they wished they had the course before their internship and how much they "missed" as a result if they had a chance to teach physical education in their internship.

I will continue to run this course in the same manner as it has been perfected at this point, while remaining open to modifications or extensions as they arise. I will continue to acquire more equipment to add to the teaching opportunities and work towards inviting new school partnerships to participate. As you can see, this class is not based around the sports paradigm. It is about teaching children and TCs the joy of movement and learning skills that can be applied to lifetime, enjoyable activities of choice; including sports. They learn about the value of being physically active and the value of choice. Opening the TC's vision of what a quality Physical Education Program should be is the mandate of this course and the valuable outcomes are exciting. When TCs leave the class believing they can be effective, passionate teachers of physical education, and they value physical education within the daily learning for children I am delighted. TCs value the body of knowledge learned in the course and feel confident to continue learning in this area. These outcomes tell me as the instructor to continue to inspire my teacher candidates in their professional practice and enjoy learning alongside of them.

About the Author

Dr. Brenda Kalyn is a faculty member in the Department of Curriculum Studies, College of Education, University of Saskatchewan. Brenda can be reached at this e-mail: brenda.kalyn@usask.ca

Bibliography

Boorman, J. (1969). *Creative dance in the first three grades.* Don Mills, ON: Longmans Canada, Ltd.

Graham, G.; S. A. Holt/Hale & M. Parker (2007). *Children moving: A reflective approach to teaching physical education.* New York, NY: McGraw Hill.

Hopper, T. & R. Bell (2016). *In the beginning: Field based teacher education course in physical education: Impact on pre-service teachers and teacher educators.* Retrieved April, 2016 from http://web.uvic.ca.

Hutchings, P. & A. Wutzdorff (1988). Experiential learning across the curriculum: Assumptions and Principles. In P. Hutchings & A. Wutzdorff (Eds.), *Knowing and Doing: Learning through experience* (pp. 5–19). San Francisco: Jossey-Bass, Inc.

National Association for Sport and Physical Education [NASPE]. (2007). *Physical education teacher evaluation tool* [Guidance Document]. Reston, VA: Author.

Pangrazi, R. & S. Gibbons (2009). *Dynamic physical education for elementary school children.* Toronto, ON: Pearson Education.

Seidentop, D. (1991). *Developing teaching skills in Physical education* (3rd ed.). Mountain View, CA: Mayfield Publishing Co.

Weimer, M. (2002). *Learner-centered teaching: Five key changes to practice.* San Francisco: Jossey-Bass, Inc.

Chapter 11: Student Partnerships

Extended Flipped Classroom – using peer dynamics for integrative learning

Charlotta Johnsson, Carl-Henric Nilsson & Givi Kokaia

Background

The Extended Flipped Classroom (EFC) concept was developed for and applied to a selected group of students studying at the Technology Management programme, a cross-disciplinary master programme at Lund University, Sweden, in 2014. The main driving force for its development was a strong believe that the university can provide the students with, not only knowledge in various subject fields, but also, and equally important, a positive attitude to lifelong learning, an understanding of learning in the coming work-life, and the insight that their own role in the learning situation has an important impact on the outcome.

To be able to explicitly include these aspects in the master programme, the concept of Extended Flipped Classroom was developed, and used in the course Technology Strategies and Structures (TSS). The three main components behind the concept are; flipped classroom, subject field integration, and peer learning. These imply that the students must work through the material together with peers prior to an instructor led classroom lecture, a situation that mimics how learning is done in many work-life situations where teamwork is a common way of working. The students should also analyze and understand how various subjects are interrelated. This mimics real life learning situations in which subjects are rarely encountered as separate entities but rather appears integrated and in a context. Getting an understanding of the whole picture is complementary to understanding the parts. In addition, the students will learn to listen to each other and see each other as resources of knowledge and information, and, vice versa, start to be aware of their own role as contributors in a learning situation. Altogether, EFC with its three components exposes the students to an innovative and new teaching and learning situation that will enhance their learning and practice their life-long learning skills.

Extended Flipped Classroom

Lund University in Sweden is an international university with nine faculties, hosting more than 40 000 students annually. A selected number of students (40) from the Faculty of Economics and the Faculty of Engineering study together during their last 2 years of study in the cross-disciplinary programme Technology Management (Sörgärde and Nilsson, 2005). Their views on problems and challenges in today's industry and society often complement each other. The programme consists of six courses and a master thesis project. After graduating they receive a master's diploma, and the vast majority of the students start their work-life.

Figure 1: Logos for Technology Management programme and Lund University, Sweden.

The Extended Flipped Classroom (EFC) concept is developed for the course Technology, Strategy and Structure (TSS), which is a second semester course. The course is considered to be a half-time course (15 credits), and hence the students study other individual courses during the same time. The TSS course has two modules; the first module has its focus on knowledge and was, before the EFC introduction, composed of a set of traditional lectures; the second module has its focus on skills and is composed of a set of practicing-worklife projects.

The course is built within an already rigid curriculum, where students have been working extensively in teams for the first six months of the program. The students are therefore already exposed to each other, while being tested on new topics and areas in real-world business environments. Subsequently, the students have started to learn how to work and develop their knowledge about the dynamics of their teams. Students as well as teachers have given positive evaluations of the EFC concept with previously defined teams. The concept can be applied to newly formed teams as well. However, the need to increase knowledge about teamwork and group dynamics among team members can become more necessary, in order to create a positive momentum within the team.

The EFC concept was applied to the knowledge module in the TSS course. The module is 4 weeks long. Traditionally, the schedule for the module was composed of 4 traditional classroom lectures, each one 3 hours long, see Figure 2 (left). After the introduction of EFC, the schedule is instead divided in approximately 6 mini-lectures, each max 20 minutes long including a task, plus a final 4 hour integrative discussion workshop in the classroom, see Figure 2 (right). The course is terminated with an exam.

Schedule before introduction of EFC	Schedule after introduction of EFC
Each lecture covers a topic and is presented by a teacher in the classroom. Students are encouraged to attend the lectures.	Students divided in groups of 5. Each group decides its schedule (time and place) for listening to the mini-lecture and do the tasks. The integrative discussion workshop is held in the classroom.
Lecture 1: Topic 1	Topic 1: 6 mini-lectures + tasks
Lecture 2: Topic 2	Topic 2: 6 mini-lectures + tasks
Lecture 3: Topic 3	Topic 3: 6 mini-lectures + tasks
Lecture 4: Topic 4	Topic 4: 6 mini-lectures + tasks
Final Exam	Integrative discussion workshop in classroom
	Final Exam

Figure 2: Conceptual presentations (no details) of the schemas for the TSS course, before (left) and after (right) the introduction of EFC concept.

The main idea behind the Extended Flipped Classroom (EFC) concept is to extend traditional classroom learning with concepts that enhance learning and mimic work-life learning situations. In traditional classroom learning the instructor prepares the material to be delivered in class, the students listen to lectures and guided instructions in class while taking notes, and the students are assigned homework to demonstrate understanding. This means that the instructor plays a major role and various subjects are treated separately and in sequence, a situation seldom encountered in work life. The three main components behind EFC are; flipped classroom, subject field integration, and peer learning. The three are closely intertwined and enables enhanced learning and is based on a lifelong learning attitudes.

Flipped Classroom

In the *flipped classroom* (Bergmann & Sams, 2010) what is traditionally done in the classroom is done at home and vice versa. In our case the instructors record and share the lectures outside of class, the students watch and listen to the lectures before coming to class. The class time is devoted to applied learning activities and more higher order thinking tasks, and students receive support from instructors as needed. In the TSS course the concept of flipped classroom is used, however with some adjustments. The lecture was not recorded as one cohesive lecture (normally 45 minutes) but rather broken down into smaller mini-lectures of approx. 5–20 minutes, each followed by a task. In this way the discussion and interaction among the participants becomes more natural and an integral part of the stream of mini-lectures.

The students were told to watch/listen to the sequence of mini-lectures in groups of five and to pursue the tasks together before listening to the next mini-lecture. Since each traditional lecture is replaced by (a set of) pre-recorded mini-lectures and tasks, the students are convened to the classroom for applied learning activities and higher order thinking tasks. One instructor is responsible for each subject along with their mini-lectures and tasks. The course contains a number of different subject fields, in the same way as a traditional course can contain several subject fields, each often with a separate instructor. Hence, the TSS students are faced with material from different subjects from several instructors.

Subject Field Integration

An additional classroom session is held at the end of the course, with the focus on *subject field integration*. In the subject field integration session, the focus is on synthesis of the various subjects brought up in the course. In the TSS course this is e.g. to discuss what implications technology strategies such as "just in time" (subject in one mini-lectures and tasks) can have on actual technical implementations in a production plant (subject in another mini-lectures and tasks), or how personal characteristics of employees (subject in one mini-lectures and tasks) can be leveraged on in lean-production philosophy (subject in another mini-lectures and tasks). Subject field integration session supports understanding of the whole picture, which is complementary to understanding the parts (Bell, 2011).

Peer Learning

The applied learning activities, higher order thinking tasks, and the subject field integration sessions are guided by the instructors, however, the hard core of the work is carried out by the students. The original groups that were formed for the students to watched/listened to the pre-recorded mini-lectures are split and new perpendicular groups are formed. The perpendicular groups spend time by discussing and explaining what was learned while in their original groups. In the master programme, in which the TSS course is part, the academic backgrounds of the students are either management or engineering, which implies that their views on problems and challenges brought up in the mini-lectures often complement each other. The students are given ample room for peer teaching and *peer learning* since explaining your view to someone else, as well as trying to understand someone else's opinion, provide new insights, structure knowledge and build professional opinions.

After concluding the programme, the students join the workforce, hence an important task is to prepare them for the transition by e.g. toning down the role of the instructor as the main knowledge provider and demonstrating peer learning. Learning will not end because the educational programme comes to an end, lifelong learning is available if peers are seen as valuable sources of knowledge.

Pedagogical background

EFC also has a strong connection to pedagogical ideas such as *Zone of proximal development* (Vygotsky, 1978) and *Didactic triangle* (Uljens, 1997). In order to grasp, understand and find subject matter knowledge as something interesting, it is critical to understand the learner's point of origin and associated pre-knowledge. If the new material is "too far away" from previous knowledge, there is no way to connect the dots and extend the body of knowledge. This phenomenon is referred to as the Zone of proximal development.

In recent years, discussions related to teaching has shifted from "how to present and transfer knowledge from a teacher to someone else" to "how information and knowledge provided is perceived by the receiver" (Kolb & Kolb, 2005), i.e. from a teacher-student-transfer focus in which the subject is only the transported goods, to the student-subject-relation focus in which the teacher is only the medium used. The task for the teachers is to help the students to learn. The relations between teacher, student and subject, can be illustrated by a triangle in which each has its corner, see Figure 3. The important side in this *didactic triangle* is the one between student and subject.

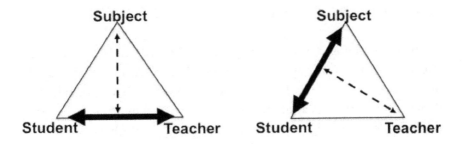

Figure 3: An interpretation of the Didactic Triangle showing a shift from the teacher-student-transfer focus (left) to the student-subject-relation focus (right) (Johnsson et al., 2014).

By using flipped classroom, subject field integration, and peer learning – the three components in EFC – the relation between the student and the subject can be put in focus, and the students are given ample opportunities to extend their body of knowledge starting from their own point of origin, all together this results in enhanced learning and lifelong learning attitudes.

Outcomes

Learning outcomes are statements that specify what learners will know or be able to do as a result of a learning activity. Learning outcomes are usually expressed as knowledge, skills, or attitudes (Biggs & Tang, 2011). The learning outcomes from the course itself are described in the course syllabus. In addition to the course learning outcome, there are learning outcomes from applying EFC, both from the perspective of instructors/ professors and students.

Instructors' view

After termination of the course, each student is given the possibility to fill out a standardized course evaluation questionnaire (CEQ). Two of the questions are of extra importance, Question–17 and Question–26. Question–17 concerns the students' perception of the relevance of the course, i.e. should the course be part of the curriculum? Question–26 concerns the students' perception of the quality of the course, i.e. is the course well taught? The grading is from −100 (very bad) to +100 (very good).

The TSS course got the grades Question−17= +96 and Question−26= +81. Out of the 702 courses that were evaluated with CEQ during the same academic year, only 3.1% (21 courses) were graded equally high or higher. This is an indication of success. Figure 4 shows the distribution of the 702 courses with respect to Question−17 and Question−26 (left part of figure) as well as a magnified view of the top ranked courses with the TSS course marked in white-color (right part of figure). The x-axis of the two figures corresponds to the result of Question−26 and the y-axis corresponds to the result of Question−17.

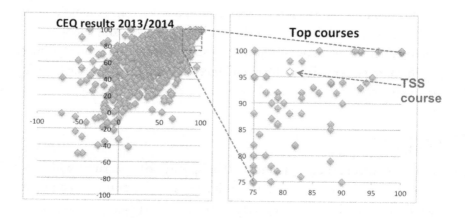

Figure 4: An overview of the results of all 702 courses (left) and the top ranked courses (right) with the TSS course marked in white.

Students' view

As a student, the course provides an opportunity to learn scholastic material in a unique way. The main take-away from the EFC methodology is that you "learn more about the subject-fields by teaching others". Additional student reflections attending the TSS course are collected in post-course evaluations. Examples are:

Students that are happy with the course state (translated, statement originally in Swedish): *"An incredible informative course! It treats many aspects; group dynamics, personal development, and academic advancement. I feel that I have learnt more in this course than in any other."*

Students less happy with the course state (translated, statement originally in Swedish): *"The activities in the flipped classroom could have been motivated upfront, resulting in a better understanding of what was expected from me. The workload in the course has been very high, which made the course a tough one."*

How to apply the EFC method to a new course

When introducing the EFC concept to a course, there are aspects to take into consideration. These aspects can be divided in the chronological order; prerequisites, before, while and after running the course. Based on our experience of introducing EFC to the TSS course, we have highlighted what we believe are the most important aspects.

Prerequisites

Before the introduction, when investigating if EFC is something that would suit your course, there are a number of aspect that we believe are worth considering.

It will be considerably easier if the students are used to work in groups and have experience of working with each other. We believe that an upper limit of the number of students in the class is approximately 80. With more students, it will be difficult to make sure that all students are sufficiently involved.

The instructors/professors involved in the course represent their subject. Even if one single instructor/professor is capable of making the full course by him/herself, there is a point in having more instructors/professors involved. One aim is that the students should start to appreciate each other as valuable sources of information and it is therefore important the the instructors act as role models and live what they teach.

Lectures should be pre-recorded into mini-lectures, i.e. some technical tools are needed. Remember that the content of the mini-lecture is important, not their technical quality, hence the mini-lectures can be recorded via a normal smart phone or laptop.

Before running the course

The pedagogics of the students' learning journey have to be designed before-hand. In the Extended Flipped Classroom the majority of the work for the teacher is in this phase. On the good side, when this work is done once, it can with very limited resources be reused several times. Life-expectancy of most of the material prepared in this phase is 5 year (five or more classes into the future), so it is an investment on behalf of the teacher that will save time later.

The job involves splitting of the traditional lectures (normally 2 or 3 lectures a 45 minutes) into a logic set of set of mini-lectures (approximately 5–6 in number). These mini-lectures (5–20 minutes each) are then recorded. Based on the teacher's experience as film director, cameraman, producer and actor, all in one person. This task can be complex and tedious at first. However please remember that it is the content that matters not the technical quality of the film. Quite on the contrary we have got feedback from the students that the films were more interesting to look at since some bloopers survived the cutting, lights were not perfect etc. From a technical point of view, we aim for a "good enough" quality level (Dogme 95). For each film element a corresponding task is designed in order to propel the student groups from film to film. We use simple text files to guide students along this journey of consecutive films and group discussion tasks. Often the question raised at the end of film X is shortly discussed in the beginning of film X+1.

We also recommend to prepare a presentation f the holistic perspective of the course content, how the course is build up, what subject matters will be treated in the course (the what) as well as about the pedagogical thinking behind (the why). This can be done physically or via a film.

The job also consists of splitting the students into groups of approximately 5 students. This is the group that should watch the mini-lectures and do perform the corresponding tasks, together.

While running the course

When the course it started it is important to inform the students about the EFC concept, so that they understand what and why the course is structured in a different way compared to traditional courses. The first mini-lecture should include the holistic perspective of the course.

The students should be informed about the groups and know to what group he/she belongs. An important aspect when running the course, is that the students watch the generated material together in groups to secure a serious and joint effort. It will also increase the level of discussions, while the material is on top of the students' minds.

Another important aspect is find a structure that works for the whole group, when presenting the material to each other. As all individuals take in new information in different ways and methods, a positive approach is to have the group spend a short time discussing how the new material should be presented to the entire group.

At the last subject integration discussion workshop, the original groups are split and new perpendicular groups are formed. The instructor guides the students through the process of finding new perpendicular groups, see Figure 5.

The perpendicular groups spend time by discussing and explaining what was learned while in their original groups. It is important to dedicate time to these discussions (recommended time is 2 hours). By letting the students discuss extensively among peers, the role of the instructor as the main knowledge carrier is toned down, and the power of peer-learning is demonstrated. When the the discussion time is over, each perpendicular groups is asked to come back to the classroom and make a presentation for the full class concerning their learnings. Since all topics covered in the course are discussed in these presentation, it is imperative that all teachers involved in the course participate in order to represent their area of expertise. The role of the teachers is to guide the discussions, to add comments, and provides opportunities to learn from peers (students and teachers). The act of having all teachers present in the classroom, make them become role-models of the EFC concept (they live what they teach).

After running the course

After the termination of the course, it is recommended to let the students make a course evaluation. At Lund University, the Course Evaluation Questionnaire developed by a committee at Lund Institute of Technology (CEQ) is used for all courses. In addition to the standard questions included in the CEQ questionnaire, the course responsible can add additional questions to the students. There are various ways of making course evaluations, our suggestion is to use one that fits with your university's, department's or personal strategy.

It is also recommended to organise a meeting with all instructors/professors involved in the course in order to review the results of the course evaluation, to speak about lessons learned and to take notes and agree on improvements for next year's course.

Moving Forward

The Extended Flipped Classroom (EFC) concept was developed based on a strong believe that the university can provide the students with, not only knowledge in various subject fields, but also, and equally important, a positive attitude to lifelong learning, an understanding of learning in the coming work-life, and the insight that their own role in the learning situation has an important impact on the outcome.

EFC has been implemented at the Technology Management master programme at Lund University, Sweden. After concluding the programme, the students join the workforce, hence an important task is to prepare them for the transition. The main idea behind the EFC concept is to extend traditional classroom learning with concepts that enhance learning and mimic work-life learning situations. The three components behind EFC are; flipped classroom, subject field integration, and peer learning. The three components are closely intertwined. Feedback from students, alumni and instructors is strongly positive, indicating that the EFC concept is a successful and innovative teaching and learning practice suitable for higher education.

About the Authors

Charlotta Johnsson is Associate Professor at Department of Automatic Control, Faculty of Engineering at Lund University, Sweden. CJ was co-program director for the Technology Management program 2008–2015.She can be reached at this e-mail: charlotta.johnsson@control.lth.se

Carl-Henric Nilsson is Associate Professor at Department of Business Administration, Lund School of Economics at Lund University, Sweden. CHN was co-program director for the Technology Management program 1997–2015. He can be reached at this e-mail: carl-henric. nilsson@fek.lu.se

Givi Kokaia is currently working as management consultant. He is an alumni from the Technology Management program at Lund University, Sweden. He can be contacted at this e-mail: givi.kokaia@kunskapspartner.se

Bibliography

Bell P. (2011). Understanding the whole and not just the parts. BAtimes, Webarticle.

Bergmann, J. & A. Sams (2010). The Flipped Classroom.

Biggs J. & C. Tang C. (2011). Teaching for Quality Learning at Universities. Open University Press, UK.

CEQ: Course Evaluation Questionnaire at LTH Lund University.

Dogme 95: Online Resource: https://en.wikipedia.org/wiki/Dogme_95 [Accessed May 28, 2016].

Johnsson C.; Q. Yang; C.-H. Nilsson; J. Jun; A. Larsson & A. Warell. (2014). Fostering Automatic Control students to become innovators. In proceedings of 19th World Congress International Federation of Automatic Control (IFAC), South Africa, September 2014.

Kolb A. Y. & D. A. Kolb (2005). Learning style and learning spaces: Enhancing experimental learning in higher education. *Academy of Management Learning & Education*, Vol. 4, No. 2, pp. 193–212.

Sörgärde N. & C.-H. Nilsson (2005). Technology Management, A Multidisciplinary Master's Program in Lund. International Association for Management of Technology.

Uljens, M. (Ed.) (1997). *Didaktik – teori, reflektion och praktik*. Studentlitteratur. Lund, 1997.

Vygotsky L. S. (1978). *Mind in Society: Development of Higher Psychological Processes*. Harvard University Press.

An Introduction to Teaching and Learning Innovations Using Modern Technologies

Clifford De Raffaele, Hani T. Fadel & David Watson

Traditional Lecturing as a Problem

Despite the clear evolution in modern technology and its use, particularly in education, traditional lecturing remains the most common method of teaching across disciplines (Brown, 1987). Teachers tend to prefer traditional lecturing since it gives them the opportunity to comfortably determine the aims, content, organization, pace and the direction of a particular session. It also helps them clarify and directly arouse interest in a certain subject. More importantly, it facilitates simultaneous large-class communication (Eggen & Kauchak, 1988). However, when looking at the one-way passive format along which traditional lecturing usually runs, a number of drawbacks were repeatedly observed. These include low scoring during exams, decreased class attendance rate, and an observed negative student perception towards the educational process as a whole (Maloney, 1998). Traditional lecturing is known to follow a single learning pace, something that does not allow for addressing the intrinsic differences in learning preferences between students (Kharb *et al.*, 2013). This can be explained in part by the fact that the attention span of the average human brain is thought to last between 10 to 15 minutes, after which one would gradually lose concentration (Burns, 1985). If the rapid availability of common distractors nowadays, such as smartphones and personal devices are added to the equation, maintaining full concentration during a 1-hour traditional lecture becomes a challenge for most students (Tindell & Bohlander, 2012).

Active Learning as a Solution

Educators have continuously strived to overcome the aforementioned shortcomings that are associated with traditional lecturing. Repeated attempts have led to the introduction of the term Active Learning (Bonwell & Eison, 1991). Active learning is when students are actively or experientially involved in the learning process (Weltman, 2007). In any given learning session, students are expected do more than just listen. They should, for example, read, write, discuss with peers, and/ or be engaged in problem solving tasks (Bonwell & Eison, 1991). Aside from being knowledgeable about a particular piece of information, Active Learning focuses more on the process of obtaining the information rather than the information itself (Weltman, 2007). As a result of being more student-centred, Active Learning has been associated with a significant change in student behaviour towards sessions, a more positive perception of the learning process, and higher exam scores when compared to those following traditional lectures (Freeman, 2014).

The Flipped Classroom or Flipped Learning is a popular example of an active learning method. It refers to an instructional strategy that reverses the traditional learning environment by delivering instructional content outside of and before coming to the classroom (Bergmann & Sams, 2012). In addition, it moves activities that were traditionally meant to be performed at home (or elsewhere) back into the classroom. Different types of flipped learning have been proposed, collectively divided into front loading and non-front loading types of flipped classroom. This depends mainly on the provision of pre-sessional readable, audible and/ or visual material to the students by the teacher (Bergmann & Sams, 2012). In a front loading type of flipped classroom, students would go through the provided material, collaborate in discussions, and/or carry out some research before coming to class. They would then be engaged in exercises that focus on key concepts in the classroom with guidance from the teacher, who acts more as a facilitator in such instances. In the non-front loading type, on the other hand, students would come to class and tackle a certain task that has been carefully constructed by the teacher, who would then provide guidance and further elaboration throughout the process as needed. Generally, the implementation of the Flipped Classroom has led to a notable positive impact on many different aspects, regardless of the area or discipline (McLaughlin *et al.*, 2013).

Technology as an Opportunity

The exponential growth experienced in educational technology within the last decades has astounded both computer scientists and educators alike (Dabbagh *et al.*, 2016). The transformation of computer systems into personal devices has led both academics and students to explore the vast abilities of this technology to assist in their perusal. Moving away from isolated devices and resources, communication advancements such as the Internet made information availability evermore enriched and diverse (Williams, 2002). This was in turn closely followed by the popularisation of social networking sites such as MySpace, Facebook and others, leading to internet users directly sharing information and knowledge in informal and synchronous interactions (Johnson *et al.*, 2013).

It is evident within classrooms today that open educational resources have been made the de facto standard, and that both industry and academia are resorting to these technologically available sources for the attainment of information (Forsyth, 2001). Nonetheless, this vast availability quickly presents a downturn to stakeholders, since the time spent in retrieving the required information is constantly increasing despite advancements in data searching algorithms (Sopan *et al.*, 2016). Employees and students alike are becoming ever more challenged in finding the right type of knowledge to seek. It is thus commonly agreed that merely accessing open educational resources is not an effective way of learning (Branch *et al.*, 2015).

Rather than delivering knowledge and data content, educators today are required to explain and provide skills for students to progress through data and acquire the intended knowledge from their available repositories (Jones & Sallis, 2013). Consuming this data is a daunting task with most technology enabled learners today quickly finding themselves overloaded with information and not capable to keep abreast with its rapid advancement (Chen *et al.*, 2012). This has led to an ever-increasing interest from academics to visualise content and information in a more effective manner. Rather than being the recipient of data, students are taught how to directly engage with the presented information and further their exposure in a dynamic manner (Sun *et al.*, 2015). Thus, teaching within a technological context is becoming far more process-driven rather than the knowledge transferring approach that it traditionally was (Vu *et al.*, 2015).

Technology as a Solution

The emergence of technology as a suitable solution for education requires, not only the availability of resources; but also a well-designed study plan to properly integrate and exploit the brought over advantages (Takahashi *et al.*, 2015). The inherent ability of technology to engage students within their learning environment presents a repertoire of options which allows for more interactive involvement with the learning process (Mellecker *et al.*, 2013). Rather than being a platform for educational provision, different technologies can be combined to influence the educational experience of students, allowing for the customisation of learning to be collaboratively explored.

This aspect has been sought after with varying success in primary education, whereby student engagement and interest is given particular attention (Abdul Razak & Connolly, 2013). Adopting these tools in higher education, however, brings along a number of interesting possibilities. Being enabled within a more mature audience provides the ability for technology to promote the self-driving aspect of teaching and learning. This is carried out whilst capitalising directly on experimental approaches and innovative solutions devised by the students themselves. To this end, a number of technological tools such as personal devices are being creatively used to add value to the students' learning experience in either providing or visualising data (Pinto *et al.*, 2012). Similarly, new tools are also being developed which aim at presenting a completely new paradigm to users in interaction and information experience, hence facilitating their ability to interact and engage with their learning content (Schneider & Blikstein, 2016).

Challenges to Overcome

Adopting modern technologies results in a transition period for both students and faculty members, meaning new skills and techniques may need to be developed and applied for innovations to be successfully implemented. Naturally, there has always been a certain amount of resistance to change from the faculty's side (Knight, 2009). Conscious effort must be made to transform the mind-sets of the initial resistors, something which can be achieved with considerable guidance and support. Structured and efficient training can nourish confidence in adopters, which will ultimately grow with time and eventually lead to their consistent application of new practices. This training in itself has evolved from traditional face-to-face methods to incorporate online platforms, screencasts, videos and documents, which provide step-by-step instruction and guidance.

Resistance to change is not exclusive to educators. Students may also be apprehensive to new learning experiences (Dembo & Seli, 2004). For example, traditional instructor-led methods such as lectures are a stark contrast to the collaborative nature of active peer-learning, where students work in groups to discuss themes or develop solutions to problems. The concept of being more active and self-sufficient in their learning as opposed to the process of instructor-student knowledge transfer can be an alien concept to some students who have been used to the traditional methods (McKay & Kember, 1997). In addition, students associating the use of their personal smart devices with their social activities and personal lives, may be introduced to the concept of using these tools for their learning, consequently blending their social activities with the educational process.

Likewise, time constraints for educators to be able to experiment new technologies, along with economical restrictions and the ability to purchase tools and software, can result in educators remaining with traditional tried and tested practices, despite these methods not necessarily being the most effective (Altbach et al., 2009). However, the evident benefits of utilising modern technologies in addition to capitalising on students existing digital skills means that educators must make a conscious effort to remain informed about the development and availability of modern technologies, to enhance their teaching approaches and the students' learning experiences.

Innovative Application of Modern Technologies

The relentless evolution of technologies and emergence of today's digital native students has initially resulted in the use of technology to enhance learning in higher education, and has enabled the effective application of distance learning – expanding on the traditional face-to-face campus-based education. Despite this leap, Puentedura (2009) claimed that current Higher Educational practices offered no real challenge or change, and that little advantage is taken of the possibilities for technology to transform the act of learning. However, modern technologies, led by the innovation of smart devices, has presented educators with revolutionary platforms to transform the way teaching and learning is performed. The model introduced by Puentedura (2009) highlights how technology could transform learning, representing the level of modification of the activities. With the ultimate goal being 'Redefinition' of tasks "that have been previously inconceivable without the technology", the SAMR model (Figure 1) begins with technology acting as a substitute for an existing tool, before employing technology as a tool to 'Augment' the functionalities.

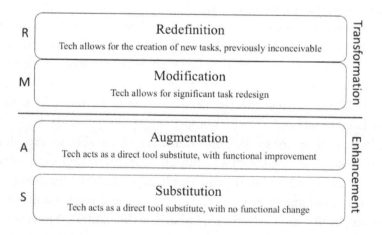

Figure 1: The SAMR Model describing the evolutionary role of technology in education (adopted from: Puentedura, 2009).

Traditionally, one of the most notable observations in Higher Education is smart devices being perceived as distractors to learners that come to class with these devices as part of their toolkits (Tindell & Bohlander, 2012). Previously, students have been asked to switch their devices off during class-time, however, we should be encouraging students to make use of these devices for their learning. This can be achieved by educators redesigning their teaching activities and tasks to utilise the digital tools and skills which the students possess. Adopting innovative usage of available tools and software in different settings such as Audience Response Systems (ARS), Augmented Reality (AR), and/or Tangible User Interfaces (TUI) would ensure that the students are utilising technology to aid their learning, thus adding value to the learning experience.

While it is an essential practice for educators to adopt an explorative mentality in their approach to modern technologies, it is of equal importance, however, to note that modern technologies should only be adopted where they add value and enhancement to a particular teaching activity or task. If traditional methods are the most effective methods of teaching a particular activity, then those methods should be the ones deployed, regardless of the use of technology. In this section, the authors have adopted a variety of modern technologies innovatively to enhance and add value to their teaching practice. Hani T. Fadel (chapter 12) is using a combination of recorded lectures and a simple mobile phone application as an ARS in a Modified Flipped Classroom-Peer Instruction format to provoke peer discussion and learning. David Watson (chapter 13) on the other hand is using AR to create digitally interactive 360° physical learning environments in a hybrid style of Flipped Classroom. Finally, Clifford De Raffaele et al. (chapter 14) are making use of TUIs for non-front loaded Flipped Classrooms to aid in the Teaching and Learning of Abstract Concepts within Higher Education. Each of these cases has been developed with the aim of addressing the common issues and challenges highlighted above, and to ensure that learners are more engaged, focused, positive and ultimately achieving the intended learning outcomes.

Disclaimer

The authors highlight that the practices documented in this section work independently of the chosen software, applications and/or tools mentioned. Educators are free to select the software, applications and/or tools which they feel the most at ease with or which they have access too. The authors bare no affiliation with the brands, organisations or products utilised in these practices.

Acknowledgement

The authors would like to thank Dr. Doaa Al Harkan from Taibah University, Madinah, Saudi Arabia for her active participation and stimulating ideas during the writing of the section overview.

About the Authors

Clifford De Raffaele is Senior Lecturer and Academic Programme Coordinator in the field of Computer Science and Engineering at the school of Science and Technology in Middlesex University Malta. He can be contacted at this e-mail: c.deraffaele@ieee.org

Hani T. Fadel is an Assistant Professor of Periodontology with a degree in Medical Education. He currently works at the Taibah University Dental College and Hospital (TUDCH), Madinah, Saudi Arabia. Hani can be reached at this e-mail: hani.fadel@yahoo.com

David Watson is an Instructional Design Specialist in the Educational Development Centre at The Hong Kong Polytechnic University. He can be contacted at this e-mail: david.watson@polyu.edu.hk

Bibliography

Abdul Razak, A. & T. A. Connolly (2013). *Using games as a context for interdisciplinary learning: A case study at a Scottish primary school.* Paper presented at the Global Engineering Education Conference (EDUCON), Berlin.

Altbach, P. G.; L. Reisberg & L. E. Rumbley (2009). *Trends in Global Higher Education: Tracking an Academic Revolution.* Paper presented at the The UNESCO 2009 World Conference on Higher Education.

Bergmann, J. & A. Sams (2012). *Flip Your Classroom.* Eugene, Oregon. Washington, DC: International Society for Technology in Education (ISTE).

Bonwell, C. & J. Eison (1991). *Report No. 1: Active Learning: Creating Excitement in the Classroom.* Washington, D.C.: Jossey-Bass.

Branch, J.; P. Bartholomew & C. Nygaard (2015). Introducing technology-enhanced learning.. In J. Branch; P. Bartholomew & C. Nygaard (Eds.), *Technology-enhanced learning in higher education.* Oxfordshire, UK: Libri-Publishing.

Brown, G. A. (1987). Higher Education: Lectures and Lecturing. In M. J. Dunkin (Ed.), *The International Encyclopedia of Teaching and Teacher Education.* Oxford: Pergamon Press, pp. 284–288.

Burns, R. A. (1985). *Information Impact and Factors Affecting Recall.* Paper presented at the Annual National Conference on Teaching Excellence and Conference of Administrators, Austin, TX. ERIC Document No. ED 258 639.

Chen, C.-Y.; S. Pedersen & K. L. Murphy (2012). The influence of perceived information overload on student participation and knowledge construction in computer-mediated communication. *Instructional Science*, Vol. 40, No. 2, pp. 325–349.

Dabbagh, N.; A. D. Benson; A. Denham; R. Joseph; M. Al-Freih; G. Zgheib; H. Fake & G. Zhetao (2016). Evolution of Learning Technologies: Past, Present, and Future. In N. Dabbagh; A. D. Benson; A. Denham; R. Joseph; M. Al-Freih; G. Zgheib; H. Fake & G. Zhetao (Eds.), *Learning Technologies and Globalization.* Springer International Publishing, pp. 1–7.

Dembo, M. H., & Seli, H. P. (2004). Students' resistance to change in learning strategies courses. *Journal of Developmental Education*, Vol. 27, No. 3.

Eggen, P. D. & D. P. Kauchak (1988). *Strategies for Teachers: Teacher Content and Thinking Skills.* Englewood Cliffs, NJ: Prentice Hall.

Forsyth, I. (2001). Teaching and learning materials and the internet (3rd ed.). London: Kogan Page.

Freeman, S.; S. L. Eddy; M. McDonough; M. K. Smith; N. Okorafor; H. Jordt & M. P. Wenderoth (2014). *Active learning increases student performance in science, engineering, and mathematics.* Paper presented at the Proceedings of the National Academy of Sciences (PNAS).

Johnson, L.; S. Adams Becker; M. Cummins; V. Estrada; A. Freeman & H. Ludgate (2013). *The New Media Consortium Horizon Report: Higher Education Edition.* Austin, Texas.

Jones, G. & E. Sallis (2013). *Different Types of Knowledge. Knowledge Management in Education: Enhancing Learning & Education.* Routledge Publishing.

Kharb, P.; P. P. Samanta; M. Jindal & V. Singh (2013). The learning styles and the preferred teaching-learning strategies of first year medical students. *Journal of Clinical Diagnosis Research*, Vol. 7, No. 6, pp. 1089–1092.

Knight, J. (2009). What Can We Do About Teacher Resistance? *Phi Delta Kappan*, Vol. 90, No. 7, pp. 508–513.

Maloney, M. (1998). The relationship between attendance at university lectures and examination performance. *Irish Journal of Education*, Vol. 29, pp. 52–62.

McKay, J. & D. Kember (1997). Spoon Feeding Leads to Regurgitation: a better diet can result in more digestible learning outcomes. *Higher Education Research & Development*, Vol. 16, No. 1., pp. 55–67.

McLaughlin, J. E.; L. M. Griffin; D. A. Esserman; C. A. Davidson; D. M. Glatt; M. T. Roth; N. Gharkholonarehe & R. J. Mumper (2013). Pharmacy student engagement, performance, and perception in a flipped satellite classroom. *American Journal of Pharmaceutical Education*, Vol. 77, No. 9, pp. 196.

Mellecker, R. R.; L. Witherspoon & T. Watterson (2013). Active Learning: Educational Experiences Enhanced Through Technology-Driven Active Game Play. *The Journal of Educational Research*, Vol. 106, No. 5, pp. 352–359.

Pinto, M.; R. Raposo & F. Ramos (2012). *Comparison of Emerging Information Visualization Tools for Higher Education*. Paper presented at the 16th International Conference on Information Visualisation, Montpellier.

Puentedura, R. (2009). *As We May Teach: Educational Technology, from Theory to Practice. TPCK and SAMR Models for Enhancing Technology Integration*. Online Resource: http://www.hippasus.com/rrpweblog/archives/000025. html [Accessed June 5, 2016]

Schneider, B. & P. Blikstein (2016). Flipping the Flipped Classroom: A Study of the Effectiveness of Video Lectures Versus Constructivist Exploration Using Tangible User Interfaces. *IEEE Transactions on Learning Technologies*, Vol. 9, No. 1, pp. 5–17.

Sopan, T. M.; D. A. Vilas & S. S. Suresh (2016). An Efficient and Secure Technique for Searching Shared and Encrypted Data. *Imperial Journal of Interdisciplinary Research*, Vol. 2, No. 3, pp. 295–297.

Sun, X.; Y. Wu; L. Liu & J. Panneerselvam (2015). *Efficient Event Detection in Social Media Data Streams*. Paper presented at the IEEE International Conference on Computer and Information Technology; Ubiquitous Computing and Communications; Dependable, Autonomic and Secure Computing; Pervasive Intelligence and Computing (CIT/IUCC/DASC/PICOM), Liverpool.

Takahashi, A.; Y. Kashiwaba; T. Okumura; T. Ando; K. Yajima; Y. Hayakawa, M. Takeshige & T. Uchida (2015). *Design of advanced active and autonomous learning system for computing education*. Paper presented at the IEEE

International Conference on Teaching, Assessment, and Learning for Engineering (TALE).

Tindell, D. R. & R. W. Bohlander (2012). The Use and Abuse of Cell Phones and Text Messaging in the Classroom: A Survey of College Students. *College Teaching*, Vol. 60, No. 1.

Vu, X. T.; M. H. Abel & P. Morizet-Mahoudeaux (2015). A user-centered approach for integrating social data into groups of interest. *Data & Knowledge Engineering*, No. 98.

Weltman, D. (2007). *A comparison of traditional and active learning methods: An empirical investigation utilizing a linear mixed model.* (Ph.D.), The University of Texas at Arlington, Ann Arbor.

Williams, C. (2002). Learning On-line: A review of recent literature in a rapidly expanding field. *Journal of Further and Higher Education*, Vol. 26, No. 3, pp. 263–272.

Utilizing Recorded Lectures and Simple Mobile Phone Audience Response Systems in a Modified Flipped Classroom-Peer Instruction Format

Hani T. Fadel

Background

Passive, one-way traditional lecturing has been associated with a number of drawbacks, namely gradual loss of attention (Burns, 1985), reduced attendance rates and relatively low exam scores. In order to overcome such drawbacks, educators began the search for ways to better engage with their students during class time. Although he personally likes lecturing and considers himself pretty good (and creative) at it, the author came to the conclusion that active, two-way learning is the only sensible way for the attainment of the above stated goal of better student engagement. A number of active learning strategies, such as problem-based learning, group discussions and group exercises showed promise and potential. However, what struck the author the most was highlighted during a workshop conducted in 2012 by Professor Eric Mazur from Harvard University. During that event, Professor Mazur introduced his idea of Peer Instruction (Mazur, 1997), and how it fits very nicely within a Flipped Classroom format (Bergmann & Sams, 2012).

The Original Method and The Buildup

The Flipped Classroom-Peer Instruction concept, as described by Professor Eric Mazur, seemed logic, straight forward and readily applicable. Before coming to class, students (or better termed "the learners") would first receive the core or bulk of knowledge outside the classroom, e.g. pre-reading material, audio material, recorded lecture, online video, or other. In-class time is then dedicated to focusing on key concepts and elaborating on them in order to achieve the specific topic objectives. This is carried out in the form of interactive polling exercises. Briefly, the teacher (or "preceptor") poses a number of ConcepTests, which are basically short conceptual questions on the subject being discussed (Mazur, 1997). These could be multiple-choice or short answer questions. The learners are first allowed to answer the questions individually without communicating with their colleagues by means of an Audience Response System (ARS), such as hand signs, flash cards or clickers. The preceptor analyzes the answers without revealing them and takes notes of the learners' initial level of understanding of the topic in hand. The learners are then encouraged to look for a classmate who answered differently and start discussing with him/her the reason behind choosing that particular answer while giving their own reason/justification for choosing their answer. This process of peer discussion and learning is termed peer instruction, which is suggested to provide numerous benefits, such as leading to high levels of student engagement, interaction and deep learning (Mazur, 1997). Following a few minutes of peer instruction, the preceptor then poses the same question again and at this point he/she may choose to reveal the answers. Depending on the answer trend, the preceptor decides on how the next step would be, i.e. Would he/she decide to elaborate further on the topic? To move on to the next point? Or to take questions in the case a group struggle is noted? And so on. One indication that may suggest that the class is grasping the explained topic is when more than 80% of the learners have reached the desired answer (Lancaster, 2015). Otherwise, further elaboration and re-explanation is warranted. After a designated number of ConcepTests and peer instruction exercises, the preceptor may choose to take a few minutes to elaborate on certain points related to the topic, and perhaps open a question and answer (Q & A) window before ending the lesson. The preceptor may also give room for the learners to absorb the information and send any questions afterwards via email.

Taken all together, a direct application for the Flipped Classroom-Peer Instruction concept in the "traditional" educational settings at a university level was already foreseen by the author. This was in light of the continuous emphasis made by the various educators, stating that active learning strategies may be applied in different fields, subjects or class sizes, with undeniable benefits, and with only some fine tunings and adjustments (Prather *et al.*, 2009).

The First Attempt

At Taibah University in Madinah, KSA, in which traditional lecturing is the main method of teaching across schools and disciplines, the author attempted to implement the Flipped Classroom–Peer Instruction concept for the first time during the 2014/2015 academic year. For convenience and accessibility, the Periodontology I and II courses/modules as part of the Bachelor of Dental Surgery (BDS) program were selected as a setting for the quasi experiment. The objective of implementing the Flipped Classroom-Peer Instruction concept was to further engage the learners during the session and to stimulate their critical thinking abilities. At that time, the implementation was sudden and for a single lesson only, merely a proof of principal to show the potential benefits the method may bring. In addition, the degree of resistance to change from both the learners and the teachers at the institution was to be explored (Dembo & Seli, 2004; Knight, 2009). Thus, no prior preparation or arrangements were sought. Polling exercises were informal, mainly to gain and observe some initial responses. Management of class time was not optimal since the approximate discussion time could not be anticipated. Nevertheless, and upon conclusion; the learners thought it was a new, interesting and engaging experience (Figure 1). The learners also scored in the following quizzes just as good as in those which followed the usual traditional lectures. However, and despite all that, the learners were quite unsure and insecure regarding the new method and how they may benefit from it, compared to what they were traditionally used to for a very long time (McKay & Kember, 1997). A more detailed account of the findings from this initial attempt is to be published elsewhere.

Figure 1: Learning atmosphere among dental students at Taibah University in a Flipped Classroom-Peer Instruction format.

The Practice

During the following academic year (2015/2016), the author re-implemented the Flipped Classroom-Peer Instruction concept with some modification and a slight shift in strategy. Moreover, areas of deficiencies from the previous year in terms of staff training, learner preparation and session refinement, were addressed.

Briefly, a focused 20- to 30-min audio-visual lecture is recorded by the teacher/preceptor at home (or elsewhere) using the same presentation software used to build up the presentation slides e.g. Microsoft Power-Point®, Keynote®, or other. The lecture recording includes the main/key concepts of a given topic. The recording is then uploaded in a suitable movie file format appropriately in advance before the scheduled lesson time on a common platform for the learners to access such as Google Drive® or Dropbox®, together with carefully-selected reading material, e.g. book chapter, article, or other. The learners are expected to watch (and listen to) the recorded lecture, and go through any pre-supplied reading material before coming to class.

Meanwhile, the preceptor would construct ConcepTests that address key issues and cover the topic's specific objectives very carefully, in order to be tackled in class. ConcepTests are ideally in the form of case scenarios, which target higher cognitive skills and provoke debate, rather than being mere recall questions. For the purpose of ConcepTest construction and as a means of ARS, an online platform and voting system is selected by the author (Poll Everywhere, Inc. San Francisco, CA). The Poll Everywhere program has the advantage of being detailed yet very user-friendly, with mobile phone and tablet applications readily available for downloading. After registering on the selected ARS site, the preceptor can construct ConcepTests (or polls) under his/her account and keep them inactive till the time of the actual exercise (Figure 2a). The preceptor would also plan ahead the number of tests to be posed during the lesson, the estimated time for each segment, and the possibility to incorporate any necessary new ideas that fall within the learning objectives of the topic in hand. To overcome previously encountered time management issues, it is recommended to time-box each segment of the session by means of a timer or an alarm.

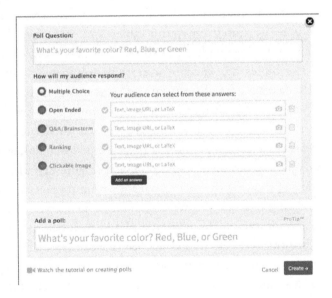

Figure 2a: Creating the polls (i.e. ConcepTests) by the preceptor in the online program platform.

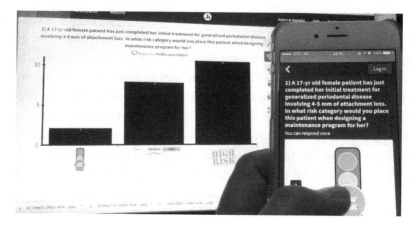

Figure 2b: Learner responding to the posed poll through personal device application, with real time results appearing on the preceptor's screen.

Before coming to class, the learners are instructed to be on time and to be seated in a way that would facilitate group discussion. The best arrangement is to be seated on round tables and in groups. However, compromises may be inevitable since the former is not always possible, especially if the tables are fixed in a certain arrangement within the classroom. The learners are also instructed to access and register at the selected ARS to record their responses to the ConcepTests when posed.

In class, the preceptor would activate the polls at a particular moment and ask the learners to respond either via provided poll web link or through the program application in their personal devices (Figure 2b). The program gives the option of showing the poll responses within presentation slides in real time if desired (Figure 2b). However, it is recommended to withhold the results at the first instance. The preceptor would then ask the learners to discuss their answers with each other via peer instruction before activating the poll again and asking them to respond one more time. Depending on the answer trend, one can decide on how to precede with the remainder of the session. At this point, the preceptor can show the results to the learners and comment on them constructively. The preceptor would then continue with the planned number of ConcepTests and peer instruction exercises, followed by a brief elaboration on certain points if needed, before ending with an open Q & A segment. For anonymity, learners have the choice of using the selected online ARS platform for the Q & A segment as well. Further, the preceptor may choose to leave his/her email address to receive any further questions that the learners' may need addressing after the session has ended (See Box 1 for more details on preparatory steps and instructions).

- *Training the trainers.* Training should at least include construction of ConcepTests, effective time management, and moderation of class discussions (Jambi et al., 2015).
- *Preparing the learners.* Providing information ahead of time with explanation of anticipated benefits is essential to avoid any negative impact of sudden method implementation.
- *Course/module schedule modification.* Ask for more than the classical 1-hour class time so you could deliver a hustle-free interactive session.
- *Ensure adequate seating arrangements.* Providing an appropriate learning environment positively adds to the experience. Give the learners clear seating instructions beforehand.
- *Construct a concise, focused lecture.* Following the specific topic objectives is an integral part of the process.
- *Record the lecture in a clear, dynamic multi-tonus voice.* It is advised to "rehears before recording" and "review before uploading".
- *Upload the recording for the learners in advance.* Choose an accessible, easy-to-use platform.
- *Give clear instructions.* Instruct on how to access the selected electronic voting system.
- *Register/open an account.* Remember to register on the selected electronic voting system webpage/program.
- *Construct your ConcepTests based on the specific topic objectives.* Construct more ConcepTests than what you actually need in case time or situation permits for more questions. In contrast, rank your ConcepTest according to importance, and make sure you cover the ones you designate as most important first. You may find yourself running out of time before covering your key questions!
- *Time box each segment of the session.* Use an alarm or timer to give alerts at each segment for better time management (Tip: Use your personal mobile device. It may act as your very own personal assistant!).
- *Give your email address to the learners at the end of the session.* They may need to ask you some questions later on.
- *Don't feel disappointed if the method doesn't work out well the first time!* It may take a few attempts for you to be comfortable with the process and implementation.

Box 1: Things needed to prepare/consider (and tips) when implementing the proposed Flipped Classroom-Peer Instruction strategy.

Outcomes

After a number of sessions, the learners noted a very interesting learning experience, informative class sessions, increased understanding of initially complex topics, and improvement in various personal skills, such as their self-studying abilities (Figure 3). The learners appreciated that they had access to the recorded lecture at any time to accommodate for the intrinsic differences in learning pace and preferences between them (Kharb et al., 2013). They also valued the easy-to-use electronic voting system and the stimulating peer instruction exercises. Further, the learners positively perceived themselves as finally being the center of the learning process.

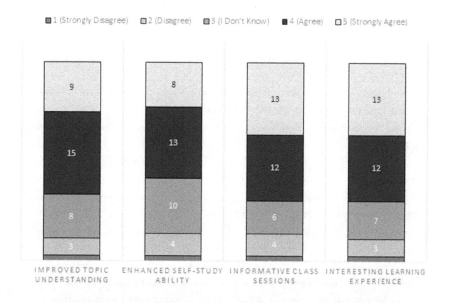

Figure 3: Frequency distribution of the learner responses (N=36) to the statements concerning the Flipped Classroom-Peer Instruction strategy using a 5-point Likert scale (Note: Differences between responses within each statement were statistically significant at $p < 0.05$ using one sample chi-square test).

In addition, positive feedback from colleagues, who were invited to observe the class sessions; was obtained. They observed enjoyment and engagement within the class, with notable eagerness to debate and learn.

The observing colleagues also hailed the effort of transforming potentially distracting personal devices into usable tools as part of the learning process. Such positive feedback from both the learners and and the faculty motivated the department's decision to implement the Flipped Classroom strategy in the entire course starting from the following year. The school administration was also inspired by the potential success story and is promoting the revisiting and implementation of such engaging strategies by other departments.

Highlights

The main feature of the proposed strategy in comparison to traditional lecturing is the achieved level of engagement. Learners are more actively involved in a fun and stimulating environment, and are actually more enthusiastic about learning. The method is considered to be more learner-centered opposed to the teacher-centered traditional lecturing. In fact, the teacher/preceptor acts more as a facilitator rather than simply being a person who delivers knowledge.

Moving Forward

The positive feedback from the learners, as well as the faculty; is an important indication of the inherited potential the proposed method carries. This alone may give a hint on how such an experience may be rewarding and motivating for the teacher. However, a successful teacher should always be self-critical and strive for continuous improvement. In the context of the proposed method, a number of areas may be addressed for an improved learner experience. One of the things that may be explored is the concept of Just-in-Time-Teaching (JiTT) (Novak et al., 1999). In this pedagogical concept, the structure of the class sessions, ConcepTests and assignments are formulated based on learner feedback, arguably making the learning process even more appealing for them. Moving into details, a number of learners suggested for example adding some illustrative video clips within the recorded lectures – again something worth evaluating for possible future consideration.

Aside from the details, areas of improvement are always present, since what works for some doesn't necessarily work for others. Generally speaking, there are no limits for creativity and innovation, particularly in the field of education. It's also important to note that there are no absolute rights or wrongs in the context of teaching and learning. It is the added value that the innovative practice has on the learning experience what matters the most, and forms the key motive for continuous improvement.

Acknowledgement

The author would like to thank Dr. Wesam Abu Znadah from King Saud Bin Abdulaziz University for Health Sciences, and Doctors Ayman Khalifah, Rawan Kamal and Faisal Hakeem from Taibah University for their support in conducting the initial attempt.

Disclaimer

The author reports no conflict of interest related to the described methods or the used programs/softwares mentioned.

About the Author

Hani T. Fadel is an Assistant Professor of Periodontology with a degree in Medical Education. He currently works at the Taibah University Dental College and Hospital (TUDCH), Madinah, Saudi Arabia. Hani can be reached at this e-mail: hani.fadel@yahoo.com.

Bibliography

Bergmann, J. & Sams, A. (2012). *Flip Your Classroom*. Eugene, Oregon . Washington, DC: International Society for Technology in Education (ISTE).

Burns, R. A. (1985). *Information Impact and Factors Affecting Recall*. Paper presented at the Annual National Conference on Teaching Excellence and Conference of Administrators, Austin, TX.

Dembo, M. H. & H. P. Seli (2004). Students' resistance to change in learning strategies courses. *Journal of Developmental Education*, Vol. 27, No. 3.

Jambi, S.; A. M. Khalifah & H. T. Fadel (2015). Shifting from traditional lecturing to interactive learning in Saudi dental schools: How important is staff development? *Journal of Taibah University Medical Sciences*, Vol. 10, No. 1, pp. 45–49.

Kharb, P.; P. P. Samanta; M. Jindal & V. Singh (2013). The learning styles and the preferred teaching-learning strategies of first year medical students. *Journal of Clinical Diagnosis Research*, Vol. 7, No. 6, pp. 1089–1092.

Knight, J. (2009). What Can We Do About Teacher Resistance? *Phi Delta Kappan*, Vol. 90, No. 7, pp. 508–513.

Lancaster, S. (2015). Innovative pedagogies series: *Engaging Chemistry students*. Higher Education Academy York Science Park, Heslington, York: I. Way.

Mazur, E. (1997). *Peer Instruction: A User's Manual*. Upper Saddle River, NJ: Prentice-Hall.

McKay, J. & D. Kember (1997). Spoon Feeding Leads to Regurgitation: a better diet can result in more digestible learning outcomes. *Higher Education Research & Development*, Vol. 16, No. 1, pp. 55–67.

Novak, G. N., Patterson, E. T., Gavrin, A., & Christian, W. (1999). *Just-in-Time Teaching: Blending Active Learning and Web Technology*. Saddle River, NJ: Prentice Hall.

Prather, E. E.; A. L. Rudolph; G. Brissenden & W. M. Schlingman (2009). A National Study Assessing the Teaching and Learning of Introductory Astronomy. Part I. The Effect of Interactive Instruction. *American Journal of Physics*, Vol. 77, No. 4, pp. 320–330.

Chapter 13: Modern Technologies

Enhancing the Physical World with Augmented Reality (AR)

David Watson

Background

This innovative teaching and learning practice was designed primarily for the Professional Development of Academic, professional and support staff, however, its success and popularity has enabled its transition into student facing professional seminars for students engaged in MA in Bilingual (Digital) Corporate Communication. Although the use of Augmented Reality (AR) is not subject nor activity specific, I believe its features and application provide great benefit and enhancements to a diverse range of subjects, particularly medical, clinical skills, engineering and laboratory environments. A concise summary of AR's features as a valuable asset for teaching and learning (Bloxham *et al.*, 2013; Johnson *et al.*, 2011; Luckin & Fraser, 2011) can be considered as:

- by overlaying information onto real world situations, it can link higher level, abstract concepts with tangible, real world environments;

- fits with constructivist learning and acts as scaffolding for learners;

- stimulates sensory feedback and audio-visual and kinaesthetic appeal;

- offers the potential for 'frictionless learning' – reducing the cognitive load of the learner;

- does not involve URL bars – thus reducing the risk of users 'roaming';

+ utilises 'curiosity, mystery & intrigue' to draw even reluctant learners into an activity;

+ initial 'gimmick' attraction begins to give way to a serious way to engage learners.

Furthermore, *"Augmented Reality can also help students learn by placing course content in rich contextual settings that more closely mirror real-world situations in which new knowledge can be applied,"* (Johnson et al., 2016:40) which enables educators to expose learners to unfamiliar environments, leading to the development of new knowledge and skills in preparation for real-world situations.

The Practice

On successful participation in this session, participants or students are able to:

+ understand the principles of Augmented Reality (AR) and hold a basic knowledge of the technology used to develop AR;

+ analyse how AR is being used in education (HE), industry and different disciplines;

+ examine with your peers areas where AR can enhance your teaching (and learning) practice and/or benefit practice & services;

+ understand the parameters and consideration needed when applying AR to education (or Digital Communication);

+ create AR content using the appropriate application by linking images to instructional multi-media content.

As part of my facilitation of Continuing Professional Development for Academic, professional and support staff at all levels, this innovative teaching and learning practice enables me to adopt the practice which I am teaching to facilitate the session, or put simply, using Augmented Reality (AR) to teach Academics how to use AR effectively in their teaching practice. This is achieved via a blended approach, online (30%) and face-to-face (f2f) (70%), although this innovation is focused more on the f2f component of the teaching and learning and encourages active learning and a constructivist approach. By 'flipping' the session, participants attend the f2f component with a prior acquired knowledge of AR which has been developed via the online materials, such as videos, articles and demonstrations of its use. Had the session been solely f2f, participants may attend the session with no knowledge of AR, therefore valuable time would need to be dedicated to establishing a core knowledge of AR and its potential – time which otherwise could be spent on more constructive discussion and activities.

Simplified into six (6) sequential activities and taking no more than 1 hour, the online component is hosted on the institutional Virtual Learning Environment (VLE) and begins with participants completing a short survey [1] on their prior experiences and understanding of AR. This enables me to tailor the f2f component accordingly, before participants engage with multimedia and learning content focusing on 'What is Augmented Reality' [2] and 'How AR is being used in education & industry' [3]. Following this, participants engage in online discussion [4] sharing their experiences and expectations of AR, before submitting a blog [5] in which they briefly summarise a video, article or paper on how AR is being used to enhance a process, activity or learning experience, before preparing for the f2f component [6].

Whilst participants are engaged with the online component, for which I aim to provide at a minimum of 7 days before the face-to-face (f2f) session, I actively interact with their discussion posts and blog articles to stimulate engagement and to develop a sense of community in the online environment, thus increasing the knowledge base which is established before the f2f session. In addition, I utilise this time to develop the interactive AR content which provides the scaffold for constructivist learning during the f2f session. In this instance, my AR content is developed using Aurasma App (iOS & Android) and Aurasma Studio, its web-based platform. Primarily consisting of content which introduces participants to AR, examples of its use, its impact on education (or specific corporate fields), pedagogic principles and what the future holds, I design unique images which are used to trigger interactive content via a smart device, which typically consists of instructional videos, case studies and quizzes. When complete, I share this AR content to a channel which is set as public, which means that anybody following that channel on the Aurasma platform can activate that AR content with a smart device.

Representing 70% of the session, participants are requested to download the Aurasma App, create an account and follow my pre-determined channel before attending the f2f component, as this enables them to fully immerse themselves into the session and the learning activities within. Typically 90 minutes in length in a traditional classroom setting, I design the f2f session to ensure a balance between active and constructivist learning, supplemented with discussion and 'free roaming.' Beginning by summarising the online survey results, I ask participants to elaborate on their answers in a group discussion to establish a common understanding of AR and a sound platform on which build upon. At this point, the sessions true format is established, as rather than a traditional instructor-led approach I position AR content around the learning environment. Utilising all four walls, I transform the conventional classroom into a 360° interactive learning tool, encouraging participants to explore, engage and interact with different multimedia and learning content that is attached to the walls [*Figure 1, Figure 2*]. This self-paced free roaming at key intervals of the session allows students to absorb digital content which is overlaid onto the real world, providing a more transformational experience using the smart devices which they already have in their possession, before coming together again as a group to analyse, dissect and discuss constructed knowledge in peer-to-peer learning and interaction.

Figure 1: AR content on walls.

Figure 2: Learner activating content.

Focally, the session is sculpted around a key learning activity in which participants are asked to bring along a book, CD or DVD which they then use to develop AR content of their own. First of all, another free roam to trigger step-by-step instruction to guide them through the creation process informs participants to film a short video of each other introducing their book, CD or DVD using their smart device. They then take a photograph of the book, CD or DVD cover to use as a trigger image, and via the Aurasma App link both the image and video together to create functioning AR content. Specifically, this learning activity teaches participants how to incorporate digital information into real-world spaces, whilst at the same time affording them a first-hand user experience, developing an appreciation and awareness of the impact AR can have on teaching and learning.

Including being aware of the potential impact AR could have on teaching and learning, developing an appreciation of the process required to develop and maintain AR content is an essential outcome of this innovative practice, as it exposes participants to the preparation which is required to apply AR to teaching practice, whilst also experiencing how effective AR can be. Introducing new concepts and ideas of how to incorporate AR into teaching and learning stimulates alternative thinking and approaches, such as using AR for formative assessment, adding new dimensions to poster presentations, short quizzes and tutorials embedded in course materials; things which are only possible if participants have a clear understanding of AR and the confidence to facilitate its application. Likewise, MA students in Bilingual & Digital Corporate Communication acquire a robust understanding of how AR is developed, and also how AR is adopted by large corporations as an effective communication and marketing tool to engage with stakeholders and customers. Constructing knowledge and skills in AR development and its application in industry, MA students can not only apply these factors to their course work, but also have the potential to apply them in a professional capacity.

Differing from traditional teaching and learning practices AR blends reality with the virtual environment, allowing students to interact with both physical and digital objects; a flexible practice which can be used in traditional classroom settings, and clinical, medical, laboratory or workshop environments where equipment and/or machinery can be used to trigger AR content rather than unique static images. Utilising free roaming at key points, students are exposed to a new learning experience which stimulates audio-visual senses and interactions using existing technology and tools with which they are familiar with; an immersive environment in which they construct their own knowledge and actively apply it to learning activities and peer interactions. Although not considered a 'traditional' approach, I believe AR and the principles of social constructivism achieve an innovative and dynamic teaching and learning practice, activating and stimulating ideas in participants who are strengthened by knowledge acquisition and highly visual learning.

Preparation and Materials

Essential Tools
Smart Device, Aurasma iOS/Android app, access to studio.aurasma.com, Virtual Learning Environment (VLE), online survey tool, colour printer, physical learning environment/classroom.

Although the preparation and props required for this innovative teaching and learning practice may differ depending on the instructors approach, the core fundamentals remain the same. Additionally, whilst adopting a blended approach traditionally increases the preparation time and requires an online environment, this is not essential and this innovation could be as effective in a solely face-to-face (f2f) delivery with a more instructor-led approach.

Essential to this innovation is access to a smart device (iOS or Android) which can install the Aurasma App (free), with access to its online platform Aurasma Studio (studio.aurasma.com) required to develop, manage and track your AR creations; a simple and free account creation process. To begin, it is advisable to use Aurasma Studio to create a 'campaign' which acts as a channel in which all of your AR creations sit, therefore it is recommended that this channel is named after the subject/course/faculty which will be developing and publishing AR content in this area.

Focus must now turn to your learning content and the design and implementation of 'Auras,' which is a term used by Aurasma to describe AR content that consists of a Trigger Image and an Overlay.

- A trigger image is that which when a smart device running the Aurasma App is pointed at it, triggers the start of an Overlay. A trigger image may be an image designed by the instructor or a photograph of a piece of machinery/equipment or location;

- An overlay can be a video, 3D model, web page or another image, however it is essentially the engaging component of the Aura.

Both triggers and overlays can be uploaded to the 'Assets' area of Aurasma Studio, allowing easy management of asset libraries before proceeding to create a new Aura. The process of creating a new Aura begins by uploading or selecting an existing trigger image, before uploading or selecting an existing overlay. It is then possible to add actions to that overlay, for example; when tapped load URL etc. It is also possible to resize and edit the positioning of the overlay and set 3D views in the event of using 3D models. Finally, after the option of previewing the Aura, an Aura name is required before the process is complete, and the trigger image and overlay are linked to form a complete Aura. It is at this stage that it is possible to share the Aura with a channel, which is required to enable student engagement; changing the default setting of 'Private' to

'Public' allows the selection of a relevant channel under which the Aura shall be listed, allowing followers to trigger the Aura when using the Aurasma App.

Perhaps the key stage would now take place; testing. Although you have the option to preview the Aura before you finalise the creation process, it is good practice to test the Aura before students engage with them in an f2f setting. Aside from creating a test account yourself, ask a colleague to download the Aurasma App, create an account, follow your channel and try to trigger Auras using the trigger images which you have defined; this will allow you to establish and resolve any issues in the performance or quality of image and/or overlay before they are visible to students.

Once satisfied with your creations it is advised that students are sent a preparation email and/or announcement with a request and clear instruction to download the Aurasma App, create an account and to search for and follow the channel which you have created to enable them to successfully engage with your innovation during the f2f session. You may also consider students that may not have access to a smart device, and if necessary arrange for supplementary devices to be provided for the session with the Aurasma App already pre-installed.

Depending on the physical environment in which your f2f session will be set, it may or may not be required for you to print trigger images for your session. If you intend to use photographs of machinery/equipment in a lab or workshop environment as a trigger image then printed materials may be minimal, however, if you use self-designed images then printing these images for locating around the learning environment is essential and will need to be pre-planned. It is worth noting however that trigger images are also effective via a digital screen, providing students have easy access to reach the screen to activate the aura. As a supplement, it may also be beneficial to print some short and concise instructions of how to use Aurasma and/or trigger an Aura should students need gentle instruction and encouragement at first.

Outcomes

Aside from evaluation data and feedback, I consider my innovative teaching and learning practice a success as it benefits both Academic & professional staff, enhances the student learning experience and also empowers students to integrate AR into their work, assignments and presentations. What's more, I consider this teaching and learning practice a success as I see smiles on people's faces and I see a learning environment being brought to life; a conventional classroom transforming into a vibrant 360° interactive learning tool, with Academics and students engaging in learning activities with curiosity, mystery and intrigue.

Success of this innovation can be measured via two strands; Firstly, Academic & professional staff learn how AR can link higher level abstract concepts with tangible real world environments by overlaying information onto real world situations. Via both an online environment and face-to-face session, Academics learn the importance of the pedagogy behind AR's effective use for teaching & learning, how it promotes a constructivist approach for students and also acts as a scaffold for their learning. They then essentially become the student in a f2f setting to experience AR first hand, and engage in activities to nurture the development skills required to implement AR effectively in the classroom; this allows them to experience AR as their students would, enhancing their appreciation and consideration for its successful application.

Secondly, students are engaged in a new and stimulating way, a whole new dimension to their learning experience in which they can actively interact with learning content using their smart devices, removing themselves from the traditional classroom practice and setting. These factors stimulate sensory feedback and audio-visual & kinaesthetic appeal – features associated with immersive environments, and offers the potential for 'frictionless learning' – reducing the cognitive load of the learner. Likewise, AR is instantaneous and therefore does not involve URL bars – reducing the risk of students 'roaming' to other websites or detracting from the appropriate media, keeping students focused on the task or learning content with which they are engaged.

Participants and students of this innovative teaching and learning practice particularly valued the flexibility and freedom of the 'free roaming' in the f2f learning environment. Being exposed to a new learning experience which is removed from the traditional instructor-led approach, with the instructor being the focal point of the session added a new vitality to the learning experience which participants find refreshing. In addition, being encouraged to use their mobile devices and to engage in learning activities which have an aspect of fun and playfulness to them resonates with participants and encourages interaction with activities and peers. The reduced cognitive load and self-paced nature of the session allows participants to immerse themselves in the learning content, rather than being a passive learner, which enables a deeper understanding of AR and more sustainable engagement and learner focus.

Using a personal item such as a book, CD or DVD adds a personal investment to the learning activity, with participants emitting a certain level of excitement, interest and pride in the artefacts around which the learning activity is based; something which they can take with them from the session to show friends and family or share through social media. In addition, participants valued the blended or flipped approach of the online component, allowing them to attend the f2f session with an existing understanding of AR upon which knowledge and skills can be established, whilst having also interacted virtually with colleagues or peers, therefore adding a familiarity and friendliness to the atmosphere during the f2f session.

Using AR to teach participants and students how to effectively use AR has been a popular and effective approach, with all parties being exposed to both the development process and the user experience, heightening the understanding and appreciation of AR and its role in education and industry. Using AR to break down the step-by-step process of its construction allows participants to deeper understand the process and particularly become accustomed to the Aurasma App which is integral to the teaching and learning practice. Academic, professional & support staff valued the innovative practice highly, and have requested a series of workshops aimed at different levels of AR, ranging from beginner through advanced, such is their appetite to be able to develop more advanced and interactive AR in the future – something which would not be possible without the design, implementation, healthy participation and success of this innovative teaching and learning practice.

Moving Forward

Forward facing, it is envisaged that rather than a stand-alone blended workshop consisting of 90 minutes f2f exposure with a flipped online component, the workshop is to be developed as a series of workshops or short course. Feedback received suggests that there is demand for a more advanced approach, therefore, it is planned to re-sculpt the workshop as 3 f2f interlinked workshops at beginner, intermediate and advanced levels, enabling participants to progressively acquire and fine-tune skills in developing AR content and generate achievable ideas for its adoption in their teaching practice. Facilitated over a 3 week period, the workshops will culminate in an advanced session where participants learn how to add menus within AR content and integrate assessment and quizzes into their AR creations.

For Higher Education there is endless opportunity to harness AR and shape it into a valuable educational tool, no more so than to empower students with the skills to engage with digital storytelling, bringing their poster presentations to life with digital media. Following a successful seminar with MA students in Bilingual & Digital Corporate Communication, there are intentions to adopt digital storytelling as an assignment based activity, enabling students to move away from the one-dimensional poster based presentations to incorporate descriptive video content when triggered by a mobile device. This will allow assessors to view an in-depth elaboration and commentary of the poster itself without the student being present, transforming a simple poster into a digital portfolio documenting the student's journey or project contents, something which could result in a more engaging experience for students, educators and assessors alike.

About the Author

David Watson is an Instructional Design Specialist in the Educational Development Centre at The Hong Kong Polytechnic University. He can be contacted at this e-mail: david.watson@polyu.edu.hk

Bibliography

Bloxham, J.; A. Crawford-Thomas; S. Wileman (2013). *Advancing Education Autumn Edition; Immersive Learning Experiences through Augmented Reality.* Online Resource: http://legacy.naace.co.uk/2481 [Accessed May 11, 2016]

Johnson, L.; S. A. Becker; M. Cummins; V. Estrada; A. Freeman & C. Hall (2016). *NMC Horizon Report: 2016, Higher Education Edition.* Austin, Texas: The New Media Consortium.

Johnson, L.; S. A. Becker; V. Estrada, V. & A. Freeman (2014). *NMC Horizon Report: 2014 K–12 Edition*. Austin, Texas: The New Media Consortium.

Luckin, R. & D. S. Fraser (2011). Limitless or Pointless? An Evaluation of Augmented Technology in the School and Home. *International Journal of Technology Enhanced Learning*, Vol. 3, No.5, pp. 510–524.

Puentedura, R. (2009). *TPCK and SAMR Models for Enhancing Technology Integration (Transcript). As We May Teach: Educational Technology, from Theory to Practice*. Online Resource: https://itunes.apple.com/gb/itunes-u/as-we-may-teach-educational/id380294705?mt=10 [Accessed June 5, 2016].

Vygotsky, L. S. (1978). *Mind and society: the development of higher mental processes*. Cambridge, CA.: Harvard University Press.

The Application of Tangible User Interfaces for Teaching and Learning in Higher Education

Clifford De Raffaele, Serengul Smith & Orhan Gemikonakli

Background

The proliferation of smartphone and tablet technology has seen consumers opting to move further away from the classical interaction notions of keyboards and mice, and closer towards more physical interactions (Ozkan & Gokalp-Yavuz, 2015). Furthering this drive, Tangible User Interfaces (TUI)s present an augmented interaction domain whereby real-life physical objects are used to interact and manipulate digital information (Ullmer et al., 2005; Ullmer & Ishii, 2001). This inherent ability to interplay between the physical and digital domains makes TUI systems even more intuitive and thus, has gathered interest for application in numerous domains.

Within teaching and learning, the notions of computer-based education have long been in the centre of technologically enhanced learning initiatives (Nasman & Cutler, 2013) which consistently underline the benefits of active learning and student engagement (Blasco-Arcas et al., 2013; Mellecker et al., 2013). The facilitation of computer usage to students coupled with additional benefits such as collaborative interaction has consequently made TUI systems an interesting and attractive technology to be employed in classrooms (De Raffaele et al., 2016).

The ability to captivate student attention as well as provide physically engaging activities led to numerous studies investigating these benefits in young children whilst learning mathematical concepts (Price & Rogers, 2004), spatial reasoning (Rogers et al., 2002) and musical impressions (Xambo et al., 2013).

The proposal of this work lies at the confluence of the introduced streams. Whilst the majority of TUI research in literature target subjects covered by young children, more complex adaptations are restrained to industrial contexts in which simulation scenarios are made use of (Maher & Kim, 2006; Underkoffler & Hiroshi, 1999). As a contrast to such TUI literature, this chapter considers the innovative adaption of TUI systems for the integration within Higher Educational Institutes (HEI)s. The contribution lies in investigating the suitability and relevance of such tangible systems in explaining complex abstract notions within university courses. Specifically, the proposed TUI system is evaluated on its appropriateness for aiding teaching and learning of threshold complex concepts in the disciplines of Science, Technology, Engineering and Mathematics (STEM).

The deployed implementation, highlighted within this research, assessed the effectiveness of the proposed technique with respect to traditional lecture-based delivery within the undergraduate programmes of Computer Science and Information Technology. The efficacy of concept delivery was hence assessed by using this modern technology in explaining the threshold concept of database normalisation. This compulsory topic within computer studies was principally chosen since it routinely presents a tough challenge for lecturers to deliver and students to grasp successfully within their university's studies.

The Practice

In light of the above requirement, and in tandem with the TUI and active learning literature, the system was designed so as to present students with the ability to interactively manipulate and visualise the presented concept. Specifically, students were enabled to interact with the various databases and table attributes during the normalisation sequential processes whilst visualising the underlying principles being adopted throughout each stage.

System Overview

To this end, the tangible table-top system was designed in line with the MCRpd interaction model (Ishii, 2008) and ReacTIVision framework (Kaltenbrunner & Bencina, 2007). The developed physical construction as illustrated in Figure 1, comprises of a wooden enclosure with a semi-transparent acrylic glass panel is placed on top. The table was designed at a height of 80cm and with a workable area of 1m x 0.7m. These dimensions were implemented to explicitly enable a collaborative approach whereby a number of users were allowed to view and comfortably interact together on the system. Inherently the setup further provided a platform where teaching and learning can occur simultaneously both from a tutor instructive perspective as well as from an experimental learning approach by students.

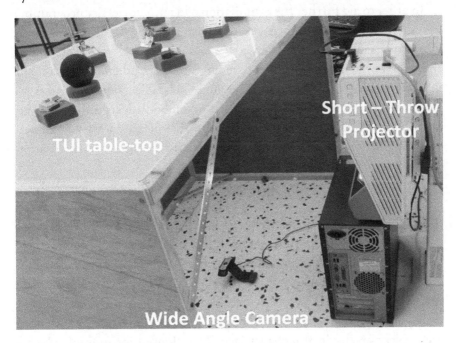

Figure 1: Hardware used for Interactive table-top setup.

A wide angle camera was installed beneath the table to wirelessly monitor interactions and a short-throw projector used to illuminate the interactive surface with digital data. This enabled the TUI design to also provide perceptual coupling to the users, allowing students to visualise and interact on the same surface hence directly promoting system feedback. Intrinsically, this functionality aids to provide a consistent and concretised understanding of the system's state allowing peer students to comprehend better the highlighted concepts being interacted with.

The interactive engagement of students with the system was achieved via the manipulation of dedicated 3D objects. These physical components, shown in Figure 2, were aptly selected to represent concrete real-world models and thus embody the various attributes qualities of data fields used in the considered database. These physical objects were therefore sourced from familiar student environments so as to represent an inherent understanding on their meaning and association, thus allowing students to focus on the normalisation task without needing to decode or shift attention towards the utilising the computer interface.

In order to aid further the assimilation of data, a university programme transcript was considered as the database scenario for engaging with in normalisation. Apart from reflecting commonly used attributes and inherently familiar data for undergraduate students, this domain further enabled the creation of evermore relatable tangible devices as described for Figures 2a–2d. This strong embodied cognition allowed for a more engaging interaction with the abstracted data fields as well as an augmented focus on interacting with the described normalisation processes.

As shown in Figure 2, each object was mounted on a wooden platform (6cm x 6cm) onto which a reacTIVision 'amoeba' fiducial was attached (Kaltenbrunner & Bencina, 2007) as captured in Figure 2f. The size of tangible devices was determined to enhance the usability and comfortable interaction with devices by students, whilst occupying minimal spatial area on the interface so that to allow for virtual projected data. The reacTIVision 'amoeba' symbols, specifically designed with inter-symbol orthogonality, further assisted the system camera to locate and identify each object on the interactive surface. This allowed for multiple objects to be used in conjunction, whilst providing the user with the ability to spatially drag the components on different areas of the screen.

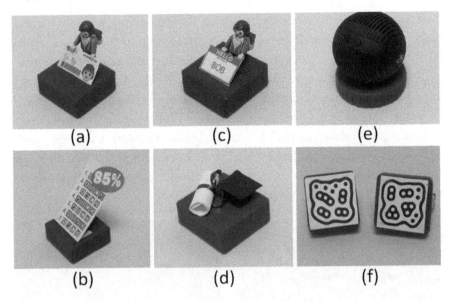

Figure 2: Tangible objects representing the attribute fields of selected database.

  a) Student ID – Small figurine holding university identification card.

  b) Grade Achieved – Corrected multiple choice questionnaire with score.

  c) Student Name – Small figurine holding nametag.

  d) Degree Programme – Miniature graduation cap and certificate scroll.

  e) Setup Controller – Rotatable speaker with Bluetooth® connectivity.

  f) Tangible objects underside – ReacTIVision 'amoeba' fiducial symbols.

The other aspect of the system, which was undertaken subsequent to the physical construction described, was the design and development of the software component. The latter was responsible for embedding the necessary concepts of database normalisation which the students would be subject to. This digital element interlaced with the TUI system dynamic data on the tangible objects, hence providing students the ability to augment their understanding of the manipulated objects.

The Graphical User Interface (GUI) of the system was developed using the Unity platform and C# programming language. As portrayed in several screenshots within Figure 3, the projected digital interface makes use of a number of graphical components to provide the student with the necessary ability to undertake the different conceptual alternations at each stage of normalisation technique. Different GUI's and visualisation cues are thus employed, to aid students in understanding their current stage-related task as well as receive visual feedback on their interactions. The digital interface, as captured in Figures 3a-d makes use of graphical placeholders to assist students in understanding the physical movements expected at each normalisation stage. These are accompanied by virtual messages that instruct the student on the TUI operation and database normalisation related tasks. Hence, two types of messages are employed, with static instructions relating mostly to the current normalisation stage aspects, whilst dynamically changing messages change continuously in relation to the operations done by the user.

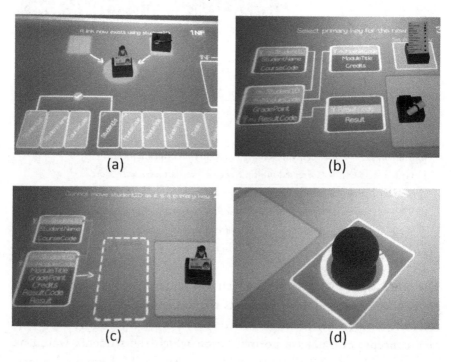

(a)   (b)

(c)   (d)

Figure 3: GUI screenshots of proposed TUI system.

a-c) Different instructions provided to students in order to progress through the processes and concepts of normalisation with various placeholders and visual cues dynamically displayed.

d) Setup Controller – Projected information prompting the user to rotate the tangible object so as to change normalisation stages adjacently displayed.

The illustrated GUIs in Figure 3 automatically changes the component colour scheme (from orange to purple) throughout the procedural execution, allowing the user to appreciate when a tangible object has been correctly placed and/or identified by the system. Furthermore a number of dynamic links, arrows and messages as illustrated in Figures 3a-c are presented by the system indicating to the users what is expected and even visualising some of the underlying processes occurring.

Additionally, the proposed TUI system makes use of a further feedback channel; audio. This is integrated within the 'setup controller' tangible devices, shown in Figure 2e and Figure 3d. This device is able to provide additional information and instructions to students via the internal speaker and voice messages are played providing details on the respective stages of the normalisation system. Incorporating and carefully integrating these interactive approaches, hence provides the TUI system the ability to gain a substantial cognitive and social advantage for students. It also allows a more engaging teaching and learning activity whilst allowing students to explore, assimilate and express their knowledge on the subject.

Teaching and Learning Session

The proposed TUI system was implemented at Middlesex University Malta within the undergraduate degree programmes of Computer Science and Information Technology. The identified normalisation concept, is present as a compulsory scheduled topic within the databases course, and is traditionally perceived as a particularly difficult topic to teach and learn. To this end, once the TUI system was assembled, programmed and implemented as described in the previous section, the innovative practice was able to integrate naturally within the academic curriculum of the identified course.

The session was directly scheduled to coincide with the formal introduction to the main threshold concept of normalisation within the databases course. Sixteen (16) first year students, who were all enrolled for this course, were selected based on a convenience sampling technique. To establish an a-priori baseline of student knowledge before the evaluation session, a multiple choice questionnaire was provided to students so as to test their former knowledge on the subject. Following this test, the class was randomly split such that seven (7) students would serve as a control group, whilst the remaining nine (9) students formed the experimental group. The former would undergo a traditional tuition session whereby normalisation was explained and exemplified using a traditional lecturing approach using projected slides and whiteboard setup. The experimental group on the other-hand undertook an introduction of normalisation concepts using the proposed TUI system by the same lecturer as illustrated in Figure 4.

Figure 4: Evaluation session of the proposed TUI system for teaching and learning database normalisation concepts.

Outcome

The teaching and learning effectiveness of the proposed TUI system was evaluated using both summative and formative techniques. Diverse examinations were designed to audit the ability of students to answer both theoretical and practical sessions on the topic whilst a number of probing questions were posed to derive a more formative assessment of the system.

Summative Appraisal

Following the teaching sessions on database normalisation using either the TUI framework or traditional lecturing, both cohorts of participants were subjected to a second different multiple choice questionnaire re-examining their acquired knowledge on the identical concepts covered within either session. These post-test results have been compiled for both teaching methodologies and illustrated in Figure 5a adjacent to the respective pre-test scores achieved by the same students

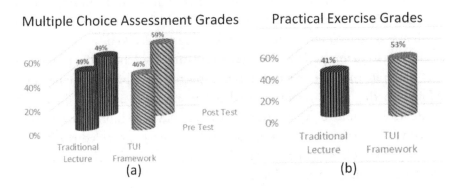

Figure 5: Comparative analysis of grades achieved in.
a) Theoretical multiple choice assessment.
b) Practical case-based exercise.

As can be derived from the comparative analysis of the results in Figure 5a, students being exposed to the concept of database normalisation using the proposed TUI framework were able to achieve a grade improvement of 13% (SD 22.3). This was achieved with respect to their traditional lecture counterparts at a 90% confidence interval. Another assessment provided to students following their respective learning session was aimed to assess their ability to employ the learnt concept during a practical session in normalising a database scenario. The results, represented in Figure 5b, highlight that the same improvement was replicated with respect to understanding and learning the abstract concept using a TUI framework.

Formative Appraisal

The positive achievement registered from the summative assessment was further collaborated via formative feedback derived from students. Participants in the TUI demonstration highlighted that the interactive aspect of the system provided an opportunity to interact and experiment with the various stages of data normalization, a task which proved to be enjoyable. Furthermore, it was commonly noted that the visualization aspect of the virtual data being manipulated, allowed for easier understanding of the abstract concepts at each normalization stage. This was further complimented by visual and audio feedback which allowed students to understand better the task being undertaken.

From a lecturing perspective, the system furthered the ability to explain and illustrate to students the different aspects of database normalisation. Moreover, the TUI system allowed for an interactive session in which students were able to express their knowledge and collaborate together in deriving the correct task processes. This inherently provided the ability to assess the individual understanding of students and deliver formative feedback instantly on the subject.

Moving Forward

The TUI framework presented within this work was developed following the recognised necessity at Middlesex University Malta to aid the teaching and learning of database normalisation within its undergraduate programmes. The proposed framework was developed using TUI based on the strong knowledge of the visualisation and interaction capabilities afforded by this novel technology.

In light of the successful outcomes obtained by the described implementation and the positive feedback received from learners and the faculty, the proposed TUI framework is currently being investigated for further application. At a system level, a number of modifications have been conceived on the tangible and digital aspects of the framework which will further capitalise on the inherent benefits afforded from the TUI system as well as add additional functionalities. On a more conceptual aspect, the adaptation of the TUI system will be analysed for its effectiveness to provide a similar benefit in teaching and learning diverse abstract concepts within the STEM disciplines offered at university. This will ultimately enable HEIs to utilise TUI systems as a value adding technology in a wide range of aspects and stem a range of creative and innovative uses of technology enhanced learning.

About the Authors

Clifford De Raffaele is Senior Lecturer and Academic Programme Coordinator in the field of Computer Science at the school of Science and Technology in Middlesex University Malta. He can be contacted at this e-mail: c.deraffaele@ieee.org

Serengul Smith is Associate Professor and Director of Programmes of Computer Science at the school of Science and Technology at Middlesex University in London. She can be contacted at this e-mail: s.smith@mdx.ac.uk

Orhan Gemikonakli is Professor of Telecommunications at Middlesex University in London. He can be contacted at this e-mail: o.gemikonakli@mdx.ac.uk

Acknowledgment

The authors would like to thank undergraduate students Mr. Matthew Borg Carr, Mr. Norbert Muscat, Mr. Nigel Debbatista and Ms. Rebekkah Baldacchino at Middlesex University Malta for their instrumental contribution in the development, implementation and evaluation of this work.

Bibliography

Blasco-Arcas, J.; I. Buil ; B. Hernandez-Ortega & F. J. Sese, F. (2013). Using clickers in class. The role of interactivity, active collaborative learning and engagement in learning performance. *Computers & Education*, Vol. 62, pp. 102–110.

De Raffaele, C.; S. Smith & O. Gemikonakli (2016). The aptness of Tangible User Interfaces for explaining abstract computer network principles. 46th IEEE International Frontiers in Education Conference (FIE 2016), Eire, Pennsylvania, USA, pp. 1-8.

Ishii, H. (2008). Tangible Bits: Beyond Pixels. *2nd International Conference on Tangible and Embedded Interaction*. Bonn, Germany.

Kaltenbrunner, M. & R. Bencina (2007). reacTIVision: a computer-vision framework for table-based tangible interaction. *1st International Conference on Tangible and embedded interaction*. Louisiana, USA.

Maher, M. L. & M. J. Kim (2006). Studying designers using a tabletop system for 3D design with a focus on the impact on spatial cognition. *1st IEEE International Workshop on Horizontal Interactive Human-Computer Systems (TableTop 2006)*. Sydney University, NSW, Australia: IEEE.

Mellecker, R. R.; L. Witherspoon & T. Watterson (2013). Active Learning: Educational Experiences Enhanced Through Technology-Driven Active Game Play. *The Journal of Educational Research*, Vol. 106, No. 5, pp. 352–359.

Nasman, J. & B. Cutler (2013). Evaluation of user interaction with daylighting simulation in a tangible user interface. *Automation in Construction*, Vol. 36, pp. 117–127.

Ozkan, N. & F. Gokalp-Yavuz (2015). Effects of Dexterity Level and Hand Anthropometric Dimensions on Smartphone Users' Satisfaction. *Mobile Information Systems*.

Price, S. & Y. Rogers (2004). Let's get physical: The learning benefits of interacting in digitally augmented physical spaces. *Computers & Education*, Vol. 43, pp. 137–151.

Rogers, Y.; M. Scaife; S. Gabrielli; E. Harris & H. Smith (2002). A Conceptual Framework for Mixed Reality Environments: Designing Novel Learning Activities for Young Children. *Presence*, Vol. 11, No. 6, pp. 677–686.

Ullmer, B. & H. Ishii (2001). Emerging Frameworks for Tangible User Interfaces. In J. M. Carroll (Ed.), *Human-Computer Interaction in the New Millenium*. Addison-Wesley, pp. 579–601.

Ullmer, B.; H. Ishii & R. J. Jacob (2005). Token+Constraint Systems for Tangible Interaction with Digital Information. *ACM Transactions on Computer-Human Interaction (TOCHI)*, Vol. 12, No. 1, pp. 81–118.

Underkoffler, J. & I. Hiroshi (1999). Urp: a luminous-tangible workbench for urban planning and design. *SIGCHI conference on Human Factors in Computing Systems*. Pennsylvania, USA.

Xambo, A.; E. Hornecker; P. Marshall; S. Jorda; C. Dobbyn & R. Laney (2013). Let's Jam the Reactable: Peer Learning during Musical Improvisation with a Tabletop Tangible Interface. *ACM Transactions on Computer-Human Interaction*, Vol. 20, No. 6.

Section 4: Case-based Teaching and Learning

An Introduction to Case-based Teaching and Learning

Martin Eley, Dario Faniglione & Lisbet Pals Svendsen

Introduction

Cases were being introduced in the classroom around the turn of the 20th century, originating out of Harvard University which developed its case-writing activities into a lucrative business with universities around the globe buying its cases and case solutions. According to Courtney *et al.* (2015:1) *"Characteristically, the traditional approach to teaching would start with the premise that the teacher has a superior knowledge in the subject area compared to the students. Following the traditional approach, the goal of the teaching would therefore be to transmit the teacher's knowledge to the students in the lecture hall. The students would continue to attend their educational institution until this transmission of knowledge has been successful. The typical student will leave academia after a number of years, will wander out in the world and start to test out the theories that he or she has learned. Often this meeting with the empirical world will prove to be a shock for the ex-student. Although the process of transmission might have been successful, the transformation from theoretical knowledge to practical ability is a challenge that is left to the ex-student and the businesses she or he is working with."*

In the words of Hannan & Silver (2000:9), *"From the 1980s [...], it was clear to many staff that the old forms of lecture and seminars were not working. Student constituencies were becoming greatly more diverse, expectations were different, the burden of assessment was becoming alarming, the new and pervasive shapes of modular and semesterized courses were changing teaching and learning styles and rhythms, and the outcomes of higher education were being questioned by employers and professions. The results at institutional or professional levels included a wide variety of strategies, such as the adoption of problem-based learning for the professions relating to medicine, and the adoption of new staff development programmes for new and existing teachers."*

In the experience of the authors in this section, however, the idea of transmission of knowledge from lecturer to student does not work exactly in the way noted above, and the following three chapters will give some illustrations of other perspectives. The aim here is to use the case method in the classroom, but to apply it in different contexts of higher education, which requires a break with the traditional, one-size-fits-all way of looking at and using cases in the classroom.

The three chapters in this section will show the three authors' very different ways of approaching cases in the classroom, but in discussions when forming this section it became evident that a number of common themes from both students' and teachers' perspectives were shared, particularly with regard to how the use of cases may foster critical thinking and metacognition in students in higher education. It became clear to the authors that this development is taking place in a wider context, institutional as well as national and cultural, in terms of e.g. internationalization, far greater numbers of students and the breaking down of cultural barriers.

The Student Perspective

Even if institutional policies, and individual lecturers' preferences and approaches, may find traditional lecturing inadequate for contemporary higher education, resistance from certain parts of the student population may be observed, for example the increasing internationalization in the classroom means that students will come from different cultures and thus also from different teaching and learning traditions; in some cases this may mean that students have been brought up not to question 'The Professor', therefore making their participation in this type of exercise problematic.

Another challenge is the politically driven (although often based on competitive economic rationale) increase in student numbers (OECD, 2016), which has implications for the level of motivation, interest, cognitive abilities and prior knowledge that students bring into the classroom.

The third main challenge area is the students' expectations as they enter university as 1st semester students progressing into a different set of expectations when, for example, they reach the final semesters of their master's degree as experienced learners. For the 1st semester students entering university, there is the additional challenge of negotiating the expectations of, for example, parents, community and their own expectations.

For what does a 1st semester student expect when s/he sees the curriculum that states 'lecture' or 'seminar'? Probably not the same as the experienced lecturer who has been working at the university in question for a number of years.

A key challenge of higher education would then be the one of creating an environment where students feel empowered to engage in active and independent learning. As such the case-based teaching could become the trigger for a progressive mindset and ultimately foster a change in student perceptions of learning culture. This would, however, require a move away from the frequently seen student 'anxiety' of making mistakes in front of their peers. Still, that challenge might be addressed by re-thinking how cases used in the classroom are created, segmented and used; here a tool like the Casemaker (Courtney *et al.*, 2015) may prove its worth in allowing incremental progression and answer building.

From the Teacher Perspective

One of the challenges of moving away from the traditional transmission model relates to the perceived identity of the teacher and the definition of his/her role as 'The Professor' in a context where the content is ubiquitous.

The changing student population in terms of numbers and educational backgrounds means that the role of the teacher also needs to undergo some degree of change in order to align with student needs. Such change would require teachers to move away from the traditional perception of what it means to be a university teacher towards, for example, a more mentoring, coaching, facilitating role. This development requires a move away from the pedagogical stance towards emphasis on andragogy, which Knowles (1984) suggests consists of the following four main principles:

1. Adults need to be involved in the planning and evaluation of their instruction;

2. Experience (including mistakes) provides the basis for the learning activities;

3. Adults are most interested in learning subjects that have immediate relevance and impact to their job or personal life;

4. Adult learning is problem-centered rather than problem-oriented. (Kearsley, 2010).

Taking our starting point in Knowles' principles, we believe case-based teaching aligns with these principles. For example in constructing and co-creating cases and learning resources with students, learners become deeply involved in the construction of their 'exercise spaces'. According to Holtham (2015:135) *"These differ from the sort of place where people work; they provide an environment in which the focus is on coaching to augment intellectual agility. Athletes training for events do not prepare simply by running; they also exercise in a gym to develop specifics that support and enhance the final performance method"*. In a similar way, the areas of the curriculum which would benefit from deeper links between theory and practice are identified and developed. This allows the co-creation of those experiences which trigger learning at a deeper level (Biggs & Tang, 2011).

In fact, the closer links we can create between what goes on inside and outside the university environment, the better the chances of involving students in challenging themselves with active learning on areas which they recognize as being beneficial and applicable for their future lives and practices.

Finally, the problem-centered learning which Knowles refers to can manifest itself in the carefully crafted and sectioned case-based learning activities. Still, applying principles of this nature means that there has to be a negotiation of mutual expectations in the classroom between students and teacher(s) to reach common understanding of how the student learning experience can best unfold and what the common 'terms of engagement' are supposed to be for the best outcome. So rather than relying on traditional and implicit roles, a new 'contract' needs to be arrived at between students and teacher(s) outlining expectations and responsibilities on both sides so that there is a common 'code of conduct' that guides what goes on in the classroom, and beyond. Over time, if this is repeated, it would become embedded into the system.

The aim would be working towards authentic, transformative learning, and offering this through the development of learning communities to explore a given subject area, and support critical articulation of personal and professional development throughout. The aim would be to challenge students' existing knowledge through engagement with innovative learning activities, supporting them to become agents of change and creative innovators within their future professional and community lives.

Practical Challenges

Traditionally, case-based learning has been specific for management studies and associated with Harvard-style cases. However, many commentators (Branch *et al.*, 2014; Minzberg, 1990; Gloeckler, 2008) have highlighted the need for rethinking case-based teaching and learning into a variety of subject areas that may each require a distinctive case format. This means that the availability of ready-made cases is limited, and as a consequence greater time must be spent by teachers on developing appropriate studies. This requirement is not always reflected in the time allowances given to teachers (Gregory & Lodge, 2015) for activities that are not directly linked to their delivery and assessment in research.

Therefore, depending on the subject area to be taught, the appropriate case format to the given learning situation and whether the case required is designed ad hoc or 're-cycled' and modified, teachers will need to spend different amounts of time on such activities in order to ensure constructive alignment of the learning activities with the learning outcomes and how these facilitate students' working towards their assessment (Biggs, 1996).

Another practical challenge can be encountered during the face-to-face sessions with students who may for some reason not have prepared. This teaching methodology relies on students being independent learners, who take responsibility for their own learning, and so the real challenge lies in managing the situation where some students have prepared and the rest haven't. Therefore strategies have to be developed to counter for this eventuality; this could be handled by developing a joint 'code of conduct' at institutional level.

Brief Description of Chapters

Chapter 15 by Martin Eley & Dario Faniglione is entitled "Collabora-tive engagement in case-studies through Learning Technology". In their chapter they look at an approach to address, at least in part, the issue of limited collaborative case-study engagement by students outside the classroom environment. They describe a trial study of an innovative plat-form for collaborative and progressive work on, and use of, case-studies. Additionally they go beyond the trial itself and attempts to contextualise some of the opportunities and findings within a wider view of the issue.

In chapter 16, "Teaching Responsible Management Practices via Cases", Lisbet Pals Svendsen gives an insight into the reflections of the teacher in connection with organizing a course on corporate communi-cation and including reflections on responsible management practices to fulfill the strategic aims of the university. Her chapter also contains reflec-tions on how best to facilitate student learning through the use of cases that play into the corporate communication and responsible management philosophy and what the teacher's role should be in this process.

Chapter 17, "Psychology students as co-creators in designing an inno-vative case-study based learning resource" by Dario Faniglione, Olga Fotakopoulou & Graham Lowe, present innovative approaches related to students as partners at Birmingham City University. Academic staff and students have been working in partnership to identify areas of the Psychology curriculum which could benefit from greater links between theory and practice. Consequently, the proposed solution was the co-creation of an interactive multimedia resource that allows learners to explore all the stages involved in taking a clinical, assessment or devel-opmental history interview. Embedding this resource in the Educational Psychology module would contribute to give students an opportunity to both challenge their skills with a real-life case study and contribute to a more constructively aligned curriculum.

Common issues moving forward

The innovations we have experienced and articulated in the chapters of this section should be seen as our sharing our practical experiences from the collaboration with our students in different settings. The underlying motivation of engaging with innovative learning and teaching approaches arises from previous experience which have identified issues and challenges that need resolving. The solutions presented in the chapters all stem from the individual or teaching team experimentation rather than having been brought about at institutional level. If you are frameworked within institutions that support this kind of thinking, that would help implementing these innovative approaches. And – as we have experienced – if you try to do new things, it doesn't hurt.

About the Authors

Dr Martin Eley is Associate Professor – Management Practice at Birmingham City University. He can be contacted at this e-mail: Martin. Eley@bcu.ac.uk

Dario Faniglione is Senior Lecturer in Learning and Teaching Practice at Birmingham City University. He can be contacted at this e-mail: Dario. Faniglione@bcu.ac.uk

Lisbet Pals Svendsen is associate professor at the Department of International Business Communication (IBC) at Copenhagen Business School, Denmark. She can be contacted at this e-mail: lps.ibc@cbs.dk

Bibliography

Biggs, J. & C. Tang (2011). *Teaching for Quality Learning at University.* 4th ed. Maidenhead: Open University Press.

Biggs, J. (1996). Enhancing Teaching through Constructive Alignment. In: *Higher Education,* Vol. 31, No. 3, pp. 347–364.

Branch, J.; P. Bartholomew & C. Nygaard (Eds.) (2014). *Case-Based Learning in Higher Education.* Oxfordshire: Libri Publishing Ltd.

Courtney, N.; C. Poulsen & C. Stylios (Eds.) (2015). *Case Based Teaching and Learning for the 21st Century.* Oxfordshire: Libri Publishing Ltd.

Gloeckler, G. (2008). The Case against Case Studies, *BusinessWeek,* February 4, pp. 66–67.

Gregory, M. S. J. & J. M. Lodge (2015). Academic workload: the silent barrier to the implementation of technology-enhanced learning strategies in higher education. *Distance Education,* pp. 1–21.

Hannan, A. & H. Silver (2000). *Innovating in Higher Education: Teaching, Learning and Institutional Cultures.* Philadelphia: Open University Press.

Holtham, C. (2015). Towards New Genres for 21st Century Business School Case Studies. In N. Courtney; C. Poulsen & C. Stylios (Eds.), *Case Based Teaching and Learning for the 21st Century.* Oxfordshire: Libri Publishing Ltd., pp. 121–135.

Kearsley, G. (2010). *Andragogy (M. Knowles). The theory into practice database.* Retrieved from http.://tip.psychology.org. [Accessed 11 May 2016].

Knowles, M. (1984). *Andragogy in Action.* San Fransisco: Jossey-Bass.

Mintzberg, H. (1990). The Design School: reconsidering the basic premises of strategic management. *Strategic Management Journal*, Vol. 11, No. 3, pp. 171–195.

OECD (2016). Population with tertiary education (indicator). Websource: doi: 10.1787/0b8f90e9-en [Accessed 11 May 2016].

Chapter 15: Case-based teaching and learning

Collaborative Engagement in Case-studies through Learning Technology

Martin Eley & Dario Faniglione

Background

Experience to date was of limited collaborative case-study engagement by students outside the classroom environment. Up to this point such engagement had primarily relied on face-to-face meetings among students. The opportunity therefore seemed to be available to address this issue, at least in part, and at the same time contribute to two strategic objectives: student inclusion and engagement, and greater emphasis on effective problem-based learning.

In order to deliver a meaningful contribution to both strategies, an open access online platform was identified, allowing for groups of students to work collaboratively with case-studies and problem-based learning. Open access outputs from recent collaborative EU initiatives were considered. The Casemaker (The Casemaker, 2015) platform was selected, as it was perceived that it was likely to fulfil given strategic requirements for ease of use in delivering student inclusion and engagement.

The Practice

In order to improve upon our student engagement strategy, a platform was implemented to deepen the engagement with business case-studies, going beyond the standard university technology platforms and systems, such as Moodle. This has allowed students to interact on a more frequent, personalized and collaborative basis, leveraging communication and interaction strategies aligned with ones of social media and technology-based media, with which they are already familiar due to use in personal lives.

In delivering the implementation described here, an appropriate project plan was constructed and communicated, aiming at empowering stakeholders throughout (Bartholomew & Freeman, 2010). To achieve holistic buy-in and successful adoption at delivery level, the head of department was kept informed and the programme director was involved in the decision-making process; both supported the approach. The module leaders and tutors collaborated in this new approach, constructing the implementation and, during the module learning activities, benefited from the empowerment in taking ownership of the learning experience with both students and tutors. The teaching staff identified an area of the module learning design, which was likely to be enhanced through the adoption of new technology fostering contemporary collaboration with the teaching material.

The Casemaker online platform has been designed with the aim of facilitating and enhancing case-based teaching approaches (Courtney *et al.*, 2015). The online interface is structured around three main components: the case database, the case editor (author/teacher view) and the case analyser (teacher/student view). Both the case editor and the case analyser features were at the core of this implementation.

Following the identification of the session topic, the teaching team identified an appropriate case-study which facilitated the application of theory into practice. The case-study used in this trial was the development of a progressive induction programme for a baby and child equipment retailer. The case-study was segmented and adapted by the tutors to be delivered through the Casemaker platform, by following simple processes which are supported where necessary by the user manual (The Casemaker, 2015).

Students were introduced to the Casemaker analyser at the start of the selected face-to-face sessions. The particular sessions were selected to provide a good mix of international students. In this trial the introduction was undertaken by staff who were familiar with the Casemaker. A demonstration, followed by a Q&A session, was delivered covering how they could interact with the software and what was expected of them.

The student learning experience in this instance is designed around small-group work, in solving problem-based challenges. The Casemaker interface fully supports this approach, therefore student groupings were identified by tutors to provide a good mix of skills in each group, and these groups were set-up on the system.

Within the demonstration, it was important to engender student enthusiasm through a high-energy introduction, designed to create interest, a higher level of interaction and debate, within and beyond the session. The high energy element is based on existing tutor skills and while complementing the Casemaker trial are not unique to it. This interest generated includes ongoing collaboration through the Case-maker, any-time and any-place in order to suit the student preferences on time and location. The platform allows for asynchronous individual contribution to the group development work and output. Students access case materials through the analyser interface. If required, the case can be split in parts, which automatically unlock to the student view in a sequential fashion. The analyser allows student groups to access the textual, multimedia (i.e. videos, pictures, audio) and complementary (i.e. diagrams, spreadsheets, etc.) elements of the case. Most importantly, they can collaboratively annotate these elements. Videos can actually be anno-tated on specific time-codes throughout the timeline. This feature allows students to collaborate remotely on the case analysis, which is often the necessary trigger for constructing links and connection between the inci-dents and situations portrayed in a case study and the relevant theory. There is an expectation that students would recognize the Casemaker interface as familiar tools of communication and interaction (i.e. social media). In the process, they could give, receive and act upon peer-feed-back encouraged by a more familiar interface. Additionally, students can collaboratively draft an analytical document, though the Casemaker report editor, which provides collaborative editing in real-time.

The Casemaker platform offers students a structured way of engaging with the case analysis, and provide teachers with a means to access and deconstruct student interactions. Through the case analyser individual student contributions are exposed and presented to the tutor chronologi-cally, allowing a tutor view of how the group developed their thoughts around the case over time. The tutor dashboard also allows for individual and group overviews, providing a brief visualization of overall student engagement with the learning activity. Therefore, the teaching team is empowered to monitor student participation. This facilitates the planning for personalized and/or group interventions. Also feedback and feed-forward opportunities are enriched by the overview of all individual and group contribution to the learning activity.

In a typical classroom-based learning environment, lectures and tutors would hand out a case study in a face-to-face session, then wait for another face-to-face session to follow up with student-led learning activities, such as group presentations, plenary discussions, etc. In-between sessions, students would need to arrange meetings and engage with a learning process, which often educators have no evidence of. The lack of evidence extends to the student's own 'solutions' such as WhatsApp and other methods.

In addition to the more traditional case-based teaching affordances (i.e. application of theory to practice), students are exposed to contemporary online collaboration, which enhances team-working skills and mirrors many workplace environments. This can help in developing core management skills of team-working and collaboration.

Outcomes

An immediate positive result of this practice can be appreciated in the construction of a "blended learning" environment. Student contribution outside of the face-to-face interaction with the teaching team can be observed, measured and quantified by the teaching team. This is a clear improvement on more traditional approaches, which heavily relied on contact time to take a view on overall and individual student contributions. Also, being able to identify student input beyond the classroom and the provision of a safe, peer-led online environment has enabled the breaking of certain cultural barriers, such as those related to deference to tutors (i.e.: not-questioning). As a consequence of engaging with these environments, core business skills are developed in the areas of collaboration, planning, organization, online etiquette, and respect.

After using this platform a tutor commented that "it is easy to use and gives a real insight into who is doing what in collaborative problem-based learning tasks". This is in line with the aim of continuing a hands-on approach beyond the classroom, one that is designed to encourage discussion and debate, and to share student progress. Additionally, in a network of students the identification of 'the star' may allow a tutor to work 'through the star' to diffuse knowledge and insight quicker by using the network effect.

It has been found in the authors' experience to be engagement that inspires both teachers and students. It is fundamentally about bringing the future into the present, and it demonstrates an understanding of what technology does for younger people, both in enabling and inspiring them. This facilitates capture of enthusiastic and tremendous efforts of particular learners.

The implementation of Casemaker in the 'Individual and People Management' module of the MSc Management program has been formally evaluated. As part of the evaluation, two cohorts of students (N=35) were asked to provide their views after the engagement with a case-study in Casemaker for the first time. Students were asked to collaborate in small-groups, to produce an analysis of the case and deliver a presentation of their findings in the following face-to-face session (one week later). Students were invited to access to case material and work collaboratively on the task through the Casemaker interface. Feedback on the experience has been collected though an evaluation form, which students filled-in individually and anonymously in a follow-up face-to-face session.

The key findings highlighted that students in this particular module enjoyed the engagement with new ways of interaction with the course material and their peers. In particular, they appreciated the value of using cutting edge web technology, such as the real-time editor and video annotation tool. Most comments around the Casemaker user interface highlighted the ease of use, and the contemporary look and feel. Some comments related to how this differs to the "clunky" Moodle interface, the VLE (virtual learning environment) they normally use for online learning activities. No particular problems were highlighted in accessing and navigating through the platform. Perhaps more interestingly, positive comments related to group-work dynamics. Two students noted the benefit of online group collaboration in allowing for a more transparent group interaction, where most group members can voice opinions, with less susceptibility to group dominators and "loud voices".

Not all students, however, contributed to the Casemaker tasks, and two of the seven groups decided to physically meet-up anyway, in order to prepare a report and make arrangements for their presentation. It has been observed and concluded that it would take some time to build student engagement with a (any) new online interface, as increasing use is dependent on the level of familiarity and confidence with the platform and the approach. Informal feedback questioned whether students may be sceptical in adopting social-media style interaction for their learning and teaching practice, as this may blur any distinction between their social and study activities, and it has not been readily seen so far that this is something which all students would necessarily like.

Moving Forward

Depending on the complexity of the case study, this approach can be utilized for a single session topic (i.e. face-to-face, seminar cycle) or an entire module, and even across a course. The key differences from more traditional approaches of engaging students with case-studies include:

+ Flexibility of student working and contributing "any time / any place" (McLinden, 2013);

+ Real-time monitoring of student contributions to the task;

+ The possibility of personalized interventions beyond the face-to-face sessions;

+ A key part of "blended learning" approaches in module learning design, breaking the face-to-face/seminar/presentation cycle, by leveraging on meaningful online student collaboration.

Although this innovative teaching and learning practice has been implemented through a dedicated platform (i.e. the Casemaker), there is the possibility of replicating similar interventions through a variety of Virtual Learning Environments (i.e. Moodle). This would require some initial customization of the workflow. However, the benefit could be a high level of integration with existing systems and user familiarity across the institution. If it is to be used in other contexts such as Executive MBA groups where the student population would typically be older than the students involved here, it would need to be tested whether their age would be a barrier, either real or perceived.

These initial results, although limited and therefore indicative in nature, are certainly encouraging for further adoption of this approach. The overall conclusions relate to the need of Higher Education institutions to cater for more diverse and changing student populations that are tech-savvy, especially in terms of social media use. Innovative approaches, similar to the one described here, can contribute in to shaping an inclusive student learning experience, where learners with varied commitments and extra-curricula responsibilities have an equal chance to engage in richer peer-led learning activities, in their own time and at their own pace. However, this may not be universal at present as in Africa technology is still a differentiator and can be a barrier; a digital divide. The context of this trial however is in a developed environment and infrastructure.

From the trial undertaken encouragement for others can be taken in trying some new options that work better for programme inclusion and contemporary mixed methods of engagement. In strategic terms it is part of continuing to take steps forward in a fast moving environment and exploring more avenues to challenge the learners.

About the Authors

Dr Martin Eley is Associate Professor – Management Practice at Birmingham City University. He can be contacted at this e-mail: Martin. Eley@bcu.ac.uk

Dario Faniglione is Senior Lecturer in Learning and Teaching Practice at Birmingham City University. He can be contacted at this e-mail: Dario. Faniglione@bcu.ac.uk

Bibliography

Bartholomew, P. & R. Freeman (2010). The ladder of engagement. Adapted from 'Levels of learner voice participation'. In Rudd, T; F. Colligan & R. Naik, *Learner Voice: A Handbook from FutureLab*. Bristol: FutureLab.
Courtney, N.; C. Poulsen & C. Stylios (Eds.) (2015). Case Based Teaching and Learning for the 21st Century: an Introduction by the Editors. In N. Courtney; C. Poulsen & C. Stylios (Eds.), *Case Based Teaching and Learning for the 21st Century*, Oxfordshire: Libri Publishing Ltd., pp. 1–17.

McLinden, M. (2013). Flexible pedagogies: Part-time learners and learning in higher education. *Flexible pedagogies: Preparing for the future.* The Higher Education Academy.

The Casemaker (2015). Online Resource: http://www.casemaker.dk [Accessed July 20, 2016].

Chapter 16: Case-based teaching and learning

Teaching Responsible Management Practices via Cases in the Corporate Communication Classroom

Lisbet Pals Svendsen

The Background

In this chapter I will elaborate and discuss the practical use of cases in the corporate communication classroom with students who are in their very first semester of their B.Sc. International Business programme at Copenhagen Business School (CBS). The fact that the students in the classroom are 'new' to the university setting offers a range of challenges of a more general nature in terms of university teaching and learning that go beyond the core content of the course, which in this case would be their course in Corporate Communication. These challenges will be elaborated further in this chapter.

"CBS is a pioneer in embedding UN Principles for Responsible Management Education (PRME) and is currently reviewing everything we do through this lens. The ambition is to make responsible management education an integral part of our core activities both in research and education while leading by example through our own organisational practices in delivering our services" (CBS, 2016).

Responsible Management is therefore taught as an underlying principle across courses, disciplines, curricula, levels and programs. In fact, the first day of the autumn semester each year is designated Responsibility

Day where new students are introduced to this central issue in CBS thinking and teaching.

In a 'historical' perspective, the format and content of the Corporate Communication course have changed over time from a more traditionally taught course with the title Intercultural Corporate Communication where focus was to a large extent on cultural challenges in connection with corporate communication, to today's course where the intercultural dimension has been integrated in the course in a way that sees interculturality as a natural consequence of globalization and therefore not as something that needs to be addressed separately as a novelty, but rather as a fact of life in the world inhabited by students and faculty. New topic areas are still being introduced to the course content when the development in the corporate environment calls for adjustments to the curriculum; most recently (in 2015), the topic of social media in corporate communication was introduced.

The Practice

The Corporate Communication classroom is huge: around 175 students are admitted into the programme each year, and the grade point average at entry level is the highest in Denmark. The students admitted are Danish as well as non-Danish, so the classroom environment is truly international and intercultural, and all of them come to CBS with a very high level of personal ambition.

Timewise, the course is placed in the 2nd quarter of the students' 1st semester at CBS, the students have approx. seven weeks with 2 x 3 lessons, and parallel to the classroom activities, they are required to write a 30-page exam project in groups of four to five students, for which they will sit for an individual oral exam at the end of the semester. Therefore there are usually three teachers involved in the teaching of this course; the teachers participate in the classroom sessions two and two in varying constellations so that at the end of the teaching period, all students know all three teachers ahead of the oral exams.

In line with the Responsible Management vision of CBS, the Corporate Communication course is intended by the teachers to be much more than 'just' a communication course where focus is on working with and explaining a series of communication episodes; rather we attempt to take a holistic view of the organization and reflect upon how in a given situation communication might impact the different levels of the organization and what effects it may have on the identity, image and reputation of the organization in question.

The students who take the Corporate Communication course have a parallel course in the 2nd quarter of their studies, viz. microeconomics. And since that topic is new to most of the students while they feel much more at home with communication challenges, one of the challenges of the course is that there is a somewhat 'distorted' balance between the perceived relevance of the two courses in the students' minds with the microeconomics course being the absolutely heavier of the two.

The Teacher Perspective – Underlying Considerations

From my perspective, the Corporate Communications course rests on the premise that a solid theoretical foundation is required for communication practitioners to make the best strategic choices in terms of level of formality, level of politeness, cultural knowledge, vocabulary, style, genre etc. On the other hand, theory cannot stand alone. As is the case with all skills, communication skills need to be developed intro true competences by being practiced by the individual in order for him/her to be able to make the right choices on the spot, which is required in oral communication – and especially if this communication takes place in a language that is not the communicator's first or native language. In popular terms: Professional language competence is a muscle that needs to be exercised on a daily basis!

In a course like this, two sets of theory come into play: The first set is the theory relevant to the core of the course, for example classical communication theory as expressed in the Shannon & Weaver model (Communication.Theory.org, 2010), the theory of reputation, identity and image (Hatch & Schultz, 2008), the theory of crisis communication and image restoration (Coombs, 2007; Benoit, 1997), the theory of change communication (FitzPatrick & Valskov, 2014) as well as the theory of social media in corporate communication (Li & Bernoff, 2008).

The other set of theories is more aimed at equipping the teachers with an insight into what 'makes students tick', for example how teaching activities may be organized to support students' progression from knowledge via skills towards competences where the skills and the knowledge are harnessed and can be reused in different contexts (Nygaard *et al.*, 2008), motivation (Dörnyei & Skehan, 2003), evaluation (Svendsen, 2011), adult learning (Hermansen, 2005) and Bloom's taxonomy of learning domains (Bloom, 1956 *in* Clark, 1999).

The Course Plan

Over the now (2016) seven years that I have been in charge of planning, managing and teaching this course, the course plan has been developed from being a rather traditional one-page plan with indications of weekly readings and not much more into an elaborated, seven-page plan with a lengthy introduction to the students about the foundations for the course in terms of *what* we do, *why* we do it and *how* we do it as well as an explanation of how I expect the students to handle the theoretical topics that they will be in charge of presenting to the class.

Next comes a highly detailed course plan with dates, times and room indications as well as weekly themes and the relevant literature, which is colour-coded (cf. below) to facilitate students' preparation. The weekly themes are selected with a view to who we might attract as guest speakers and when they would be available, who in the three-person teacher team has what area(s) of special interest and when is each of the three teachers able to be in the classroom.

The topics in the course plan can be seen as puzzle pieces that can be moved around to fit the teacher team of a given year and match the calendars of busy guest lecturers. Just as an example, the 2015 – the most recent – course plan contained the themes of Stakeholder Management, Branding & Reputation, Crisis Communication, Leadership and Corporate Identity, Culture and Communication, Campaigning, Financial Communication (to provide a mental link to the parallel course in micro-economics), Media Relations, Employee Communication, Change Communication and CSR. Indeed, in 2015 the pieces of the puzzle were moved around compared to the year before, since the teacher team was supplemented with a new member who already had obligations in her calendar before being assigned to co-teach this course.

The last point in the course plan is the literature list and general advice on how to access materials from the CBS Library electronic database, followed by an indication of the date when the students have to hand in their exam project report and the dates for the oral exam.

The practice of colour-coding the course literature in red, yellow and green, thus indicating what literature is absolutely central to the course (red), and which references might be somewhat less central (yellow or green) is a feature of the course plan that the students highly appreciate, since it allows them to gain a quick overview of essential readings for a specific class and lets them follow up with the supplementary readings after class.

The Materials Used

The materials used in the Corporate Communication classroom are – perhaps in contrast to the underlying thoughts and visions of the course – rather traditional, as the students are new to CBS and to student life in general; therefore the introduction in the classroom of highly innovative materials could be a bit 'too much', given that many students new to university life have relatively rigid expectations of what it means to study and what they expect from their teachers and from the work they are supposed to be doing themselves.

One bone of contention for many of the students in this particular classroom is that they are enrolled in a B.Sc. programme with focus on economics and management, and so they do not necessarily see the Corporate Communication course – a 'soft' topic – as being just as important as the more 'hard-core' economics courses. It is in fact frustrating to many of these students that there is no 'one correct answer' to communication questions, but that usually there are several 'correct' solutions depending on the participants or the context.

Student evaluations of the course support the notion that students feel comfortable and 'safe' with the somewhat traditional materials used in the classroom: A textbook presenting theory and cases in parallel, additional readings uploaded to the Moodle-based learning platform used at CBS, PowerPoint and/or Prezi presentations uploaded to the platform and guest lecturers invited to give an outside view of communicative practices in corporate life.

As already indicated, cases are a central feature of this course, and students are encouraged to contribute actively with materials, suggestions, models, texts etc. to these activities during the course.

A natural feature of the whole process of preparing for classes is of course to review the course plan and the literature list every year before the course starts in order to ensure that the literature references are up-to-date, and that the latest articles and new insights relevant to the course are used to the widest possible extent. It also goes without saying, that a critical review of what cases to use for what purpose when and how must be made.

The Classroom Activities

The weekly 2 x 3 lesson-classes fall into two equally important parts: A theoretical part and a practical part, and we work with both parts in all sessions. Classes take place in three-lesson time slots, and each class consists of a (brief) theoretical introduction to the theme of the week by either the teacher or selected student/s, followed by practical work in groups where the teacher functions as mentor and discussion partner; each class ends with a brief sum-up and evaluation of the day's activities and learning outcomes.

The purpose of this structure is that the approach combining the traditional delivery of content with the student-led discussions and negotiations of meaning, supports not just the lower levels in Bloom's taxonomy (knowledge and understanding) but that allowing students to make sense of theories and concepts for themselves and applying them to a case helps facilitate higher cognition levels in the students through the strengthening of their selection, application and analysis skills.

In order for the students to be as active as at all possible in the classroom, it is necessary that not only the teacher is involved in the work on the theoretical texts, so from time to time students are invited to introduce the various themes from a theoretical point of view based on the readings outlined in the course plan; for these student-led introductions, the procedure is as follows:

- One group will facilitate approx. 30 minutes of class discussion. The discussion is based on an article, case or discussion points. They are not to make presentations in the traditional form, but rather to take responsibility for starting a discussion, explaining main points of texts, criticizing (or highlighting the merits of) texts, finding additional material, asking questions, drawing parallels, etc.;

+ The group submits a plan to me before the lesson with keywords of how they want to facilitate the discussion, for example brief introduction by a group member, buzz groups, questions to peers, workshop, quiz, role play etc., etc.). Teacher's role: consultant, discussion partner.

In addition, evaluation is a central element in the classroom sessions and the main reason why all sessions consist of three classes, as this time-frame leaves room for evaluation. Ideally, the most important form of evaluation would be students reflecting on their own learning. According to Hermansen (2005), the learning process takes place along three dimensions: Feedback and feedforward, habitus and reflection as well as toil and exuberance. In regard to the evaluation process in class, the dimension of habitus and reflection comes into play in the sense that according to Hermansen (2005:5) *"Habitus is unconscious learning. It is learning without knowing what is being learned or why... [and] Reflection is conscious learning. Reflection is said to occur when you think about what you are learning, where you are learning, how you are learning and why you are learning. Reflecting about what you are learning is when you are able to compare the current input with other knowledge, skills and competencies, to create meaning in what you are learning and find the connections with what has previously been learned".*

Self-evaluation may thus be described as 'students connecting the mental dots' and is therefore an essential activity in the collaborative classroom where meanings are negotiated and student satisfaction hinges on individual accomplishment.

In addition to self-evaluation, peer evaluation may also be used but in other contexts, as peer evaluation will be used to discuss for example answers to specific questions, notes taken in connection with a lecture or the like. Often students are uncomfortable with the idea of engaging in peer evaluation, since they do not know how to politely offer critical comments, but then again that's all part of becoming a competent communicator.

Teacher evaluation is of course also an important element, but should ideally in my experience come last, as the true learning takes place when students self-evaluate and not when the teacher offers them their view of what was 'good', 'poor', 'correct' or the like and students can mentally tick off a box depending on whether they had arrived at the same suggestion or not.

Cases and the Responsible Management Perspective

The cases used in class illustrate various communication choke-points where there communication is at risk of going wrong or being misinterpreted or misunderstood for various reasons, for example if the communication strategy chosen is in conflict with the vision, strategy and goals of the organization, if it fails to live up to the intercultural conventions and expectations inherent in a given situation or if for example the vocabulary or grammar of the communicator (student) fails to live up to the level of formality required of the communication context etc. These examples show communication choke-points at a micro-level.

Micro-level considerations relate to the choices made by the individual student/communicator, but in the classroom it is also necessary to take the macro-level perspective of Responsible Management Practices into consideration, and this to a great extent hinges on the choice of cases used in the classroom. Therefore the 'ideal' case would be one that addresses the specific topic(s) of the week and at the same time feeds into the Responsible Management philosophy to allow students to see the wider implications of the communication in the narrow perspective of for example a crisis situation and also to see the wider implications in terms of responsible management when for example the CEO fails to get his message across.

Some cases are used for one specific purpose only, for example The Heineken-Mongolia case from the textbook used (Cornelissen, 2014) which was used to illustrate a clash between western CSR standards and Mongolian cultural tradition and which actually led to some heated discussions in class between the various student groups. Other cases are used across a number of themes such as the CBS Goes Green case (Svendsen, 2014:152–155) or the case I wrote in 2014 about Marius the Giraffe that was killed in early 2014 by the Copenhagen Zoo, dismembered in public and fed to the lions, which led to a multitude of reactions from around the world (the case is available from the Case Centre as part of the free CBS collection).

In all case situations, however, we encourage the students to attempt to take a holistic view of the organization and reflect upon how the communication in a given situation might impact the different levels of the organization and what effects it may have on the identity, image and reputation of the organization in question and hence on its responsible management practices.

The Outcome

The Student Perspective

Post-course evaluations are a regular feature linked to all courses at CBS, and they are used by programme directors, teachers and heads of department to assess whether a given course is 'on the right track' and fits into the relevant course portfolio in a sensible manner. In their post-course evaluations of the 2015 course, the students mention positively the variation in topics, the use of cases that gives a feel for what goes on in 'real' corporate life, the discussions they had in their groups during case work time and the fact that the cases added a 'hands on' dimension to the course.

In spring 2016, the CBS Dean of Education's Office decided to compile a report across the 19 bachelor programmes mapping the various courses and activities that play into the Responsible Management Practices philosophy that is so central to CBS strategy, and in an interview with a group of 'my' B.Sc. IB students, the students contribute to that report with the following comments on the corporate communication course:

"Corporate Communication investigates what constitutes good communication practices in a corporate context. The course identifies and examines elements of different corporate communication strategies, pointing out their respective strengths and weaknesses. The course balances corporate communication and interpersonal communication theories with practical exercises that allow students to develop strategic corporate communicative competences. The course draws upon cases from the current corporate environment, allowing students to arrive at the best solutions to present and past communication

dilemmas. This enables students to know how to communicate in multicultural corporate environments. Furthermore, students are introduced to several cases such as the Heineken dog fight case set in Mongolia."

The Teacher Perspective

I have found the above student comment particularly encouraging, as it demonstrates that the students have latched on to the underlying premises and visions of the course. The students express that in the classroom we literally pick up various elements of communication strategies, examine them, 'turn them over' to see what they look like from the other side and evaluate whether they actually fit into the given communication context and what they contribute to that context.

To me as a teacher, I am convinced that my teaching practice is a success because the Responsible Management perspective makes sense to the students, which contributes to increasing their motivation to participate actively and contribute in class. This approach has, however, forced me to rethink my own role in the classroom, and in this process, I was reflecting on the considerations shared in the general introduction to this section, particularly the question of how to change students' expectations that 'The Professor' would teach them 'The Truth' and that learning would be a one-directional process beyond their control into creating a learning space where learning is not only two- but multi-directional and is co-constructed by active participants in an exchange of thoughts, ideas and insights that would facilitate the students' development as not only students but as active participants and communicators, allowing them to develop from having knowledge to possessing competences (Nygaard *et al.*, 2008).

To reach this goal, I have had to embrace the idea of Ghasemi & Hashemi (2011:3100) that *"The modern educator in the ICT era is no longer described as 'a sage on the stage' but 'a guide by the side'"*.

Moving Forward

In my view, learning is a dynamic process. In addition, the development of communication competence is also paradoxical in the sense that the learning process is taking place inside the individual but cannot be

triggered without collaboration with others in a dynamic process. Therefore the course plan for a course like the corporate communication course
also needs to be seen as a dynamic tool and must in itself offer an example
of the type of learning that I wish for the students to walk away with at
the end of the course.

In writing this chapter, I have had the possibility to reflect on my own
practices and the learning that I can draw from collaborating with my
students, and one point that I plan to implement in the coming version of
the course plan is that I will clearly outline what the vision, mission and
strategy of the course are, thus playing into the business context that the
students are engaged in in their studies and their future aspirations. By
clearly specifying vision, mission and strategy for the course, the students
will get a clear impression of 'the contract' we enter into when we meet in
the classroom to discuss and contribute to the co-creation of knowledge.

In addition, I am aware that it would be wise to include in the course
description and plan an explanation of the usefulness of evaluation –
in particular self-evaluation – in order to encourage students to actively
take part in this to support their own learning. Also I need to consider a
format for peer evaluation that will not deter students from participating
in this very central activity that develops their own competence just as
it allows them to negotiate meaning in collaboration with their fellow
students.

Also, for each year that I am involved in teaching in general and this
course in particular, it becomes increasingly clear that in order for the
students to truly be motivated to develop their insight into the corporate
communication framework, into the philosophy of responsible management practices and not least their personal communication competences,
the cases selected for the course need to fit into the framework at all
three levels. This means that ideally students should become increasingly
involved in the co-creation of cases, and therefore the next step for me
would be to develop a framework that facilitates this, whether this be in
the e-learning environment used at CBS or through other channels.

The remark by the students (cf. above) about the course that it is
"allowing students to arrive at the best solutions to present and past
communication dilemmas" is encouraging and would suggest that the
course is well on the way towards meeting the development goals I
have for my students, but as new generations of students will have new

expectations, the course must remain dynamic to continue to support student learning.

About the Author

Lisbet Pals Svendsen is associate professor at the Department of International Business Communication (IBC) at Copenhagen Business School, Denmark. She can be contacted at this e-mail: lps.ibc@cbs.dk

Bibliography

Benoit, W. L. (1997). Image repair discourse and crisis communication. *Public Relations Review*, Vol. 23, No. 2, pp. 177–186.

Case Centre, The (2014): Marius the Giraffe. Online resource: http://www. thecasecentre.org/main/ [accessed 11 May 2016]

CBS, Principles of Responsible Management Education. Online resource: http:// www.cbs.dk/en/knowledge-society/strategic-areas/office-of-responsible-management-education, downloaded May 2016 [accessed April 2016]

Clark, D. R. (1999). Bloom's Taxonomy of Learning Domains. Online resource: http://www.nwlink.com/~donclark/hrd/bloom.html [accessed May 2016].

CommunicationTheory.org (2010). Shannon and Weaver Model of Communication from: http://communicationtheory.org/shannon-and-weaver-model-of-communication.

Coombs, W. T. (2007). Protecting Organization Reputations During a Crisis: The Development and Application of Situational Crisis Communication Theory. *Corporate Reputation Review*, Vol. 10, pp. 163–176.

Cornelissen, J. (2014). Corporate Communication – A Guide to Theory and Practice. London: Sage Publications

Dörnyei, Z. & P. Skehan (2003). Individual differences in Second Language Learning. In Doughty, C. L. & M. H. Long (Eds.) *The Handbook of Second Language Acquisition*. Malden, Oxford, Melbourne, Berlin: Blackwell, pp. 589–630.

Ghasemi, B. & M. Hashemi (2011). ICT: Newwave in English language learning/teaching. *Procedia Social and Behavioral Sciences*, No. 15, pp. 3098–3102. Elsevier Ltd.

Hatch, M. J. & M. Schultz (2008). *Taking brand initiative: How companies can align strategy, culture, and identity through corporate branding*. San Francisco: Jossey-Bass.

Hermansen, M. (2005). *Relearning*. Copenhagen: Danish University of Education Press / CBS Press.

Li, C. & J. Bernoff (2008). *Groundswell – Winning in a world transformed by social technologies*. Forrester Research. Harvard Business Review Press.

Nygaard, C.; T. Højlt & M. Hermansen (2008). Learning-based Curriculum Development. *Higher Education*, Vol. 55, No. 1, pp. 33–50.

Svendsen, L. P. (2011). Didactic Experiments Suggest Enhanved Learning Outcomes. *International Journal of Business and Social Science*, Vol. 2, No. 22, pp. 35–44.

Svendsen, L. P. (2014). Using Cases in the 'Social Software Classroom'. In J. Branch; P. Bartholomew & C. Nygaard (Eds.) *Case-Based Learning in Higher Education*. Oxfordshire: Libri Publishing Ltd., pp. 137–159.

Chapter 17: Case-based teaching and learning

Psychology Students as Co-creators in Designing an Innovative Case-study Based Learning Resource

Dario Faniglione, Olga Fotakopoulou & Graham Lowe

Background

As a mechanism for quality enhancement of the curriculum and the student learning experience at Birmingham City University (BCU), students are asked to provide feedback about the content and delivery of modules and courses. This might take the form of a group feedback session or they may be asked to fill in questionnaires. The results of the evaluation of each module are considered by the course team as part of the monitoring process and provide good opportunities to listen and make sense of student voice. The teaching team of the Educational Psychology module (Level 5 – second year undergraduate), part of the BSc Psychology course, in analysing student responses to module evaluation questionnaires, discovered that a common theme in student feedback for their module related to missing opportunities of linking theory to practice throughout the learning on the module, and generally within the Psychology curriculum as a whole. This was also reiterated in other informal feedback opportunities, such us one-to-one tutorials and learning activities in plenary face-to-face sessions.

Work experiences, placements and enriched mentoring programmes could be put in place as possible solutions. However, when considering the specific subject area and level of study, anecdotal evidence and previous studies (Reddy & Moores, 2012) seem to suggest that these opportunities tend to be limited in scope, and benefit only a small number of learners in a given formal educational experience. Therefore, the teaching team decided to experiment with an innovative approach to learning activity design. Rather than passive recipients of knowledge, students have become active participants in facing real-life problems and scenarios. Furthermore, some of them have also had the opportunity to identify the specific areas of the curriculum in need of improvement and have co-created those scenarios and learning resources aimed at encouraging problem-solving and active learning.

The Practice

Innovative approaches related to students as partners and co-creators of learning activity and resources seem to have gained momentum in the past few years (Carey, 2013; Nygaard et al., 2013; Bovill et al., 2011). The teaching staff on the undergraduate Psychology course at BCU were willing to challenge the traditional conception of academic staff being in control of every aspect of the learning design (Mann, 2008). Meaningful collaborations amongst students, and between students and academic staff have been identified as having the dual purpose of enhancing existing learning and teaching approaches, and, at the same time, creating the conditions for transformative learning to take place, as described by Biggs & Tang (2011).

A call for student partners was communicated to current and previous students on the Educational Psychology module. Three students showed interest in co-creating resources and, together with the teaching staff, they contributed to the submission of an application for funding to the existing Student Academic Partners (SAP) scheme, run by the Centre for the Excellence in Learning and Teaching (CELT) at BCU. The scheme has been in existence at BCU since 2008, and allows students to be employed by the university, working in partnership with staff. The main aims of partnership projects funded by SAP relate to shaping collaboration and communities working on pedagogy and research. The funding pays for student time, while they are employed to work together with staff to transform and enhance areas of the curriculum and the learning experience across the University (Bovill et al., 2015). At present, the SAP scheme funds around 50 projects per year, and some of these experiences have been documented in a previous publication (Nygaard et al., 2013). The idea of partnering with students in the co-creation of learning resources is not a new invention per se within the institutional context. In fact, the commitment to the philosophy of 'students as partners' has over the years become deeply embedded in the organisation and these types of implementation are often seen as a manifestation of the BCU institutional core values (BCU, 2014). The novelty and the perceived added value of the innovation described here relate to a specific context in which this has been applied, and the intended output of Psychology student and staff collaborative efforts. The application for SAP scheme support was successful, and this was essential to commence and sustain the partnership work in the following months. Being an established platform and framework for collaboration, the SAP scheme handled the administrative side of the partnership (i.e.: funding, student employment) and CELT also provided technical and pedagogical support to the initiative.

Having established the administrative dimension and identified additional institutional stakeholders, the next step was the articulation of roles and responsibilities, to be shared between the academic and student partners. It seemed clear from the outset that the end product would need to create a legacy, which would positively impact on the learning experience of future students on the course. However, the shared view of staff and student partners was that, first of all, the team needed to identify a specific area of the curriculum that could be enhanced by such a product. Further, the team had to articulate how this area could be made more relevant and engaging. Finally, the technicalities of the actual multimedia resource were to be decided.

Addressing the "muddiest point"

Psychology students in the project team had been already experienced the Educational Psychology module in its original format. They were therefore in a position of providing unique insights and alternative perspectives to the teaching team. Student partners were initially reminded and re-introduced to relevant literature, in order to strengthen their understanding of core concepts and boost their confidence in dealing with subject specific topics. The initial team meeting allowed time and space for students to identify the "muddiest point" (that aspect of their understanding that seems to them to be the least clear) in the syllabus, which was narrowed down as being the design of effective interviews with the parents of a child. This did not come as a surprise to the teaching team. One of the learning outcomes of the Educational Psychology module relates to making effective choices when conducting interviews, and articulating a rationale for these choices. Also, the development of an interview schedule is part of the assessment for the module. However, even if the theoretical background is presented and explained, the existing learning design of the module did not appear to provide enough opportunities to plan and experiment with those choices. In other words, the student partners highlighted the need for more explicit connections between theory and practice for this particular area of their curriculum. According to the principles of constructive alignment introduced by Biggs (1996), the learning activity design should aim to facilitate and support students in working towards and successfully meet the learning outcomes set at modular level. Therefore, the teaching staff saw an opportunity here to implement and apply this principle to the Psychology curriculum.

The obvious challenge was then creating a working solution to address the issue, by crafting a safe learning environment, in which students on the module could make mistakes and learn from those mistakes. Practising with subjects in real life was not a viable and scalable option, given the level of study, the limited previous experience of students and ethical implications, which are specific to the subject area. At this level of study, it is not considered appropriate for Psychology students to find parents or carers of a child with learning difficulties, intellectual disabilities or Attention Deficit Hyperactivity Disorder or Autistic Spectrum Disorder and conduct a developmental history interview. This would require a lengthy process of institutional ethical clearance and approval, besides additional training, supervision, access to educational or clinical settings, and a process of risk management associated with the procedure of collecting information on sensitive topics. Undergraduate students usually do not have access to these resources and opportunities.

Two alternatives were identified: role-play and interactive case studies. One of the initial brainstorming meetings identified as a possible solution and potential outcome of the SAP project the creation of an interactive multimedia resource that would allow a student to explore all the stages involved in taking a clinical, assessment or developmental history interview. Embedding this resource in the Educational Psychology module would contribute to giving students an opportunity to both challenge their skills with a real-life case study and provide "exercise spaces", as described by Holtam (2015). The expected outcome would ultimately relate to the enhancement of the overall student experience and a further step towards a more constructively aligned curriculum (Biggs, 1996).

Co-creating the learning resource

As part of the assessment for the Educational Psychology module, students are required to produce a developmental history interview, write an educational psychological assessment report and justify the choices made in structuring the interview, with articulation of relevant theoretical frameworks. This type of assessment is practice-led and would ideally benefit students wanting to pursue a career as an educational or clinical psychologist. Following the summative assessment, students had an opportunity to receive feedback which would guide them in addressing further educational needs and contribute to strengthen their clinical and employability skills. However, the formative feedback and opportunities for reflection throughout the module were limited and probably not adequate for the development of these skills, which usually require clinical practice and exposure to real life situations. The student partners stressed the importance of the fact that the learning resource to be created had to address this weakness.

As the interactive case study approach seemed to be the preferred solution to try and address the issue, the learning technology team in CELT introduced both academic and student partners to an in-house technology solution known as Shareville, and openly available at http://shareville.bcu.ac.uk/index.php. Shareville provides simulations, interactive case studies and an explorative type of interface which resembles the real world. It hosts learning activities aimed at providing students with 'real-life' experiences of the kind that are difficult to provide in a traditional educational environment. The types of cases and real life scenarios which can be found in Shareville are varied and are crafted to support holistic learning experiences across the university.

The default workflow for the production of Shareville learning resources involves academic staff presenting a rough idea to learning technology developers, who then design and implement one or more ad-hoc interactive scenarios. Through the collaborative project described here, there was an opportunity to experiment with the empowerment of students as co-creators in most of the idea generation, planning and design of the interactive elements of a Shareville resource. A series of brain-storming sessions were put in place, letting both academic and student partners free to imagine what they would like to see and experience, as a concrete product of the collaboration. The brainstorming sessions were followed by a series of writing labs, where a few case-studies were co-drafted by student and academic partners. The case-studies detailed the context, realistic characters (i.e.: children, parents) and real-life situations (i.e.: pathologies, triggers, issues). These drafts were intended to inform the design of the learning resources and provide the necessary realism and context that the Shareville scenarios and simulations need to make the necessary impact. The term 'simulation' as applied to the field of education and training is a contested one and any definition offered is therefore only to be taken as convenient shorthand for the type of simulation being discussed in this work. Encyclopaedia Britannica defines simulation as, "a research or teaching technique that reproduces actual events and processes under test conditions," and notes that the word stems from the Latin word simulatio meaning 'an imitating or feigning'. Smith (1999:2) defines simulation as, *"the process of designing a model of a real or imagined system and conducting experiments with that model."* We would echo this view with the caveat that these 'experiments' relate to the application of prior learning by individual students to specific scenarios.

A question that is sometimes asked of this kind of simulation is, 'Aren't they just playing at it?' We would answer the implicit criticism by stating that there is no 'just' about it and that 'playing' in this context is as valid a usage here as it is in early years education (Moyles, 2010). Indeed, the convergence of simulation with computer technology is probably most easily identified in the 'Serious Games' movement. The concept of using a game (which Clark Abt (1960), who first coined the phrase 'serious game', often used interchangeably with simulation) to support learning seems to fit in well with a constructivist epistemology and pedagogy. Dewey's ideas regarding 'active learners' (Schubert, 2005), Piaget's ideas about the need to modify and change environments to know them (Huitt & Hummel, 2003) and Bruner's insistence that learners find things out for themselves (Smith, 2002) can all be taken as key elements of serious games and simulations.

It was made clear to both student and academic partners, that the level of the details needed particular consideration in crafting characters and simulated scenarios. Therefore, providing insights from experiences in real clinical settings was the essential role of academic partners in facilitating student partner contributions to the case-studies. From the student perspective, they were contributing to the case-studies by highlighting those aspects of the subject area where further exemplification was required, and where the theoretical models could benefit from further links to the complexity of real-life contexts. The overall co-writing process followed an iterative dialogical approach, and contributions from both sets of partners were enriched at each revision point by individual partner's comments.

The student partners needed more guidance from the academic partners in the following stage of development of the learning resources, where multimedia scripts needed to be produced. The idea of an interactive interview was put forward, so a bank of questions had to be developed. These questions had to be based on the drafted case-studies and cover the areas of clinical practice, assessment and developmental history. The overall project would include three phases: the scripting phase, where student and academic partners create the scenarios, the characters and the interview questions; the production phase, where the interactive interview learning resource is set-up and implemented in the curriculum, and the evaluation phase.

At the time of writing, the scripting phase has been completed and the production phase is ongoing, under the supervision of the learning technology team in CELT that have highlighted the high quality of the case-study and multimedia script provided.

The ingredients of success

An institutional framework for staff-student partnership is definitely helpful in setting up co-creation projects and contribute in shaping motivations and the sense of community (Nygaard et al., 2013). Alternatively, students could be employed with temporary or ad-hoc contracts. In this case, leadership, authority and power issues must be carefully considered to avoid unhealthy imbalances which may harm co-operation (Bovill *et al.*, 2015). An ongoing dialogue with student partners is paramount. This would include aspects of the subject area, motivation and project aspirations in terms of learning and teaching practice. Relevant studies, research papers, lived experiences and real-life stories are helpful in inspiring the drafting of realistic case-studies, which are pertinent to identified area of the curriculum. Beyond the scripting, the implementation of the actual resource would require support from learning technology experts or instructional designers.

Outcomes

The student partners felt empowered in making an important contribution to the curriculum. As a result, there was an opportunity to positively impact on future student learning experiences. The variety of learning opportunities and teaching methodologies is often perceived as a de-facto offer in contemporary learning and teaching practice. However, if that innovation is largely a tutor-led one, the student voice may get lost in the process. The innovation described here is not only a response to student voice, but also the result of a staff-student partnership approach. Student partners have played an important role in shaping learning design which benefits their peers. This certainly constitutes a learning experience in itself, and perhaps it has provided opportunities for reflection, when considering how these students have contributed to the academic community of our university. For end user students, the outcomes of this partnership should positively impact on academic and employability skills. In particular, aims include the enhancement of student transition from the undergraduate to the postgraduate studies and life in practice by providing a 'flavour' into the applied aspects of qualified professional psychologists. Student partners reported that having a role in shaping aspects of the learning and teaching practice had a positive impact in their confidence in dealing with the actual subject area. They themselves appreciated the value of linking theory to practice, and made connections with other topics they have encountered in their current level of study. They become more engaged with the entire curriculum and their experience in the University. This acted as a motivator in deepening their research around their interests and they engaged more deeply in independent learning activities. They have also had a chance to appreciate some of the learning design processes, which go beyond the delivery of content and other learning activities within the face-to-face sessions.

Moving Forward

As the Shareville project is largely self-funded by CELT, resources are limited in scope. The design and production of innovative multimedia resources and simulation which are successfully embedded in the curriculum heavily relies in the academic staff being willing to experiment and try new learning design approaches. The collaboration project described here has paved the way for further meaningful collaborations with students, at different levels. In the first instance, being an active participant in the learning design experience, they can identify and highlight the areas of the curriculum which need further improvement. Additionally, they can also contribute ideas, perspectives and enthusiasm to the following stages of production and implementation of Shareville scenarios and simulations. Beyond these contributions, we aim to involve and empower students in evaluating the effectiveness of online problem-based learning and simulation, in a context in which time, expertise and other resource allocation needs to be fully justified.

Simulation type activities are most closely associated with military and medical training applications and have been for many years but, whilst there is an ever growing body of research literature surrounding the topic, many researchers in these fields have been cautious not to overstate the benefits and little controlled research identifying benefits in terms of learning gain have been carried out. In particular, there is criticism that, despite the obvious (and possibly superficial) links with constructivism as described above the literature lacks a strong theoretical background linked to a clear pedagogy that can establish, in principle as well as in practice, whether learning through simulation is a 'good thing'. In essence, the question has become 'whether, learning by simulation can become self-referential and offer a simulation of learning' (Bligh & Bleakley, 2006:606). Our research into the use of simulations, for example in the area of Initial Teacher Training (Lowe *et al.*, 2015), through Shareville have shown some marked improvements in student confidence and self-evaluation of skills development and we continue to both implement and research our use of simulated activity through Shareville with the desire to establish such a framework. However, more research is necessary to assess the value of these efforts, and we believe that students can be involved as co-researchers and add depth to this explorative inquiry.

About the Authors

Dario Faniglione is Senior Lecturer in Learning and Teaching Practice at Birmingham City University. He can be contacted at this e-mail: dario. faniglione@bcu.ac.uk

Olga Fotakopoulou is Senior Lecturer in Developmental Psychology at Birmingham City University. She can be contacted at this e-mail olga. fotakopoulou@bcu.ac.uk

Dr Graham Lowe is Head of Learning and Teaching Practice at Birmingham City University. He can be contacted at this e-mail: graham. lowe@bcu.ac.uk

Bibliography

Abt, C. C. (1970). *Serious games*. New York, Viking Press.

BCU (2015). *Core Value Frameworks*. Online resources http://www.bcu.ac.uk/ Download/Asset/213421b3-a41d–4163-b9d0–5516fe8d6122 [Accessed on May 11, 2016]

Biggs, J. (1996). Enhancing Teaching through Constructive Alignment. *Higher Education*, Vol. 32, No. 3, pp. 347–364.

Biggs, J. & C. Tang (2011). *Teaching for quality learning at university*. Berkshire: McGraw- Hill.

Bligh, J. & A. Bleakley (2006). Distributing menus to hungry learners: can learning by simulation become simulation of learning? *Medical Teacher*, Vol. 28, No. 7, pp. 606–613.

Bovill, C.; A. Cook-Sather & P. Felten (2011). Students as co-creators of teaching approaches, course design and curricula: Implications for academic developers. *International Journal for Academic Development*, Vol. 16, No. 2, pp. 133–145.

Bovill, C.; A. Cook-Sather; P. Felten; L. Millard & N. Moore-Cherry (2015). Addressing potential challenges in co-creating learning and teaching: overcoming resistance, navigating institutional norms and ensuring inclusivity in student–staff partnerships. *Higher Education*, pp. 1–14.

Carey, P. (2013). Student as co-producer in a marketised higher education system: A case study of students' experience of participation in curriculum design. *Innovations in Education and Teaching International*, Vol. 50, No. 3, pp. 250–260.

Holtham, C. (2015). Towards New Genres for 21st Century Business School Case Studies. In N. Courtney; C. Poulsen & C. Stylios (Eds.), *Case Based Teaching and Learning for the 21ˢᵗ Century*, Oxfordshire: Libri Publishing Ltd., pp. 121–135.

Huitt, W. & J. Hummel (2003). Piaget's theory of cognitive development. *Educational Psychology Interactive*. Valdosta, GA: Valdosta State University.

Lowe, G.; D. Faniglione; M. Hetherington & L. Millard (2015). Real World Cases in Virtual Environments. In N. Courtney; C. Poulsen & C. Stylios (Eds.), *Case Based Teaching and Learning for the 21ˢᵗ Century*, Oxfordshire: Libri Publishing Ltd., pp. 199–220.

Mann, S. J. (2008). *Study, power and the university*. Maidenhead: Open University Press.

Moyles, J. (2010). *The excellence of play*. Maidenhead. Maidenhead: Open University Press.

Nygaard, C.; S. Brand; P. Bartholomew & L. Millard (2013). *Student engagement: identity, motivation and community*. Oxfordshire: Libri Publishing Ltd.

Reddy, P. & E. Moores (2012). Placement year academic benefit revisited: effects of demographics, prior achievement and degree programme. *Teaching in Higher Education*, Vol. 17, No. 2, pp. 153–165.

Schubert, W. (2005). Active learning as reflective experience. In D. Breault & R. Breault, *Experiencing Dewey: Insights for today's classroom*. Indianapolis: Kappa Delta Pi.

Smith, M. K. (2002). Jerome S. Bruner and the process of education. *The encyclopedia of informal education*.

Smith, R. D. (1999). Simulation: The engine behind the virtual world. *Simulation 2000*, Vol. 1.

Introduction to Authentic Learning – Environments, Experiences and Field Work

Susan Benvenuti, Sami Heikkinen, Tiffany Ip & Zeinab Younis

Introduction

Current demands of higher education include the requirement that students enter the working world with the knowledge and skills needed to support employability. This means that learning outcomes defined by universities need to focus both on developing knowledge and the skills needed to apply the knowledge in its appropriate context (Bransford *et al.*, 1990). Previous studies (e.g., Brown 1997) suggest that students need to be exposed to authentic learning situations in order to be able to apply theoretical knowledge in context to create real meaning and learning.

A further reason to engage in authentic learning practices is the potential to increase student motivation for deeper engagement with the learning activities (Ames, 1992). Vroom's expectancy theory (1964) as applied to the educational setting talks to the idea of students responding to educational practices that are seen as manageable, likely to yield anticipated results, and offering valuable outcomes for them. By creating authentic learning experiences for students, the various authors in this section hope to demonstrate the relevance of the curriculum to students and thereby raise the level of motivation for deeper and more sustained engagement.

In this introduction we briefly discuss the concepts, origins and some practices relating to authentic learning, particularly those which are used by the various authors to create the authentic learning environments and experiences.

Authentic learning

Authentic learning and the concepts of authentic learning environments and authentic learning tasks emerged originally from Lave & Wenger's (1991) work on situated learning, as well as work done by Brown *et al.* (1989) and Collins *et al.* (1989) on theorising apprenticeships for application to teaching and learning in higher education. Collins (1988:2) defined situated learning as: "...*the notion of learning knowledge and skills in contexts that reflect the way the knowledge will be useful in real life.*", while Brown *et al.* (1989) described situated cognition as learning within a context that reflects both the social and physical environment in which it will be later be applied. Lave & Wenger's (1991) work on "legitimate, peripheral participation" looks at the role of the guide or master in shaping the gradual learning experience of the apprentice as they progress from limited participation on the periphery of a "community of practice" to full engagement in the activities of the working community. Herrington (2006) summarised characteristics of situated learning environments drawn from previous research in the field:

+ authentic context;

+ authentic activities;

+ modelled examples of expert performances, ways of thinking and processes;

+ varied roles and perspectives;

+ collaborative knowledge construction;

+ reflection;

+ articulation;

+ coaching and scaffolding;

+ authentic assessment.

The innovative practices described in this section of the handbook use various tools, techniques or methods through which to support authentic learning. The focus varies in terms of emphasis on authenticity of the environment, the learning tasks or as an overall authentic learning experience. The following sections discuss some of these approaches.

Project-based learning

Project-based learning is commonly defined as a teaching method in which students gain knowledge and skills by working for an extended period of time to investigate and respond to an engaging and complex question, problem, or challenge (Blumenfeld et al., 1991). This method is regarded as both authentic and student-directed. Project-based learning requires the completion of an end product, which, according to Blumenfeld et al. (1991), drives the learning process and provides an authentic purpose for engaging in the project work. With teacher guidance, students aim to produce real-world products or projects (Harwell, 1997; Larmer & Mergendoller, 2011). When students are allowed to make choices, monitor their progress and reflect upon their work in a contextualized environment, they become more strategic and metacognitive. Benvenuti's chapter in this section demonstrates how students are encouraged to set their own individual learning goals and to reflect on their progress and achievement. Students are found to be able to apply the skills they have learnt from the project-based learning experience to other situations. Students gain deeper understanding of content – acquired from not only the traditional forms of instruction but hands-on work as well – with the most significant gains often found among lower achieving students (Barron & Darling-Hammond, 2008).

Researchers have warned that this approach can be difficult to implement and might be *much more complex than teachers' direct transmission of knowledge to students via textbooks or lectures* (Barron & Darling-Hammond, 2008:53). Teachers may encounter various obstacles such as having limited time teaching and preparing all the possible materials for the project. Some teachers might simply find it difficult to give up control and let students take control instead. However, formal classroom instruction alone does not necessarily result in effective learning, because the learner is ultimately the one who is in charge of the natural learning process. A capacity to initiate and manage one's own learning is equally, or even more, essential. This echoes the centrality of the constructivist paradigm. In accordance with the view that *"knowledge cannot be taught but must be constructed by the learner"* (Candy, 1991:252), learning is most effectively achieved when students actively participate in and assume control of their own learning process, during which teachers provide more facilitation and guidance than lecturing. Project-based learning becomes an increasingly favorable instructional approach since it under-lies student's engagement in the ongoing process of education.

Learning in teams

Project-based learning generally happens in groups. Hackman (1990) suggests that working in groups requires a special skill set. Dedicated groups for single projects are often called teams. A team is a group of people with different skills and different tasks, who work together on a common project, service, or goal, with mutual support. The purpose, mission, or main objective has to be known and understood by all team members. Teams are effective once communication within the team is open, direct and honest.

To achieve their goals, teams need sufficient leadership skills. Teams must evaluate their performance in order to identify developmental needs and to make action plans to achieve them. There should also be an agreed organisational structure to the team. Teams cannot achieve their goals if they have insufficient resources for the task. Resources include skills, tools, facilities and budget. When teams work properly there exists synergy, so the team performs in a way that is greater than the sum of its parts (Hackman, 1990).

Teams can also be used as a tool for learning. Michaelsen *et al.* (1982) propose that team-based learning is a process-driven way of learning, happening in three stages of a cycle: preparation, in-class readiness assurance testing and application-focused exercise. According to Michaelsen and Richards (2005) team-based learning implementation is based on four underlying principles:

* teams should be intentionally formed to support learning outcomes;

* students are accountable for their pre-learning and for working in teams;

+ team assignments should promote both learning and team development;

+ teams should receive frequent and immediate feedback.

Interdisciplinary and multicultural teams

Derry & Schunn (2005) propose that solving complex problems often requires teams with participants from multiple disciplines. Universities are therefore developing cross-disciplinary programs as seen in Heikkinen and Ahonen's chapter or even cooperation between universities as can be found in Ip's chapter. Knowledge diversity has been identified as a positive factor in team innovation (Mannix & Neale, 2005). Interdisciplinary knowledge transfer increases the chances of efficient knowledge utilization for innovation (Seufert et al., 1999; Szeto, 2000). This can further be understood as an enabling platform for radical innovation (Malerba, 2002).

Frequent and voluntary interaction within groups results in sharing and discussing ideas, opinions and perspectives. This has been shown to directly affect the occurrence of innovation (Drach-Zahavy & Somech, 2001). The voluntary interaction requires good team dynamics; therefore team building must be done carefully, fostering relationships between team members. Nonaka & Takeuchi (1995) explain that the superiority of the Japanese continuous innovation approach has been due to their strong emphasis on socialisation (i.e. sharing tacit knowledge directly) and internalisation (i.e. individuals' own participation in learning-by-doing). This requires collaboration between different participants. The same aspect should be taken into account when universities are designing their own authentic learning activities.

Paletz & Schunn (2010) developed a social-cognitive framework for interdisciplinary team innovation. They found that effective cooperation requires shared mental models, knowledge diversity, formal roles, communication norms and cognitive processes. Shared mental models refer to convergent thinking needed for creative solutions for existing problems. This includes not only explicit knowledge but also implicit knowledge such as heuristics and unspoken assumptions about a given scientific or technological field. Knowledge diversity offers a broader base of information to be shared but also offers conflicting and contradictory norms and assumptions regarding what might be considered optimal solutions or normal work practices. Information about the tasks, roles, and processes of the team itself should also be shared with team members, otherwise knowledge diversity would simply result in a collection of diverse mental models. Shared conceptions of team roles are the key to coordinating activities and thus the key to performance. Assigning experts can help increase a group's likelihood of sharing unique information. The ideal zone in which multidisciplinary teams can work is the shared mental model trading zone based on a common understanding of the task and work. This does not mean that each individual becomes an expert in each other's domain, but that enough of a shared language exists to facilitate team work.

Prohl (1997) undertook a literature review of 26 articles published between 1992 and 1995, noting that the definitions of an effective team share five characteristics that can also be thought of as requirements for effective multi-disciplinary cooperation: shared identity, common goal, interdependence, personal interaction, and mutual influence.

There are also several reasons why interdisciplinary cooperation might fail to achieve a team's goals (Lencioni, 2002). These include absence of trust, fear of conflict, search for artificial harmony rather than constructive debate, lack of commitment and avoidance of responsibility. To overcome these challenges teams need to work together for some time, otherwise it is not possible to achieve the effective working phases presented in Tuckman & Jensen's (1977) model of team development phases. The performing phase is the fourth stage of team operation, which follows forming, storming and norming.

As universities continue to attract foreign students, many courses will include teams that are multicultural. Further, as will be seen in Ip's chapter, teams may be multicultural in nature by design. If this is the case, cultural factors have to be considered during facilitation. According to Hofstede et al. (2010) these include power distance, individualism, masculinity, uncertainty avoidance, long-term orientation and indulgence. Cultural background can determine how individuals perform their role in a team.

Student peer assessment and reflective learning

Wherever teamwork is involved, peer assessment is important to establish contribution levels by individual student team members. This helps to reduce occurrences of social loafing or dominance by individuals, and provides students with some degree of control. Peer assessment is also grounded in active learning. While there are many issues linked to student peer assessment (Falchikov & Goldfinch, 2000), learning to make informed judgements on student work is in itself a valuable learning opportunity (Boud, 1988). Software tools such as the Comprehensive Assessment of Team Member Effectiveness (CATME) tool can help lecturers manage student peer assessment within teams, as done by Benvenuti in her work (www.catme.org).

Closely linked to the idea of student peer assessment is the concept of reflective learning, usually by individual students on their own learning and the learning process. According to Boyd & Fales (1983) reflective learning is the process of internally examining and exploring an issue of concern, triggered by an experience, which creates and clarifies meaning in terms of self, and which results in a changed conceptual perspective. Furthermore, they suggest that this process is central to understanding the experiential learning process. Gibbs (1988) proposes that effective learning requires reflection on the learning process, otherwise the learning is soon forgotten. Besides the knowledge, the feelings and thoughts that emerge are valuable in making the learning outcomes a part of the personal learning continuum.

Employability and graduateness

Universities preparing undergraduate students for the workplace need to consider broader issues than simply disciplinary knowledge. Graduates need to compete for job opportunities in a potentially saturated market that needs innovative ideas and work-place skills. Gaps between theory and field work practice on the one hand, and employers' criticism of higher institutions for failing to produce the sets of skills needed by these students to face global market challenges on the other, suggest that more authentic approaches to learning and teaching have merit.

Lankard (1990) defines employability as the set of transferable skills needed by students to make them employable. Universities are therefore increasingly focusing on the development of soft skills or transferable skills. These skills include communication, interpersonal skills, problem solving, self-motivation, team building, adaptability, managing diversity and negotiation. These skills were further developed by Bagshaw (1997) under an umbrella of flexibility and adaptation, as one of the pillars of attributes that ensures employability.

Glover *et al.* (2002) and Yorke (2004) regard graduateness as consisting of three types of graduate attributes: field specific, generic and shared achievements. The first refers to the possession of the body of knowledge particular to the field of study, and the other two to the possession of generic attributes relevant to most graduates whether from shared achievement or generically on the level of most graduates. Graduateness can be seen as a subset of employability as it considers student attributes related to the university degree, not the other sets of skills or aspects linked to achieve employability. Bell (1996) and Walker (1995) advocate that tension might arise between graduateness as a state after the completion of a course and employability as an assessment of the value of the student economically in the market.

All four chapters in this section use innovations and methods that take cognisance of issues of graduateness and employability. Ahonen & Heikkinen's chapter presents ways in which students can become familiar with starting up new a business venture. This is especially important for business students, as it helps them to understand the overall context which they will face after graduation. Ip's chapter discusses an innovative practice which aims to develop not only student academic writing skills but transferable social and communication skills useful in any professional situations. Benvenuti's chapter specifically focuses on demonstrating what future employers will be looking for in graduates, and asking students to focus on developing some of these skills in a self-directed personal development portfolio. Finally, Younis's chapter talks about the multiple tools that enhance the transfer of knowledge from theory to practice to prepare students for future employment opportunities.

Introduction to the chapters using practice

In various ways, the innovative practices adopted by authors in this section of the handbook all attempt to support student learning by providing a guided or facilitated learning environment in which students are engaged in activities which are either situated in real-world contexts, draw the real-world into the classroom or are the kinds of activities that they will one day undertake in the work environment. In this way, all seek authenticity in some form to support teaching and learning outcomes that focus on developing usable knowledge that is directly applicable to context-based practice and graduate employability.

In Chapter 18, Ahonen & Heikkinen focus on developing and testing business ideas. This is a method used to demonstrate to business students what kind of aspects they have to consider when creating new business ideas. The method aims to create an authentic learning experience for students. The authentic experience creates strong memories which can be used later in their studies as a framework for knowledge to be attached into. Simultaneously it is offering the students opportunities to identify their own strengths and become familiar with their fellow students.

In Chapter 19, Tiffany Ip introduces the innovative teaching and learning practice designed for an academic writing course. Students experience a complete, systematic and authentic research process organized according to the project-based learning approach. The process is achieved through an inter-university collaboration. Students in small teams collect data relevant to any social issues of their own interest. The data are used to generate two outcomes – an academic research paper for students of one university and a business plan for students of the other university. With this practice students develop hands-on research skills and learn academic literacy more effectively. The collaborative experience also enhances their social and communication skills through working in multidisciplinary and multicultural teams.

In Chapter 20, Zeinab Younis describes an actual experience of the multiple tools that are used to ensure the transfer of knowledge from theory to practical field work application. The tools are used in the British University in Egypt where a variety of modules are taught in the Business Department to ensure meeting the intended learning outcomes and developing transferable skills in order to ensure a high degree of employability in the market. The intention is to prepare graduates for both local and international employment through the application of several methods in the course of their higher education at university.

Susan Benvenuti in Chapter 21 describes an approach to curriculum design and implementation that encompasses not only consideration of what students need to know and be able to do, but a broader view that looks at the context in which they will one day need to do it. Learning outcomes for the courses include a focus on the personal attributes and values related to students' future careers, and an aspect of self-directed learning in which students define their own specific learning outcomes and ways in which to develop these. By strongly emphasizing the relevance of the curriculum to their future desired careers, it is hoped that high student engagement over a sustained period of time will be encouraged.

About the Authors

Susan Benvenuti is a lecturer in Information Systems and Assistant Dean for Teaching and Learning in the Faculty of Commerce, Law and Management, at the University of the Witwatersrand, Johannesburg, South Africa. She can be contacted at this e-mail: susan.benvenuti@wits.ac.za

Sami Heikkinen is senior lecturer at Lahti University of Applied Sciences. He can be contacted at this e-mail: sami.heikkinen@lamk.fi

Dr. Tiffany Ip was Postdoctoral Fellow in the Centre for Applied English Studies at University of Hong Kong and is now a lecturer at Hong Kong Baptist University. She can be contacted at this e-mail: tiffip@hkbu.edu.hk

Dr. Zeinab Younis is currently the head of the Center of Innovation, Governance and Green Economy; General Business Specialisation Coordinator and lecturer at the Business Department, Faculty of Business Administration, Economics and Political Science at the British University in Egypt. She can be contacted at this e-mail: zeinab.younis@bue.edu.eg

Bibliography

Ames, C. (1992). Classrooms: Goals, structures, and student motivation. *Journal of educational psychology*, Vol. 84, No. 3, pp. 261–281.

Bagshaw, M. (1997). Employability- creating a contract of mutual investment. *Industrial and Commercial Training*, Vol. 27, No. 6, pp. 187–189.

Barron, B. & L. Darling-Hammond (2008). How can we teach for meaningful learning? In L. Darling-Hammond (Ed.), *Powerful learning: What we know about teaching for understanding*. San Francisco: Jossey-Bass, pp. 11–70.

Bell, J. (1996). *Graduateness: some early thoughts*. Paper to Given Credit Network Leeds.

Blumenfeld, P. C.; P. Soloway; R. W. Marx; J. S. Krajcik; M. Guzdial & A. Palincsar (1991). Motivating project-based learning: Sustaining the doing, supporting the learning. *Educational Psychologist*, Vol. 26, pp. 369–398.

Boud, D. (Ed.) (1988). *Developing student autonomy in learning*. London: Kogan Page.

Boyd, E. M. & A. W. Fales (1983). Reflective learning key to learning from experience. *Journal of Humanistic Psychology*, Vol. 23, No. 2, pp. 99–117.

Bransford, J. D.; R. D. Sherwood; T. S. Hasselbring; C. K. Kinzer & S. M. Williams (1990). Anchored instruction: Why we need it and how technology can help. In D. Nix & R. Spiro (Eds.), *Cognition, education and multimedia: Exploring ideas in high technology*. Hillsdale, NJ: Lawrence Erlbaum, pp. 115–141.

Brown, A. L. (1997). Transforming schools into communities of thinking and learning about serious matters. *American Psychologist*, Vol. 52, No. 4, pp. 399–413.

Brown, J. S.; A. Collins & P. Duguid (1989). Situated cognition and the culture of learning. *Educational Researcher*, Vol. 18, No. 1, pp. 32–42.

Candy, P.C. (1991). *Self-direction for lifelong learning*. San Francisco: Jossey-Bass.

Collins, A. (1988). *Cognitive apprenticeship and instructional technology* (Technical Report No. 6899): BBN Labs Inc., Cambridge, MA.

Collins, A.; J. S. Brown & S. E. Newman (1989). Cognitive apprenticeship: Teaching the crafts of reading, writing, and mathematics. In L. B. Resnick (Ed.), *Knowing, learning and instruction: Essays in honour of Robert Glaser*. Hillsdale, NJ: LEA, pp. 453–494.

Derry, S. J. & C. D. Schunn (2005). Introduction to the study of interdisciplinarity: A beautiful but dangerous beast. In S. J. Derry; C. D. Schunn & M. A. Gernsbacher (Eds.), *Interdisciplinary collaboration: An emerging cognitive science*. Mahwah, NJ: Erlbaum, pp. xiii–xx.

Drach-Zahavy, A. & A. Somech (2001). Understanding team innovation: The role of team processes and structures. *Group Dynamics: Theory, Research, and Practice*, Vol. 5, No. 2, p. 111–123.

Falchikov, N. & J. Goldfinch (2000). Student peer assessment in higher education: A meta-analysis comparing peer and teacher marks. *Review of Educational Research*, Vol. 70, No. 3, pp. 287–322.

Gibbs, G. (1988). *Learning by doing: A guide to learning and teaching methods.* Birmingham: Sced.

Glover, D.; S. Law & A. Youngman (2002). Graduateness and Employability: Student Perceptions of the personal outcome of university education. *Research in Post-compulsory education*, Vol. 7, No. 3, pp. 293–306.

Hackman, J. R. (Ed.) (1990). *Groups That Work (and Those That Don't): Creating Conditions for Effective Teamwork.* San Francisco: Jossey-Bass.

Harwell, S. (1997). Project-based learning. In W. E. Blank & S. Harwell (Eds.), *Promising Practices for Connecting High School to the Real World.* Washington, DC: Office of Vocational and Adult Education, pp. 23–30.

Herrington, J. (2006). *Authentic e-learning in higher education: Design principles for authentic learning environments and tasks.* Proceedings of E-Learn: World Conference on E-Learning in Corporate, Government, Healthcare, and Higher Education, Chesapeake, Va, pp. 3164–3173.

Hofstede, G. H.; G. J. Hofstede & M. Minkov (2010). *Cultures and Organizations: Software of the Mind: Intercultural cooperation and its importance for survival.* New York: McGraw Hill.

Lankard, B. A. (1990). *Employability: the fifth basic skill.* Eric Digest, Washington, department of education.

Larmer, J. & J. R. Mergendoller (2011). *The main course, not dessert. How are students reaching 21st century goals? With 21st century project-based learning.*

Larmer, J., & Mergendoller, J. R. (2011). The main course, not dessert. Buck Institute for Education. Retrieved from http://bie. org/object/document/main_course_not_dessert

Lave, J. & E. Wenger (1991). *Situated learning: Legitimate peripheral participation.* Cambridge: Cambridge University Press.

Lencioni, P. (2002). *The five dysfunctions of a team.* San Francisco, CA: Jossey-Bass.

Malerba, F. (2002). Sectoral Systems of Innovation and Production, *Research Policy*, Vol. 31, No. 2, pp. 247–264.

Mannix, E. & M.A. Neale (2005). What differences make a difference? The promise and reality of diverse teams in organizations. *Psychological Science in the Public Interest*, Vol. 6, No. 2, pp. 31–55.

Michaelsen, L. K.; W. E. Watson; J. P. Cragin & L. D. Fink (1982). Team-based learning: A potential solution to the problems of large classes. *Exchange: The Organizational Behavior Teaching Journal,* Vol. 7, No. 4, pp. 18–33.

Michaelsen, L. & B. Richards (2005). Drawing conclusions from the team-learning literature in health-sciences education: A commentary. *Teaching and Learning in Medicine: An International Journal,* Vol. 17, No. 1, pp. 85–88.

Nonaka, I. & H. Takeuchi (1995). *The Knowledge-Creating Company: How Japanese Companies Create the Dynamics of Innovation.* New York: Oxford University Press.

Paletz, S. B. F. & C. D. Schunn (2010). A Social-Cognitive Framework of Multidisciplinary Team Innovation. *Topics in Cognitive Science,* Vol. 2, pp. 73–95.

Prohl, R. (1997). Enhancing the effectiveness of cross-functional teams. *Team Performance Management,* Vol. 3, No. 3, pp. 137–149.

Seufert, A.; G. Krogh & A. Back (1999). Towards Knowledge Networking. *Journal of Knowledge Management,* Vol. 3, pp. 180–190.

Szeto, E. (2000). Innovation capacity. *The TQM Magazine,* Vol. 12, No. 2, pp. 149–157.

Tuckman, B. W. & M. A. C. Jensen (1977). Stages of small group development revisited. *Group and Organizational Studies,* Vol. 2, pp. 419–427.

Vroom, V. H. (1964). Work and motivation. Oxford, England: Wiley.

Walker, L. (1995). *Institutional change towards an ability based curriculum in higher education.* Sheffield: Employment department.

Yorke, M. (2004). *Employability in higher education; what it is and what it is not,* Higher Education Academy: Esect, Edinburgh.

Chapter 18: Authentic Learning

Integration Method to Create Innovative Business Ideas and to Learn Multicultural Team Working Skills

Tarja (Terry) Ahonen & Sami Heikkinen

Background

In the beginning of their studies, novice students traditionally sit through a week long orientation program, listening to lectures – morning and afternoon – relating to the practicalities of their degree programs. After orientation they begin different courses of their studies – separately, in their own degree program groups. The orientation programs focus on supplying the newbie students with as much information as possible, in as short a time as possible. The roles are traditional: teachers as lecturers lecturing material and the students as listeners. This does not however lead into expected results. Students quickly forget parts of the information given and become frustrated already in the beginning of their studies. With the new method presented, there is active learning in the beginning and the roles of the participants have changed. The teachers are facilitators and supervisors while the students are the active participants. The implemented method encourages students, coming from different degree programs and different cultures, to innovate and create together. In addition, the method aims to integrate the students into their studies.

The Practice

The implemented method is targeted for first year business students. The method involves setting up and running a new venture at a trade fair. The target of the method is to have students experience actual business operations right from the beginning of their studies – thus, giving them an opportunity to experience authentic fieldwork business in practice. Furthermore, the project aimed to help students – coming from two different degree programs and from different countries – learn skills in team working and working in a multicultural environment, learn the basics of start-up development, become acquainted with each other, and encourage social networking between the students in order to help them develop a close connection to each other.

With this method, the students – throughout the whole project – are integrating, are learning to work together regardless of differences in cultural backgrounds, are making decisions, and are implementing their choices – and all outside of a regular classroom. What is more, the project leaves permanent memories for students. This includes both mistakes and successes. When the same topics are later faced during the studies, there is a personal reference point available which can be used to connect the theoretical concepts into the real world that is actual for each and every student.

To succeed in the project, the students need a good understanding on working in multicultural teams, generating business ideas and idea generation methods. These should be taught to students before they can start working on their project. These are also skills that are included in the curriculum and especially these skills are needed in working life. The experience and knowledge are tightly connected as in the model of experiential learning (Kolb & Fry, 1975).

Process

The method starts with preparatory lectures concerning the principles of business development, business idea (Osterwalder & Pigneur, 2013), idea generation, and multicultural team working (Hall, 1959; Hall, 1977; Hofstede *et al.*, 2010; Kaplan, 1966; Loughborough University, 2015). In this setting, the project started on Wednesday. Preparatory lectures took four hours. This is the only lecture part of the entire project. It is strongly recommended that the students receive learning material that they could use throughout the project to better develop their ideas further. The material given, in this case, was partly in the form of videos, partly in written documents, and partly in PowerPoint lecture material.

After the lectures the students are divided into prearranged multi-cultural groups. Each group includes students from both degree programs, i.e., International Trade and International Business. The nationalities are divided equally in the teams. This ensures not only gaining cultural competence – understanding how working is different in multi-cultural teams – but the different backgrounds also help the students find more innovative initiatives for their venture. In these groups, the students have exactly one-week time to plan, prepare, and implement their project.

After the division students get to know their team mates. This is done via group discussions, based on pre-arranged discussion questions. One of the first tasks is to create a business-related name for their group. Once the business name is created the students need to brainstorm what product or service they would create and sell at a business exhibition. The product or service could be anything that meets the needs of prospective customers and is legally approved of – either tangible or intangible. The student teams get the first evening of the first project day to consider their product ideas. The ideas of groups' chosen products or services is then presented to the rest of the groups in class the following day. This gives students a glimpse on the presentation skills they will need later on during the project. Each team needs to present three prioritized product ideas to the rest of the teams during the first milestone, on Thursday. This practice allows the elimination of any overlapping of product or service ideas. This also ensures that the competition is not too fierce. In addition, this allows the teams more opportunities on being successful at the trade fair.

Once the ideas are approved, each group creates a project plan. This will ensure that they are taking all the necessary actions required on making the project successful. The project plan should include the tasks the groups have to do before the trade fair, responsibilities of the group members, scheduling and budgeting, and other practicalities such as transporting of their goods to the venue (e.g. Turner, 2014). The project plan needs to be approved by the supervising facilitators before the groups can proceed with their plans.

Each group is given 50 Euro as their budget, to cover the expenses incurred in the implementation of their product or service, such as raw material costs and other costs. After the event, the groups are required to pay the 50 euros back. Any profit they attain from their sales, they are allowed to keep. As the project is a competition – thus practicing real business life – the group earning the most profit is declared the winning team and is awarded.

Project guidance is arranged in forms of milestones. There are four milestones throughout the project. The milestones are utilized to ensure the progression of the project and the development of the business ideas, i.e., keeping students on track with the schedule, as well as to support the students throughout the project and helping them solve any problems or questions they may have with the project or with their group members. Also, with the milestones the project facilitators can give guidance, tips and hints as well as steer the progress of the project in the correct direction.

There is one milestone (compulsory and voluntary) arranged for each day of the project – with prearranged time slots for each group. The second milestone, arranged on Friday, is voluntary. The groups need to participate in this second milestone only if they face problems or have questions which they cannot find answers to, themselves. The third milestone (Monday) and the fourth milestone (Tuesday) are mandatory. For both of these, 15–20 minutes time were reserved for each group for guidance.

The day before the trade fair, in this setting Tuesday, the students need to visit the venue. There they have to check the location of their booth and make preparations for the trade fair. In addition, before the trade fair the students need to organize the roles of each group member for the trade fair and consider the schedule for each group member so that everyone gets a chance to take coffee, lunch and bathroom breaks. They also need to plan the logistics of their project.

On the trade fair day, Wednesday in this setting, the students arrive to the venue at least an hour before the doors open. They make the final decorations and preparations of their booth. Once the doors are opened, they do their best to sell their product or service so to make as good sales as possible. The doors open to the public at 8 am and close at 4 pm.

Once the trade fair ends, the groups clear their booths at the venue. The sales' results of each group is also counted and the results are given to the project facilitators. All of the material, which each group brought to the venue, is also taken away from the site. Figure 1 illustrates the complete process.

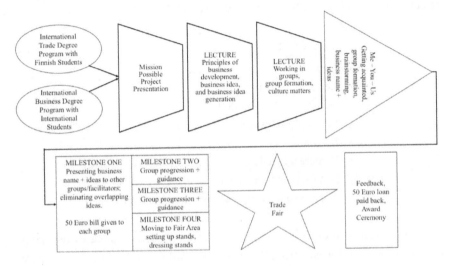

Figure 1: Process of method used.

The following day, the final compulsory session, a feedback meeting session is arranged. The groups are required to give feedback on the project. Also, the sales' results of each group is announced to the rest of the groups and the winning group is awarded.

Preparations

The method needs some preparation before it can be started. In box 1 these are presented. The method requires a group of students that have enough time available for the project. In this setting, one week was intensively and exclusively used for this project. This means that there were no other educational activities running during this week. The facilitators of this project also need one week's time to prepare and plan the project. Facilitators need to prepare the lecture materials, the schedule for the project and rehearsals for the groups to get familiar with each other. During and after the project the facilitators need sufficient time to take care of all matters relating to the project, e.g., attaining the 50 Euro per group budget money, arranging milestone spaces, arranging key and name tags to the trade fair venue, to other practicalities relating to the actual venue such as water posts and electrical outlets.

> Preparations (Box 1)
>
> • Clear the schedule of the students
> • Lecture material
> • Arrange budget for students
> • Make group division
> • Book a venue
> • Prepare schedule
> • Book stands at trade fair
> • Get prepared to help with marketing material

As well, a venue should be available, where the students can meet their prospective customers. This kind of venue could be e.g. trade fair, exhibition, marketplace or mall. It is important that there are plenty of people passing by the stands. The booking of the venue should be taken care of well in advance.

The groups need marketing material to promote the stands. The quality and quantity of the material depends greatly on the product or service the student groups are going to be offering to sell. Because the schedule is so tight, it would be a great help if there is already pre-negotiated prices for printing services available in the very beginning.

Stands as well as other needed trade fair facilities should be organized. This can be done by the university but in some cases it is possible to give this task to the students as well.

Starting capital is required also, and should be provided by the university. The money, a loan, is to be paid back to the university later, after the project is completed. But, it is required in the beginning in order for the project to be implemented and to succeed.

Outcomes

The students participating in the project were able to practice, in an authentic environment (see Lave & Wenger, 1991), what their studies will be teaching them. With the help of the project, the students have acquired skills that are beneficial in both their studies as well as the business world. For example, many of the students realized what they are really good at. Some students realized that they are good at selling things, others found out they are not so good but that they are good at planning or carrying out some other task required for the project. Also, many of the students expressed that they really learned to understand what is needed when a business is set up. Students also benefitted by creating social networks at the trade fair – when they were selling their products to other business employees/entrepreneurs, etc. And, the students learned how to contact companies to get support for their business ideas, sponsors etc. – selling skills for sure.

According to the feedback received, every single participating student was extremely satisfied with the project. Also, they expressed how exciting and educative it was to really learn what the business concept means for real. Furthermore, they emphasized how well they got to know each other throughout the implementation of this project. Completing the project in multicultural groups helped the students acquire skills in team working as well as cultural skills (see Hall, 1959; Hall, 1977; Hofstede *et al.*, 2010; Kaplan, 1966; Loughborough University, 2015). In addition, the students learned to make good use of the strengths of each team member. Other acquired skills included: leadership skills, socializing skills, time-management skills, entrepreneurship skills, sales and marketing skills, communication skills, and problem-solving skills.

Moving Forward

The execution of the project has been an interesting chance for both the students as well as the project facilitators. Furthermore, this project helped the students to integrate more quickly into their business studies. Once the student get their learning experience from the project, they remember it for a long time. This means that they have personal reference points, which can be used later on, e.g., when topics of various courses introduce further details of theoretical models. These models can then be connected with the personal memories of the students. This helps the teachers control the linkage between theory and practical experiences. Months after the project, students from both study groups, still maintain contact with each other as well as spend time together, both in the classroom as well as outside the classroom. Furthermore, working intensively, for one whole week with the newbie students allowed the facilitators to get to know the students well – thus really connecting with the students.

The university does have a new kind of learning environment in use by using this learning method. The authentic learning environment is more thrilling for students. This can be used as an advantage in promotion of the degree programs. Benefits contribute to the university level in this manner. The method used is going to be extended by using it in the orientation programs of student groups in future. The number of degree programs applying the method is increased. Thus, this type of student integration through involvement model is worth trying in other universities.

About the Authors

Tarja (Terry) Ahonen is senior lecturer at Lahti University of Applied Sciences. She can be contacted at this e-mail: tarja.ahonen@lamk.fi

Sami Heikkinen is senior lecturer at Lahti University of Applied Sciences. He can be contacted at this e-mail: sami.heikkinen@lamk.fi

Bibliography

Hall, E. T. (1959). *The Silent Language*. New York: Doubleday.
Hall, E. T. (1977). *Beyond Culture*. New York: Anchor Books.
Hofstede, G. H.; G. J. Hofstede & M. Minkov (2010). *Cultures and Organizations: Software of the Mind: Intercultural cooperation and its importance for survival*. New York: McGraw Hill.
Kaplan, R. B. (1966). *Cultural Thought Patterns in Inter-cultural Education*.
Kolb. D. A. & R. Fry (1975). Toward an applied theory of experiential learning. In C. Cooper (Ed.), *Theories of Group Process*. London: John Wiley.

Lave, J. & E. Wenger (1991). *Situated learning: Legitimate peripheral participation.* Cambridge: Cambridge University Press.

Loughborough University. (2015). *Working in Groups.*

Osterwalder, A. & Y. Pigneur (2013). *Business Model Generation: A Handbook for Visionaries, Game Changers, and Challengers.* New York: John Wiley & Sons.

Tuckman, B. (1965). Developmental sequence in small groups. *Psychological Bulletin*, Vol. 63, pp. 384–399. The article was reprinted in *Group Facilitation: A Research and Applications Journal*, No. 3, Spring 2001.

Turner, J. R. (2014). *The handbook of project-based management*, Vol. 92. McGraw-Hill.

Chapter 19: Authentic Learning

Teaching Academic Writing against the Grain: A project-based approach

Tiffany Ip

Background

The innovative teaching and learning practice is designed for a course titled "Dissertation Writing for Social Sciences". This is a credit-bearing English enhancement course at the University of Hong Kong (HKU), and was offered for the first time in the second semester of the 2014–15 academic year. The two sub-classes of the course are taught by the two investigators of the project respectively. The course objective is to prepare third-year students of Social Sciences (who are in a four-year degree program) to write a final-year dissertation with a research component. During the first launch students could only rely on imaginary data to write up their research reports. In response to student feedback about the difficulty of completing a dissertation without actual data, we therefore hope to make curriculum innovations and improve the course by giving students an opportunity to be involved in an authentic data collection process which is essential in actual research practice. This process is achieved through an inter-university collaboration in which the project-based learning approach is embedded.

Curriculum innovations are made for the second launch of this course (in the second semester of 2015–16 academic year) – by cooperating with Chung Ang University (CAU) in Seoul, Korea. Throughout the course HKU students experience a complete, systematic and authentic research process organised according to problem-based learning approach (Blumenfeld *et al.*, 1991) in terms of these four steps – Step 1) collaborate in small teams with CAU students to identify a research topic featuring social problems in Hong Kong and Seoul and design a research project; Step 2) do literature search; Step 3) collect and analyse data; and Step 4) write up an academic research paper in the form of a mini-dissertation. CAU students follow the first three steps, but with their focus on transforming the collected data to a business plan instead of a research report. In other words, the data are used to generate two outcomes – a research essay for students of HKU and a business plan for their CAU counterparts.

This teaching and learning practice marks significant differences from the traditional academic writing classes. In the traditional classes, students are taught to read and write in the style and register required for academic study. Emphasis tends to be placed on the writing process. Problems may arise because without having to conduct a full research study (probably due to time and resource constraints), students usually spend most of their time on literature review writing practices. The discussion section, although being a key component of most dissertations, remains a struggle for students. A dissertation demands the input of original work and student's new information or ideas within the chosen topic. Even though students may know all the principles in a writing class and become able to provide a constructive critical review of existing theories, they still do not have the experience of offering new viewpoints and presenting the findings from the data gathered by themselves. Furthermore, merely being introduced to the principles of academic writing does not make one a good writer, just as only reading published literature does not make one know what works and what fails to get published. The authentic experience of carrying out a real and complete research project empowers students to conduct research and write academic papers independently in the future – or at least in the short run they get more confident of producing their final-year dissertations.

On top of offering research and academic writing skills, this innovation which involves inter-university collorative work gives extra learning benefits for our HKU students as well. While business administration does not fall within social sciences in HKU, it is a major discipline in the Faculty of Social Sciences at CAU. Working with students of CAU allows HKU students to link their research ideas to a business context, seeing how a research idea may generate different possible applications although they are not directly involved in the final write-up of a business plan. A business plan is also a new writing genre which is not in the formal syllabus of our dissertation writing course, offering a great learning opportunity for HKU students. This is a point where knowledge transfer and exchange takes place (Seufert *et al.*, 1999; Szeto, 2000). Given the chance to engage in teamwork, students need to effectively interact with team members who share different academic and cultural backgrounds. Multidisciplinary and multicultural teamwork is prized in higher education, and could reap learning benefits for small groups (Guerin *et al.*, 2013) and even in short courses (Hazelton *et al.*, 2009). It is no easy task to come up with a project topic (from a broad array of possible alternative viewpoints) that interests all members and allows them to make use of their respective experiences and capabilities. In the process they learn to develop convergent thinking skills which allow them to speak in a common language and resolve conflicting ideas (Paletz & Schunn, 2010). Working in teams therefore not only gives them a chance to investigate a social problem that might be too complex for an individual, but develops transferable social and communication skills useful in professional situations (Jones, 2013).

The Practice

The participants in this project are 52 undergraduates: 28 from HKU and 24 from CAU from a range of academic disciplines. They are divided into 12 teams, each with a mix of students from both universities. Students of the two universities engage in a social venture project related to Hong Kong and Seoul in teams of four or five. On the basis of project-based learning, students worked in teams, selected a social problem shared by Hong Kong and Seoul, and embarked on an investigation of its seriousness with a dual aim – to take an evidence-based approach to studying problems, and to propose solutions.

What students do in different stages

At the first stage, HKU students start liaising with their research collaborators at CAU through video conferencing at the beginning of a course to brainstorm about a project topic, which is likely a social problem of common interest, ranging from education, cultural issues, nature and environment, to politics. During the second stage, students of the two universities get involved in face-to-face discussions and group presentations of initial project plans, when CAU students stay in Hong Kong for a week. HKU students need to explore how to effectively communicate with their Korean collaborators, and work together to decide how data are to be collected. For instance, they need to identify and access participants including the appropriate community stakeholders and the social groups they would like to target in their project for data collection. After the week, preparation work for research activities is mainly done through video conferencing before actual data collection takes place. The teams spend approximately one month fine-tuning their project ideas and collecting data in their own cities.

At the same time of collecting the data, HKU students need to write a literature review draft with a skeletal outline of what they have read and what they plan to write. This is, on the one hand, to ensure students have thoroughly reviewed current knowledge on the topic and placed their own projects within the context of previous, related research, and on the other, to see in which direction they are heading and whether they are on the right track. Upon receiving teacher feedback, students have the chance to modify the literature review which will be incorporated in their final research report. Guiding students through this process is crucial. Many novice writers regard literature review writing as one of the most difficult and time-consuming processes; but once they are able to construct a decent literature review section, other sections of the writing, all of which develop from the literature review, turn out to be relatively easy (Ip, 2016). The outline further makes a good head start on writing a full research report.

Using the same set of data, CAU students present their business ideas, and HKU students present their preliminary research findings at the third stage. The presentation is one of our course assessments since we hope students to be able to academically present research inquiries – not just in writing but orally as well – to an audience comprising people with or without knowledge of their own research area. During the process students give, receive, and use feedback to improve each other's work and are inspried by more ideas on proposing solutions to the social problems.

At the final stage of the project, HKU students each write an academic research report, which is another (and major) course assessment. HKU students are further encouraged to write a reflection on their project-based learning experiences, including but not limited to identifying their personal strengths and weaknesses, challenges encountered in the research work, issues related to intercultural communication, and insights gained from this international and collaborative experience.

What teachers do in different stages

We identify a university from another country for inter-university collaboration and have been liaising through e-mail with collaborators from CAU specialising in project-based learning since June 2015 – six months before the course. After finalising a project theme for students of both universities to investigate, we apply for project funding and arrange a week for students of the two universities to meet. A face-to-face meeting is not a must, but it allows for a chance to know each other better so that students can more easily decide on a topic and allocate responsibility. We also touch base with relevant organisations which can offer guest lectures and site visits for all students during that period.

During the face-to-face meetings, we organise an orientation session in which, following the team building activities, we give advice to students about how to formulate project plans and research questions, arrange logistics of data collection and conduct effective meetings. What students can produce at the end of the orientation is a preliminary research plan that includes the research aims, hypotheses or research questions, methods they would like to use to collect data, and the expected project outcomes. At the end of the week we meet with student teams to finalise their research plans, and also create and supervise an online platform (i.e., Moodle) to facilitate regular communication between students of the two universities. It is particularly important to have a shared database to store and share ideas after the week of face-to-face meetings when students return to their respective cities.

Our role is mainly advisory and facilitative at all stages – initiation, conduct and conclusion – leaving more scope for student centredness. During the preparation stage, i.e., the first stage, we prepare documents that clarify to students the project rationale and rundown of the project, and a statement of intent that helps students set a clear target for each phase of the project. In addition to providing students with feedback regarding their project plans to ensure they are feasible and researchable, we offer as many out-of-class learning activities as possible at the beginning of the course (e.g., site visits to catering ventures, including a café and a convenience store run by non-profit organisations working with the disabled, guest lectures by representatives from social enterprises explaining the start-up and operation of their enterprises and the challenges they have encountered, etc.) to make the project-based learning experience as gratifying as possible.

New and relevant course materials need to be created and blended with the project. Designing appropriate teaching and learning materials also helps provide the flexibility for a move away from pure lecturing to a more student-centred environment with continuous task-oriented interaction. In our first two lectures, we teach our students basic research skills and methodology and cover some skills in reviewing literature because students are required to decide on a project topic within a short period. These skills enable them to work more effectively of their own accord in the following months.

Students take an active role in data collection, but we nevertheless offer assistance to them if needs arise (such as suggesting names of non-governmental organisations or social enterprises they may explore and approach for research) during the second and third stages. Each team's project progress is monitored on a weekly basis. We give interim feedback (in the forms of both formal course assessment and informal tutorial discussions) at various stages – on their literature review drafts and on their oral presentations – and make suggestions for changes and improvements where necessary. We also provide specific guidelines to students for giving peer feedback when they present their preliminary findings halfway through the project.

When it comes to the final stage, we organise and summarise all the project outcomes and arrange for them to be disseminated. With the exchange of final products (i.e., academic research reports and business plans) students are enabled to see the flexible use of data to produce different written outcomes. In our case – as our main goal is to enhance students' academic writing skills – we focus more on demonstrating the contrasting features of different writing genres, and analysing the writing styles in the academic and professional contexts.

We address students' self-reported challenges and limitations encountered in this project according to what students write in the reflections. Quality research reports are selected and respective student authors are contacted to explore the possibility of disseminating their findings in academic seminars and/or academic journals.

In sum, throughout all three stages we facilitate different kinds of in-class and out-of-class learning activities, on top of teaching students academic writing skills during regular weekly lectures.

Outcomes

Inspired by a quote from Confucius: "I hear and I forget; I see and I remember; I do and I understand", we strongly believe our practice in the previous academic year of asking students to write a research report based on imaginary data is insufficient and less than desirable for their learning. As a result we make curriculum innovations by incorporating this project into the academic writing course so that students can activate their existing knowledge base and combine it with real-life issues. In the process of such integration, students develop their capability of academic writing as well. The fundamental aim of this innovative practice is to transform a conventional language course into one that places emphasis on authentic learning experience and application. The project serves as an anchor for and gradually permeates through students' writing experience. Write-up is only a part of the whole research process. The final written product produced by our HKU students is actually a lot more than a normal essay assignment. It requires a large amount of both independent and team efforts resulted from students undertaking their own fact-finding and analysis, from both library and internet resources and from gathering data empirically.

We examine students' perceived effectiveness and challenges of this teaching and learning practice by means of a post-course questionnaire survey and focus-group interviews. Results show that our students benefit a great deal from the following three areas, which are also the three intended learning outcomes of this innovative practice:

+ to learn academic literacy more effectively through using actual data and applying their knowledge in social sciences to their writing;

- to develop hands-on skills valuable in conducting research;

- to enhance social and communication skills through collaborating with team members of different cultural and academic backgrounds.

Learn academic literacy using actual data and prior knowledge

Researchers do not always have perfect data. Writing with reference to imaginary data is easier, but the gains are less substantial and students are probably unable to tackle actual data by this allegedly quicker mental route. Actual data gives students an opportunity to make connections with their prior knowledge. This can be used to reflect upon a topic that matters to them and consider its real life applications. Getting students to solve real life problems during their studies promotes important processes of knowledge application and restructuring, which in turn are essential for expertise development (Coombs & Elden, 2004). With actual data in hand, students are motivated to look for research papers that support both or even more sides of arguments and those that contradict their arguments in order to defend their conclusion. By so doing students truly learn how to interpret the data and develop the skills of problem solving and critical thinking. There is no better way than "learning to solve problems through the experience of solving problems" (Weaver, 1999 as cited in Helle *et al.*, 2006).

It is encouraging that students themselves see the value of learning academic writing with a real research project component: "*When using actual data, I have the incentive to observe and find out their patterns, whether or not they show a common or different direction. This helps me develop analytical skills. But writing based on imaginary data would only require make-up points and examples, which do not involve analytical exploration*". While the majority (84%) of students find their writing experience with actual data easier and more authentic, a few raise doubts as they deem it sufficient to use imaginary data to learn academic writing, which to them, is all about writing skills and style, They nonetheless acknowledge that the real research project component provides them with the hands-on experience of conducting research.

Student centredness emphasised in this course leaves plenty of room for students to use their prior knowledge and experience in a personally meaningful way. A student who examines the consumer buying behavior in the context of social enterprises utilises her knowledge of self-determination theory and theories of persuasion learnt in psychology classes. Another student applies her earlier skills of conducting comparative studies of Hong Kong and other cities on low fertility rate to this project, which she compares to the traffic safety issues in Hong Kong and Seoul.

Develop hands-on research skills

Often universities expect students to read and write academic papers as well as being able to give quality presentations without offering the hands-on training necessary to achieve these skills. Many Hong Kong English-as-a-Second-Language (ESL) learners, for example, indicate that their learning experience with English writing in school is highly word-level or sentence-level oriented with much less attention being paid to the development of appropriate discourse organisation (Ip & Lee, 2015). While they are expected to master how to write academically after several years in college, the truth is even graduate researchers still experience difficulties in writing for publication. Such difficulties include referencing published literature, structuring arguments, and textual organisation, in addition to many more discourse-level writing difficulties identified by Ip & Lee (2015). Some universities run a one-off technical course on how to write and present academically, but such introductory courses are usually of limited value as it tends to be too generic.

Of course it is a good idea to have academic writing courses at the undergraduate level, but it will be even better if they are available as part of a broader training programme. Training students to write a good essay does not necessarily enable them to write and work at a scholarly level. Such methods fail to let students have a taste of what works and what does not work to get a research project done. In our course students are inculcated with a research model by going through all the stages of a research process, from the very basics such as project topic and hypothesis formation to the development of a fully-fledged paper. Each step is carefully guided and critiqued. While experiencing setbacks and making countless modifications to the study design, students grow to understand it is not only about how they write, but also *why* they write. This is exactly what we aspire to achieve through the project-based learning approach: students acknowledge the presence of a problem, and seek ways to construct a final product which addresses the problem (Blumenfeld *et al.*, 1991).

A student comments that *"reading journal articles in the courses of my major (psychology) has given me an idea of what a dissertation is roughly like – the format, the content and the language style. This course however provides me with a much more solid idea of what exactly I should take note of"*. Another student thinks the failure experience is invaluable in that *"after experiencing the failure in making good hypotheses due to reviewing insufficient literature, I learn how to do a more comprehensive and critical literature review next time. I am more capable of anticipating problems regarding conducting research after this course. This will make me better prepared for writing a dissertation in the future"*. It is all very uplifting that 84% of students believe the course increases their confidence in writing a dissertation in their own disciplines, and all of them are convinced they can actually transfer the knowledge and experience obtained from this course to future writing.

Enhance transferrable social and communication skills

Students in this course play roles as co-teachers and learning partners for their peers. In most traditional courses students work with those within the same major(s) undertaking the same coursework. This limits the learning community and fails to represent what teamwork in real and professional life looks like. In modern working practices people of different backgrounds, beliefs and aspirations develop accountability and work together for a common cause by making the combined use of (interdisciplinary) knowledge and skills (Helle *et al.*, 2006). Higher education goes beyond creating and transmitting knowledge. This is one major reason why project-based learning – which makes possible the knowledge exchange capacity of individual and professional communities – tops the agenda (Eraut, 1985). Our course requires students to cooperate and collaborate with those possessing different discipline-specific knowledge and cultural backgrounds. When exchanging ideas and providing peer feedback they learn how to communicate with a lay audience or an audience outside of one's discipline. This forces them to thoroughly understand and break down some very complex scientific or theoretical principles when articulating their deliverables (in terms of research reports and oral presentations). The communication is not simply a one-way street. Our students benefit from understanding their Korean team members' business ideas generated from the same set of data, from which they also realise they are able to contribute to and complement each other's work. Not only do they learn what a business writing genre is like, many find the business plans impressive and express that they *"have never thought of such an innovative way to look at the topic"*.

Finally it is delightful to see that our students enjoy not only the knowledge exchange but also the cultural exchange with the Korean team members both during and outside of the class time; and in the meanwhile, discover themselves and learn more about their personal strengths and weaknesses in the world of work within the educational context. Learning through social interaction brings students to a higher state of development (Vygotsky, 1978) and the edge of many more possibilities including sharing visions and understandings, all of which are gains that individual learning may hardly achieve.

Encountered challenges and solutions

Since the project involves inter-university collaboration, one of the biggest challenges is to compromise between the very different course schedules and objectives of the two universities. Another challenge is to decide on a project theme that students from a multidisciplinary background find interest in (although teachers can encourage students to explore areas they are not specialised in), and teachers have the sufficient expertise to supervise the various topics derived from it. It takes considerable planning time to overcome both challenges.

Similar to what other project-based learning cases have reported (Nye læringsmetoder, 2000 as cited in Helle *et al.*, 2006), the uneven distribution of workload across the semester leads some students to overestimate the overall workload. Students may find it tough to decide on a project topic, do literature search to identify areas for investigation, and discuss research plans with their Korean teammates all within the first month. Only 26% of students find it easy to formulate a research plan for their projects. This relates to the first challenge we encounter: the Korean students finish their course earlier than our students do, and hence all these have to be settled in a month to allow Korean students more time to kickstart their business plans.

We are aware of the possible problems arising from the different course schedules, and we want to avoid students from rushing into the hands-on work without properly designing their research. They are therefore given plenty of opportunities to receive peer and teacher feedback before actual data collection takes place. Additionally, students are urged to take responsibility for active monitoring among members and voluntarily consult with teachers so as to ensure the teams work effectively and problems are detected early on. Despite the challenges, student evaluation regarding inter-university collaboration is particularly positive, with 100% indicating they have learnt how to put forward practical and realistic ideas through teamwork, and 89% having learnt how to communicate more effectively and professionally with people of a different culture and background after this collaboration. A student even highlights it is the challenge of working with teammates with a different course timeline in another country that drives him to "make timely and clear communication in order to smoothly finish the project".

Moving Forward

Effective language learning takes place in the context of social negotiation and construction of meanings among interlocultors. We envision this inter-university collaboration is a good opportunity to bring our students into contact with the community, and to bring the community into the classroom. Besides teaching academic writing, the course is meant to strengthen students' awareness of different cultural and social expectations and norms in relation to communication practices. In other words, our students are able to benefit from academic and intellectual communication with their peers through an authentic project-based learning experience. It also helps alert students to the fact that language is not to be learned in isolation.

The project itself can be regarded as an authentic learning environment where students participate in a community of practice (Wenger, 1998). Students tend to become more engaged when being put in a natural learning context than in a conventionally structured classroom setting. Learning academic literacy in this way creates a bigger purpose: students write with a 'voice' that serves a meaningful purpose and real world applicability.

Possibilities abound with project-based learning in higher education. Lattery (2001) probably gives the best summary of what a project should be like: beginning with a simple-to-approach and workable question that unfolds into profound and long-lasting outcomes, from which students can see the relevance to the course and to the authentic learning environment. With the project putting all these together, significant learning benefits of project-based courses are guaranteed to be derived from its application. Lastly, let us not forget educators' and teachers' benefit as well – from finding an approach that, apparently, accommodates learners of all levels and across multiple disciplines.

About the Author

Dr. Tiffany Ip was Postdoctoral Fellow in the Centre for Applied English Studies at University of Hong Kong and is now a lecturer at Hong Kong Baptist University. She can be contacted at this e-mail: tiffip@hkbu.edu.hk

Bibliography

Blumenfeld, P. C.; E. Soloway; R. W. Marx; J. S. Krajcik; M. Guzdial & A. Palincsar (1991). Motivating Project-Based Learning: Sustaining the Doing, Supporting the Learning. *Educational Psychologist*, Vol. 26, No. 3–4, pp. 369–398.

Coombs, G. & M. Elden (2004). Introduction to the Special Issue: Problem-Based Learning as Social Inquiry – PBL and Management Education. *Journal of Management Education*, Vol. 28, No. 5, pp. 523–535.

Eraut, M. (1985). Knowledge Creation and Knowledge Use in Professional Contexts. *Studies in Higher Education*, Vol. 10, No. 2, pp. 117–133.

Guerin, C.; V. Xafis; D. V. Doda; M. H. Gillam; A. J. Larg; H. Luckner (2013). Diversity in Collaborative Research Communities: A Multicultural, Multidisciplinary Thesis Writing Group in Public Health. *Studies in Continuing Education*, Vol. 35, No. 1, pp. 65–81.

Hazelton, P.; M. Malone & A. Gardner (2009). A Multicultural, Multidisciplinary Short Course to Introduce Recently Graduated Engineers to the Global Nature of Professional Practice. *European Journal of Engineering Education,* Vol. 34, No. 3, pp. 281–290.

Helle, L.; P. Tynjälä & E. Olkinuora (2006). Project-based Learning in Post-Secondary Education – Theory, Practice and Rubber Sling Shots. *Higher Education,* Vo. 51, No. 2, pp. 287–314.

Ip, T. (2016). Writers' Workshop: How to write a literature review in the 'write' way. *The Language Teacher,* Vol. 40, No. 1, pp. 37–39.

Ip, T. & J. Lee (2015). Difficulties in Mastering Psychology Writing: A Student Perspective. *Frontiers of Language and Teaching,* Vol. 6, pp. 12–21.

Jones, E. (2013). Internationalization and Employability: The Role of Intercultural Experiences in the Development of Transferable Skills. *Public Money and Management,* Vol. 33, No. 2, pp. 95–104.

Lattery, M. (2001). Thought Experiments in Physics Education: A Simple and Practical Example. *Science and Education,* Vol. 10, No. 5, pp. 485–492.

Paletz, S. B. F. & C. D. Schunn (2010). A Social-Cognitive Framework of Multidisciplinary Team Innovation. *Topics in Cognitive Science,* Vol. 2, No. 1, pp. 73–95.

Seufert, A.; G. Krogh & A. Back (1999). Towards Knowledge Networking. *Journal of Knowledge Management,* Vol. 3, No. 3, pp. 180–90.

Szeto, E. (2000). Innovation Capacity. *The TQM Magazine,* Vol. 12, No. 2, pp. 149–57.

Vygotsky, L. S. (1978). *Mind in Society: The Development of Higher Psychological Processes.* Cambridge, MA: Harvard University Press.

Wenger, E. (1998). *Communities of Practice. Learning, Meaning and Identity.* Cambridge: Cambridge University Press.

Multiple Tools for Innovative Interdependent Learning Techniques in Higher Education to Foster Employability Skills

Zeinab Younis

Introduction

Albert Einstein once said: *"we cannot solve our problems with the same thinking we used when we created them"*. So innovation entails thinking outside of the box in a lateral creative way to solve complexities. This type of thinking is needed at the level of higher education institutes to prepare students for future careers. Therefore, institutions have to underpin the process of change by supporting their students in building the new. Modernising a tool of education or a technique entails deviating from traditional ways of delivering information to enhance field experiences and practices for future student employability. According to De bono (2014), lateral thinking reflects the origination of new ideas through creativity and does not depend on the logic of vertical thinking, where a problem would be worked out step-by-step. So it is about exploring unusual ways to solve the problem and not just the problem itself. Lateral thinking concerns teaching students to think creatively and develop a new position on where they are, and where they want to be, in the future. So if we understand lessons in life by looking backward, still life has to move forward, and so does innovation in the field of higher education. You cannot simply build a new invention from scratch without understanding the value of it. One has to look to new inventions to upgrade the past tools and techniques used, to move from one known idea to constructing new ideas to be used by future generations, in an era of fast growing modernisation. Students have to learn how to find causal relationships between problems, and reasons behind those problems, to escape from old ideas and create originality. This is usually happens when there is an open venue for brainstorming, intuitive thinking, and creating diversion.

Background

The need to use innovative multiple techniques in improving higher education field learning practices arises from the increasing records of unemployment worldwide that are invading the global market. This leads a number of undergraduate students to face the problem of a lack of job opportunities when they graduate. They may believe a magic wand to get them a job is in their certificates alone, however, they can wake up to find a saturated market that needs innovative ideas and a spirit of lateral thinking, to ensure their chances of work. Lauder (2013) identified that the jump in the working age, the skills shortage, the shift in economic power and a gap between theory and real needs for the market are different reasons behind the gap. Employers criticise higher education institutions for failing to produce the sets of skills needed by students to face global market challenges and, on the other hand, students complain for not being absorbed into the market. According to a CBV survey in 2011, 70% of employers want to see the development of employability skills among students at both schools and universities in their higher education level. The urgency of the matter is that employers look to transfer academic skills into a set of employability skills, for the field practices needed in today's market. Students need to display a wide range of attributes in innovation and methods to serve a magnitude of job requirements that cannot be underestimated. The paradigm is shifting towards an era where acquiring employability skills in higher education stands out as a primary requirement, if universities want to meet the competitive edge of the local and the international market for their graduates.

Employability is about making closer links between education and the world of work. In 1997, the report of the National committee of Inquiry into Higher Education, Chaired by Lord Dearing (INCIHE 1997), raised the issue of employability and pointed to the need of enhanced opportunities for students to undertake all the skills of a work related environment in their curriculum of higher education. Among universities all over the world there has been a cultural shift to a requirement to develop skills to meet market needs through innovative techniques of learning in higher education and to relate academic learning to fieldwork practices (Mason et al., 2002). According to Lankard (1990), employability is the set of transferrable skills needed by students to make them employable. Moreover, for Hillage & Pollard (1998), employability focuses on the ability to acquire and maintain work. It can be broken down into four categories: the asset which refers to knowledge, how the individual employs his assets effectively towards developing his self-awareness to reap the benefits of his knowledge, presentation which helps the applicant to demonstrate his abilities to his potential employer, and the context which relates to how individual employability is influenced by personal circumstances and the labour market. For Biggs & Tang (2007), complex learning is more likely to achieve graduates' attributes leading to employability which are listed as critical thinking, ethical practice, creativity, independent learning, problem solving, communication skills and team work. Glover (2002) and Yorke (2004) discussed the graduate attributes that are a necessity to employability as field specific, generic and shared achievements. The first refers to knowledge possession particular to a field of study, and the other two to the possession of more general attributes and shared achievements at the level of most graduates. Bell (1996) and Walker (1995) advocated that a tension might arise between *graduateness*, as a state after the completion of a course and *employability*, as an assessment of the value of the student economically in the market. The early work of Bagshaw (1997) and the Institute for Future Education (2011) added to these another set of skills including novel and flexible adaptive thinking patterns towards complexities and a design mind set for acquiring social, as well as emotional intelligence. These findings were also driven from the early work of Dacre & Sewell (2007) regarding employability as a lifelong complex process involving a number of interlinking areas. It is not about passing an interview or writing a good CV to be accepted in the job, but it is about becoming a major stakeholder in one's career and position, from whom managers would also expect to see achievements in a specific context. The set of skills that we give our students in their path of education is their tool and it yields dual responsibility from both sides: the students as fresh graduates and the employer in his demand for specific skills. The career edge developed by Dacre & Sewell (2007), presented several approaches to developing employability skills in levels of higher education, including students' engagement and innovation, experience of work and life, a degree which is their subject knowledge, generic skills and emotional intelligence. In most higher education institutes, the intended learning outcomes of most modules taught try to meet these career edge requirements for future opportunities. In The Egyptian case, policy makers of the higher education sector are eager to involve academia in innovative field practices to respond to international trends in education. According to Kirby (2015), the British university in Egypt, is one of 23 private universities in the country, holding in total 60,000 students competing with 20 public universities of over 20 million students and trying to create the means to implement this cause, to alleviate the quality of higher education and training.

The Practice

The implementation method is targeted for the department of business in the faculty of Business Administration, Economics and Political Science, in the British university in Egypt. The target population is the students of the business department in their first, second and fourth year in different module applications. The target is to get students exposed as much as possible to real life field practices during the course of their academic studies, hence applying all the skills needed for future job opportunities waiting for them upon their graduation. The process of preparation itself is very clear to students during their orientation week, where the entire junior and senior staff members act as mentors for guidance for what students will expect in their four years study at the business department. Moreover, the students get several induction sessions to explain the different specialisations available at the business department and the requirements of the employability market for each. The schedules are prepared and the modules' specifications are reviewed by our UK university partners – London South Bank University and Loughborough University – before the beginning of the academic year, to ensure skills are inclusive in our programs. A set of multiple tools of innovative techniques in learning practices are used in the British University of Egypt, in the business department to ensure the delivery of employability skills for the BUE graduates, comprising as an umbrella the lateral thinking methods of solving complexities to ensure that emotional intelligence, blended learning, co-teaching methods and case studies-based learning are used to improve delivery of knowledge. Here is a collection of different tools used, for applying innovative techniques to field study in The British University in Egypt inside the Business Administration department, to ensure employability.

Emotional intelligence

During the past fifty years there has been a change in the curriculum of higher education towards a growing interdisciplinary connection between theory and practice. The emotional intelligence tool, as a paradigm shift in teaching and learning patterns of education, creates a social bonding to feel connected with students and colleagues. According to Goleman (1996), emotional intelligence refers to the ability to perceive, control and evaluate emotions, to also understand emotions and emotional knowledge and to reflectively regulate emotions so as to promote emotional and intellectual growth. These skills involve how to handle oneself to work in teams and they are also responsible for business success and job retainment. Panju (2008) saw emotional intelligence as the ability to monitor one's own, and others feelings and emotions, to discriminate among them and to guide one's own thinking and actions. According to Serrat (2009) the key factors for success in academic achievements and ensuring tenure as an employee lie in the essential components of emotional intelligence which are:

+ Self-awareness: implying an accurate self-assessment of capabilities, strengths, weaknesses and develop self-confidence;

+ Self-management: self-control, honesty and consciousness to take responsibility for actions;

+ Social awareness: entailing the development of several social characteristics as empathy, cooperation in developing and helping others, managing diversity and ability to handle situations;

♦ Social skills: the capacity of the individual to exercise conflict management and negotiation, not to create an adverse atmosphere in the organisation and develop soft skills at the workplace.

Studies showed that emotional intelligence is related to academic performance, because it involves a great deal of ambiguity, so the student has to possess this attribute to solve stressful situations. Teachers are required to develop activities for students to enhance their own self-image, which creates a mind-map for students to assess their strengths and weaknesses, roles and qualities. The approach is to mainly acquire soft skills to let the feeling facilitate the action, rather than making it difficult (Kawarsky, 2016). In our preparatory year at BUE, emotional intelligence is an important tool used to encourage students to fit in their first year and meet the transitional changes between the last year in high school and the beginning of university life. The high doses of using this concept, both in assignments and projects in the first and the second year of university, proved a great success. It is even considered as a therapy and not only a tool towards breaking the ice between concepts learned and the way to approach these concepts in real life situations. Firstly, we do the induction week for both staff and students to get to know each other and exchange new knowledge and prospects for the new academic year and to embrace new staff members into the system. Secondly, we work in the first three weeks of the semester to have a door open to students at any time upon their convenience and we don't stick to office hours. Thirdly, in both Introduction to Management and Organisational Behavior modules, staff members gather with the students in most social events that are run by clubs during the first quarter of the semester. In the personal effectiveness module, two lectures are dedicated to the topics of self-awareness and negotiation in order to prepare students for real life situations of bargaining and presentations in their field of work in the future. Working in teams to prepare for their assignments and projects in all of the above three modules paves the way for building knowledge capacity, together with interpersonal skills.

The feedback that staff members give to their students after their presentations requires a high degree of emotional intelligence to tackle the weak points, without the accusation of being a failure. By your inner psychological framework as a teacher, you can develop with these students emotional and social skills that collectively establish how well they perceive and express themselves to cope with challenges. It also implies how we develop and maintain the relationship between us as educators and students. Using different ideas like convincing them that today's presentation is in front of their colleagues and teachers, but tomorrow's will be in front of their managers and CEO's, they learn for the future, which motivates them a lot. They are sometimes given the freedom to choose topics that they would see themselves presenting in the future according to their areas of specialisation. Moreover, these presentations develop their competencies for empathy, mutual understanding, team leadership and managing diversity.

So, between the stimulus of teaching the material of the module and the response of the students in the classroom session, in the form of participation or in class presentations, lies a space for emotional intelligence to interfere. Lecturers were able to identify areas of angry feelings and weaknesses and analyse alternatives to stressful situations. Students with additional needs were able to access longer examination times and special coaching in specific circumstances and feedback was given on a regular basis to them. Students are provided in these modules with an open venue for lateral thinking where they can take their minds outside the box. This comes usually after the brainstorming techniques used in some sessions, where light is shed by the instructor to open the door for discussion and allow differences to prevail in a constructive way, building an argument rather than arising conflicts. By working hard with the students in their first and second year using this technique, success arises from the notion that by reaching their 4th-level year they would have already passed small areas of conflicts. They will have mastered the talents of working in groups, presentation skills enhancing effective communication, engaged in empathic listening and handled the differences of the multicultural environment of work that lies ahead of them.

Blended learning

Blended learning enables the instructor to enhance the student's ability to dig into the field of real work environments for answers to their questions and assignments. According to Horn (2014), traditional face-to-face instruction is replaced by web-based online learning, where 30 to 70 % of instruction is delivered online. There are several kinds of blended learning techniques, but the most adopted one is the flipped classroom, where the students participate in online learning off site in place of traditional homework and this is considered the best tool to ensure the delivery of employability skills of self-learning and relating theory to field practices.

At BUE, blended learning tools were used for a variety of modules during the last couple of academic years. We used a technique called *flex-model* where online learning is the backbone of student learning and the teacher is on site providing face to face support for the student in their assignments, which are usually uploaded on the e-learning site a week ahead. Students are given the opportunity to research the problem of the question before presenting it in class. What is unusual about this experience is that 70% of the material of blended learning study is researched first by students then delivered by the teacher, which opens the thinking patterns of the students to more ideas. It started as a pilot study experiment facing success and challenges, then it was adopted in year two and four. Blended Learning as a tool for approaching theory to practice uses the stimulus of giving the material of the module and the response of the students in the classroom session in the form of participation or in class presentation, and provides a space for transferrable skills. Students are given an open venue for lateral thinking outside the box, following brainstorming techniques and light shed by the instructor, to open the door for constructive discussions. This helped in developing a panel discussion between alumni of the university and successful stories behind businessmen, to expose students to more field experience and develop a construct of lessons learned that could be useful in real working life. A new section of employability will be added next September to all lecturers' modules specifications, in order to highlight the areas to be researched in blended learning.

Three modules applied this technique:

1. Public administration module (year four);

2. Contemporary Issues in leadership (year four);

3. Organizational Behavior and Personal effectiveness module (year two).

1. Public administration module (year four)

The instructor challenged the students to blend their learning of exploratory competencies in answering two questions related to the process of Egyptian parliament elections and lessons learned from the administration of the logistics of the electoral operation itself. This allowed the students to look for information needed in the field with the help of the university by organising trips to parliament and granting access to the students to discuss matters related to the election process with elected members. The number of students in this module did not exceed the 50, which was a big advantage in controlling the experiment towards a successful result. The students used innovative techniques of comparative analysis to answer the questions, by presenting individually for ten minutes each on what they learned from their field visits. They used small plays and theories of comparative administration to reflect on other countries' systems of elections.

2. Contemporary Issues in leadership (year four)

The blended learning tool was used in three intervals during the module: Week 4, 8 and 11. The students were asked to present blogs of 1000 words each describing a real life experience of their summer training, or of an incident that they were involved in and how this experience reflected on their leadership skills, on both academic and personal levels. The total of the three blogs carried 30% of their grade, which was the first attempt to grade a blended learning experience and it proved a great success, as the students were highly committed to deadlines and the quality of the work presented. At this level, we asked for a peer review for their blogs from several teaching and lecturers' assistants which added value to the work done and opened a great prospect for future lessons learned. The idea was mainly to encourage a research related field experience where the student is mixing theory and practice to prepare himself for a future career.

3. Organizational behaviour and Personal effectiveness modules (year two)

The idea of blended learning was adopted in these two modules as they contain a lot of theoretical approaches that have to be tackled on a practical field level. Two topics were chosen from the OB module "motivation and leadership", and one topic from the PE one (Team building). The students were asked to relate how the management functions intersect in real life by reflecting on concepts respectively in assigned lectures. They were asked to review real life companies that apply high motivation and team building techniques to their employees, whether locally or multi-nationals located in Egypt. Also, specifically in PE, they addressed two online questions they were required to research beforehand and give their answers in a panel discussion in class reflecting on real life experiences. The blended learning started in weeks 9–10 after the theories in both modules were discussed and the functions of managers vs leaders were well explained. The experiment was challenging, as the number of students in these modules exceeded 200, and it was a BUE decision to divide them into teams and to motivate them by an extra bonus if they solved their blended learning assignment.

The advantages of this experience of blended learning as a part of our teaching patterns in the British university in Egypt, is that it proved by evaluation from staff and the students to be a way to promote intellectual skills of the students guided by the instructor. The questions and module materials were uploaded as an e-learning assignment to promote the research capacities of the students and students set their timetable starting week 3 to manage their effort and time in relation to other modules. The BUE is planning to continue using these tools by developing a panel of discussion between alumni of the university, successful stories behind businessmen, and the winners from the start up competition that was held few weeks ago for students' innovations in the business field. This exposes students to more field experience and develops a construct of lessons learned that could be useful in real working life. Blended learning is a new part of our module reports for two academic years now, and a new section of employability will be added starting next September to our module specifications in order to highlight the areas to research in blended learning.

Co-teaching

Co-teaching is a very useful tool in higher education as it allows the broadening of the module scope through the mutual work of lecturers. Two minds are better than one in the co-teaching spirit and the material covered is from all aspects and reflecting two or more different experiences and backgrounds. The co-teaching team share in preparing, planning and delivering the material of the course both academically and practically. So the expert in theory would complement the expert in the field to transfer both the hard and the soft skills needed for the students for their future careers. At the same time, it can be a double edged sword presenting some challenges, when two different styles of teaching create preferences towards one form of instruction more than another. So the idea is to complement each other to bridge the gap, not to widen it, and that's the challenge. The benefits will be to access more instructional support and increased opportunity for meeting students' needs, learning from peers, more social interaction and more understanding of students' minds. There are different approaches to co-teaching and according to Friend & Cook (1996) it enhances personal effectiveness skills in students, as teachers are actively involved in the management of the lesson, the discipline and establishing a rapport. One of these approaches is parallel teaching where two teachers plan jointly and split the classroom into half to teach the same information at the same time. This method proved very tedious and the students lost focus in previous semesters in the middle of the topic of both OB and Personal effectiveness. Another one is the alternative method, where one teacher manages most of the class whilst the other teacher works with a small group of student's parallel to the main theme and they alternate roles during the session. This method was ineffective in the past, in both C 2nd and fourth H levels as BUE students' numbers are enormous, so they lose concentration as well as both instructors. Co-teaching is also used where both teachers are responsible for planning and they share the information and instructions in material delivered and in course-work projects and this is the technique used in BUE. This proved to be the best way and it was highly appreciated by our supervisors when co-teaching happened in Personal Effectiveness. Materials were uploaded two weeks ahead of the semester under headlines and subtitles agreed upon. We attended each other's lectures to build up both knowledge and skills and the presentations were double marked and peer reviewed by both of us in an alternating way to ensure subjectivity.

To ensure the effectiveness of the delivery of co-teached material the department ran a survey among students in the modules where co-teaching was applied. The result was very challenging, as the open-ended questions carried students comments such as "*it brought us to real life as theory from one professor was complemented by practice from the other*", "*we took the best from both to carry on in our future careers*" and finally "*one taught us soft skills and the other taught us hard skills and we will learn both the hard way in our future jobs*".

Guest speakers in fields of leadership training were brought to lectures to complement the practical part. My role as Head of the Innovation Center at BUE was to try to mingle industry and academics at an earlier stage of student life, and bringing in guest speakers was the platform for that.

Case studies

By case studies, students learn not only the 'what' but the 'how', as they are a part of the authentic learning experience to put theory into context of practical applications. Case studies work too as a reflection for a number of intended learning outcomes where students can argue and develop analytical and logical skills to solve their complexities and discuss their problems. According to Halldorsdottir (2013) higher learning institutions exist to change people's mindset towards more employable skills for market requirements, so how can case studies change students? The answer lies in the concept of delivering transformative learning through case studies via the teachers who have to act as facilitators and not only deliver knowledge. The only disadvantage of this practice is that it might not be the base for generalisations in some specific situations, so the student can act as the student and not the real businessman who is asked to draft a presentation about the future of his company in an economic crisis.

A continued use of case studies application to the modules taught at BUE is one of our innovative teaching techniques. In BUE, I experienced this technique in an Organisational Behaviour module, where I taught level "C" students the certificate 2nd level in the cohort. The technique was to bring examples of case studies to successful stories and provide an experience of learning via examples of how managers and leaders of several companies provided motivational schemes for their employees. The case studies were both national and multi-nationals, but with most of them located in Egypt, so that the students wouldn't have a difficulty in visiting their site and interviewing their management staff. The case study works from inception to application in an OB class where it turned out to be very good tool for analysing business issues and strategies. Students who are very bright and articulate formulated a full business plan presentation from one of these cases discussed in class. They assessed the basic strengths and weaknesses that the business was trapped into and they had the opportunity to invite the CEO of the related company under study for a free consultation. This led afterwards to invitations from several of these companies for summer internships for those students, thus ensuring field work during their holiday. The in-class experience is usually taught once a week in "OB" in one of the two hour's lecture frames that are left in weeks 11, 12 and 13, after finishing the basic theories and models of the first 10 weeks of the module. Before that the students are given free slots where they can go and interview management and survey the company. The application of case studies on concepts learned provided dynamic selected working teams with opportunities to solve the case and develop a strategy for solving complexities and gaps in the business environment. They learned in class how to use lateral thinking and not the typical systematic kind in solving some techniques in the business world where they had to work on the problem in an innovative way. One of the challenges met in this practice was that we insisted that students had to work on a pre-selected team from our side of 4–5 members. So the problem was that they were acquainted with a new technique for working and a new company of colleagues that they had not dealt with before. We tried to give them 'break the ice' sessions during class and organised their seating with their project team members, convincing them that in a couple of years this is going to be the real situation in an actual working life environment. Still we discovered some cases of unfriendliness and social loafing which created conflicts, but those who succeeded to work out their differences, were good to go in their future and they won a good summer internship too.

The outcome

Employability skills are becoming of higher importance and many employers are now offering soft skills training to ensure that graduates possess the skills they are seeking. They are prepared to bridge what most institutions and the market suffer from as a skills gap. For BUE students, their modules prepare them for the following:

+ Academic skills including reading, writing, numeracy, presentation skills, listening and understanding;

+ Thinking skills: analysis (problem identification), creativity, decision making, problem solving skills, logical vs lateral thinking, and critical thinking;

+ Personal attributes: leadership, team working, adaptability, self-motivation, self-management, honesty and integrity.

For all of the above skills to be put into action, these depend on the modules discussed on Classroom management. The ideal teaching patterns use different techniques and organise challenging work. The instructional goals were clear in meeting the students' expectations, and providing feedback. The classroom management in this case entailed all the practices and procedures that allow a lecturer to deliver and students to learn. These include effective guidance in time management, clear and challenging goals explained to the students through induction and mentoring week, pre-study guide material uploaded on the e-learning site at least 1–2 weeks ahead and a positive classroom atmosphere, arising from a cooperative and productive collaborative work depending on resources that were provided by the university. In BUE there is a compulsory 20 credit personal effectiveness module. this helps students to develop many of these skills, the course work in several preparatory and 2nd year levels helps to assess these skills, as required by major companies locally and internationally in the real life work place. These encompass knowledge acquisition with understanding subject specific practical skills and key transferrable skills. The BUE classrooms replicate the features of the workplace, as students are often required to work on real-world problems and if possible in the real world place itself. They can relate and appreciate the relevance of their learning and recognise the behaviour required from them in the future.

Since December 2015, the strategy of BUE has been designed in parallel with employability requirements, helping students to broaden their experience for the employment market, to get and retain a job after graduation and to empower the students to develop critical learning skills. According to the UK Commission for Employability and Skills, universities have to recognise any students' initiative for innovation and creativity in the work provided specially in the coursework and research and raise awareness of the staff lecturers to practice these skills in the module curriculum.

The structure of the four modules I personally taught at BUE mentioned earlier: Introduction to Management as preparatory level, Personal effectiveness and Organizational behaviour as core business modules to year two, Contemporary issues in leadership and public administration taught at level H which is year 4, were designed to meet the strategy of December 2015. It is modified also to meet the post graduate studies management department that will be in action next academic year. In applying this in post graduate studies, the challenge will be in diversity management, from the side of the students in their groups. Most of them will be from different working backgrounds, with challenges for meeting deadlines and time constraints in a conflict of interest between real work commitment and MBA requirements. The advantage will be that these candidates can help in being mentors from real field practices to their fellow undergraduates and provide guidance for how the skills are related to the actual work environment.

On the undergraduate level the four modules provide the opportunity for students to master the following set of skills:

- ◆ Personal attributes: they are ready to participate and make suggestions, accept new ideas and constructive criticism and take accountability for the outcome. Also to understand the impor-tance of adaptability, to ensure the acceptance of change and the lack of resistance to an ever changing working environment. They need to understand the importance of performance under pres-sure and inspiring a result-driven approach, as a direct experience from the exposure that the modules require in their projects. They start acquiring these skills from the module of Introduction to management level one, to their graduation year modules in Public Administration and leadership.

- Functional skills: the students can express ideas clearly, convey information appropriately and demonstrate effective communication, presentation and listening skills. This is mainly because of the different case studies based learning experience that they were subjected to in both modules of leadership and organisational behaviour.

- Self-management skills: students exercise time management, crisis management in overcoming challenges and punctuality in delivery. They moreover develop self-awareness of their strengths and weaknesses during the feedback period given by their instructors.

- Organisational skills: the student graduate from BUE with the skill of understanding the concept of person-job fit acknowledges the idea of relating academic theory to the reality of the organisation. They succeed to manage conflicts and disruption because of the negotiation skills that they learned in Organizational Behaviour and Personal effectiveness modules.

- The modules taught at BUE help them to generate imaginative ideas that can be applied in different situations, and demonstrate effective planning and analysing situations to determine the most appropriate way to solve complexities in real life afterwards. They encourage them to learn the concept of diversity and the respect of different perspectives in thinking laterally and demonstrate global awareness in effective team leadership with academic staff colleagues and peers, so that in the future they can organise their relationship in the workplace.

Moving Forward

In our modules at BUE we create a proactive spirit of mutual cooperative methods of teaching, which results in motivation of the students. The Research Center for Innovation.developed a student research community to promote the spirit of success and positive direction towards research and entrepreneurial start-up in collaboration with the student union to create a firm body that has the capacity to envision the needs of the students and act accordingly. One of the most proactive experiments lately was launching a collaboration for a CV writing workshop between the student union and the student research community. This was highly welcomed by students in level H, which is year 4 and almost graduating. They felt that they are delivering a benefit by themselves to themselves and this increased commitment. Our students grasp knowledge and are able to succeed in their working life experiences, as they possess articulate creative capacity in addressing problems and complexities that arise due to their exposure to real life experiences of working environments in business ahead of their graduation. This is a result of the innovative tools used in their teaching and learning through the 4 years spent at BUE. Their capacity knowledge building gets better every year and they get marvellous job opportunities after graduation. Last month we launched the first Start-Up Week of entrepreneurship try outs and our BUE students were in the first ranking places among other universities in Egypt, getting grants and funds from several local businessmen to start their projects. As a result of these practices, the BUE University was ranked number one on the Middle East for the year 2014–2016. This rank is giving us the opportunity as a business department to launch a call for partnership for post graduate studies with several other universities in the UK for an MBA. Moreover, the Organisational Behavior module with expansion is one of the core courses in both MBA and MPA (Master of Business Administration and Public Administration), So by implementing our tools for students in their undergraduate year in this course we are preparing them for higher levels of talents, not only in their academic post graduate careers but also in future jobs.

About the Author

Dr. Zeinab Younis is currently the head of the Center of Innovation, Governance and Green Economy; General Business Specialisation Coordinator and lecturer at the Business Department, Faculty of Business Administration, Economics and Political Science at the British University in Egypt. She can be contacted at this e-mail: zeinab.younis@bue.edu.eg

Bibliography

Bagshaw, M. (1997). Employability- creating a contract of mutual investment. *Industrial and Commercial training*, Vol. 27, No. 6, pp. 187–189.

Bell, J. (1996). *Graduateness: some early thoughts.* Paper to Given Credit Network Leeds.

Biggs, J. & C. Tang (2007). *Teaching For quality Learning at Universities.* Maidenhead 3rd edition. Open University Press.

Branch, J.; P. Bartholomew & C. Nygaard (2004). *Case-based Learning in higher education.* Oxfordshire UK: Libri Publishing Ltd.

CBV-EDI (2011). Education and skills survey. *Building For growth: Business priorities for education and skills.* London: CBI.

Coopers, L. (1998). *Skills development in higher education.* Report for CVCP/DFEE/HEQE. Committee of the vice chancellors and principals of the universities of UK. London.

Dacre, P. L. & P. Sewell. (2007). The key to employability: Developing a practical model of Graduate employability. *Education training.* Vol. 49, No. 4, pp 277–289.

De Bono, E. (2014). *Lateral thinking.* IP development corporation: UK.

Friend, M. & L. Cook (1996b). *The Power of 2: Making a difference through co-teaching.* Indiana University/ on-site, Bloomington, IN 47405–1006.

Friend, M. & L. Cook (1996a). *Interactions:* collaboration skills for School Professionals. White Plains: Longman.

Glover, D.; S. Law, & A. Youngman. (2002). Graduateness and Employability: Students perception of the personal outcome of university education. *Research in Post-compulsory education*, Vol. 7, No. 3, pp. 293–306.

Goleman, D. (1995). *Emotional intelligence.* Bloomsbury: London.

Halldorsdottir, S. (2004). The cycle of case-based teaching for transformational learning. In J. Branch; P. Bartholomew & C. Nygaard (Eds.), *Case-Based Learning in Higher Education.* Oxfordshire, UK: Libri Publishing Ltd.

Harvey, L.; W. Locke, & A. Morey. (2002). *Enhancing Employability, recognizing diversity: Making links between higher education and the world of work.* Centre for research and evaluation: universities UK and CSU.

Hillage, J. & E. Pollard (1998). *Employability: developing a framework for policy analysis.*

Horn, M. B. & H. Staker (2014). *Blended Learning: using disruptive Innovation to improve schools.* Jossey Bass: San Fransisco.

Jones, E. (2013). Internationalization and employability: The role of intercultural experiences in the development of transferable skills. *Public Money & Management*, Vol. 33, No. 2, pp. 189–201.

Institute for the Future (2011). *Future Work skills*. University of Phoenix Research Institute, Arizona.

Kawarsky, D. (2016). *Soft Skills volume*. Lulu Publishing services: North Carolina: USA.

Kirby, D. & H. El Hadidiy (2015). Universities and innovation in a factor driven economy: The Egyptian case. *Industry & Industry Higher Education*. Vol. 29, No. 2, pp. 151–160.

Knight, P. & M. Yorke (2003). *Assessment Learning and Employability*. Open University Press, UK.

Lees, D. (2002). *Graduate Employability- Literature review*. Learning and Teaching Support Network Generic Centre, UK.

Lankard, B. A. (1990). *Employability: the fifth basic skill*. Eric Digest, Washington, department of education.

Lauder, A. (2013) *Employability skills: The connection between skills and Employement*. Bliip Global employability, Queensland: Australia, March 2013.

Mason, G.; G. William; S. Cranner & D. Guile. (2002). *How higher education enhances the employability of graduates*. Institute of Education and NIESR for HEFCE.

National Committee of Inquiry into Higher Education (NCIHE, 1997). *Higher Education in the Learning society*. HMSO, London.

Nygaard, C.; S. Brand; P. Bartholomew & L. Millard (Eds.) (2013). *Student Engagement: Identity, motivation& community*. Libri Publishing: UK.

Panju, M. (2008). *7 Successful strategies to promote E.I. in the classroom*. Library of congress catalogue: New York & London.

Preeti, B. (2013). *Role of Emotional Intelligence for Academic achievement for students*. Research Journal of Educational Science. India.

Rees, C.; P. Forbes & B. Kubler. (2006). *Student employability profiles: A guide for higher education practitioners*. The Higher Education Academy: September.

Serrat, O. (2009). *Understanding and Developing Emotional Intelligence*. Cornell University. ILR School: USA.

The British university strategic plan, December 2015. www.bue.edu.eg.

The Employability Challenge, UK commission for Employability and Skills, 2009.

Walker, L. (1995). *Institutional change towards an ability based curriculum in higher education*. Sheffield: Employment department.

Walsh, J. J. & D. Snyder. (1993, April). *Cooperative teaching: An effective model for all students.* Paper presented at the annual convention for the council for exceptional children, San Antonio, TX.

Yorke, M. (2004). *Employability in higher education; what it is and what it is not,* higher education Academy: Esect, Edinburgh.

Chapter 21: Authentic Learning

Building Motivated Student Engagement through Demonstrated Curriculum Relevance

Susan Benvenuti

Background

Students undertaking an undergraduate degree are often far removed from the realities of their eventual careers and working environments. Courses they take don't always resonate with them and they do not always see the relevance of what we as lecturers ask of them. For many of them, their future career is still conceptual or theoretical – they have little real understanding of what they will be doing on the job. Students also view academics and textbooks as removed from the realities of the working world.

Many educational researchers have identified student motivation as central to student success. Some see motivation as either a facilitating or limiting factor depending on its presence or absence, while others view it as a more "dependent variable" – something that can possibly be affected given the appropriate strategies or conditions. Research that particularly resonates with us is the application of Vroom's (1964) Expectancy Theory, originally and extensively shown to be a valid and reliable measure of motivation in the workplace, to the classroom.

Expectancy theory views people, in our case students, as purposeful, who behave or act in ways that support an expectation that their efforts and actions will result in an outcome that they value (Hancock, 1995). Hancock cites several studies (including Brophy, 1988; Eccles & Wigfield, 1985; Feather, 1992; Hancock, 1991, 1994; and Howard, 1989) that have demonstrated that expectancy theory can be reliably transferred to the classroom, where it is interpreted as: strong student motivation to learn or engage in a course or learning activity is dependent on a student's expectation that the learning activities or requirements are within their ability to achieve and that the resultant outcomes are of real value to them.

Hancock's (1995) work looks at the possibility of identifying peda- gogic approaches or teaching strategies that could be used to build student motivation in view of this knowledge. The approaches or interventions can focus on one or more of the components of expectancy theory from a student's perspective, namely: expectancy ("will I be able to do what is required?"), instrumentality ("if I do what is required how likely am I to actually achieve my desired outcome?") and/or valence ("what real value will I get from the outcome?").

We also believe that the most valuable motivation to encourage deep and ongoing engagement in learning is intrinsic rather than extrinsic motivation. Extrinsic motivation is typically reward focused (or seeks to avoid punishment or negative results) but only has influence for as long as the reward or otherwise is in effect. Intrinsic motivation, by compar- ison, is driven by internal influences such as self-esteem, self-satisfaction, self-concept, interest, relevance and valence, personally held values, or personal needs, drivers or ambitions. Intrinsic motivation is said to be more long-term or enduring, often continuing despite set-backs, and lack of progress or short-term rewards.

The rationale behind the teaching and learning approach in this course is to motivate students to engage deeply and consistently in our course as we believe that sustained engagement over a period of time (Chickering & Gamson, 1987) builds stronger knowledge in comparison with a more "fragile knowledge" that is obtained through short bursts of effort and engagement focused on "passing the exam".

Guided by expectancy theory overall, we have therefore tried to "influ- ence" students' perceived valence of the course by foregrounding the relevance of what we are requiring of them to their future careers, and creating a more authentic learning experience (Stein et al., 2004) within the formal higher education setting. In focusing on a longer-term value we are hoping that students will invest more sustained effort over a longer period if the return on that investment of time is likely to deliver long-term value.

Though on a smallish scale, we have also tried to give students some input into what the outcomes of the course should be. This enables students to choose outcomes that have personal relevance (and therefore potentially high value to them) and provides for some control of the expectancy aspect of the theory as students are also able to define what actions they personally will undertake towards meeting those outcomes.

The Practice

Our approach to curriculum design encompasses not only consideration of what students need to know and be able to do, but a broader view that looks at the context in which they will one day need to do it. We therefore include learning outcomes that focus on the personal attributes and values often mentioned in recruitment advertisements related to their future careers, "the graduateness" or employability aspect. Further, our teaching seeks to move largely away from lectures to facilitating learning within project teams and requiring student defined and driven personal development.

The course adopts a team-based project approach which is not in itself innovative, but the creation of a rich, real-world context together with a focus on developing the required professional attributes and values of their future career, ensures that students appreciate the relevance of the course and therefore engage more deeply, readily and consistently. By combining team-based project work, individual experiential learning through role-play and focused self-directed personal development, we have tried to create an authentic learning environment that motivates student engagement and learning. Chickering & Gamson's (1987) "Seven Principles for Good Practice in Undergraduate Education" provided a strong framework for conceptualising what we were trying to achieve in this approach. These principles emphasise student and faculty engagement, cooperation between students, active learning, timeous feedback, engagement with tasks over a period of time, expectation of high standards and diversity in learning approaches. Furthermore, we have tried to achieve both constructive alignment in terms of learning outcomes, ways of teaching and learning and assessment (Biggs & Tang, 2007) and authenticity in developing and evaluating students. Figure 1 shows the overview of our course.

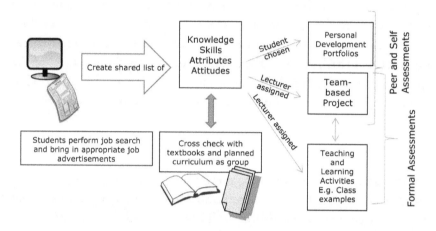

Figure 1: Overview of the course.

Demonstrated Curriculum Relevance

Our opening week of "lectures" involves demonstrating the relevance of the course curriculum to students' future careers. In our opening lecture, we explain the overall philosophy of our course as team-based collaborative learning with a focus on real-world projects and problem solving. Students are then asked to look for and bring to the second class of the course, a recruitment advertisement that really resonates with them – i.e. we ask them to bring us an advertisement that spells out their dream job.

Small groups then work together on extracting employer requirements relating to knowledge, skills, personal attributes etc. Almost immediately it becomes clear to students that many of the requirements looked for by employers are common across a variety of jobs in the industry. As a class we then spend some time analysing and discussing what employers are looking for and then map these requirements to the course curriculum – in terms of both content and approach.

In our discipline, Information Systems (IS), we work with both technological and business knowledge and skills. Many of the jobs require attributes or skills such as teamwork, time management, conflict management, presentation skills, report writing, etc. We are therefore able, in these early discussions, to demonstrate to the students the benefits of our team-based, collaborative learning approach. While many students dislike teamwork, we are able to show them that there is value in learning to manage the challenges inherent in teamwork.

On the content side, unfamiliar discipline terminology, which might appear in a job advertisement, can be shown to be located in the chapters of the textbook or appear in an assessment task outline. We have found it very useful to create a representation or diagram of our course at a high-level, which includes core terminology that we know from experience, appears in recruitment advertisements. We use the diagram in our first session together to talk students through the course and expectations, and then re-present it to the class towards the end of the second "lecture" session. Having gone through the discussions, made lists of valued personal attributes, and looked at IS specific terminology, the diagram now takes on far more meaning for the students. In gaining meaning, we hope that the course requirements and promised outcomes (particularly as they relate to future employment in personally chosen dream jobs) grow in value to the students and therefore encourage an early personal engagement with the course.

"A Bonus": one of the unintended yet valuable benefits of using student sourced recruitment adverts in demonstrating curriculum relevance, is that we quickly become aware of shifting trends in employment requirements and opportunities in our industry. When we undertake curriculum review and hold discussions with our industry advisory board, changes in requirements are easily identified and discussed, and changes to the curriculum adopted as we see fit. This does not mean that we are governed or driven exclusively by recruitment demands, but it does help us to better prepare our students for the workplace, particularly in the absence of a formal professional body.

Using a "manufactured" rich context to encourage deep learning and engagement

The concept of a team-based project working environment in industry is linked to the major teaching and learning aspect of our courses: milestone based project deliverables. Again, team-based project work in our discipline is not innovative, rather it should be expected, but how we attempt to deliver it in terms of providing a real-world context is different.

Throughout the course, case studies involving role-play of the students in their future professional roles are used for in-class teaching, project work and assessment tasks such as presentations, tests and exams. Every piece of work delivered by the student teams is written for their "client" – they therefore need to learn to write using business language focused for an executive or managerial reader. This helps us to identify the extent to which students really understand what they are doing and why, as they cannot hide behind technical jargon that they may or may not understand.

Students are quickly shown that ongoing engagement is key, and that success in assessment tasks is related to their level of engagement in class and project work. Lecturers try to keep lecturing to a minimum and instead work as much as possible with in-class examples which get progressively more complex as the layers of detail get added. In these classes, students work in their project teams and lecturers engage with them on the examples as "technical experts" or "project managers" as applicable. In playing these roles they require students to talk them through their questions relating to the examples as though the experts know little about the client context. This helps students to learn how to work collaboratively by "unpacking problems", talking through their understanding and debating the potential solutions. The goal is to support students in learning these techniques through modelling them in class within the teams, so that as they work on the bigger more complex problems contained in their main project, they are able to use this approach.

When working with the teams as the client for their major project, the lecturers take a different approach. Students wishing to consult with the course lecturers on project work are given a limited number of vouchers per semester which equates to time with a busy executive. If teams arrive for meetings unprepared, the value of the consultation is affected. Lecturers purposely do not volunteer information that is not sought, and they will respond to technical language or use of jargon with questions or feigned confusion.

To summarise, lecturers are creating a context rich teaching and learning environment which demonstrates the relevance of the course content and approach, through a close approximation of a real-world working environment.

Student activity – how are they learning and engaging?

The students, in response to the course context, are engaged in small group cooperative learning within the larger class context. As described above, students are engaged in working on small chunks of a larger project over the period of a whole semester. In class they are given short lectures or demonstrations of techniques, and then work within their teams on completing examples or tackling similar problems.

As they work, lecturers are present to talk through difficulties they might be experiencing, to pose questions both to the groups (or as similar misunderstandings arise) to the whole class, and to encourage discussions and debates amongst students. Generally solutions to the examples are presented by one of the student groups (by rotation) to the rest of the class, and questions and comments are made by the other teams. Where possible the students handle the questions or debate the disagreements until they resolve the issues, with lecturers asking appropriate questions where necessary to guide discussions. At first students are not confident in engaging with other students and look frequently to the lecturers for judgement. Over time, their confidence and expertise grows, the questions become deeper and more members of the class participate willingly.

Development of skills and knowledge through role-playing, experiential learning and peer and self-assessment

Over the course of the project, students are required to take on specialist roles and rotate through these. The major role which is under development in this scenario is that of the project manager. While we have a session on the importance of project management, each student is required to research the role of the project manager and compare that role in industry with the role they play in the student teams. They are expected to identify learning opportunities, undertake self-assessment and report on their learning and successes through peer and self-review of their project work, reflective writing and critical incident reporting. Development of some of the knowledge and skills is thus based almost purely on experiential learning.

In order to support students with their self-reflection and reflective writing, we provide some guidance through templates, readings on the difference between reflection and reporting, and require them to build up a record of what they have been doing and how they feel about it. In some years we have used learning journals and more recently online blogs. Sometimes we provide questions for them to respond to, while at other times we ask for critical incident reports or leave the writing entirely up to the students. We generally start with smaller requirements and build over time and the assessment criteria clearly prioritise effort, engagement with task and attempts at reflection, over content and relevance, particularly early on. It is all about building confidence and recognizing progress to begin with.

Peer assessment of project teamwork is always a difficult undertaking. We have adopted an online tool, CATME (Comprehensive Assessment of Team Member Effectiveness) which poses specific questions to students and provides them with summarised feedback relating to their self-assessment of their contribution to teamwork and how their peers collectively rated their performance. As an external tool that identifies patterns of conflict, over- and under-rating of self-assessment and good performers, we have found that students more readily accept individually adjusted marks based on CATME results. The tool also provides a good starting point for discussions if team conflict arises (www.catme.org).

Assessment of student work on an individual level is again based on mini-case studies which require students to do much of the work that they have been undertaking in their team towards the main project, on their own. We are gratified that many students work collaboratively in preparing for tests and exams as they start to value the input and advice that their team members are able to give them.

Using personal development portfolios (PDPs) to build motivation

While focusing on demonstrating relevance of the curriculum to students and providing a context rich environment in which to deliver and assess the course, we have also tried to build student motivation and engagement by requiring them to personalize and focus their learning by allowing them to choose aspects of professional attributes to focus on based on their desired future career. We use personal development portfolios (PDPs) which give students the responsibility for planning, executing and evaluating their growth. These PDPs while allowing individual choice to students, tie back to curriculum relevance as they require students to select their learning goals from their "dream job advert".

The PDP takes the form of a learning contract and asks students to choose between one and three learning goals that they will work on during the course. Students need to identify and define their learning goals, explain the rationale behind choosing each one and then articulate their proposed learning plan (what activities they might undertake, what criteria they will use to judge their progress and success, and how they will measure their achievements). We also ask students to give us a one page CV which gives us insight into who they are, where they come from and their general goals and aspirations.

Using the PDP is not only useful in giving students some real input into their learning outcomes for the course and thereby increasing both the valence and expectancy discussed above, it also introduces students to the very important concepts of self-directed and lifelong learning. In our discipline, and in a growing number of others, the so-called half-life of knowledge continues to shrink more and more rapidly. In the technology arena, we need to ensure that our students are both aware of the need for ongoing professional development, as well as able to identify specific areas of necessary growth and to take the steps to achieve this.

We encourage students to look fairly broadly for ways in which to accomplish their goals – in particular we encourage them to look for online resources such as TED talks, MOOCs, surveys to measure learning gaps or achievements, and a variety of readings. In this way we expose them to potential sources of ongoing professional development and also guide them in discerning value in what they find and use.

Some practical considerations

This approach is adopted over two semester long courses in the students' second academic year of study, and defines the whole approach to the courses, i.e. it is a full semester long approach for a course. It should however be possible to use the approach over parts of a course where specific knowledge, skills or attributes can be treated in isolation.

The PDP specifically is a useful tool to use within any course. By setting a task that has real relevance to a student's future career (or allowing students to set their own defined tasks) and requiring them to define how they will both accomplish that task and demonstrate their success, students can take some ownership of the learning process. A PDP can run for a few weeks or across a semester, depending on the level of learning you wish students to engage in.

Lecturer guidance in what constitutes appropriate goals is very important to the PDP – students need to engage with something sufficiently challenging but which can be achieved within the available time. Advice on scoping their goals is thus critical. We use a "set-up" phase in which students set goals, identify learning activities and set up criteria for demonstrating progress and success. Lecturers provide feedback to the students within a week to ten days so that they do not undertake learning goals which are compromised from the start. We use a dropbox facility provided by our learning management system for each student. They deposit their PDP in the dropbox and we are able to provide feedback directly to them by posting rubrics in return. Students are also encouraged to put a link to their online learning blog or pages of their learning journals in their dropbox. Any resources used or work done is also placed in their dropbox to gradually develop their portfolio of evidence relating to their goals.

Adjusting from traditional teaching and learning practices as a teacher to facilitator and guide

Using both the team-project and the PDP, means that our role changes from that of teacher imparting and testing knowledge to facilitator of growth and change. While we remain responsible for ensuring that students cover and learn the appropriate knowledge and skills, we pass responsibility to the students for constructing their understanding of the knowledge of what to do and how to do it through teamwork, in-class engagement and group-based consultations.

We spend little time lecturing content and process, and instead spend the majority of our face-to-face time facilitating small group work within project teams and helping students to judge their own and other team's work in terms of criteria. Student teams are also given parts of the content to prepare and deliver to the class, particularly sections which are not complex conceptually. This also enables us to provide various opportunities for students to demonstrate their personal goal development e.g. students who wish to work on presentation skills may choose to be the ones to present team prepared content to the class. Students who want to develop leadership skills may choose to undertake early opportunities as the team project manager, or students wanting to improve their writing skills might undertake document quality assurance for their team.

As stated earlier, we ask teams to present their solutions to problems to the class and then get the rest of the class to offer comments and feedback to the team on their solutions. We do our best not to offer solutions but encourage debate and iterative improvements using questions to both the presenting team and the class as a whole. The idea is to help students "work it out" but not to allow them to waste too much time heading in the wrong direction. Over time their questioning and feedback becomes more focused and useful, and they are more confident in engaging with the other teams and the lecturers. Participation is valued, encouraged and built on, even while ensuring that students move from incorrect solutions towards better ones.

Students' roles and experiences – a whole new student-centred world

Students are required to do a few things differently from traditional classes. Firstly, students are required to engage in the course from day 1; after their first lecture they are looking for recruitment advertisements in our field, becoming familiar with the expectations of future employers, and doing some personal reflection on their strengths and weaknesses as future professionals.

Very early on, students are defining some personal development goals for the semester that are strongly related to their future employment. This exposes them to the idea of self-directed learning through the use of personal development plans and learning contracts. These in turn expose them to the idea of learning outcomes, learning resources and activities, and the concept of evidence based assessment – how will I demonstrate what I have learned or what I can now do? The idea of assessment criteria and standards therefore become more accessible to students as they determine what they would put forward as a basis for judgement of success. Discussions and sometimes negotiations are necessary but these too are useful in helping students to understand assessment and perform better in assessment tasks set by lecturers.

Secondly, the team-based learning and "doing" aspect of the course is often difficult for students early on. Although we allow students to choose their own teams in the first of the two semester courses, team work is still challenging for many of them. We use the teams very much as a learning resource; all class activities are done in these small groups so that discussions and debates over time lead to ongoing understanding. When they are working on their assessment project milestones outside of class time they are able to return to their group thinking and discussions on a similar problem as worked through in class.

In trying to demonstrate relevance of our course curriculum to the students, we set in motion the idea that courses offered in their degree programme can all contribute towards their development and future careers. Students begin to look for value in what they are doing and often push lecturers in other courses or disciplines for more.

Lastly, we draw on our graduates as resources to further support the idea of relevance of curriculum to their future careers. Many employers bring past students back into the classroom to encourage students to consider joining their organisations – in return, our graduates are able to answer questions from our students relating to their careers and to what degree the courses they have undertaken at university prepare them for the working world. The extent to which companies look for time in front of our classes in order to attract students also speaks to the fact that students completing our courses are in demand. We have been lucky to be able to invite graduates working in "cool" organisations such as Google or Facebook back into the classroom to really fire up our students and support our claims that what we are teaching them is really relevant. All our undergraduate students are also encouraged to sign up on LinkedIn and we connect them to our graduates through a LinkedIn group for IS graduates and current students.

Outcomes

While students initially find the difference in approach difficult and the change in established roles a bit uncomfortable, they exhibit tremendous personal growth over the two semesters and their confidence in taking responsibility for their own learning grows.

They also exhibit far more confidence in engaging with challenging content and demonstrate through their questioning a desire for deep understanding. The core knowledge and skills covered in this course are not built on in further years of study, yet employers and recruiters regularly comment on the "corporate readiness" of our students when taking up roles directly related to the content of this course.

Students appreciate the relevance of the work that they are expected to do and the way in which lecturers engage with them. While they initially find the uncompromising stance on attention to detail and professionalism difficult, they later report confidence in job interviews, in graduate internship programmes and in the first few months of working. This suggests that students are actually developing some so-called employability skills (Fallows and Steven, 2000) through this approach.

They also enjoy not having to study for tests and exams by learning volumes of information by rote. Even more theoretical concepts have been worked with in sufficient depth within class and through their projects for students to feel equipped to deal with them based on their ongoing work.

Moving forward

The power in using the teaching and learning approach across an entire course or year of study, is that it becomes almost a guiding philosophy or way of being for both lecturers and students. In the past we used team –based project work as a vehicle for teaching the knowledge and skills required to perform many of the tasks associated with systems development – a core function in our field. At the same time we used the PDP independently to try to develop a sense of the value of self-directed learning for students given the frequent changes in disciplinary knowledge in our field.

Over time we have integrated these to a large degree and are now able to build a more holistically authentic learning environment and hence experience for our students. Each year we undertake a reflective review of the course and try to use the exercise to improve the teaching and learning in the course. Students' reflective work, comments on evaluations and feedback from external examiners and employers are all used to reshape our courses. In addition the student research work on dream jobs and the knowledge and skills that is valued in the market, helps to ensure that our curriculum remains relevant and responsive.

In order to continue to pursue improved teaching and learning for our students, we will continue to fine tune our courses and approaches. We are currently exploring thinking around how best to expose students to a wider variety of development tools and techniques, as well as encourage them to explore new forms of technology to enhance team work and communication.

In considering how best to apply this type of teaching and learning innovation, lecturers would need to think about what constituted an authentic learning environment and how best to build or construct that. The power of using student research to help create the motivation for developing the specific knowledge, skills, attitudes and attributes is also an important factor. While our course provides us with a fairly manageable field within which to work, broader courses may require different approaches. Work done by Dörnyei and Ushioda (2011) on motivation in language education, and using the concept of the visualised "ideal self" and "future self" may be worth exploring, along with related work by Magid and Chan (2012).

About the Author

Susan Benvenuti is a lecturer in Information Systems and Assistant Dean for Teaching and Learning in the Faculty of Commerce, Law and Management, at the University of the Witwatersrand, Johannesburg, South Africa. She can be contacted at this e-mail: susan.benvenuti@ wits.ac.za

Bibliography

Biggs, J. & C. Tang (2007). *Teaching for Quality Learning at University* (3rd ed.) Buckingham: SRHE and Open University Press.

Brophy, J. (1988) Research Linking Teacher Behaviour to Student Achievement: Potential Implications for Instruction of Chapter One Students. *Educational Psychologist*, Vol. 23, pp. 233–286.

Chickering, A. & Z. Gamson (1987). Seven Principles for Good Practice in Undergraduate Education. *AAHE Bulletin*, March, 1987. American Association for Higher Education.

Dörnyei, Z. & E. Ushioda (2011). *Teaching and Researching Motivation*. Harlow: Longman.

Eccles, J. & A. Wigfield (1985). Teacher Expectations and Student Motivation. In J. B. Dusek (Ed.), *Teacher Expectancies*. Hillsdale, NJ: Erlbaum, pp. 185–226.

Fallows, S. & C. Steven (2000). Building employability skills into the higher education curriculum: a university-wide initiative. *Education and Training*, Vol. 42, No. 2, pp. 75–83.

Feather, N. T. (1992). Values, Valences, Expectations, and Actions. *Journal of Social Issues*, Vol. 48, No. 2, pp. 109–124.

Hancock, D. R. (1995). What Teachers May Do to Influence Student Motivation: An Application of Expectancy Theory. *The Journal of General Education*, Vol. 44, No. 3, pp. 171–179.

Hancock, D. R. (1994). Motivating Adults to Learn Academic Course Content. *Journal of Educational Research*, Vol. 88, pp. 102–108.

Hancock, D. R. (1991). *Effects of Conceptual Levels and Direct and Nondirect Instruction Patterns on Achievement and Motivation in Course Content*. Diss. Fordham U.

Howard, K. W. (1989). A Comprehensive Expectancy Motivation Model: Implications for Adult Education and Training. *Adult Educational Quarterly*, Vol. 39, pp. 199–210.

Magid, M. & L. Chan (2012). Motivating English Learners by Helping Them Visualise Their Ideal L2 Self: Lessons from two Motivational Programmes. *Innovation in Language Learning and Teaching*, Vol. 6, pp. 113–125.

Stein, S. J; G. Isaacs & T. Andrews (2004). Incorporating authentic learning experiences within a university course. *Studies in Higher Education*, Vol. 29, No. 2, pp. 239–258.

Vroom, V. H. (1964). *Work and Motivation*. Oxford: Wiley.

Section 6: E-learning

Introduction to Innovative Teaching and Learning Practices using e-learning

Jeff Lewis, Didem Koban Koç, Jülide İnözü, Ayşe Görgün,
Chris Perumalla, Engin Koç & Andries Du Plessis

Introduction

This section of the book embraces several different applications of e-learning in various different contexts that encompasses a wide geographical area; including Canada, South Africa, Turkey and UK. All of these courses are either for credit or credit equivalent and offered for undergraduate students. The authors describe in their individual chapters how they implement e-learning using a variety of digital tools in their respective fields of study, all within a Higher Education context. The practices presented illustrate how e-learning is used across different disciplines by providing contextualized examples.

Several programmes within the field of education utilised digital technologies, such as, Moovely and Concordance Analysis Programme and these were used to encourage students to be independent learners through strategy training. Blogging and Podcasting were used to extend exposure to foreign language input through a self-study mode in an English as a Foreign Language environment. Moodle, Webspiration and YouTube facilitated internal communications and developed independent learning pathways. Google+ was used in the absence of a traditional Learning Management System to allow access to learning materials, implement assessment and also administer student information. Health Sciences used the BlackBoard for course management, including posting videos, administering online assessment and submitting assignments. The final example used Adobe Connect Pro, Moodle and Mahara to increase access to dental technology programme for geographically remote and academically disparate learners.

Historical context

E-learning includes all learning and teaching activities that are electronically supported focusing especially on computer related *"transfer of skills and knowledge"* (Darwesh, et al., 2011). E-learning is ubiquitous assuming minimal hardware requirements are met and is also one subset of Distance Education, which has evolved through three generations of technological advancement, ranging from simple correspondence courses in late 19th century to mass communication media – through radio in the 1950s, use of cassette tape recorders in the 1960 through 80s, and more recently through computer assisted instructions (Bernard et al., 2009; Sims, 2008). The onset of 21st century has resulted in an exponential explosion of technologies and the simultaneous evolution and availability of faster internet access has revolutionized E-learning in the past decade. Online learning is praised most for its ability to improve access to learning materials and educational content without the restrictions of time, space or distance (Means et al., 2010).

The ability of application of internet technologies to break through time and space constraints, and cross over geographical boundaries and break language barriers, have taken learning to altogether a different level. Recent survey in 2011 by The Sloan Consortium reported that in United States alone, there has been a phenomenal increase in students taking at least one online course; the report added that number of students enrolled in at least one online course in autumn 2010 has surpassed 6.1 million. The report added that online enrollment accounted for nearly one-third of the total enrollment in higher education in the US (The Sloan Consortium). Anecdotally, many post-secondary institutions in Canada offer online courses but according to the Canadian Council on Learning's report (2009), Canada is falling behind in their e-Learning achievements compared to other western countries such as United States,

Australia and the United Kingdom. There is a trend for the increased use of e-learning globally.

With the e-Learning courses experiencing almost a decade of success in various disciples, the educational literature is providing some insights on the efficacy of online learning in various disciplines such as, mathematics (Yates & Beaurdrie, 2009), psychology (Dell et al., 2010) business (Peters et al., 2011) and health sciences (Chapman et al., 2011). One of these insights is that there is general agreement that E-learning is proving to be on par with traditional methods of teaching at least with regard to learning outcomes (Cook et al., 2008; Cook et al., 2010; Kee et al., 2014).

Overview of chapters

The paragraphs below give an overview of the chapters in this section, demonstrating how and where e-learning has brought added value for both students and tutors within the relevant programmes:

A Concordance Program and the Moovly tool were the technological tools used in the teaching and learning practice featured in Chapter 22 by Didem Koban Koç. The main reason for using these tools in this learner-centered classroom was to encourage students to be independent learners. The concordance analysis program extended students' vocabulary by allowing them to see and search for lexical combinations used in different contexts on their own. The Moovly tool gave students an opportunity to work together to create presentations independently while they decided what kind of information was to be extracted from the different websites they accessed. By using these tools students improved their cognitive and social strategies. Students not only scanned and searched for information but they also evaluated information and made independent decisions. They worked collaboratively and with peers in groups.

The use of blogging and podcasting are demonstrated in Chapter 23 by Julide Inozu and Ayse Gorgun to provide students with ample amount of listening experience in foreign language learning process. The main motive for using these digital tools was to extend in-class work to outside of the classroom, so that the students could have access to teacher-structured materials and activities delivered in a self-study mode. Integration of digital technologies enables the teacher to extend the classroom beyond its physical borders and allows the students to study in their private or preferred environment without time and place constraints. Lower levels of anxiety, improved self-efficacy perceptions and increased motivation are the further benefits of this instructional design.

Chapter 24 described by Chris Perumalla *et al.* presents the online courses in Faculty of Medicine at the University of Toronto (UofT) using the Blackboard (Bb) Learning Management System which is licensed for UofT courses. The flexibility and robustness of Bb provides instructors in creating a "virtual learning environment" and the ability to manage the course content including posting videos and other learning modules, administer online assessments (quizzes), submit assignments and also to manage Grade Book where students can access their respective grades. For the students, it provides a "one stop shop", where they access course material, create a community of learners through chat and discussion boards, and can easily and conveniently access bulk announcements.

Chapter 25 by Engin Koç shows examples that allow freedom for learners to create their own learning path using Webspirationpro with feedback from teachers in the form of a concept map. As the learners choose their own path, they can use the necessary resources from the videos uploaded by the teacher. Also the freedom of learners was extended to create evaluation schemes by negotiating with the teacher and peers in line with self-directed learning principles. Moodle and YouTube were used for assignment and resource sharing.

Chapter 26 by Andries Du Plessis at University of Mpumalanga in South Africa proposes the use of freely available solutions such as Google Applications. The absence of a Learning Management System necessitated the use of time-saving scripts such as Doctopus in conjunction with Google Drive and Flubaroo in conjunction with Google Sheets. This proved particularly useful for efforts to teach both *with* and *about* technology as part of the students' teacher training, and the implementation of certain social media applications created opportunities to model these applications use to help facilitate teaching about technology.

Utilisation of the following digital technologies in Dental technology were adopted in Chapter 27 by Jeff Lewis. Adobe Connect Pro (videoconferencing software) used polls, presentations, collaboration, and breakout groups. This increased access to the programme for geographically remote and academically disparate learners. Moodle (VLE) including the use of Lessons, Books, Quizzes and Mahara (eportfolio). Work Based Learning and Professional Practice outcomes provides a single point of access for learning resources (to increase access and consistency of material presentation and format). YouTube allows access to practical demonstrations. The benefits to students are that we provide contextualisation and application of learning to the workplace – and workplace activity to the learning. Access to practical demonstrations of processes through video clips and rewards work related activity with academic credit.

In Chapter 28 Willie McGuire describes his work with an online course at the University of Glasgow. It is a global, free, completely open, online course, with no entry requirements, not targeted at a specific group. It is a trans-discipline initiative that is cross-cutting in that it is targeted at all careers and is also supportive of academic-professional/work transitions. Its aim was to improve employability through the development of 'digital' or online *curriculum vitae* (CV) writing skills and it involved liaison with a wide range of internal and external partners.

Synchronous or Asynchronous?

In regard to the activities outlined above, there is the consideration of whether they are undertaken synchronously or asynchronously. This depends on the activity and whether this is for delivery, or whether it is an assessment event. Many of the activities run asynchronously and allow students to access learning material online and work through the modules at their own pace. Some of them are activities that are delivered to classes synchronously and all students work through them together, with a tutor facilitating. There are also examples where both synchronous and asynchronous activities are used and this depended primarily on the purpose and nature of them. Where there are assessments within the practices that are held at the same time, these were considered to be synchronous. Other assessments which are run over a dedicated time (e.g. 24 hours or more) then this was considered by the group to be asynchronous.

About the Authors

Dr. Didem Koban Koç is an assistant professor in the English Language Teaching Program at the Department of Foreign Languages at Hacettepe University, Ankara, Turkey. She can be contacted at this e-mail: dkoban@hacettepe.edu.tr

Dr. Jülide İnözü is an associate professor in the Department of English Language Teaching at Çukurova University in Turkey and is interested in the psychological perspectives of ELT including individual learner differences in language learning. She can be contacted at this e-mail: julideinozu@gmail.com

Dr. Ayşe Görgün is a lecturer at ELT Department, Çukurova University, Adana, Turkey. She specializes in Educational Technology. She can be contacted at this e-mail: pentimento8@gmail.com

Dr. Chris Perumalla is an Associate Professor, Teaching Stream, Department of Physiology, and Director of the Division of Teaching Laboratories, Faculty of Medicine, University of Toronto. He can be contacted at this e-mail: c.perumalla@utoronto.ca

Dr. Serdar Engin Koç is an assistant professor at the Department of Computer Education and Instructional Technologies at Başkent University, Turkey. He can be contacted at this e-mail: sekoc@baskent.edu.tr.

Dr Andries Du Plessis is Senior Lecturer in the Early Childhood Department at the Siyabuswa Campus of the University of Mpumalanga, South Africa. He can be contacted at this e-mail: andries.duplessis@ump.ac.za

Jeff Lewis is Principal Lecturer in Dental Technology at Cardiff Metropolitan University, Wales, United Kingdom. He can be contacted at this e-mail: jlewis@cardiffmet.ac.uk

Bibliography

Bernard, R. M.; P. C. Abrami; E. Borokhovski; C. A. Wade; R. M. Tamim; M. A. Surkes & E. C. Bethel (2009). A meta-analysis of three types of interaction treatments in distance education. *Review of Educational Research*, Vol. 79, No. 3, pp. 1243–1289.

Canadian Council on Learning. (2009). *State of e-Learning in Canada*. Ottawa. Online Resource: http://www.ccl-cca.ca/pdfs/E-learning/E-Learning_Report_FINAL-E.PDF

Chapman, C.; C. B. White; C. Engleberg; J. C. Fantone & S. K. Cinti (2011). Developing a fully online course for senior medical students. *Medical Education Online*, Vol. 16.

Cook, D. & F. McDonald (2008). E-Learning: Is There Anything Special about the "E"? *Perspectives In Biology And Medicine*, Vol. 51, No.1, pp. 5–21.

Cook, D.; S. Garside; A. Levinson; D. Dupras & V. Montori (2010). What do we mean by web-based learning? A systematic review of the variability of interventions. *Medical Education*, Vol. 44, No. 8, pp. 765–774.

Darwesh, M. G.; M. Z. Rashad & A. K. Hamada (2011). From Learning Style of Webpage Content to Learner's Learning Style. *International Journal of Computer Science & Information Technology*, Vol. 3, pp 6–14.

Dell, C. A.; C. Low & J. F. Wilker (2010). Comparing student achievement in online and face-to-face class formats. *Journal of Online Learning and Teaching*, Vol. 6, No. 1, pp. 30–42.

Kee, N.; D. Sarkis & C. Perumalla (2014). *Engaging Local and Global Learners in an e-Learning Environment-University of Toronto Experiences*. Proceedings of the 9th International Conference on e-Learning: ICEL 2014, pp. 104–118.

Means, B.; T. Yukie; R. Murphy; M. Bakia & K. Jones (2010). *Evaluation of Evidence-Based Practices in Online Learning: A Meta-Analysis and Review of Online Learning Studies*. U.S. Department of Education.

Peters, L; S. Shmerling & R. Karren (2011). Constructivist pedagogy in asynchronous online education: Examining proactive behaviour and the impact on student engagement levels. *International Journal on E-Learning*, Vol. 10, No. 3, pp. 311–330.

The Sloan Consortium (2011). *Going the Distance – Online Education in the United States*. Sloan Review.

Yates, R. W. & B. Beaudrie (2009). The impact of online assessment on grades in community college distance education mathematics courses. *The American Journal of Distance Education*, Vol. 23, pp. 62–70.

Chapter 22: E-learning

Promoting Self-Regulated Language Learning through a Technology Enhanced Content-based Classroom

Didem Koban Koç

Background

This teaching and learning practice incorporates self-regulated learning (SRL) combined with the use of technology in a content-based classroom. This practice involves English language learners at an intermediate level in an immersion program. The most important characteristic of this form of learning is students are independent learners who take responsibility for their own learning. When SRL is incorporated in a classroom it is expected that students are actively involved in the learning process and have control over their own learning (Usuki, 2007). In addition, students are expected to develop their metacognitive, cognitive, affective and social skills, such as planning, organizing and evaluating tasks, sharing information as well as solving problems that come up during the learning process. SRL also enables students to manage their time and their learning and learn to evaluate their own progress. All of these features make SRL an important form of learning that students can integrate into their everyday lives.

Although SRL in technology enhanced learning environments (TELE) has become an influential practice in education and thus been used in many schools and language teaching institutions worldwide, unfortunately, in most language classrooms, learning is still mostly teacher-centered, that is, teachers initiate what is going on in the classroom and they are the primary information providers. The reason for implementing this kind of innovative practice is that in contrast to traditional teaching and learning, teachers in SRL, instead of just transferring information, give guidance and feedback to students, motivate them to work independently and help them make their own decisions. Students' behavior is also different in SRL. They are the decision-makers and researchers. They set goals, make plans, monitor themselves and reflect on their learning process. However, SRL combined with TELE can be a demanding practice for teachers as they are required to update their skills in certain areas.

According to Zimmerman (2000), SRL involves three processes: *forethought*, *performance*, and *self-reflection*. In these processes students perform several cognitive, metacognitive, and motivational functions. In the *forethought* process, students first analyze the situation, instruction and available resources. Based on this analysis, they identify their own goals (Pintrich 2000; Zimmerman 2000) and determine appropriate activities related to their goals (Narciss *et al.*, 2007). The *performance* process requires learners to search for information and evaluate whether the information is relevant for their goals. According to Proske *et al.* (2007), taking notes during this process is an important activity that contributes to students' learning. This process also involves self-observation which refers to students' monitoring themselves (Kuhl, 2000). In the *self-reflection* process, students evaluate the learning outcome with respect to whether or not the goals of the learning process are satisfied. They also determine whether or not the activities they selected in the forethought process should be changed (Bannert & Mengelkamp 2008; Narciss *et al.*, 2007; Zimmerman 2000). Thus, students make self-judgements about their performances. As Pintrich (2000) states, SRL can be very demanding for some students as they constantly have to observe and self-reflect on their performances and update their strategies.

According to Bernacki *et al.* (2011) SRL has many advantages. First, it promotes metacognitive functions, that is, students have the opportunity to plan, organize, analyze tasks, and monitor their progress. Second, they use strategies such as taking notes, which help them understand and remember important information better. Third, students are able to adapt themselves easily to changing situations. Fourth, if students are given appropriate training in SRL, they are able concentrate on the task. Last, students do not necessarily need others to begin tasks, organize themselves and use strategies because they are aware of the fact that SRL contributes to their success.

The Practice

This teaching and learning practice involves intermediate level adult English language learners enrolled in a content-based classroom. Content-Based Instruction is considered as a student-centered language teaching approach that involves a subject area through which the target language is learned indirectly (Brinton et al., 1989). In other words, students learn the target language through studying a subject. For example, students use the English language to learn about 18th century British literature. The rationale behind Content-based instruction lies in the fact that if students study a subject that they are interested in they are more motivated to learn the target language. In addition, working on a content allows students to improve their higher-order thinking skills as they think about the content and less about the structure of the target language.

In this course, students explained the meaning of unfamiliar words in a given text, created sentences using the unfamiliar words in the given text, skimmed the given biography to look for the main idea, scanned the given biography to look for supporting ideas and created a presentation using the Moovly tool in groups of four. At the beginning of the term, surveys were distributed to students in order to learn their opinions about the use of technology. Also, the rationale for using technology was explained to the learners ahead of time. The majority of the students' opinions about using technology in the classroom were positive, so the teacher guided the students regarding the technological tools to be used in the class. These were concordance analysis, the Moovly and rubrics for web evaluation. This way, students knew the reasons why they had to complete certain tasks. If the students were not willing to use the technological tools, then the importance of using such tools in the learning process would have been explained to the students.

With respect to using technological tools in the classroom, it is important that in a TELE environment teachers are trained to use the necessary software before asking students to use it. Otherwise students will not know what to do with the software and will not be able to use the strategies they possess. Note that the teacher is already trained to use the tools in this practice and the programs that students need to use are already installed in their computers. Moreover, before the students were engaged in the tasks, the teacher gave the students some training in SRL. Several studies showed that students who receive training are likely to use learning strategies more effectively than those who are not trained in SRL (Azevedo *et al.*, 2002, 2003). These strategies include taking notes, reviewing them, managing time and activating prior knowledge. The teacher also monitored and evaluated students' work.

As the first task, the teacher introduced the famous pop-art artist, Andy Warhol, and asked students to brainstorm about his life and pop art. This way, students activated their prior knowledge (10 minutes). The students then looked at the images of Warhol and read about the techniques he used for his art at different websites. The students were free to choose the web sites. They reported their findings to the class (20 minutes). Next, the instructor asked students to read a biography of the artist online. Once again, the students were required to choose the biographies online themselves and answer several questions about the artist while reading the passage. Students read the biography online and answered the questions. Then they discussed the answers in the class (45 minutes).

Sample Questions

1. When and where was the artist born?

2. Was there a person who was influential to him as a child?

3. Describe the artist, both socially and academically.

4. Did the artist attend college? If so, which one? If not, why?

5. What subject(s) did he study and why?

6. Did he get a degree? In what?

7. What was his first job?

8. Who was the biggest influence in his career?

9. Did he have children? If so, how many and what age and gender are they?

10. Describe the artist's art.

The next task involved improving the vocabulary knowledge of the students. The teacher asked students to search for the meanings of unfamiliar words in the texts through the Collins Cobuild Corpus. The students did a concordance analysis. A concordance is a computer program which gives the lexical combinations of a certain key word once it is searched. It also gives the context in which the word is used and the frequency of occurrence of the lexical combinations. Therefore, it is an effective program that helps students to learn the uses of words in different contexts. Students entered each word on the website and retrieved the meaning of the words and lexical combinations. The students also made sample sentences with the new words in pairs and discussed the meanings of the words in the class (60 minutes). The following Table is an example of a concordance analysis ("Sample concordance program," 2016).

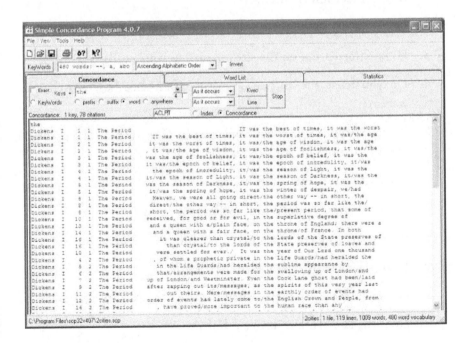

Table 1: Sample Concordance Analysis.

As the last task, the teacher divided the class into groups of four. She gave each group the name of a contemporary pop artist (Keith Haring, Claes Oldenburg, Coosje van Bruggen, Robert Raucshenberg, Richard Hamilton, Roy Lichtenstein, Peter Blake, and David Hockney) and asked them to search for the biography and works of each artist online. After the students retrieved information and took notes, they were asked to come up with a presentation using the Moovly tool. The Moovly is a software program which is used to create animated videos and presentations. Students prepared the presentation according to several points determined by the instructor. While the students searched for the websites, they were also required to evaluate the websites using a rubric (80 minutes). After they prepared their presentations, they presented it to the whole class (20 minutes).

Sample Questions in the Rubric

1. Is a personal author, publisher or an institution provided along with contact information?

2. Does the website have an .edu, .org, or .gov ending in its URL?

3. Is the information on the site relevant to your needs?

4. Do you trust the author or organization that has created the website?

5. Based on the reading you have already done on the subject, does the information on the site seem accurate?

6. Is factual information referenced in footnotes or a bibliography?

7. Are there any grammar and spelling mistakes?

8. If there are links to other pages, are they to reliable sources?

9. Is the date the site was created provided?

10. Is there a date that shows when the site has last been updated?

11. Does the site contain "broken" links?

("Website evaluation checklist," 2016).

Outcomes

This practice promoted behavior changes both in the students as well as in the teachers. First of all, encouraging students to search for information online helped students take control of their own learning. When students were free to choose their own texts, they became motivated and engaged in the lesson while they improved their literacy skills. According to Skehan (1991), choosing texts on the web increases students' intrinsic motivation. In addition, since the students were exposed to different biographies when they were searching for websites, they reported that they learned more interesting facts about the artist than when they were exposed to a single biography. This also led to interesting and motivating discussions in the class.

The students were also engaged in data-driven language learning which involves planning, monitoring, and evaluating (Wenden, 1991). Data-driven language learning plays an important role on motivating students to take responsibility for their own learning as well as improving their language skills and strategies. For example, when learning vocabulary through concordance analysis, students learned collocations, their uses and the grammatical contexts in which the words were used. As a result, students were exposed to natural language use (Friedman, 2009) and were personally involved in the learning process. Data-driven learning also gave the students the opportunity to organize and evaluate their work.

Regarding teachers' behaviors, although in SRL there seems to be a shift from teachers to students in terms of control and teachers do not seem to play a dominant role on providing information, their role as feedback givers is still very effective. Several studies indicated that learners are better at acquiring knowledge if they are given immediate feedback (McKendree, 1990; Gao, 2003; Graesser et al., 2004). Moreover, teachers' guidance and their role as information givers and observers combined with appropriate technological tools can be very influential in terms of student success. As the label TELE suggests, learning environments are only enhanced with computers and their software (Bernacki et al., 2011). In this practice, the usage of technology was supported by teacher feedback and the students received the necessary input. In addition, appraisal plays an important role in this practice. According to

Boekaerts & Niemivirta (2000), appraisal comes first and is an important factor that motivates students to complete the given tasks successfully. If students do not receive appraisal at the right moment, they may lose their motivation and choose not to finish the task. Therefore, it is important that teachers should value the role of appraisal.

This form of learning is successful because students have the opportunity to use metacognitive, cognitive, affective and social strategies such as planning, organizing, evaluating, and working with others at different stages of the lesson. The students used their metacognitive and cognitive strategies when they activated their prior knowledge before reading biographies, looked up unfamiliar words during a concordance analysis, read the biographies to answer certain questions as well as evaluated information. The students also developed metacognitive skills when they approached the task of creating a presentation, made decisions about what to include in their presentations and solved problems that came up during the tasks. In addition, students developed affective and social strategies when they interacted with each other to construct sample sentences during the vocabulary learning phase and prepared a presentation using the Moovly tool and participated in class discussions.

The practice also integrated technology to help learners plan, monitor and in some phases evaluate their learning. Data-driven learning not only allowed students to be exposed to authentic use of language when dealing with lexicon and reading texts, but it also allowed them to focus on real tasks such as searching for appropriate texts online, extracting specific information from the text, organizing information based on the feedback from the teacher and reporting it to an audience. Further, working with the Moovly tool gave the students the opportunity to share information with one another and work collaboratively.

Further, like in every learning situation, motivation is an important factor that facilitates learning. In this practice, the fact that learners were actively involved in the activities and had much more control over their learning process led to increased motivation in TELE (Moos & Azevedo, 2008a). In addition, SRL was incorporated into content-based context in which the target language was learned through a topic or subject-matter. The topic for the course was art and since both the students and the instructor decided on this topic at the beginning of the course, their motivation was already high.

In sum, the students had some control over the tasks when they selected, shared, created and evaluated information. While doing these they had support from the teacher and their peers. They worked in teams, which allowed them to acknowledge and use their social skills.

Moving Forward

This chapter offers and discusses several suggested technological tools through which self-regulated language learning is promoted. In order to enhance learning, several factors need to be taken into account for future practices. Firstly, using different forms of technology, which, according to Hiemstra (1988), serve as motivational factors for fostering independent learning. Nowadays students' use of technology in their everyday lives is increasing day by day. They depend on technology and use various technologies. Therefore, the use of additional forms of technological tools such as e-portfolios, Moodle, Blackboard, or blogs in future practices can increase students' interests in learning and involve them more in the learning process. For instance, it was found that blogs, in particular, are helpful for students who have difficulties in expressing themselves in the classroom (Koban Koç & Koç, 2016).

Another important factor to consider for future practices is students' characteristics. Before having students to use the right technological tool, students' characteristics have to be taken into consideration as TELEs must be adapted to students' needs (Bernacki et al., 2011). More importantly, since student characteristics may change over time, teachers should monitor students at each task and adjust activities according to the characteristics of the students. According to Bernacki et al. (2011) teachers should take a process approach and reassess pre-task characteristics in task periodically to monitor change.

Recall that the current practice involved tasks that took place in the classroom. What can also be done is that students can work on the same tasks through online learning platforms where the instructor and the students can communicate with each other by means of technology outside the classroom. Virtual learning platforms allow both students and instructors to access any information about the course when they are not in the classroom. The benefit of this is that students have the opportunity to work at their own pace outside of class time.

About the Author

Dr. Didem Koban Koç is an assistant professor in the English Language Teaching Program at the Department of Foreign Languages at Hacettepe University, Ankara, Turkey. She can be contacted at this e-mail: dkoban@ hacettepe.edu.tr

Bibliography

Azevedo, R.; J. G. Cromley; L. Thomas; D. Deibert & M. Tron (2003). Online Process Scaffolding and Students' Self-regulated Learning with Hypermedia. *Annual Meeting of the American Educational Research Association*, 31.

Azevedo, R.; D. Seibert; J. T. Guthrie; J. G. Cromley; H. Wang & M. Tron (2002). *How Do Students Regulate their Learning of Complex Systems with Hypermedia?* Paper presented at the annual meeting of the American Educational Research Association, New Orleans, LA.

Bannert, M. & C. Mengelkamp (2008). Assessment of Metacognitive Skills by Means of Instruction to Think Aloud and Reflect When Prompted. Does the Verbalisation Method Affect Learning? *Metacognition and Learning*, Vol. 3, No.1, pp. 39–58.

Bernacki, M.; A. C. Aguilar & J. P. Byrnes (2011). Self-Regulated Learning and Technology-Enhanced Learning Environments: An Opportunity-Propensity Analysis. In G. Dettori & D. Persico (Eds.), *Fostering Self-Regulated Learning through ICT* Hershey, PA: Information Science Reference.

Boekaerts, M. & M. Niemivirta (2000). Self-regulated Learning: Finding a Balance between Learning Goals and Ego-protective goals. In M. Boekaerts; P. R. Pintrich & M. Zeidner (Eds.), *Handbook of Self-Regulation*. San Diego, CA: Academic Press.

Brinton, D. M.; M. A. Snow & M. B. Wesche (1989). *Content-based Second Language Instruction*. New York: Newbury House.

Friedman, G. L. (2009). Learner-created Lexical Databases Using Web-based Source Material. *ELT Journal*, Vol. 63, No. 2, pp. 126–136.

Gao, T. (2003). The Effects of Different Levels of Interaction on the Achievement and Motivational Perceptions of College Students in a Web- based Learning Environment. *Journal of Interactive Learning*, Vol. 14, No. 4, pp. 367–386.

Graesser, A. C.; S. Lu; G. T. Jackson; H. Mitchell; M. Ventura; A. Olney & M. M. Louwerse (2004). Auto Tutor: A Tutor with Dialogue in Natural Language. *Behavior Research Methods, Instruments, and Computers*, Vol. 36, pp. 180–193.

Hiemstra, R. (1988). Self-directed Learning: Individualizing Instruction. In H. B. Long (Ed.). *Self-directed Learning: Application and Theory*. Athens, GA: University of Georgia, Adult Education Department.

Koban Koç, D. & S. E. Koç (2016). Students' Perceptions of Blog Use in an Undergraduate Linguistics Course. *Journal of Language and Linguistic Studies*, Vol. 12 No.1. pp. 9–19.

Kuhl, J. (2000). A Functional-design Approach to Motivation and Self-regulation: The Dynamics of Personality Systems and Interactions. In M. Boekaerts; P. R. Pintrich & M. Zeidner (Eds.), *Handbook of Self-regulation*. San Diego, CA: Academic Press.

McKendree, J. (1990). Effective Feedback Content for Tutoring Complex Skills. *Human Computer Interact*, Vol. 5, pp. 381–413.

Moos, D. C. & Azevedo, R. (2008c). Self-regulated Learning with Hypermedia: The Role of Prior Domain Knowledge. *Contemporary Educational Psychology*, Vol. 33, No. 2, pp. 270–298.

Narciss, S.; A. Proske & H. Körndle (2007). Promoting Self-regulated Learning in Web-based Learning Environments. *Computers in Human Behavior*, Vol. 23, No. 3, pp. 1126–1144.

Pintrich, P. R. (2000). The Role of Goal Orientation in Self-regulated Learning. In M. Boekaerts; P. R. Pintrich & M. Zeidner (Eds.), *Handbook of Self-regulation*. San Diego, CA: Academic Press, pp. 451–502.

Skehan, P. (1991). Individual Differences in Second-Language Learning. *Studies in Second Language Acquisition*, Vol. 13, No. 2, pp. 275–298.

Usuki, M. (2007). *Autonomy in Language Learning: Japanese Students' Exploratory Analysis*. Nagoya, JP: Sankeisha.

Wenden, A. L. (1991). *Learner Strategies for Learner Autonomy. Planning and Implementing Learner Training for Language Learners*. London, UK: Prentice Hall.

Zimmerman, B. J. (2000). Attaining Self-regulation: A Social Cognitive Perspective. In M. Boekaerts; P. R. Pintrich & M. Zeidner (Eds.), *Handbook of Self-regulation*. San Diego, CA, USA: Academic.

Chapter 23: E-learning

Promoting Language Skills through Teacher-structured out-of-class ICT Activities in Higher Education Context

Jülide İnözü & Ayşe Görgün

Background

It is an undeniable fact that rapid technological advances and global communication have changed the life of people in the 21st century irrevocably in every aspect. The Internet explosion and the information and communication technologies (ICTs) at the end of the 20th century opened new opportunities and are bringing about dramatic changes in teaching and learning (Brown, 2002; Lewin, 2000; Beebe, 2004; Oblinger, 2005, 2006; Mellow, 2005; Solomon & Schrum, 2007; Traxler, 2007; Bonk, 2009; Green & Hannon, 2007). New digital technologies and the Internet have particularly been effective in the field of language teaching and learning (Kukulska-Hulme, 2006). Research findings (Lee, 2000; Thorne et al., 2009; Zhao & Lai, 2007) indicate that digital technologies and access to Internet offers language teachers and learners a profuse amount of English resources and activities for in and outside the classroom.

Educational researchers often claim that with the widespread use of new technologies and electronic resources, all education has been revolutionized (Spreen, 2002; Baird & Fisher, 2006; Imperatore, 2009; Abel, 2005; Cochrane, 2006). Along with constructivism, a paradigm shift is taking place in the approaches to education in terms of method and structure: from teaching to learning, from classroom to real life, from one-time training to life-long education, and from stand-alone to networking. These shifts accommodate with the European Union's aims for education (Oliveira, 2003, cited in Brown 2005): learning resources should be digital and adaptable to individual needs and preferences; e-learning platforms should support collaborative learning; and ICTs should not be an add-on but an integrated part of the learning process.

It is imperative that the educators of modern times recognize the fact that their roles have changed from simply transferring knowledge to facilitating learning. They should become fully aware of new concepts and opportunities offered by ICTs to increase the effectiveness of their teaching through skilful integration of digital technologies into the school environment. This is necessary not only for enhancing their way of teaching, but also preparing students to meet the challenges of fast-paced globalization and high-tech environment of the future. Despite its acknowledged importance, it should be noted that technology itself is not a method; and we cannot improve teaching and learning just by putting materials online (Alexander & McKenzie, in Kirkwood & Price, 2005; Kellner, 2004; Blass & Davis, 2003; Henry & Meadows, 2008). What really matter is how creatively and properly it is applied and constructively integrated in an educational program (Taylor & Clark, 2010; Beetham & Sharpe, 2007). Without proper resources, pedagogy, and educational practices, technology might be an obstacle or burden to genuine learning (Kellner, 2004; Chinnery, 2006; Chinien & Boutin, 2005). McKenzie (in Kirkwood & Price, 2005) stated that along with a range of factors, which are necessary for a successful outcome, the most critical factor is the design of the students' learning experience.

The Practice

So far, ICTs were used in higher education mostly as a supplement to existing teaching and learning practices or sometimes just because they are convenient. In the present study, we aimed to explore the use of a combination of ICTs in learning English listening skills, which is a problematic area in language learning particularly for the students who are learning a foreign language where it is not used as the language of communication.

We think that students should be given special guidance and be involved in out-of-class activities that are designed by the instructor, until they attain the necessary skills that can make them independent and self-regulated learners. These activities should not remain only as out-of-class activities, but should be blended with the regular courses and the curriculum in order to arouse and maintain the motivation of students. In our particular case, we started with an administration of a survey to explore the activities the students are already engaged in using the Internet. The students were observed that they have already been involved in activities, such as watching films, surfing on the Internet, and watching television programs outside of the classroom. However, the students remarked that these activities were not practiced sufficiently enough to contribute to their language development. The activities employed by the students were related to entertainment mostly and receptive rather than productive in nature.

Following our survey, at the start of the course, the students were introduced to the blended program that was to be employed throughout the year. They were given information about the tasks that they were expected to do and also the procedure to be followed. In order to form a community of practice among the participant students and to establish a common communication platform, a class blog page was built. From the same blog site, each student built up their own blogs for sharing documents of their interest and comments. This blog was used for extending the classroom to beyond its physical borders, thereby creating an out of class virtual environment. One particular use was content distribution. The instructor paid particular attention to provide relevant materials that would match students' interests, tastes and proficiency levels while at the same time ensuring it remains demanding and challenging. What makes this practice different from ordinary ICT applications is that we used the classroom sessions as a follow-up of out-of-class ICT activities. The students were asked to complete these activities on their own. By its design, the procedure shared some common features with flip mode instruction in which the classroom was turned into a stage where the students had an opportunity to practice more and internalize what they had mastered outside of the classroom. The classrooms also served another purpose. They functioned like an exhibition hall for students to share their experiences, which were already communicated virtually through their blogs. This practice was implemented on a recursive basis, even during the semester break and public holidays due to the demands from the students.

Preparation and Sample Activities

We believe that the out-of-class activities, especially the ones exploiting the affordances of ICTs, are of great importance to help students improve their language skills; and students should be provided with opportunities, guided and motivated by their instructors to take the utmost advantage of these activities and the time spent out of the classroom. However, most of the learners do not take the advantage of ICTs as out-of-class activities and do not apply out-of-class activities in a conscious and systematic manner. Therefore, the instructor should be aware of the possible contributions of out-of-class activities to language skills, and try to arrange the teaching/learning process and context in such a way that students should get the optimum benefit out of them. Assigning out-of-class activities to students on an irregular basis may not help them improve listening skills – as it was evident the participants' own experiences. The same applies to efforts to establish goal-oriented habits. Therefore, these activities should be planned, arranged, orchestrated and guided by the instructor who must be well versed in digital technologies and its pedagogical and practical value. By using out-of-class ICT activities, time and space problems can be overcome and the class time can be extended in order to provide more exposure to the target language by making use of students' dead or unproductive time. However, some factors, such as referring to out-of-class activities in class, including materials and related tasks addressing various interests and learning styles, creating a collaborative atmosphere in the learning context, giving realistic and constructive feedback, being available (through the class blog, e-mail and phone) in times of need, brainstorming and discussions about the past and future activities, arranging challenging but attainable activities, and encouraging self-evaluation are among the key elements for maintaining students' interest and active involvement.

In our institution, Listening and Oral Communication is a two-term course that is taken for the duration of the academic year. We started our implementation at the very start of the first term and it went on almost until the end of the year. The students were introduced the new approach during the first lesson of the course. They were informed about what they were supposed to do. The benefits of this approach were also clarified. During this first lesson and the following ones, there was continuous brainstorming about what topics we should choose for listening activities and online searches. The introduction part is particularly important because students should believe that what they are going to do will be really beneficial to improve their language skills. The course would be covered in a regular way, using a textbook and regular listening and speaking activities in the classroom. In addition to this, the students would listen to extra passages, which are related to work being covered in the classroom. This was followed by related tasks, research about the topic or an aspect of the topic, sharing what they found on their blogs, and finally talking about it in the class as either presentation or discussion. As the first step, the instructor built a class blog and published all the passages, as well as assignments onto the blog. On the same blog site, each student built their own blogs and shared their studies. In this way, we have been convinced that it is possible to triple, even quadruple both the amount of the passages the students listen to and the time they spend on listening and speaking activities. Below are two samples illustrating the practices at the early stages of our implementation.

After covering a topic about cultural differences in the lesson, the instructor uploaded a listening passage about the same topic. There were various accompanying activities such as answering "wh" questions, fill-in-the-blank questions and vocabulary searches. Their following task was to choose an event, such as national holidays, wedding ceremonies, funerals, celebrations, etc., to do research about how they are held in English culture, share their findings on their blogs, make groups of three or four for giving a presentation and finally share what they learned in the classroom.

As for the second example, following the regular listening and speaking activities on Shakespeare's plays in the classroom session, the instructor uploaded a listening passage about Romeo and Juliet. The students' task was to listen to the passage as many times as necessary until they think they fully understood the content, to do the related exercises provided to them by the instructor to find more information about Shakespeare's plays and to prepare a brief summary of the specific play they learned about. This they were to post on their own blogs. Then, they were asked to present a summary about the specific play they chose by giving information on the main characters, the plot and the theme. In this way, each student provided insight into his or her selected play to everyone else. The next task involved a collage of Shakespeare's plays. To achieve this task, the students were asked to work in groups and to write a script for a new play. They had to communicate and collaborate through their blogs. The final stage of this particular activity was to produce this play on a stage in the classroom.

In both illustrations above, the activity stream that started in the classroom and then continued outside of the classroom was finalized in the classroom. To sum up, the whole course of activities was implemented in a blended fashion where each step followed chronologically upon each other.

Outcomes

The study contributed profoundly to the students' language skills, primarily listening and speaking skill, and they have learned many new things while doing all these activities. The project has positive effects on them in many aspects such as improved language skills, increased self-confidence and motivation, improved self-awareness, and enriched general culture. The students also pointed out that they have changed/improved their studying strategies throughout the course.

In our opinion, one of the reasons for obtaining positive results in this study stems from creating a student-centred, flexible, and collaborative study environment. This was supported by teacher scaffolding by uploading a wide range of materials and activities addressing different types of learners and interests, taking into account both cognitive and social aspects of learning. Intense comprehensible input with a low affective filter leads to motivation. In turn, motivation leads to increased effort. Increased effort leads to success. Success leads to building self-efficacy and self-efficacy leads to motivation, thus creating a virtuous cycle that results in better language acquisition.

The blended-design aspect of the course kept the student motivation high throughout the term. In blended designs, where face-to-face interactions and virtual learning environments are integrated, the likelihood of high motivation and achievement are higher than in fully traditional or fully on-line courses for they offer easy access outside of the classroom, flexibility, low anxiety, self-paced learning, student-student interaction outside the classroom, and timely feedback from the instructor thanks to the on-line component (Sitter *et al.*, 2009; Dziuban *et al.*, 2004; Bonk & Graham, 2006; Motteram & Sharma, 2009; Graham & Dziuban, 2008; Govender, 2010; Bekele, 2010; Rose & Ray, 2011). Blended learning, allowing students to study in their private or preferred environment in the absence of an authority and also time constraints, lowers the student anxiety to a considerable extent. Parallel to these arguments, the participant students were observed to feel more comfortable and free to get involved in the classroom activities willingly.

Improvement in self-efficacy perceptions of the participants was another successful outcome of the course. Self-efficacy is people's beliefs about their capabilities to organize and perform required courses of action to attain a specific goal, and these beliefs determine how people think, feel, motivate themselves and behave; choices they make, the effort they exert, the persistence and perseverance they display when they encounter difficulties and obstacles, and the degree of anxiety or serenity they experience while dealing with various tasks (Bandura, 1994). We can conclude that the students in this study are able to increase their self-efficacy with the help of ample amount of passages and the related activities. The students also realized that their success/goal attainment depended on an internal, unstable and controllable factor, effort.

Moving Forward

It should be kept in mind that simply putting materials online or giving links to students for self-study without supervising, guiding and evaluating is not as effective as the systematic integration of these materials in the regular course. As previous research (Chinnery, 2006; Mayora, 2006; Kirkwood & Price, 2005; Henry & Meadows, 2008; Puerto & Gamboa, 2009) agreed on that what makes the difference is not the device itself, but the combination of thoughtful second language pedagogy and technology. Therefore, instructors who have the purpose of facilitating and enhancing learning through ICTs should have clearly defined goals and develop a design which can provide students with utmost benefits while they are trying to achieve those goals by grounding on a sound pedagogical basis.

About the Authors

Dr. Jülide İnözü is an associate professor in the Department of English Language Teaching at Çukurova University in Turkey and is interested in the psychological perspectives of ELT including individual learner differences in language learning. She can be contacted at this e-mail: julideinozu@gmail.com

Dr. Ayşe Görgün is a lecturer at ELT Department, Çukurova University, Adana, Turkey. She specializes in Educational Technology. She can be contacted at this e-mail: pentimento8@gmail.com

Bibliography

Abel, R. J. (2005). What's next in learning technology in higher education. *A-HEC In-Depth*, Vol. 2, No. 2.

Baird, D. E. & M. Fisher (2006). Neomillennial user experience design strategies: Utilizing social networking media to support "Always On" learning styles. *Journal of Educational Technology Systems*, Vol. 34, No. 1, pp. 5–32.

Bandura, A. (1994). Self-efficacy. In V. S. Ramachaudran (Ed.) *Encyclopedia of Human Behaviour*. New York: Academic Press, pp. 71–81.

Beebe, M. A. (2004). *Impact of ICT revolution on the African academic landscape*. Working Paper.

Beetham, H. & Sharpe, R. (2007) *Rethinking pedagogy for a digital age: Designing and delivering e-learning*. London: Routledge.

Bekele, T. A. (2010). Motivation and satisfaction in internet-supported learning environments: A review. *Educational Technology & Society*, Vol. 13, No. 2, pp. 116–127.

Blass, E. & E. Davis (2003). Building on solid foundations: Establishing criteria for e-learning development. *Journal of Further and Higher Education*, Vol. 27, No. 3, pp. 227–245.

Bonk, C. J. (2009). *The world is open: How web technology is revolutionizing education*. San Francisco: Jossey-Bass.

Bonk, C. J. & C. R. Graham (2006). *The handbook of blended learning: Global perspectives, local designs.* San Francisco: Pfeiffer Publishing.

Brown, J. (2002). Growing up digital: How the web changes work, education, and the ways people learn. *USDLA Journal*, Vol. 16, No. 2.

Brown, T. H. (2005). Beyond constructivism: Exploring future learning paradigms. *Education Today*, Vol. 2, pp. 1–11.

Chinien, C. & F. Boutin (2005). *Framework for strengthening research ICT-mediated learning.* Paper presented at ITHET 6th Annual International Conference T3B–1. July 7–9. Juan Dolio, Dominican Republic.

Chinnery, M. G. (2006). Going to the MALL: Mobile Assisted Language Learning. *Language Learning and Technology*, Vol. 10, No. 1, pp. 9–16.

Cochrane, T. (2006). *Learning with wireless mobile devices and social software.* Proceedings of the 23rd annual ascilite conference: Who's learning? Whose technology. The University of Sydney.

Dziuban, C.; P. Moskal & J. Hartman (2004). *Higher education, blended learning and the generations: Knowledge is power-no more.* Center for Teaching Excellence, University of South Carolina.

Govender, D. W. (2010): Attitudes of students towards the use of a Learning Management System (LMS) in a face-to-face learning mode of instruction. *Africa Education Review*, Vol. 7, No. 2, pp. 244–262.

Graham, C. R. & C. Dziuban (2008). Blended learning environments. In J. M. Spector; M. D. Merril; J. Van Merrienboer & M. P. Driscoll (Eds.) *Handbook of Research on Educational Communications and Technology.* New York: Taylor & Francis Group, pp. 269–276.

Green, H. & C. Hannon (2007). *Their space: Education for a digital generation.* London: Demos.

Henry, J. & J. Meadows (2009). An absolutely riveting online course: Nine principles for excellence in web-based teaching. *Canadian Journal of Learning and Technology*, Vol. 34, No. 1.

Imperatore, C. (2009). What you need to know about web 2.0. techniques. *Connecting Education & Careers*, Vol. 83, No. 9, pp. 20–23.

Kellner, D. (2004). Technological transformation, multiple literacies and the re-visioning of education. *E-Learning*, Vol. 1, No. 1, pp. 9–37.

Kirkwood, A. & L. Price (2005). Learners and learning in the twenty-first century: What do we know about students' attitudes towards and experiences of information andcommunication technologies that will help us design courses? *Studies in Higher Education*, Vol. 30, No. 3, pp. 257–274.

Kukulska-Hulme, A. (2006). Mobile language learning now and in the future. In P. Sevensson (Ed.), *From vision to practice: Language learning and IT.* Sweden: Swedish Net University, pp. 295–310.

Lee, K. W. (2000). English teachers' barriers to the use of computer assisted language learning. *The Internet TESL Journal*, Vol. VI, No. 12.

Lewin, K. M. (2000): New technologies and knowledge acquisition and use in developing countries. *Compare: A Journal of Comparative and International Education*, Vol. 30, No. 3, pp. 313–321.

Mayora, C. A. (2006). Integrating multimedia technology in a high school EFL program. *English Teaching Forum*, Vol. 44, pp. 14–21.

Mellow, P. (2005). The media generation: Maximize learning by getting mobile. Paper presented ASCILITE Conference, 2005.

Motteram, G. & P. Sharma (2009). Blended learning in a web 2.0 world. *International Journal of Emerging Technologies & Society*, Vol. 7, No. 2, pp. 83–96.

Oblinger D. (2005). Leading the transition from classrooms to learning spaces. *Education Quarterly*, Vol. 1, pp. 14–18.

Oblinger, D. G. (2006). Space as a change agent. In D. G. Oblinger (Ed.), *Learning Spaces*. Washington DC: Educause, pp. 1–1.4.

Puerto, F. G. & E. Gamboa (2009). The evaluation of computer-mediated technology by second language teachers: Collaboration and interaction in CALL. *Educational Media International*, Vol. 46, No. 2, pp. 137–152.

Rose, R. & J. Ray (2011). Encapsulated presentation: A new paradigm of blended learning. *The Educational Forum*, Vol. 75, pp. 228–43.

Sitter, V.; C. Carter; R. Mahan; C. Masselo& T. Carter (2009). Faculty and student perceptions of a hybrid course design. In P. Smith (Ed.), *Proceedings of the ASCUE Summer Conference 42nd Annual Conference Association of Small Computer Users in Education*. Myrtle Beach: ASCUE, pp. 40–51.

Solomon, G. & L. Schrum (2007). Web 2.0 new tools, new schools. Technology and second language learning: Promises and problems. In L. L. Parker (Ed.), *Technology-mediated learning environments for young English learners: Connections in and out of school*. Mahwah, NJ: Lawrence Erlbaum Associates, pp. 167–205.

Spreen, C. A. (2002). *New technologies and language learning: Cases in the less commonly taught languages*. Hawaii: Second Language Teaching & Curriculum Center, University of Hawaii.

Taylor, L. & S. Clark (2010). Educational design of short, audio-only podcasts: The teacher and student experience. *Australasian Journal of Educational Technology*, Vol. 26, No. 3, pp. 386–399.

Thorne, S.; R. W. Black & J. M. Sykes (2009). Second language use, socialization, and learning in Internet interest communities and online gaming. *Modern Language Journal*, Vol. 93, pp. 802–821.

Traxler, J. (2007) Defining, Discussing and Evaluating Mobile Learning: The moving finger writes and having writ.... *International Review of Research in Open and Distance Learning*, Vol. 8, No. 2.

Zhao, Y. & C. Lai (2007). Technology and second language learning: Promises and problems. In L. L. Parker (Ed.), *Technology-mediated learning environments for young English learners: Connections in and out of school.* Mahwah, NJ: Lawrence Erlbaum Associates, pp. 167–205.

Chapter 24: E-learning

Impact of eLearning: Looking past the hype. The impact of two Life Science courses on global learners

Chris Perumalla, Nohjin Kee, Roula Andreopoulos
& Sian Patterson

Background

For decades, traditional in-class courses in physiology and biochemistry were offered to students in the Life Sciences programs at the University of Toronto. Although non-University of Toronto students can take these courses, it precludes those who do not live in the Greater Toronto area, and those who are working fulltime, as it would require them to physically come down to the university campus. Furthermore, with increasing numbers of people choosing a second career in health sciences, physiology and/or biochemistry are prerequisite courses for admission into these programs. Identifying this vast need of the learners for courses they can access from distance or at their own pace from their own place for those who are employed, we embarked on developing and subsequently delivering online physiology (ON-PSL) and online biochemistry (ON-BCH) courses.

Unlike several existing open forms of online courses such as the massive open online courses (MOOCs) and open educational resources (OER), both ON-PSL and ON-BCH courses are not "open" and therefore are only accessible for students who are registered in these courses.

The learners in these courses are taking them as they need either a credit or credit equivalent certificate which they can use to fulfill the requirement of their respective institution. From this perspective, both ON-PSL and ON-BCH improve access to learning materials and educational content without the restrictions of time, space or distance (Means *et al.*, 2010).

The purpose of this paper aims to provide insights for online educators based on our experiences of engaging distance learners in the E-learning format in physiology and biochemistry. These courses have a global learner contingent and consist of heterogeneous population who are taking these courses for a variety of reasons including prerequisites for second degree health science professional programs, transfer credit towards their undergraduate or graduate degrees to name a few. In spite of the demographic challenges and difference in prior background, we have created a classroom experience in providing for the students a holistic learning experience.

The Practice

Our innovative projects provide accessible education via online course delivery, enabling students to work in their own learning environment at their own pace, while maintaining the same high quality learning experience available to on-campus students. We have developed a robust and portable model of an online course, which was first used to create an ON-PSL course in 2008 and based on its generic framework, the ON-BCH course was created in 2009. Our online courses offer students the flexibility, affordability and easy access to course material, specifically for those who cannot afford the time nor have access to physically attend the courses on university campus.

We have given much thought to the instructional design and technology to ensure high standards are maintained to keep up with the 21st century learning and teaching standards, as they are essential for making an impact to our learners (Reeves & Hedberg, 2012). We have designed both our online courses to be intuitive with the use of Blackboard Learning Management System (BLMS) and have developed our own paradigms to ensure that learning is not compromised. Key features of our online courses are replicating the in-class experience of providing "real time video lectures" which are synchronized with PowerPoint slides, replicating the in-class experience.

The life-like easy-to-use, high-definition, video lectures with excellent online streaming can be accessed by students once they have registered into the course. Three lectures are uploaded on the server every week, during which time the students can watch from anywhere and any number of times; three new video lectures are uploaded every week. In this context, students "attend" three lectures per week, similar to the on-campus course with the added flexibility of watching them multiple times with the option to "stop and go" to catch up with difficult concepts.

Several other tools within the BLMS facilitates student engagement, self-directed learning with the ability to structure their learning experience so that it matches their learning style, often providing over and beyond experience to the online students compared to the in-class cohort of students. For example, the Discussion Board (DB) feature which enables students and professors to create a discussion thread and reply to the ones already created. The academic correctness of the DB is regularly monitored by a Teaching Assistant (TA). Students are encouraged to take initiative in posting a question and responding to a question posted by their colleagues. Interestingly, DB is used significantly more frequently than on-campus students, where the online learners' posts total about 1000 during the duration of the course representing a ten-fold increase compared to their on-campus colleagues. Other BLMS features which are used in the online courses include chat where students chat with each other in real-time mass email announcements, chat and email, all of which significantly enhance the student experiences in ON-PSL and ON-BCH.

- Announcements: Professors and teachers may post announcements for students to read. These can be found under the announcement tab, or can be made to pop-up when a student accesses Blackboard;

- Chat: This function allows those students who are online to chat in real time with other students in their class section;

- Collaborate: This feature allows TAs to share their computer screen and interact with participating students in real time;

- Discussions: This feature allows students and professors to create a discussion thread and reply to ones already created;

- Mail: Blackboard mail allows students and teachers to send mail to one another. This feature supports mass emailing to students in a course.

Students have access to an asynchronous learning community in a faculty-monitored online discussion forum, with 24/7 access to resources, lecturers, and TA, enabling students to learn with and from their peers. Our online courses have been designed to have a semi-structured format. The streaming lectures are made available on a weekly basis, which provides a balance between flexibility for students to customize their learning and the provision of systematic guidance to ensure timely completion of learning objectives. Secure encryption ensures protection of the course material and student information, tracking, and reporting on learning. A "virtual classroom" effect is achieved by a combination of monitored student participation on the discussion board and "virtual online office hours" monitored by the TA for two hours a week. Both student learning and program efficacy are monitored via online student evaluations and assessments, online surveys, and through a built-in capacity to track and analyze web activity.

Blackboard's built-in capacity for continuous assessment of student learning, feedback about student engagement, and evaluation of the efficacy of delivery model is also used to monitor our goals and course objectives. The assessments and evaluations in the course consist of several online quizzes occurring every three weeks and cover the material learnt during that period, and participation in the discussion board – both of which contribute towards the term mark and a proctored final exam. The proctored final exam is administered by the School of Continuing Studies (SCS) at the UofT. SCS works with their existing collaborations around the world enables students to take the final exam from any of their multiple locations around the world.

There are other self-directed elements in each of these courses to augment and reinforce concepts taught in the lectures either through "virtual labs or computer simulations" corresponding with each of the twelve body systems; in the biochemistry online course however, there are several "vignettes or case-based scenarios"; these active learning components complement the corresponding lectures. These courses balance self-directed and customized learning for students with the provision of systematic guidance to ensure the timely completion of learning objectives. Online course and lecturer surveys are carried out to allow students to share their learning experience and to allow us to use students' feedback, insights and contributions to improve our online courses. Students' comments have provided us with valuable insights into their learning experience as well as their goals and educational needs.

These courses have a global learner contingent and consist of a heterogeneous population who are taking these courses for a variety of reasons including as a pre-requisite for second degree health science professional programs, or as a transfer credit towards their undergraduate or graduate degree. The table below (Figure 1 shows the distribution of the demographics of our learners.

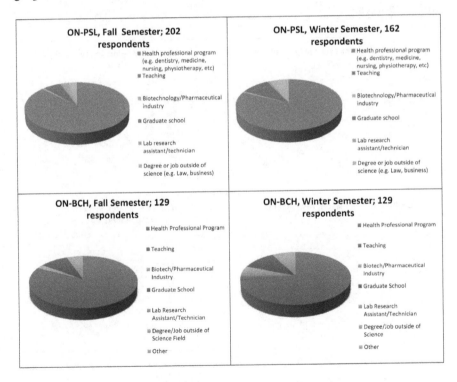

Figure 1: Distribution of the student population in ON-PSL and ON-BCH. Students were asked what their top choice for their future career was after graduation.

Outcomes

Our ON-PSL and ON-BCH courses have been offered more than 40 times over the past 7 years. From inception, we have designed and conducted student and course surveys to assess the quality, efficiency and efficacy of our online courses. To date, we have collected and analyzed the surveys and the results consistently demonstrate that our online courses provided a great and valuable learning experience. In addition, we have demonstrated that our online courses are well organized and integrated with the logical progression of subject matter. We are able to provide the depth of learning you expect in a university level course with the convenience and advantages that accompanies an online course. Figure 2 shows the results of the question of the valuable learning experience in these online courses.

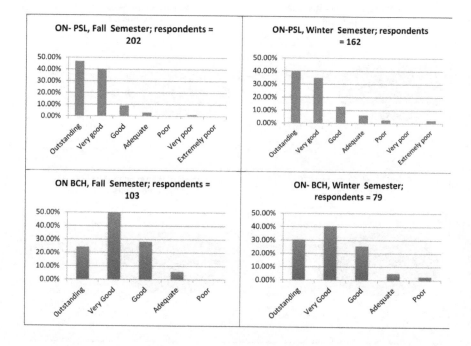

Figure 2: Analysis of the student surveys on their learning experiences in Online Physiology and Biochemistry courses.

Students' comments have provided us with valuable insights into their learning experience as well as their goals and educational needs.

Positive student comments for ON-PSL:

+ This course is taught with enthusiasm and with the required material, students can easily work to achieve a good grade and learn more about physiology.

+ I really enjoyed this course and having the opportunity to do it online allowed me to learn more about physiology. The lectures and study notes were very informative and Physio Ex (virtual lab) was a very helpful tool to review and apply the concepts that we've learned during the lectures. The discussion board was helpful to get discussions going and a safe place to ask questions that were confusing... I am happy I took this course and I would recommend it to other students looking for a physiology course.

+ I think this course has been fantastic. It is perfect for the way I learn – I am a very self-motivated and self-directed learner. I think the evaluation system is very fair. I like the online quizzes and I like that there is a final exam as well.

Positive student comments for ON-BCH:

+ The course was a valuable learning experience because I have learned a lot on the basics of biochemistry and its connection with medicine. I believe that this is very useful to my field and that it has taught me well on the biochemical foundations in relation to the medical field. The different activities also gave me the opportunity to use my creative side and work with my classmates.

+ It is rare to find a well organized online course but this one is amazing and I enjoyed it.

+ The course was a great learning experience and I really enjoyed it from beginning to end. I felt that it was a good pace and the material was continuously building from week to week which made it easy to follow along. I was able to remember things from the early weeks so the material really did stick and I think that really does show how valuable this learning experience has been.

+ The course was fascinating and challenging! It was well organized and exceeded my expectations!

Negative student comments for ON-PSL:

+ I think that the layout of this course was good, however I would have enjoyed/appreciated having more opportunities to get evaluated. I wouldn't have minded having more quizzes, or even an assignment or two.

+ One thing I don't think is 100% necessary is the 5% participation grade for posting on the discussion boards. I rarely have any questions to post on them, and when I eventually am able to make time to check the boards everyone's questions are already answered. So I'm not sure how to get my 5% without repeating others' questions or asking completely redundant ones.

Negative student comments for ON-BCH:

+ This course can be difficult because of its speed and being online. But the teachers and online lecture availability were helpful and the information was interesting.

+ The learning platform is very doable and I enjoyed being able to schedule my learning around my work schedule. That being said, I would caution those interested in taking it that it does require quite a bit of a time commitment. I didn't quite realize the extent of time that would be required to properly watch the videos and get a good grasp on most of the material. However, it is an accelerated course which I appreciate and I feel that the content is spot-on.

The need for E-Learning courses in physiology and biochemistry has become popular not only for second degree students or undergraduate students who need them towards their transfer credits, but also a new cohort of students who want to take these courses as refreshers as they prepare for Medical College Admissions Tests (MCAT). Furthermore, our subjective experiences and objective, measurable data concur with the experience of other educators that E-learning is proving to be on par with traditional methods of teaching at least with regard to learning outcomes (Cook et al., 2008, 2010; Yates & Beaudrie, 2009). Both our ON-PSL and ON-BCH have together been offered nearly 40 times and without exception, the student satisfaction in meeting obtaining the learning objectives and reaching the goals set for themselves have been exemplary and consistent. Furthermore, both ON-PSL and ON-BCH have identical on-campus courses and surveys have shown that the learning outcomes and student experiences in both types of courses (online and on campus) in these two courses are comparable (Kee et al., 2012).

Moving Forward

The initial goal which we set for ourselves in providing an accessible education via the E-learning format, enabling students to work in their own learning environment at their own pace, while maintaining the same high quality learning experience available to on-campus students has been achieved in ways which we little imagined at the onset of these online courses. Within the context of the overarching goal of providing superb educational experience for our online learners, we focused on accessibility, and quality of the students' educational experience. Both have been achieved. We have gained valuable insights and experiences, engaging distant learners through our ON-PSL and ON-BCH courses over the past eight years.

Experiences gained from creating and administering our online courses are enabling us to create new, innovative hybrid courses which will include a significant online component for the on campus students in the health sciences programs at the UofT. Furthermore, we would like to explore different ways of creating hybrid courses which include a "flipped classroom" or include different innovative, practical components of "hands on" experiences and case based scenarios to augment what the students learn watching the video lectures and participating on DB and TA-moderated online chats. We are also exploring to use our model in creating other online courses in other Life Sciences programs such as Immunology, Microbiology, Nutritional Sciences to name a few.

Furthermore, we would like to explore how machine-learning techniques to personalize learning experiences of our learners as such attempts are being made in other fields of study (e.g. Spice, 2014).

As we move forward into the next phase of creating new basic science online courses, we would like to further test the efficacy of the existing courses, new courses and develop new types of hybrid models. With the significant advances in technology and access to high speed internet by global learners, new opportunities arise to take E-learning to new heights in the next decade.

About the Authors

Dr. Nohjin Kee is an Associate Professor, Teaching Stream, Department of Physiology, Faculty of Medicine, University of Toronto. Dr. Nohjin Kee is the course director for several online physiology courses. He can be contacted at this e-mail: Nohjin.kee@utoronto.ca

Dr. Roula Andreopoulos is an Associate Professor, Teaching Stream, Undergraduate Coordinator, Department of Biochemistry at the University of Toronto. Dr Andreopoulos is the course director for the online biochemistry course. She can be contacted at this e-mail: s.andreopoulos@utoronto.ca

Dr. Sian Patterson is an Associate Professor, Teaching Stream in the Department of Biochemistry at the University of Toronto. Dr Patterson is the course director for the online biochemistry course. She can be contacted at this e-mail: sian.patterson@utoronto.ca

Dr. Chris Perumalla is an Associate Professor, Teaching Stream, Department of Physiology, and Director of the Division of Teaching Laboratories, Faculty of Medicine, University of Toronto. He can be contacted at this e-mail: c.perumalla@utoronto.ca

Bibliography

Chapman, C.; C. B. White; C. Engleberg; J. C. Fantone & S. K. Cinti (2011). Developing a fully online course for senior medical students. *Medical Education Online*, No. 16.

Cook, D. & F. McDonald (2008). E-Learning: Is There Anything Special about the "E"? *Perspectives in Biology And Medicine*, Vol. 51, No. 1, pp. 5–21.

Cook, D.; S. Garside; A. Levinson; D. Dupras & V. Montori (2010). What do we mean by web-based learning? A systematic review of the variability of interventions. *Medical Education*, Vol. 44, No. 8, pp. 765–774.

Dell, C. A.; C. Low & J. F. Wilker (2010). Comparing student achievement in online and face-to-face class formats. *Journal of Online Learning and Teaching*, Vol. 6, No. 1, pp. 30–42.

Kee, N.; J. Mak; S. Matthews & C. Perumalla (2012). Contrasting Student Experiences and Achievement between Online Distance and Online On-Campus Physiology Courses. Proceedings of the International Conference of E-Learning in Hong Kong, June 2012.

Means, B.; T. Yukie; R. Murphy; M. Bakia & K. Jones (2010). Evaluation of Evidence-Based Practices in Online Learning: A Meta-Analysis and Review of Online Learning Studies. U.S. Department of Education.

Reeves, T. C. & J. G. Hedberg (2012). MOOCs: Let's get real. *Educational Technology*, Vol. 54, No. 1, pp. 3–8.

Spice, B. (2014). Press release. Google sponsors Carnegie Mellon Research to improve effectiveness of online education. Paying attention to how people learn promises to enhance MOOCs. *Carnegie Mellon News*.

Yates, R. W. & B. Beaudrie (2009). The impact of online assessment on grades in community college distance education mathematics courses. *The American Journal of Distance Education*, Vol. 23, pp. 62–70.

Chapter 25: E-learning

Stimulating Self-Regulated and Self-Directed Learning Through Technology Enhanced Learning Environment

S. Engin Koç

Background

In this course, the students were learning the same things and some wanted to learn more whereas some wanted to focus on different parts of a lesson so it seemed like a good idea to separate the learning pathways that leads to specialization in certain types of design (i.e. interface design, general design, game design, logo design, book design, etc.) so that the students can write their own learning objectives, follow the teacher's resources and the resources they find and combine what they want to learn and come up with a learning plan. This way their learning and evaluation will be under self-directed learning where they can increase their responsibility negotiating with teacher and face the challenges that come in collaborative and individual learning. So this caused a major change in the course where it transformed the lessons from face-to-face to blended format and expanded the topics included.

The Practice

The aim is to give the control to the learners as much as possible. The factors for control are social constraints, environmental features, learner-characteristics, and educator behavior. The learners will take on activities where they will have control over their pace, troubleshooting problems and the content they prepare. They will have various tools to make content such as word processor, graphic development and animation development. The learners will be given choices to choose the programs they want to use. In such way they will have the chance to deviate from linear progress. The aim of the lesson is not memorization but to fulfill curiosity, reasoning, forming questions and seeking answer as well as judging themselves and their sources. That's why the instructions for the technology use or the homework will set some restrictions, that is the teacher will set some criteria for students they will not be totally free on their activities and obey some rules for homeworks however the learners will be given freedom of choice on most activities. In this course, there will be activities about designing educational material, designing book, designing poster, using fonts in general, choosing color, making a game and/or interface using unity and/or web design tools, ethical standards, etc...

Preparation and Materials

First a technology expert/teacher will be brought to the classroom to explain the usage of technology. Also the rationale behind technology use will be explained to the learners ahead of time. This will give ideas to learners why they are doing what they are doing. Also surveys about technology use will be delivered to the learners to gather their initial ideas. This way learner input will be the first step to control their learning as they are specializing the circumstances under which they will learn. A degree of structure is still necessary because there will be dates and information on how to send their completed projects and the process of evaluation where the teacher will have some control. The teacher also will have to know the learners' choices for taking control or using technology. While encouraging using technology and planning their own learning, for some students it is necessary to include direct teaching and finding alternatives for using technology.

Webspirationpro

The students use it as a concept map and share it with the teacher to form their learning objectives. The teacher looks at the concept maps and adds comments. The students then will create their learning pathway (most of which consists of activities and choosing videos that are compatible with each other). The benefit of Webspirationpro is that it makes the files sharable and editable by third parties and it is always reachable online. Also it is available to download or export as word document. It is a good way to express what the students want to see as their learning objectives and what they want to achieve within the boundaries of the resources appointed by the teacher.

Adobe Photoshop

The teacher uses it to teach students about designing a poster and how to make certain effects as well as basic operations. The benefit is that in Photoshop students will have a chance to practice the elements of design and design rules and be able to compare certain characteristics of good and poor posters.

Articulate

The students will use articulate to create interactive educational learning material, to make questions and to create interface (buttons, functionality and animations) to teach a subject. In this way, they will understand how interactivity and visual design rules combine to make learning easier. They are free to choose what to teach as long as they use the visual design rules and basically create motivating presentations.

Adobe Illustrator

The students will use illustrator to make logos, to choose the concept of logos and apply the right colors with the right concepts according to real world application. They will learn the critical choices and how logos reflect the principles and spirit of firms or corporates. Benefit is that quickly they can decide between good and poor designs.

Adobe Indesign

The students will use Indesign to create a book cover and inside of the book. They will learn how to use folio, what font to use, how to integrate visual elements and basically how to integrate a meaningful and easy to read pages. The benefit is that they will have the chance to compare differences between types of books and modern and classical designs.

Blog

The students will use the blog for collaborative projects. They will mainly discuss about how they choose the videos and their learning pathways. The benefit will be that those who choose similar projects will talk to each other about what they are doing, the problems they face and the solutions they find. Studies have shown that students can express themselves better and learn on their own when they use blogs (Koç & Koban Koç, 2016).

TinkerCat

Tinkercat is ideal for students who want to study 3D objects, learn basically how they can create 3D objects and use them in other contexts. The benefit is that they can use what they create in web design, game environment or any other applications that stand in their learning pathways.

Powtoon

Powtoon is great for creating short movies and animations. The benefit of the learners is that they learn to create a short movie, share it online, upload it to youtube and basically learn elements of design and how to change the screen from one scene to another.

Glogster

Glogster is easy to use application for creating posters. The students will basically learn the visual design elements and visual design rules to create interactive and good looking posters.

Unity

Unity is a game development environment. The students will learn how to use GUI elements, interactivity, writing scripts and they will develop a small game. This way they will learn to use visual elements, character movement, developing textures and objects and interacting with buttons on screen. The benefit is that they can create interactive learning games quickly and understand how to use the ready-made packages.

Kodu Game Lab

Kodu Game Lab is for developing games easy without writing codes and using basic elements that are build-in Kodu. The benefit is that they learn the algorithm without typing code and they can create learning/playing environments.

The Learning Environment

The Learning Environment will be mostly promoting collaborative learning but individual learning will be present as well. Cooperation will be valued instead of competition because it can create certain obstacles for learning. The role of the teacher will be to provide resources and basically stimulate learner control in times of difficulty. To provide learner control, the lessons will be carried out in a blended form of learning. Some of the activities will be carried out through online meetings using Anymeeting (www.anymeeting.com) and some activities will be carried out through forums. Blended here means that some lessons will be online and some will be face-to-face in class. The learners will have short and long-term plans. At the start of the term, they will review the materials and objectives. Let's say there are 30 objectives in total and each have certain points, the learners will have to complete objectives up to a certain point. They will write their own objectives for long term plan and discuss with the teacher. For short term plans they will write objectives within their chosen objectives. We can think of it as sub objectives to achieve certain skills. Every three-week, they will have short-term objectives again.

Teacher input/Evaluation

The teacher will encourage the learners to plan, evaluate and monitor their own learning. This way, learning is expected to be more relevant to their work. In traditional learning, the learners first learn then they make a project with what they learned. This is different in that learners will first decide their projects/works then learn what is necessary to achieve that. The learners will be given roles so that they can work individually. The technologies chosen will make it available for learners to save their work and reread/work difficult portions. They will also be given free time to play and explore giving them opportunity for self-development, reflection and self-evaluation. Also the format of the program will be designed in such that the skills of the learners will determine their level. The teacher and the learners will have discussions about how they will evaluate their learning. The teacher will have an evaluation plan ready in case they do not meet a consensus, but there will be peer evaluation and teacher evaluation. The learners will have a say about the quality of the educational material. Evaluation will be such that it will support the self-directed and self-regulated learning. That is why it is crucial that students decide at least some of the critical parts when designing evaluation scheme. It is also crucial that learners give complete description of what they did and how they did it using media elements if necessary so that the teacher can track their success based on their input. For this purpose, the learners will record videos of their screen and use think aloud procedures while they are working on their project i.e material preparation. In this way, they will have different forms of feedback and maintain self-regulation. First they will have feedback focused on task or product, then a second feedback on their process of information, then they will have feedback about how to better their product from their teacher and lastly they will have feedback to the 'self' which is personal rather than the task performance (Hattie & Timperley, 2007). Watching their own video will make them realize their mistakes and give them a chance to correct information. Also the feedback about these videos from the teacher will be valuable for their project. This will also allow the self-regulation process in phases where evaluation of previous performance, reflection on problem presentation and planning. The instructor will basically guide learners to maintain an effective learning environment, organize activities to help metacognitive processes, offer monitoring opportunities to learners, and provide continuous evaluation as well as self-evaluation to learners. Each of these activities will appear connected to each other with certain deviations in the form of a learning pathway. Videos will be the main resource of the course. Most of the videos will be made by the teacher but some videos will be taken from YouTube or other resources as a means of training for their projects.

Practice Map

Learners will first form a concept map of what they will learn based on the information provided by their teacher. The learning pathway will show itself when they review what they will study and do as homework through their learning process. They will use the topics as concepts and tie the activities and related information, teacher feedback to this concept map as sub topics. They will use Webspirationpro tool (www.webspirationpro.com) to create the first stage of planning their learning. They will share this concept map with their teacher and upon necessary feedback, the teacher will see if further resources are needed and s/he will make corrections if necessary. After planning their learning, the students will monitor their learning based on this concept map and write what resources they used, what information they obtain from these resources and they will create the previously explained videos while they are doing their homework and final product. They will also tell how homework create their learning process and what part of their project (final product) they will use what they learned on the homework. The teacher will also comment about these and monitor their learning, provide extra resources if necessary. For evaluation of the project, the students and the teacher will create evaluation schemes together and compare these schemes and come to a conclusion working collaboratively. It is important that the teacher is a co-learner and carry out the homework to present examples to the learners to compare themselves. The final evaluation scheme will be based on these comparisons and critical points that determine success. Such a framework is ideal for the application of self-regulated learning to ICT. In this process learners will learn from their mistakes by reviewing their processes in think aloud videos they will also learn how to form and evaluate their learning. Also by discussing their progress at the end of the lesson they will see different perspectives of how they could make better products as all the work will be reviewed by both the teacher and other learners as a collaborative learning process. This will also be done online.

Planned Learning pathways for educational material development:

1- DESIGN (Focus on elements of design)
Parameters: Using Font, Using Color, Creating Logos, Creating Web site, Book Design.
Programs used: Indesign, Illustrator, Brackets, CSS, javascript.

2- GENERAL SKILLS (A bit of everything)
Parameters: Online material preparation, online animators, colorpickers.
Programs used: Glogster, Blog, Tinkercat, Powtoon, Webspiration pro.

3- EFFECTS and TRANSFORM (focus on Transformation of photographs, effects and amazing graphics, posters from scratch)
Parameters: Illustrations, poster, small animations, drawing shapes and pathways, text, masks.
Program used: Photoshop.

4- EDUCATIONAL GAME DEVELOPMENT (Focus on rapid game production)
Parameters: Scripting C#, materials preparation, light, day-night co-routines, exploration games, GUI, downloading assets.
Programs used: Unity, Kodu Game Lab.

Note: These pathways can be mixed, the learners will decide which videos they will combine for their end product. They will use a website to choose the videos and form their learning resources.

Outcomes/Benefits

This form of learning is successful because it makes the integration of technology to help learners plan, monitor and in some phases evaluate their learning. Giving learners choices about what media they will use and what they will learn for their final product will help them regulate their own learning and the sharing of knowledge and reasons on the discussion on Moodle will help them develop their use of learning materials to create final product due to the feedback they receive from their peers and the teacher. The teacher will also experience and become a co-learner with the students since there are so many possibilities of materials and techniques using tools such as Adobe and Articulate products. Stimulating group work (social) individual work, metacognitive/cognitive aspects and using emotional motivational dimensions of teaching/learning situations will facilitate deep learning rather than transfer of information. The motivational factors at each phase of learning is the most important part of any course for the teacher so it is the ultimate purpose to make the lesson interesting that's why self-regulatory strategies are put into the course. It is clear from various literature that different forms of learning and different media such as online videos, presentation and books are more appropriate for learners of different styles i.e. some prefer to follow online videos some prefer to customize the samples of work they found and others just like to explore possibilities and finding their own resources. Self-regulated learning represents willingness to learn and self-efficacy. It was found by Zimmerman & Martinez-Pons (1986) that learners who used self-regulated learning strategies sought more help from peers and learned more compared to learners who did not use self-regulated learning strategies. Also high correlation was found between academic performance and use of self-regulated learning strategies (Zimmerman & Martinez-Pons, 1988). Furthermore, once learners learn how to control their learning, they will benefit from these skills in the future as life-long learners in all learning situations. Self-regulated learning strategies in a way fill the gap that learners experience when they do not realize they need supplementary means while they carry out instructions. Implementing factors that facilitate self-regulated learning in the course will create better learners and learning outcomes since learners will though with some restrictions plan their area of study, monitor with the help of the instructor and ask for improvements and specifications from other learners and the teacher. The teacher will have enough time for feedback and examine resubmissions of classwork since the projects will be chosen fairly close to the start of the semester. Also learners will have feedback about how they can use what they have learned in different media.

In most educational cases, the learners experience a conflict between their expectations and the teacher's expectations and they don't understand if they are successful or not. In this case, by including the learners in the process of evaluation, they will set some of the criteria and check whether they have met these criteria. So the confusion will be less and they will be evaluated for their responsible learning. Also resubmission will be possible so the learners will get appropriate feedback and they can revisit their projects if needed. In other terms, they will have more opportunities to gain success. The learners will also appreciate that the teacher will encourage them to question his own ways and comments and that the environment is secure because the teacher facilitates critical thinking and inquiry also ensuring that the teacher is a co-learner with the learners rather than someone to be always followed.

Moving Forward

There is the issue of whether self-regulated learning is taught able or not, if the learners engage in these kinds of activities where they plan, monitor and evaluate their own learning, they can pursue what they want to learn and make future plans easier. The relationship between the usage of self-regulated learning strategies and academic achievement is positive as shown by studies of Barnard et al. (2008). At the same time, according to Calabrese & Faiella (2011:165) "...self-regulation and motivation are bound together to enhance learner achievement."

That is why, for achievement schools starting from primary school should give learners different and large amount of learning opportunities and provide them with various learning materials keeping in mind that there are a lot of ways to teach one subject and learners should be able to choose their own ways. In this way, it becomes essential that learners should gain creative skills from the early stages of their educational lives.

Secondly, this chapter answers questions on how to design online educational activities that foster self-regulated learning strategies.

Thirdly it should be kept in mind that it's not the technology we use when we aim for self-regulated learning, but the method (the scaffolding, formulation of tasks, encouragement and metacognitive strategies) that are important. Still technology ensures connectivity and reachability and continuous and ubiquitous access to learners, that is why it provides necessary support.

Fourthly it is apparent that to ensure strategies are in place, *"embedding metacognitive instruction in the content matter"* is a necessity and the usefulness of the learning strategies or any strategies used should be explained to learners so that they are motivated to use the strategies (Veenman *et al.*, 2006:9).

Also tools for learning planning at the beginning of the course should be further developed to have the functions of (ClaireBout & Ellen, 2009)

+ Automatic display;

+ Instructions on how to use;

+ Automatic prompting students to use.

Furthermore, for supporting self-regulated learning, tools should be designed according to these criteria mentioned by Lizarrage *et al.* (2011:310):

+ *"Supporting self-regulated learning in diverse contexts;*

+ *Adapted to all educational levels and learning styles;*

+ *Didactic strategies that lend educational meaning to the diverse digital learning platforms;*

+ *Theoretical learning models that tap on technological advance;*

+ *Software that stimulates the creative process".*

In terms of assessment, learners should be given chances redo and evaluate their own learning. The teacher should be a role model and be a co-learner with the students to explore assessment criteria and work collaboratively with the students to reach best assessment methods and technology. New models of self-regulated learning frameworks and assessment systems should be traced and evaluated.

Next step in this chapter could be determining the nature of think aloud protocols are used when students work on their projects gave better results in terms of success and certain measures can be taken about how students will record their studies. Also using learning pathway software that can integrate videos and connect them to certain skills and objectives would make it clearer for students to see where they are and what they are supposed to be doing. The teacher can also monitor the learners easily this way.

About the Author

Dr. Serdar Engin Koç is an assistant professor at the Department of Computer Education and Instructional Technologies at Başkent University, Turkey and can be contacted at this e-mail: sekoc@baskent.edu.tr.

Bibliography

Barnard, L.; W. Y Lan; S. M. Crooks & V. O. Paton (2008). The relationship of epistemological beliefs with self-regulatory skills in the online course environment. *Journal of Online and Learning Teaching*, Vol. 4, No. 3. pp. 261–266.

Clarebout, G. & J. Ellen (2009). Benefits of inserting support devices in electronic learning environments. *Computers in Human Behavior*, Vol. 25, No. 4. pp. 804–810.

Calabrese, R. & F. Faiella (2011). Theoretical and Practical Issues in Designing a Blended e-Learning Course of English as a Foreign Language In G. Dettori & D. Persico (Eds.), *Fostering Self-Regulated Learning through ICT*. New York: Information Science Reference.

Hattie, J. & H. Timperley (2007). The power of feedback. *Review of Educational Research*, Vol. 77, No. 1, pp. 81–112.

Koban Koç, D. & S. E. Koç (2016). Students' perceptions of blog use in an undergraduate linguistics course. *Journal of Language and Linguistic Studies*, Vol. 12, No. 1, pp. 9–19.

Lizarrage, M.; O. A. Villanueva; M. Baquedano (2011). Self-Regulation of Learning Supported by Web 2.0 Tools: An Example of Raising Competence on Creativity and Innovation. In G. Dettori & D. Persico (Eds.), *Fostering Self-Regulated Learning through ICT*. New York: Information Science Reference.

Veenman, M. V. J.; B. van Hout-Wolters & P. Afflerbach (2006). Metacognition and learning: Conceptual and methodological considerations. *Metacognition and Learning*, No. 7, pp. 3–14.

Zimmerman, B. J. & M. Martinez-Pons (1986). Development of a structured interview for assessing students' use of self-regulated learning strategies. *American Educational Research Journal*, Vol. 23, No. 1, pp. 614–628.

Zimmerman, B. J. & M. Martinez-Pons (1988). Construct validation of a strategy model of student self-regulated learning. *Journal of Educational Psychology*, Vol. 80, No. 3, pp. 284–290.

Chapter 26: E-learning

Modelling the use of Google Applications for Education and Social Media as Building Blocks for Student Teachers' TPACK

Andries Du Plessis

Background

It remains a challenge to address the effects of a lingering digital divide on education in South Africa (Ndlovu, N.S. & Lawrence, D, 2012:27). South African learners, particularly in schools with limited resources, have continuously underachieved in the gateway subjects like Mathematics and Science. The government has turned to modern technology to strengthen teaching and learning and to redress past inequalities in its schools. This intervention has made little or no progress despite the availability of Information and Communication Technologies (ICTs). Working in a Higher Education environment that offers little in terms of ICT infrastructure or systems such as a Learning Management System (LMS) curtails efforts to integrate digital technologies. Furthermore, the lack of student access to any range of devices compounds the problems which lecturers face who try to teach with technology (Bingimlas, 2009; Jones, 2004). As is often the case the absence of a clear, institutional all-encompassing strategy for technological integration makes it difficult to develop training programs in which educational technology will feature (Blignaut et al., 2010). In the case of teacher training programs these and other barriers have a two-pronged impact – in terms of teaching about technology and teaching with technology.

While teaching and learning with digital technologies can be overwhelming (Jacobsen *et al.*, 2002: 367), various approaches exist to ease their integration. The Technological Pedagogical Content Knowledge framework (TPACK) provides a model along which teaching staff and student teachers alike can develop their different knowledge domains. The three domains are content knowledge, pedagogical knowledge and technological knowledge. Further combinations hereof are pedagogical content knowledge, technological content knowledge and technological pedagogical knowledge. Technological pedagogical content knowledge forms where all three main domains overlap (Archambault & Barnett, 2010; Koehler & Mishra, 2009).

Achieving any measurable degree of success with digital technology integration across academic programs is marred with difficulties. According to Ertmer (1999) obstacles include both first and second order barriers. Examples of the former include lack of and/or the unreliability of equipment, lack of technical support and other resource-related issues. Second order barriers include institutional level factors, such as organisational culture and people-related factors. The latter includes beliefs about teaching with technology and openness to change. Both first and second order barriers exist at the Teacher Education Campus in Siyabuswa – a newly established rural-based teacher training campus in the Mpumalanga province of South Africa. These barriers limit success to achieve the development of student teachers' TPACK.

SITE's three principles (SITE, 2002) – despite having been formulated over a decade ago – remain relevant to the campus under discussion. One of the SITE principles is the need for infusing technology into the entire education program. The four-year B Ed Foundation Phase program at the Siyabuswa campus offers an introductory course in digital technologies to Foundation Phase teachers in a first-year module during the second semester. Given first year students' limited computer competency levels this is insufficient to prepare them for any significant development of their various TPACK knowledge domains. Giving heed to SITE's principle that technology should be infused into the entire teacher education program, a solution had to be sought to help address this short-coming. Increased exposure to technology, it can be argued, should also result in an increase in computer competency levels. This in turn affects students' self-efficacy – an important factor to consider when developing their TPACK.

Similarly, introducing technology while remaining mindful of the context is also particularly relevant. In this environment, for example, the socio-economic realities make technology for many an expensive luxury item, thus limiting its use. Providing continuous ICT support to end-users on the campus also remains a real problem. This is especially true for students who have themselves not been exposed to well-supported technology during their own schooling. Affected by slow internet speeds, intermittent connectivity and periodic electricity outages on campus, their experiences with technology often end in frustration.

The Practice

In the case of the Siyabuswa campus where pre-service teachers are being trained digital technologies have two applications: teaching with technology and teaching about (the same) technology. One of the approaches that was followed was to start modelling the use of certain technological applications in a single course so that students can also experience it (Chai et al., 2011). The choice fell on the Teaching Studies 1A module – a first year module offered in the first semester that does not have ICT as its focus.

A dearth of technologies encompass the concepts "ICT" and "digital technologies". Therefore, a choice had to be made to limit the number of applications. From the author's perspective it was important that the applications should be easy to administer. Google offers a suite of cloud-based applications for education referred to as Google Applications for Education (GAFE). Other choices include social media applications from the gamut of Web 2.0 tools that have already been proven useful in an educational environment, e.g. Google+, Facebook, Twitter and the popular chat application WhatsApp (Pickle, 2011).

For any of this to be used it was necessary to ensure that all first year students have the necessary accounts and that they were briefed about each one's application. This was done during their first week of orientation before the academic program commenced. The first-year cohort was divided into smaller groups and assisted in the central computer laboratory during an hour long session to setup their various accounts. At this point it was evident that each student already had a Facebook account, but not everyone had a Gmail email address. Each student's Gmail address was setup and/or verified, and a digital signature added. Everyone also had to activate their Google+ profile. Students had to introduce themselves to the author by sending an email to the Gmail that was setup specifically for this course. Subsequently to this, the author added students to the course's Google circle, Google community and relevant Gmail contact groups. Approximately one hundred students enroll per year; the time spent on completing this all-important step could not be avoided since the contact list forms the basis for further lecturer-led actions using Google. Once the author's Gmail contact list was complete with first year students' information it was exported as a CSV file; data was tidied up (e.g. proper capitalization of names and surnames, while student numbers were added to the Notes column). The CSV file was then imported back into the Gmail contact list.

Rules of engagement on social media had to be established upfront for the students since this is their first experience with these applications in an educational environment. User guidelines for each application were communicated during contact class sessions as well as tutor sessions. Brief explanations were furthermore provided in the study material. The tutor – a senior student – also played an important role in assisting individual students during tutor sessions. Students were encouraged to share references to useful websites and/or assist each other as far as possible. The role of peer student support networks thus played a significant role in skills diffusion. Notably, the majority of students are active on Facebook, which made it possible to engage them via this popular social network (Madge et al., 2009; Mazman & Usluel, 2010).

Instant Messaging with WhatsApp

Students were also required to send a WhatsApp message to the author's mobile phone. To ease the administrative load of the author the tutor student was made the administrator of the WhatsApp group with the task of adding students to the WhatsApp group as well as assist with moderation. Conversations are monitored and users warned or removed when contravening the basic set of rules, i.e. appropriate language and course-related, mostly academic conversations.

WhatsApp is used extensively for administrative purposes since not all students can access their emails all the time. WhatsApp is used for an array of other reasons too, such as academic support. WhatsApp is truly useful for posing short questions related to unit topics, be it prior, during or after contact sessions. As part of revision, involving students in bursts of conversation is very fruitful.

A useful app that unfortunately stopped working after an update is a WhatsApp message scheduler. While it worked, this proved invaluable to queue messages related to a particular content lesson. Some could for example be sent a short while before a contact class, some during class and others thereafter. At the time of writing, this app has not been fixed on the Play store.

Blogs with Google Blogger

Over the years blogs have proved to be important conversational platforms (Richardson, 2008). First year students at this campus are first exposed to blogs as part of their reflective writings about their involvement in a service learning event. They post their reflections in the form of a personal blog post – for all students this is a first-time experience. For the majority of students the use of blogs is a very steep learning curve. At a technical level some steps might be particularly challenging: setting up a blog, writing the first post, transferring pictures or video clips from a mobile device to a PC, or editing the clips before uploading it to a blog post. Students explore this on their own. In some cases some start to explore freeware applications for editing purposes since the computers in the PC lab come bundled with basic software applications on a Windows 8 platform.

Apart from the service learning event students are also required to submit posts related to some units in this course. One such task is writing their personal teaching philosophies and posting it as a blog post. They are requested to comment on each other's personal teaching philosophies. This extents the typical experience many have with their personal use of Facebook to engage in online conversation – albeit longer responses. The application for academic purposes, as well as deep thought based on academic research remain difficult. It is at this point where problems with language proficiency start to surface, since English is not their home language. It is also at this point where the author could point it out to students that during the use of digital technologies it is often not the technology but students' academic prowess that needs to be developed.

Twitter

Like blogs, the majority of students are not used to Twitter. The short format messages proved conceptually difficult for some. Not every student in this course could therefore value the use of Twitter. This is, however, not unique as academics and students across the world are often slow to embrace Twitter (Evans, 2014). The author used Twitter as part of a social media mix, i.e. to draw attention to a new blog post, or website references, or discussion topics relevant to a specific unit. The fact that the majority of students do not have modern smart phones or access to the internet when away from campus meant that the use of Twitter remained limited.

Google Drive and Doctopus

In the absence of a sophisticated ICT network, the lack of an advanced computer-based administrative system as well as an LMS a considerable amount of time can be spent on setting up and maintaining networked resources such as student folders. In this regard Doctopus – in conjunction with Google Drive – proved invaluable. It requires student detail such as name and surname as well as their Gmail address. The author added students' student numbers to the name-surname mix with a simple "concatenate" function on Google Sheets. The original data was exported from the lecturer's Gmail Contact list that was setup during the first week of orientation. Upon creating a class roster using Google Sheets, Doctopus creates a teacher's folder, a class edit folder, a class view folder as well as a set of individual student folders. Student folders are shared between the student and the lecturer only.

Similar to an LMS, Doctopus makes it possible to share resources. Once the folder structure has been created individual resources can be shared in any number of ways with students. Resources can be made available in either the class view and class edit folder. In the class edit folder students can edit the resources. In the class view folder, it is view only. Another option is for resources to be copied to each student's personal folder – a process the Doctopus script handles effectively. At the time of writing, options included: individual – all the same: creates the same separate, individual resource for each student in a class; individual – differentiated: creates one copy of a resource file for each student based on their level; project groups: creates one shared copy of a resource for each project group as designated in the "Group" column on the roster; whole class: creates a single shared copy of a resource for the whole class. Furthermore, individual access and whole class access can also be set. Options are: edit, view only, or comment only. A setting also allows editors (students) to be able to change the sharing permission of a resource or not.

If students are to type answers on a template provided by the lecturer the practicality of the sharing options provided by Doctopus becomes obvious. The format for the original resources must be in Google Docs format, i.e. Google Docs instead of MS Word. The same applies if a lecturer provides a template for a presentation, in which case the shared resource must be a Google Slides file not an MS PowerPoint. When a Google Docs format is used a rubric can be attached (Google Sheet format; numeric or alpha levels) for assessment purposes using Goobric.

Goobric

For purposes of assessment Doctopus offers a feature that links a rubric to students' Google Docs via Goobric. It is a feature-packed assessment tool that offers the option for audio feedback from the assessor. Once assessed, the rubric gets attached at the end of the student's work. On the lecturer's side a separate sheet gets created on the Google Sheet that also contains the corresponding class roster. This score sheet gets populated with students' rubric scores and the assessor's comments. The administration of the feedback and assessment scores is a straightforward process; these are emailed to students' Gmail addresses, providing functionality comparable to that found in an LMS ("Top 10 Google Apps Scripts for Education – Synergyse," n.d.).

Google Forms, Google Sheets and Flubaroo

In conjunction with Google Forms Flubaroo proved particularly useful in the absence of a fully-fledged LMS such as Blackboard or Moodle at the Siyabuswa Campus. Setting up a Google Form to collect answers from students lessen the workload associated with assessment. Form data is collected and stored in an associated Google Sheet. To ensure that a student only submits one answer a setting can be activated on Google Form that requires a student to login to their Google account. Other options to be set on the Google Form include the possibility to edit responses before they are submitted, or to submit another response.

The add-in Flubaroo is activated on the response sheet which is in Google Sheet format. Once provided with an answer key that the author fills in it allows for automatic assessment. Manual grading is also possible. In comparison to an LMS the type of questions is limited to the different formats that are available on Google Form. It nevertheless serves its purpose, albeit at an elementary level. From an administrative point of view scores and the answer key can be emailed to each student's Gmail address. Flubaroo also provides basic analysis of the scores per question and overall statistics such as test average.

Boomerang

The absence of a scheduler in Google Form necessitated the use of a scheduler that works effectively with Gmail. Boomerang offers such a service. If student contacts are grouped into classes and/or project groups emails containing links to a Google Form can be directed to each in a scheduled fashion. When a Google Form is used for collecting answers by sending the link in an email Boomerang effectively becomes a test scheduler. Another feature that compares well with what is available in an LMS is closing the test. In Google Form this is achieved by restricting the responses after it has reached a certain date and time. Another setting that can be used to close the form is the number of responses. This effectively prohibits students from accessing a test when any of these conditions are met.

Hootsuite

The need to use the different social media channels before, during and after contact sessions necessitate the use of a multi-channel social media manager such as Hootsuite. Hootsuite makes scheduling across any number of social media channels possible, such as Facebook, Twitter and LinkedIn. This feature is used during planning and while preparing lessons; it results in a planned release of lecture-related messages – in the case of this course onto channels such as Facebook and Twitter. This is particularly helpful during contact sessions when a lecturer's attention is on the lecture and attending to students. Importantly, Hootsuite also provides reports for further analysis about the reach and impact of messages.

Outcomes

In terms of teaching with technology, the initial setup proved relatively easy and straight-forward. The most time-consuming aspect remains the administration of student contact detail and the initial setup of class rosters on Google Drive using Doctopus.

As mentioned earlier, a two-pronged approach was followed since teaching with technology meant that the use of these technologies could be modelled for purposes of teaching about technology. This relates closely to the aim of developing student teachers' TPACK. This process started with increasing their basic computer literacy by using Google Applications such as Google Drive and social media to help deliver content, assessment and student support. As a consequence, students were forced to increase their computer use. Amongst others, their keyboarding skills also improved, while uploading and downloading resources exposed them to file and folder management. Their knowledge of file formats also increased, thereby contributing to an increase in self-efficacy related to computer use.

Initially, students were introduced to the social media applications used in this module during the first lecture. During a tutorial session following the lectures the next step in the exposure to digital technologies followed when students were shown their Google Drive folder and how to access resources. Further explanation was given about the use of Google Docs as a way of work in the Teaching Studies 1A module for completing learning tasks as well as formative and summative assessments. Google Docs gets used in synergy with MS Word, Google Sheets as an alternative for MS Excel and Google Slides as a cloud-based alternative to MS PowerPoint.

Students were also introduced to collaborative online work using Google, either in a synchronous (live, real time) manner or in an asynchronous manner. This proved particularly difficult for some students since working collaboratively online is for everyone a first-time experience. Compounded by language barriers and entry-level computer-literacy levels working collaboratively proved to be a skill that requires continued practice. The importance of a fast reliable network also became apparent during these trial sessions with online collaboration.

In the case of the teacher students at Siyabuswa the medium-term benefits of teaching with technology during the first semester is that once they sit for the module during the second semester that does have ICT for teachers as its focus, proficiency in basic computer use, knowledge of social media as well as the use of Google applications are well established. In the long-term, however, the focus moves to teaching about technology: students can then start focusing on these technologies' use in combination with their own teaching, especially the different Add-ons applicable to Elementary education that can be added to Chrome. In this way their journey of discovery starts to develop and fuse their developing content knowledge with a growing pedagogical knowledge; it results in pedagogical content knowledge that is tightly woven with appropriate, context-sensitive technology, i.e. TPACK.

Moving forward

The success with integrating technology at an institutional level can be measured in various ways. One way is to consider the extent of digital technology integration across whole programs. A number of realities prohibit any measurable success in this regard. A reality for many HEIs is lecturers' own undeveloped TPACK that stems from a lack of basic knowledge about teaching with technology. Other reasons relate to a lack of self-efficacy amongst lecturing staff that limits their creative use of modern-day digital technologies. This creates tension with students who expect digital technologies in their educational environments since their daily lives are immersed with it.

Once students start to experience the use of social media and GAFE in one module – in this case the Teaching Studies 1A module – they inadvertently start enquiring about the use of these applications in other modules too. An additional spin-off therefore is students' influence on other lecturers. For example, students request that material and lecture notes be made available to them electronically. The skills they thus obtain in one module can get used throughout their degree program, given that lecturers also embrace such technologies (Rourke & Coleman, 2009). This is still a matter that needs to be addressed at the Siyabuswa campus. While the digital technologies used for teaching in this module might be new to other lecturers it is a welcome assurance when they are informed that students are already used to shared resources on Google Drive, for example.

Unlike some teaching staff, students are more likely to experiment and explore the creative uses of digital technologies. This is often evident from students' assignments that show the progressive use of digital solutions once they are exposed to it. Receiving a well-formatted essay in an electronic format from a student for whom this is a first-time achievement is truly noteworthy. As confidence grows the base that was initially established during the first year provides the foundation for further development at subsequent year levels. In this way the effects of the digital divide to which these students were exposed during their schooling start to dissipate. This is an important achievement for the university given its responsibility to equip students to function in a real world. However, once student teachers enter schools as newly qualified Foundation Phase teachers – as is the case with the students at Siyabuswa Campus – their newly found skills are often put to the test. Given the realities of South Africa, when they start to teach, they will once again find themselves in environments where the digital divide is a reality. It is in such instances where their tenacity as innovative teachers and the true depth of their TPACK start to matter, including their creativity and innovative use of available digital technologies.

In time the Siyabuswa campus will start to implement a university-wide e-learning strategy. This will entail, amongst others, the implementation of an LMS in conjunction with a fully-fledged student administration system. While this may in a way make the existing application of certain Google applications as described in this chapter seem redundant, it will be necessary to continue to teach about such and other technologies to the different cohorts of student teachers who enroll at the Siyabuswa campus.

The biggest change, however, will have to be made in terms of the theoretical underpinnings of teaching with technology across all courses in the various academic programs – moreover the teacher training programs. Students might enjoy certain advanced technologies while on campus, but the stark realities of the digital divide in the South African context will continue to affect them in the schools where they will be teachers. This will therefore affect their approaches to teaching and learning that will in all probability be in contrast with what they were taught in their undergraduate program. It is in this regard that fluidity and flexibility in how they adapt their TPACK will play a role, i.e. taking heed of the contextual factors in which digital technologies are deployed.

About the Author

Dr Andries Du Plessis is Senior Lecturer in the Early Childhood Department at the Siyabuswa Campus of the University of Mpumalanga, South Africa. He can be contacted at this e-mail: andries.duplessis@ump.ac.za

Bibliography

Archambault, L. M. & J. H. Barnett (2010). Revisiting technological pedagogical content knowledge: Exploring the TPACK framework. *Computers & Education*, Vol. 55, No. 4, pp. 1656–1662.

Bingimlas, K. A. (2009). Barriers to the successful integration of ICT in teaching and learning environments: A review of the literature. *Eurasia Journal of Mathematics, Science & Technology Education*, Vol. 5, No. 3, pp. 235–245.

Blignaut, A. S.; J. E. Hinostroza; C. J. Els & M. Brun (2010). ICT in education policy and practice in developing countries: South Africa and Chile compared through SITES 2006. *Computers & Education*, Vol. 55, No. 4, pp. 1552–1563.

Carpenter, R. (2015). Social media in Pedagogy and Practice: Networked Teaching and Learning. *Journal of Faculty Development*, Vol. 29, No. 2, pp. 5–8.

Chai, C. S.; J. H. Ling Koh; C.-C. Tsai & L. Lee Wee Tan (2011). Modelling primary school pre-service teachers' Technological Pedagogical Content Knowledge (TPACK) for meaningful learning with information and communication technology (ICT). *Computers & Education*, Vol. 57, No. 1, pp. 1184–1193.

Drent, M. & M. Meelissen (2008). Which factors obstruct or stimulate teacher educators to use ICT innovatively? *Computers & Education*, Vol. 51, No. 1, pp. 187–199.

Ertmer, P. A. (1999). Addressing first- and second-order barriers to change: Strategies for technology integration. *Educational Technology Research and Development*, Vol. 47, No. 4, pp. 47–61.

Evans, C. (2014). Twitter for Teaching: Can Social media Be Used to Enhance the Process of Learning? *British Journal of Educational Technology*, Vol. 45, No. 5, pp. 902–915.

Guy, R. (2012). The use of social media for academic practice: A review of literature. *Kentucky Journal of Higher Education Policy and Practice*, Vol. 1 No. 2, p. 7.

Jacobsen, M.; P. Clifford & S. Friesen (2002). Preparing teachers for technology integration: Creating a culture of inquiry in the context of use. *Contemporary Issues in Technology and Teacher Education*, Vol. 2, No. 3, pp. 363–388.

Jones, A. (2004). A review of the research literature on barriers to the uptake of ICT by teachers. BECTA.

Koehler, M. & P. Mishra (2009). What is technological pedagogical content knowledge (TPACK)? *Contemporary Issues in Technology and Teacher Education*, Vol. 9, No. 1, pp. 60–70.

Madge, C.; J. Meek; J. Wellens & T. Hooley (2009). Facebook, social integration and informal learning at university: "It is more for socialising and talking to friends about work than for actually doing work." *Learning, Media and Technology*, Vol. 34, No. 2, pp. 141–155.

Mazman, S. G. & Y. K. Usluel (2010). Modeling educational usage of Facebook. *Computers & Education*, Vol. 55, No. 2, pp. 444–453.

Nash, S. S. (2005). Learning objects, learning object repositories, and learning theory: Preliminary best practices for online courses. *Interdisciplinary Journal of Knowledge and Learning Objects*, Vol. 1, pp. 217–228.

Pickle, R. (2011). The use of Google Docs in the student teaching experience. In *Society for Information Technology & Teacher Education International Conference*, Vol. 20, pp. 635–639.

Richardson, W. (2008). *Blogs, Wikis, Podcasts, and Other Powerful Web Tools for Classrooms*. Corwin Press.

Rourke, A. J. & K. Coleman (2009). An emancipating space: Reflective and collaborative blogging. *Same Places, Different Spaces. Proceedings Ascilite Auckland 2009.*

SITE. (2002). SITE Position paper: Statement of basic principles and suggested actions. Ames White Paper.

Top 10 Google Apps Scripts for Education – Synergyse. (n.d.). Online resource: https://www.synergyse.com/blog/top–10-google-apps-scripts-for-education [Accessed July 15, 2016].

A Reduced Attendance Model of Delivery that Engages Remote Learners in the Workplace

Jeffrey Lewis

Background

Several drivers were behind the implementation of this practice, including; a reduction in qualification providers, geographically remote learners, employer demands and a requirement to hold a recognised qualification from the registering body (General Dental Council, 2013). All of these factors meant that a traditional part-time programme which required attendance to campus one day a week was not ideal and a new approach was investigated. This began with a Learning and Teaching Fellowship award that allowed a pilot study to be carried out on the implementation of a new delivery model. Now, several years on, this model has developed and we have a reduced attendance Foundation Degree programme and a full distance learning Masters programme using the practice detailed below.

The Practice

This practice has fundamentally changed the delivery of a Foundation degree, to students, by reducing the number of required attendances to the institute. Instead of on campus lectures, it utilises web-based video-conferencing (Adobe Connect Pro) to hold 'virtual classes' and relies on the use of technology to deliver material (via live meetings) to students on a weekly basis – at a prescribed time and day throughout the calendar year. These weekly online meetings are supported with a well organised, logically formatted virtual learning environment (Moodle). In addition to these, the students' work based experiences and procedures are recorded in an e-portfolio (Mahara) and forms a portable CV for students upon completion of their qualification.

Traditional attended lessons were replaced with virtual meetings, taught practical sessions were delegated out to the workplace. The validation of practical work completed by the students was stored within the e-portfolio and supervised practical sessions were supplemented by work-based mentors.

During the enrolment process, applicants are supplied with the technical specifications for the devices they will be using to access lectures. There is a tripartite learning contract that must be returned with the application that is an agreement of responsibilities between the education provider, student and employer.

Attendances: *virtual and actual*

The students log in to their virtual classroom/meeting room weekly on a specific day and at specific times, for directed learning activities rather than the traditional part-time model of travelling to the institution one day per week. Those traditional attendances occurring one day a week for the duration of the academic year at the institution has been challenged and has been reduced from 26 attendances to between 4 and 6 visits to campus across an academic year. These "actual" meetings are now for the submission of dental artefacts that have been constructed by the students in the preceding weeks/module. It also is an opportunity to carry out any formal assessment (written examinations) and for Observed Short Practical Exercises (OSPE) to take place. The use of OSPEs is a common practice in dentistry and medicine; they are short tasks, or procedures relating to the module being studied at the time that students can complete in 1 or 2hours. These OSPEs are Pass/Fail and have been introduced to allow validation of work submitted by students as their own. Students' module marks are not released unless an OSPE has been submitted to a Pass level.

These visits that occur at the end of each module (modules ordinarily last 8–10 weeks) also allow feedback discussions to take place between students and staff, allowing evaluation of delivery as well as student evaluation of previous modules to take place.

Organisation and delivery

The organisation of meetings is set out at the beginning of each academic year. A timetable is drawn up that includes all meetings that the student is required to attend; modules start and finish dates; assessment events and also required attendances to the institute. This timetable is accessible via the VLE.

Initially, one url for a meeting room was used for each module and students accessed them at the relevant time and date. This led to occasional confusion with students (or tutors) using the wrong meeting room. Now one url is used for each year as this makes it impossible for students to access the wrong room, as all meeting take place in the same place. When in the room, the delivery takes place and this varies in style from tutor to tutor – as it would in an actual classroom. An outline of the lesson is included in one of the 'pods' within the meeting room (along with any other pertinent or important info for that session. Eg. Submission date reminder), the session is recorded and the teaching activity takes place. This activity can utilise existing learning resources, such as PowerPoint presentations, pdf documents, etc – there is no need to develop different or amended material (another benefit to this method over other online approaches).

Generally, meetings are now largely based on a "flipped classroom" approach (Ryan & Tilbury, 2013) and students are requested to study learning material or undertake an activity(ies) or tasks and then in the following meeting the topics, processes, dilemmas are shared and discussed. Peer learning is promoted with the individual experiences of the students and these are brought together in these sessions. Vicarious learning has been acknowledged as taking place.

For tutors there is reduced time spent in didactic activity with students and now, time is spent on areas of complex themes, or of areas identified by the students as difficult – interestingly, these areas do not necessarily align with what lectures perceive as difficult areas. An excellent opportunity presents when students are given case studies as learning activities and they return to a later meeting where peer review can take place and a discussion ensues about the different, varying approaches to the original case presentation. Variables can be introduced to discussions and the reaction of students to those investigated.

The features within Adobe Connect Pro ® are utilised to the full within meetings – in particular the use of 'polls' and 'breakout rooms'. These can be prepared and set up before the meeting, or can be done impromptu. Polls are used to gauge understanding – such as pre and post testing a topic. Or to encourage engagement with students on a regular basis to prevent screen fatigue and to keep students attention. Breakout rooms are an excellent facility for gathering information from small groups of either the same topic, or different topics. Generally, one student is requested to make notes whilst in the breakout room and to copy that information back into the main meeting room when breakouts are closed. These notes can then be compared or explored further with all the students present. The feedback from students about the use of break-outs is excellent and they all enjoy the opportunity of contributing and actually doing something rather than responding or listening to material being presented.

Students are required to give presentations as groups and individuals during the programme and during these sessions they are in control of the pace and style of the presentation. They are visible via their webcams and answer live audio and text chat questions from peers, just as the lecturer has been. They find the software incredibly intuitive and there are very few technical problems that need to be overcome. The biggest problem has been that of being visible on the webcam, only a few are happy to have their cameras on during a session – and this issue raises an interesting question that needs separate investigation regarding engagement.

All meetings are recorded and the recording placed onto the VLE. These are kept in a dedicated area and given a title and date. Keywords are also supplied to enable students to find the appropriate meeting easily and quickly. Meeting recordings can be downloaded to watch if no internet connection is available.

Hardware choices

Headset and webcam choices are usually down to personal preference. Our experiences confirm that complicated or expensive webcams are "too clever" and try to install software over the top of any process being carried out. A good HD camera is a great choice, although cheaper, gaming style webcams and headsets are often as good as their more expensive counterparts. A wireless headset is preferred by the author. The software used updates its recommended minimum technical specifications regularly and these guidelines are supplied to all students at the beginning of each intake.

Dual monitors are preferred by staff as it allows the classroom to be viewed on the first screen and learning material to be arranged on the second screen. It makes for a much calmer meeting from a tutor perspective if all necessary materials are opened, or listed to find easily during the session on the second screen. There is of course the opportunity to utilise the content area of Adobe to share learning material, but that necessitates uploading to the server before meetings take place. Dual screen is often useful if for some reason material does not display as needed. In this case the original file can be opened on the second monitor and that screen 'shared' with attendees. The use of dual screens for this practice is highly advisable.

Staff review

There is also an excellent opportunity to hold totally unobtrusive staff peer reviews from the recordings made of the meetings. The teaching staff here hold reviews annually and discuss what they did that they felt worked well to inform colleagues. An excellent example of this is when students were asked a question via audio, but responded via a "chat" style box. It was observed that some students would wait for a series of responses to be posted in chat before entering their answer. This was overcome by asking the question, then instructing students to type the answer but not hit 'Enter' until instructed – this brings all answers into the meeting at the same time.

Work Based Learning and mentor engagement

The introduction of work based (WBL) modules now means that students are rewarded with academic credits for work undertaken in their workplace. Students study one WBL module (20credits) per academic year. Students now engage with their e-portfolio (in this case Mahara) to achieve many Professional Practice learning outcomes that the team felt were measured poorly in the past when using traditional paper based systems. These paper based systems were considered to be old fashioned, and concerns were often raised of validity and originality of the submissions. The e-portfolio allows the storage of multi-media file types to record dental artefacts constructed, or processes witnessed by the student and these can be uploaded and stored in their own private area. All, or parts of this portfolio are then shared with tutors and mentors for feedback. Areas for comment on feedback is attached to every aspect and students are able to respond to what has been said. This thinking time and response activity promotes some reflection on their work and also their perception of how they performed or are improving (Dreyfus, 1986).

One of the main issues with the traditional part-time attendance model was the poor employer 'buy-in' to their students learning and journey through the programme. Now mentors are identified in the workplace and are responsible for supervising and instructing students on the work undertaken there, thus increasing employer engagement. Work-based mentors help with reflective activities required for the e-portfolio. This is all based on the initial learning contract signed at the outset of the programme and as part of the admissions procedure.

Duration

The practice runs longitudinally for the full programme and all modules are delivered using this method. This has shown to be equally effective in any type of module and include totally theoretical (e.g. Dental Materials) and practical based modules (e.g. Orthodontics).

Benefits

Benefits for students include a reduction in the necessary visits to campus, reducing travel fatigue and also the fatigue often reported and experienced next day in work. They can access meetings they have missed (or just wish to view again) via recordings stored in a specified area of the VLE. The benefit of these recording is that they have the ability to utilise them as revision aids – at any point throughout the year. Students are able to present cases they carry out in the workplace and gain academic credit for them via the WBL modules and the e-portfolio. It has been demonstrated when measured using assessment scores that there is no detriment to student learning by using this delivery model and in some areas there has been an enhanced performance recorded. Student retention is now almost 80%, a huge increase from the 40% typical retention rate when required to attend the institution weekly. This in itself may not represent an increase in student engagement, but it does demonstrate sustainability and a lack of learners "travel fatigue" and the resulting inability to stick with a qualification to the end. An intention of this practice, was not to have to recreate or develop new learning resources, but rather be able to use those currently in existence so not creating more work for any lecturer.

Outcomes

Since the introduction of this model of delivery and student engagement we have seen a dramatic increase in recruitment and retention of our students. Recruitment has increased by 40% and our retention is now almost 80% compared to less than 50%. Analysis of assessment performance has revealed very interesting results regarding attainment. Results demonstrate that delivery by this mode has no detrimental effect on learning and in fact has demonstrated parity with (if not exceeded) traditional learner's scores on the equivalent level modules within the full-time programme. These improvements in academic performance have been noticed in both written and practical assessment events. Much of this success has been attributed to the "flipping" of the classroom and the engagement of students in activities outside of the meeting rooms. Thus creating engaging meetings *with* students rather than didactic delivery of information *to* students.

Since the introduction of registration with our profession the students are able to gain a recognised qualification that otherwise was not accessible to them for geographically remote reasons. The programme has enabled academic reward for work carried out in the workplace and has engaged employers in the education, training and development of their staff.

The practice has reduced the necessity for extended periods of commuting time and costs to gain access to a required qualification in addition to reducing the associated carbon footprint.

Moving forward

This chapter has outlined how a reduced attendance model has rejuvenated what could have been a struggling programme. The increases in recruitment and retention themselves are a great positive, but in combination with an improvement in academic performance then this is confirmation that this practice is more than capable of replacing traditional part-time delivery across programmes. It is suggested that this practice can be applied to any subject area including those that have both theoretical and practical aspects of study. An important factor to develop is the inherent 'flipped classroom' approach which allows discussion of pertinent, or difficult topics with the lecturer when in the online classroom. This model and associated student led activities should be developed to increase activities and to investigate which of them are most productive for the learner. There should be training for staff regarding the use of 'webinars' for teaching and an awareness of the 'flipped classroom' approach and how to implement this effectively. The popularity with students and staff regarding the use of e-portfolios has also been encouraging and has been very useful for recording work-based learning activities. Further development of a reflective element in the portfolio to encourage reflection through different media is being explored.

In conclusion, this practice has allowed an accredited programme to be delivered to those who may not otherwise have been able to access it. It has improved retention rates as well as having no detrimental effect on the learner's academic performance or learner experience. All this with little, or no need to develop new learning resources.

About the Author

Jeff Lewis is Principal Lecturer in Dental Technology at Cardiff Metropolitan University, Wales, United Kingdom. He can be contacted at this e-mail: jlewis@cardiffmet.ac.uk

Bibliography

Dreyfus, H. L. & S. E. Dreyfus (1986). *Mind over machine: The power of human intuition and expertise in the era of the computer.* New York: The Free Press.

General Dental Council. (2013). *Registration of Dental Care Professionals.* General Dental Council, UK.

Ryan, A. & D. Tilbury (2013). *Flexible Pedagogies: new pedagogical ideas.* York: HEA.

Chapter 28: E-learning

How Do We Hybridise x and c MOOC Architectures to Create a Course on Online CVs?

Willie McGuire

Background

The course was designed at the University of Glasgow, using the Future-learn platform, although the audience was global. It is a free, completely open, online course, with no entry requirements, so it is not targeted at a specific group. It is a trans-discipline initiative that is cross-cutting in that it is targeted at all careers and is also supportive of academic-professional/work transitions. Its aim was to improve employability through the development of 'digital' or online *curriculum vitae* (CV) writing skills and it involved liaison with a wide range of internal and external partners.

If massive open online courses (MOOCs) were considered as an educational revolution influencing the traditional model of HE (Waldrop, 2013) then their discourse is formulated in terms of polarity, and this is no better depicted than in their characterisation, as either c or x MOOCs. This typology is based on underlying pedagogical principles: the cMOOC is designed using constructivist – connectivist theories, while the xMOOC is premised on behaviourist principles. In both conceptualisations, however, educational principles predominate, while the MOOC's purpose appears to be secondary. What is clear, though, is that very careful thought needs to be applied to their macro and micro design characteristics (Scagnoli, 2014; Richter, 2014). This chapter will explore the attempts of the designers to hybridise the key strengths of both forms of architecture in order to create a construct that puts purpose first – the creation of a personalised, digital CV for real – world use.

Despite the fact that they have only been in existence for a relatively short time, since 2008, and then, later, exploding in popularity in 2012, the 'year of the MOOC', Pappano (2012), we 'feel' as if they have been with us for much longer, perhaps because their early exponential growth generated a gravity all of its own, which subsumed the whole field of e-learning, a phenomenon described by (Kesim & Altinpulluk 2015:15) in terms of the online-ness, openness, and cheap-ness of MOOCs. Indeed these strengths have also been described, paradoxically, as a major weakness-the quality of the learning according to (Bali, 2014:44) and their pedagogical effectiveness according to (Sonwalker, 2013:22).

The MOOC described hereafter titled: 'Net That Job: How to Write a CV Online' was written after a period of settlement between the x (behaviourist) and c (constructivist/connectivist) schools of MOOC design. The writing team was aware of these developments and hoped to use them to create a learning environment fit for purpose: to enable learners to improve their CVs and job chances through increased and effective use of digital technology, following the key advantage of the medium identified by (Mackness *et al.*, 2010:267) as 'reflecting a situation in which adults can take control over where, when, and how they learn.'

Many scholars (e.g. Kesim & Altinpulluk, 2015:16; Ross *et al.*, 2014:59) argue that cMOOCs are underpinned by connectivist learning theories and xMOOCs are closer to a traditional behaviourist model of learning and teaching. We aimed to create a MOOC with an x support structure, but with c depth, so we wanted to blend the behaviourist x model with the constructivist/connectivist c model in order to obviate some key issues identified in the literature and captured by Daradoumis *et al.* (2013:209–210) who explain that MOOCs pose challenges never faced before, particularly as, until not long ago, it was unthinkable to have several thousand learners participating in an online course. MOOCs then are still relatively new and online CVs are not yet fully mainstreamed, although it is highly likely that this will become more of an expectation of employers as their comfort levels with technology increase.

The Practice

In terms of design, the course lasts for three weeks, with each week containing three or four broad 'activities', within which there are three or four learning 'steps'. Each activity contains a balance of varied steps to engage learners in a variety of formats: audio, video, quiz, article, micro-exercise, peer-review and reflection, and the overall pattern is linear-sequential with students spending approximately twenty minutes on each step within an activity, which equates to four hours study each week. The following Week 3 Activity (How digital?) and its concomitant Steps (3.1–3.6) may create a clearer cross-section of insight into the student experience.

Figure 1: Screenshot from the FutureLearn online platform.

Step 3.2, for example, asks learners to scan through some interactive CVs and then to decide on which they think is most appropriate for the job for which they are applying, giving reasons. Tasks then are active and engaging and, hopefully, enjoyable as participants explore the creativity so evident in this field in a supportive environment within which their discussion area peers can help to co-create those final judgements.

In terms of 'soft' architecture, the course was written to create a specific relationship with the learners *via* authorial stance, tone, and mood, in order to promote a positive rapport to offset attrition rates so often referenced in the study of MOOCs as, according to Rivard (2013), one widely quoted dropout figure for students in MOOCs is 90 percent. Again, the attempt to create a positive authorial relationship is, perhaps, best understood through this exemplification from the introductory sequence from the course where we expose our aspirations in order to encourage the participants to explore theirs:

> I'm a senior lecturer in the School of Education at the University of Glasgow in Scotland. You might be able to tell by the accent. Before that I was a lecturer here and, prior to that, I was an education adviser in both Edinburgh and Glasgow, before which I taught in schools as a Head of English. The main thing that's important to you about my work 'story' though, is that it took me a little while to get that first job as a Head of English; I had to change my CV lots and lots of times. And it wasn't easy; I remember how hard it was very well indeed. What do I want to get from this course, then?
>
> 1. I want to help you to become successful;
> 2. I want to help you to create the best CV you can;
> 3. I want to think about my own CV! I'm a senior lecturer, but I want promotion, too; I want to be a professor. So, this course is important for me, too.

Figure 2: Introductory sequence from the course.

We also positioned the learners in an unusual way, asking them to adopt the point of view, not of potential employees, but of actual employers and this was built in to a wide range of activities consistently throughout the course, for example in the fact that each week ended with an expert panel whose views had to be critiqued by participants. Content, too, was innovative. We used, for example, Quick Response code (QR code) to showcase the CV as a 21st century digital construct. Scanning the code below, for example, will take the viewer directly to the course itself on the Futurelean platform, but the potential for such digital technology in engaging the young is profound.

Figure 3: Using a QR-code to engage.

Another example of innovative content lies in the development of competency-based interview techniques being embedded into the CV itself to better prepare learners for such interview formats. This was an entirely novel approach to the construction of the CV and had only been used, prior to this in the interview itself, as opposed to functioning as a preparatory mechanism. Moving beyond the digital domain itself, although equally interesting, is the area of teacher-student collaboration, which is evident in the composition of the design team, one of whom was a final year PhD student, with another being a third year undergraduate, while the Lead Educator was a senior academic. This also led to an international conference presentation, which was tremendous experience for the students.

The final innovation relates to our attempts to support over 25,000 students *via* the discussion groups that were linked to specific steps in the course. This was managed through thematic feedback given by the Lead Educator and one Mentor (as our PhD student had secured a Lectureship). As MOOCs are usually free, credit-less and open to anyone with an Internet connection, teaching staff cannot possibly interact with students individually (Pappano, 2012, 2). The teacher's role within a MOOC, therefore, differs from most other educational environments where teachers can know and interact with their students through such processes as selection, tutoring and assessment (Ross *et al.*, 2014, 58). Essentially, we decided that it was impossible to even attempt to engage with all of the learners on a one-to-on basis, but we could search for themes in the discussion threads, which could then become teaching and learning foci for all learners.

Inputs

The lead educator was responsible for the overall design strategy, the delegation of tasks, the creation of guidelines, the creation of drafts for upload to the Futurelearn platform, researching topics for inclusion in the course, preparing briefs for the mentors, editing materials, discussion and liaison with the mentors, and the media unit at the university.

Mentor 1 was responsible for a range of areas including: preliminary research into MOOC architecture; the creation of course materials; the construction of a literature review on design features of x and c MOOCs to present the team with the theoretical underpinnings required to allow us to begin our own construct; the editing of materials, discussion and liaison with mentor 2, the media unit and the design innovation team of the university.

Mentor 2 was also responsible for a range of areas, but the focus here was on the practice, as opposed to the theory and so this necessitated: familiarisation with MOOC architecture; developing the coding required for upload to the Futurelearn platform; the creation of materials; editing, discussion and liaison with other mentor, the media unit and the design innovation team.

Outputs: The Construct Deconstructed

Phase 1: Familiarisation

It is important to take time at the outset to become familiar with how MOOCs are constructed, and, in particular the specific nomenclature associated with them, for example: landing page, signing in page, launch page, activities, and steps. Essentially, MOOCs can last for up to six weeks, although they are more typically three weeks in duration. Each week has three or four activities and each activity has a number of steps, designed to take participants four hours to cover each week. Estimates of the time taken to create course materials will invariably be much more than that planned for and deadlines will arrive much earlier. A launch date of 1st March, for example, means course completion and readiness for Quality Assurance by 1st February.

Phase 2: Planning

A key decision at the outset is to decide on what has to be done and how to present it. Usually, a narrative thread throughout the course creates a form of intra-course cohesion, but, on the macro level, this will be an iterative process with many changes and adaptations, so it is vital to build in the time for the re-structuring and/or the re-writing of materials.

An implementation plan should be constructed in conjunction with the media/learning innovation team in which twelve months is allocated to develop the materials, which may sound peculiar in the context of a three-week course, but this will be unlike any other online course experienced to date as it is written in conjunction with the platform staff, and in-house media specialists.

Filming needs to happen much earlier than expected, so early liaison with the media unit is vital as is early thinking around what filming is likely to be required, which is difficult (or even paradoxical) as the writers are likely to be at the stage of gathering together basic ideas when the media unit will be announcing deadlines for filming.

Phase 3: Developing

The development of draft materials is certainly best done beyond the perimeter of the platform. Googledocs, for example provides an easy-to-use and access receptacle for the storage and transfer of drafts. This will enable changes to be effected simply and efficiently to any of the materials created. The online platform is much more difficult to work with as there is an element of coding required to input text, so taking time to practise the coding required to upload materials at the outset generates fewer issues later in the process. While the coding requirements are basic, they still need to be practised, which is often not factored into the design process.

Another consideration, too, during the development phase, is that MOOC platform engineers are very wary of external websites and expect the construct to be self-contained within the platform itself, so this needs to be factored into preparation time as it means that there can be few, if any, external referents. Equally, unlike book publication, there is no typesetter to autocorrect, so one problem repeated one hundred times (Upper case CV *versus* lower case cv) will mean substantial editing over, possible, forty separate pages. Additionally, it is prudent to familiarise yourself with house typesetting styles at the outset and build these into the drafts as it will save a lot of time later in the process during the quality assurance procedures. Finally, unlike working with conventional publishers the design team will be expected to have gained all copyright clearance, so it is best to avoid copyright photographs/pictures.

Phase 4: Editing

It is vital that uploads to the platform happen only occur when certain that the content is final as edits are very time-consuming because of the page-by-page organization within the platform. Consideration of the balance of broad teaching methodologies has to be factored into the design of drafts: visual, auditory, or kinesthetic present within each week and, while these do not have to be in harmonic symmetry, there is an expectation that they will be varied and appropriate to the activity being pursued. Additionally, there is also the issue to be addressed of the balance of activities within steps. MOOC platforms offer a range of varied, interactive options such as: articles, quizzes, videos, exercises, discussion topics and peer reviews. Essentially, it is better to have thought of both the balance of methodologies and activities before submission for quality assurance.

'Thank you for this wonderful course.'
'I've been looking for a course like this for ages.'
'This is just what I need.'
'My ambition is to become a doctor and I think this will help me to achieve my goal.'

Figure 4: Feedback from students.

A final key issue for the Lead Educator lies in managing online interaction and the social aspects of online learning in a realistic manner. The numbers in a MOOC course are likely to be completely beyond the tutor's previous experience and conventional approaches to the moderation of discussion forums are unlikely to be helpful. One potential way of managing such scale is to provide limited, but quality 'thematic' feedback based on the observations of sampled student work which would then allow other participants to share good practice from their peers.

Moving Forward

This is, without doubt, the largest quantitative challenge I have faced in thirty years of teaching. It has also been, at the same time, both the most satisfying and frustrating. At over 25,000 participants, it is also the largest course ever run at Glasgow University and the most geographically varied with participants from almost every continent, which creates an unmatched diversity in my experience. Additionally, there is the issue of how to manage that cultural diversity and the different expectations it engenders, which brings us into the domain of the qualitative. Feedback from students has been genuinely touching.

Paradoxically, this MOOC, while the largest delivered by Glasgow University, is actually very unusual as the recent trend in MOOC creation within my university has been in relation to the design of mini MOOCs. More recently, these have been termed small, private online courses (SPOCs) The next natural step into online learning will centre around the design of a SPOC or mini MOOC for which I have recently received funding as part of a new International MEd in Assessment Literacy. As part of the process of constructing such a course, I hope to refine some of the experience I have gained from my work on this, much larger, course to shape the end-product in negotiation with the students who will be working on the whole programme, which is an experience to which I look forward.

About the Author

Willie McGuire is a Senior University Teacher in the School of Education at the University of Glasgow and a Senior Fellow of the Higher Education Academy. His innovative work has been recognised through prestigious awards such as Teaching Excellence Awards and Student Led Teaching Awards. He has also been nominated for the Herald/Higher Education Academy Innovative Teacher of the Year Award for 2016. Willie can be contacted on this e-mail: William.McGuire@glasgow.ac.uk

Bibliography

Bali, M. (2014). MOOC pedagogy: gleaning good practice from existing MOOCs. *MERLOT Journal of Online Learning and Teaching*, Vol. 10, No. 1, pp. 44–56.

Daradoumis, T.; R. Bassi; F. Xhafa & S. Caballe (2013). A review on massive e-learning (MOOC) design, delivery and assessment. *2013 Eighth International Conference on P2P, Parallel, grid, Cloud and Internet Computing*.

Kesim, M. & H. Altinpulluk (2015). A theoretical analysis of MOOCs types from a perspective of learning theories. *Procedia – Social and Behavioural Sciences*, No. 186, pp. 15–19.

Mackness, J.; S. F. J. Mak & R. Williams (2010). *The ideals and reality of participating in MOOC*. Proceedings of the 7th International Conference on Networked Learning 2010, pp. 266–274.

Pappano, L. (2012). The year of the MOOC. *The New York Times*, November 2, 2012.

Richter, S. L. & M. Krishnamurthi (2014). Preparing Faculty for Teaching a MOOC: Recommendations from Research and Experience. *International Journal of Information and Education Technology*, Vol. 4, No. 5.

Rivard, R. (2013). Measuring the MOOC dropout rate. *Inside Higher Ed.* March 28, 2013.

Ross, J., Sinclair, C., Knox, J., Bayne, S., Macleod, H. (2014). Teacher Experiences and Academic Identity: The Missing Components of MOOC Pedagogy. *Journal of Online Learning and Teaching*, Vol. 10, No. 1, pp. 57–69.

Scagnoli, N (2014). *Thoughts on Instructional Design for MOOCs*. Working Paper/IDEALS.

Sonwalker, N. (2013). Brief. The first adaptive MOOC: a case study on pedagogy framework and scalable cloud architecture – part 1. *MOOCs Forum*, pp. 22–29.

Waldrop, M. M. (2013). Online learning: campus 2.0. *Nature*, No. 495, pp. 160–163.

Lightning Source UK Ltd.
Milton Keynes UK
UKHW021946291220
376083UK00010B/438